# Shakespeare's Theatre of War

*in memoriam*

JAN de SOMOGYI
(1923–1988)

*and*

PETER de SOMOGYI
(1954–1981)

# Shakespeare's Theatre of War

NICK DE SOMOGYI

## Ashgate

Aldershot • Brookfield USA • Singapore • Sydney

Published by
Ashgate Publishing Limited
Gower House
Croft Road
Aldershot
Hants GU11 3HR
England

Ashgate Publishing Company
Old Post Road
Brookfield
Vermont 05036–9704
USA

The author has asserted his moral right under the Copyright, Designs and Patents Act, 1988, to be identified as the author of this work.

British Library Cataloguing in Publication Data

*PR*
*3069*
*. M5*
*D4*
*1998*

Somogyi, Nick de
 Shakespeare's Theatre of War
 1. Shakespeare, William, 1564–1616—Criticism and
 interpretation. 2. War in literature.
 I. Title.
 822.3'3

Library of Congress Cataloging-in-Publication Data

Somogyi, Nick de
 Shakespeare's theatre of war/Nick de Somogyi
 Includes bibliographical references and index.
 1. Shakespeare, William, 1564–1616—Knowledge—Military art and
science. 2. Shakespeare, William, 1564–1616—Characters—Soldiers.
3. Military art and science in literature. 4. Military history in
literature. 5. Soldiers in literature. 6. War in literature.
 I. Title.
 PR3069.M5D4    1998
 822.3'3—dc21                                          98–26131
                                                         CIP

ISBN 1 84014 207 3

This book is printed on acid free paper

Printed and bound in Great Britain by MPG Books Ltd, Bodmin, Cornwall

114999

# Contents

# Notes on Procedures

All Renaissance texts are quoted from their sixteenth-century editions wherever practicable, or from modern editions that retain original spelling. This procedure is followed in order to avoid creating an artificial disjunction between modernized (apparently 'timeless') texts by such as Shakespeare and Marlowe, and the largely unedited works of their military contemporaries. The critical apparatuses of modern literary editions have in any case been extensively consulted. Where appropriate, for the sake of clarity, I have silently modernized 'j' for 'i', 'v' for 'u' (and *vice versa*), and emended contractions and superior letters. Because the range of my quotation extends to much of the Elizabethan dramatic canon, I include here a brief summary of the procedures I have adopted in quoting its main authors.

In the case of Shakespeare, for ease of reference, I have used the act- and scene-lineation of the Oxford *Complete Works* (gen. eds Wells and Taylor, 1986), keyed to the texts of the earliest 'good' Quarto (Q) when such texts exist, and of the First Folio (F) (1623) when they do not. Quotation from the Folio is from the edition prepared by Hinman (1968). One exception should be noted. In Chapter Six, I have keyed quotation of *Hamlet* to the lineation of Jenkins's (conflated) Arden edition (1982) since the Oxford *Works* relegates to an appendix the 'Additional Passages' from Q2 (775) I regard as integral to the play. My use of other modern editions of these plays and of others is signalled in my notes.

Unless otherwise specified, other canonical authors are cited in the act- and-scene lineation, or (for prose works) volume and page numbers provided by the following authoritative old-spelling editions. Dekker, *Dramatic Works*, ed. Bowers (1961-2); Dekker, *Non-Dramatic Works*, ed. Grosart (1884-6, repr. 1963); Greene, *Works*, ed. Grosart (1881-6, repr. 1964); Jonson, *Works*, ed. Herford and Simpson (1925-52); Lyly, *Works*, ed. Bond (1902); Marlowe, *Complete Works*, ed. Bowers (1981); Nashe, *Works*, ed. McKerrow, rev. ed. Wilson (1958); Webster, *Works*, ed. Gunby et al., (1995). I use the book and stanza numbers of *The Faerie Queene*, ed. Hamilton (1977). In the case of *The Spanish Tragedy* and *Soliman and Perseda*, I have used the lineation of Kyd's *Works*, ed. Boas (1901), and the texts, respectively, of the 1599 Quarto and the 1592 Quarto. In the case of certain minor plays, I have used the text and lineation of the Malone Society Reprints series (MSR). I quote from a number of Elizabethan news-pamphlets, many of them anonymous. References within the text ('News-Pamphlet 10') refer to the number I assign them in my bibliography, where they are arranged in chronological order, 1574-1605.

# Acknowledgements

A great many thanks are due, many of them owed to members (both past and present) of the English Faculty of Cambridge University, where this book first emerged as a doctoral thesis. Outstanding among them is my debt to John Kerrigan, and the patient brilliance of his supervision. I should also like to record my thanks to Jean Gooder for her very great kindness. Anne Barton, Dan Burnstone, Howard Erskine-Hill, Richard Gooder, Germaine Greer, Ralph Pite and Peter Swaab have each been a source of inspiration and support. I salute too the collectively spirited contribution made to this volume by those students of Newnham College it was my great fortune to teach between 1987 and 1993.

Thanks also are due to the Master and fellows of Pembroke College, Cambridge, and the Trustees of the Le Bas Scholarship; to the Principal and fellows of Newnham College; to Thomas Woodcock, Norroy and Ulster King of Arms; to Tony Coe and Jane Tibble of the Open University; to Patrick Spottiswoode and Deborah Callan of Shakespeare's Globe; to Ann Cooke and Toby Mitchell of Macmillan Publishing; to Colleen Collier of Robinson Publishing; to Jan Piggott and Neil Croally of Dulwich College; to Rachel Lynch and Caroline Cornish of Ashgate Publishing, and to the anonymous reader of my original manuscript. I am further indebted to the staff of the Cambridge University Library; of the English Faculty Library at Cambridge; and to the British Library for their permission in reproducing *Rumore* from Cesare Ripa's *Iconologia* (637.g.26) for the jacket of this book.

I should like to thank my close friends Mark Bridges and Nikki Ferguson for their constancy, and finally publish my debt, by far the most heartfelt, to my mother Anna-Greta, my brother Stephen, and my sister-in-law Elizabeth, without whose magnificent support, assistance and love, this book would never have found completion.

For seven years, as the scholar in Marston's *What You Will* tells us, he 'quoted, reade, observ'd and pried, | Stufft noting bookes', 'wasted lamp-oile' and 'por'd on the old print', yet all the while his spaniel slept. For many years now my cat has gained the span, weight and gravitas I hope to have bestowed on this book, and his contribution should not go unmarked: 'At length he wak'd and yawn'd and by yon sky | For aught I know he knew as much as I'.

Nick de Somogyi

# Introduction

> . . . Then, a Soldier,
> Full of strange oaths, and bearded like the Pard,
> Jelous in honor, sodaine, and quicke in quarrell,
> Seeking the bubble Reputation
> Even in the Canons mouth.
> (*As You Like It*, 2.7.149-53)

To Jaques military service is as integral a part of life as education, first love or death. For many writers of Shakespeare's generation – and for many generations since – this was no exaggeration. Jonson recalled to Drummond the highlight of his sojourn in the Low Countries, when, 'in the face of both the Campes, [he] killed ane enimie and [took] opima spolia from him' (*Conversations*, ed. Patterson, 23). Donne confessed to the 'fashion of a soldier' in 1596/7, 'which occupation for a while I professe' (Marotti, 1986, 102). Chapman's wartime editor records the 'general supposition' that he too fought in the Netherlands (*Poems*, ed. Bartlett, 427), and there is firmer evidence for Marlowe's contribution to the war effort (Bakeless, 1, 77-85, 159-62; Nicholl, 1992, *passim*). Dekker's marked concern for soldiers' welfare has been explained by his supposed military service (Hunt, 1911, 21); Tourneur's *Funeral Poeme* on Sir Francis Vere (1609) strengthens the hypothesis of his overseas employment by that family, 'concerned with military and other affairs'.[1] The examples of Sidney (killed in action at Zutphen in 1586) and Spenser (part of Lord Grey's administration of the ruthless policies in Ireland) are well known.

Nor need we seek far in what is known of Shakespeare's life and work to find evidence of the direct impact of war. His father recruited the men sent from Stratford 'with armour from the town armoury' during the 1569 rebellion (Bradbrook, 1978, 9). Henslowe (who produced some of his earliest plays at the Rose) included in his *Diary* 'a notte of what charges my Soger [soldier] petter hath stode me in this yeare 1596' (46). His later patron, Lord Hunsdon, signed 'most of the orders commanding the lords lieutenant to levy soldiers for Ireland' (Altman, 1991, 15). Sir Thomas North, the author of one of his most influential sources, held a notorious command in Ireland (H. Davis, 1949, 319-20). In the past, such evidence has been marshalled to suggest direct combat-experience in the young Shakespeare. 'Was Shakspeare Ever a Soldier?', asked William J. Thoms in 1859; 'Yes', answered A. Duff Cooper in his idiosyncratic study, *Sergeant Shakespeare*, in 1949. The question was repeated as recently as 1985, as part of Sir John Hale's enquiry into 'Shakespeare and Warfare' (1985b, 1, 89). Such conjectural biography has arisen in response to the marked frequency with which military affairs appear in the Shakespeare canon. It is important to note, however, that the overlap between 'Playwrights and Pike Trailers' (Feldman, 1953) reflects a broader presence of military elements in late Elizabethan society, unignorable for Jaques as for Jaques' original audiences.

This book explores the relations between drama and history, and seeks to illuminate the influence of wartime on the production of Elizabethan plays. Warfare 'played a role', as Hale puts it, 'between 1453 and 1618 which, if thought away, radically maims our understanding of the social experiences of those years' (1985a, 13). The same is true in respect of the London playhouses during 1585-1604 – a time of active and sustained English involvement in European theatres of war, and a period which coincides with the first performances and publication of the most enduring works of English drama.

Students of late Tudor literature remain disproportionately impressed by its most notable propagandist success, the much-celebrated victory over a Spanish invasion fleet in 1588. Ornstein is typical in his assertion that the *Henry VI* plays were composed at a time when 'the threat of invasion and the fear of civil war created by the Armada were still vivid memories' and that the 'immediate danger waned' thereafter (1972, 173).[2] The defeat of one Armada in 1588 should not obscure the fact that other Armadas were subsequently prepared. There was 'almost insuperable anxiety' in England that another might subsequently succeed (Wiener, 29). 'The war had yet to be fought' (MacCaffrey, 3). Nor should it be overlooked that Philip II's invasion-plans were known to form part of a larger European strategy.

In 1598 Barnaby Riche described how 'almost everie ordinarie about *London* may be sayde to be an Academie of martiall skill.' He dryly satirized the garrulous veterans who, 'but in one dinners discourse',

> will settle the king of *France* into a quiet government,
> they wil banish the Spaniards from out the low countries,
> they will reforme *Ireland*, they wil thrust the king of
> *Spaine* cleane out of *Portingall*, they will take from him
> his *Indies*, and they will not forget to eate their meates,
> and to drinke three or foure healthes.
> (E2r-E2v)

These jests comprise a fair summary of contemporary English war-aims. Across the Channel, France had been embroiled in a series of civil wars since the 1560s that were not resolved until 1598. Further east, in what has been called the 'cockpit of Europe' (Parker, 1975, 49), the Low Countries were in the throes of a protracted bid for independence from Spain. To both these theatres of war England had intermittently contributed voluntary bands of troops, but in 1585 the Queen officially committed resources and men to the Dutch states in an effort to resist the emergence of a Catholic continent, a fear augmented by the rebellions in Ireland, which, from the mid-1590s, threatened to 'become for England the Achilles heel that the Low Countries were for Spain' (MacCaffrey, 10). Anglo-Spanish (or Protestant-Catholic) hostilities stretched as far as the New World, prompting one historian to reflect that these wars deserve to be called the first First World War (Parker, 1975, 57). They certainly took place in a century that 'saw the transition ... from medieval conditions of warfare to modern' (Rowse, 327).

That century had begun with the *Blitzkrieg* of Charles VIII's artillery in Italy. The rise of increasingly mobile and powerful artillery had led to the development of a system of effectively defensive fortification. It is this process which in part constitutes what is now called the 'military revolution' (Parker, 1988). Shakespeare's Arcite deviates from his Chaucerian model in addressing the modern Mars as a force that 'plucke[s]'

> With hand armenypotent from forth blew clowdes,
> The masond Turrets, that both mak'st and break'st
> The stony girthes of Citties:
> (*The Two Noble Kinsmen*, 5.1.52-5)

'Armenypotent' (omnipotently armed) artillery rendered medieval 'masond Turrets' archaic and necessitated the construction of lower-slung 'girthes' about cities, the *trace italienne* 'That as a waste doth girdle you about' (*King John*, 2.1.217), to be made and broken, and made again.

As a result of such technology, the size of infantry-based armies grew while the role of cavalry diminished. A soldier's feudal loyalty to his knightly overlord was superseded by a still vaguely understood allegiance to the state. This was 'an age of siege warfare rather than of mobile warfare' (C. Wilson, 10), an appraisal confirmed by Riche's account of the 'Low Country Services, which doth rather consist in assaulting and defending fortifications, more then in any incounters in the field' (1598, G3v). Such campaigns, fought by a largely conscripted army (again reminiscent of the First World War), degenerated into expensive 'trench warfare, tedious, dangerous, murderously unhealthy' (Howard, 1976, 36). And 'usually futile' (MacCaffrey, 289):[3] for the military achievement of English intervention was, in J.E. Neale's words, 'worse than negligible' (396), and Elizabeth herself described the Netherlands as a 'sieve that spends to little purpose' (387). That unease seems to have been widespread. Elizabeth's ambassador to France was later informed that 'bothe her Majestie and her realme are become ... very weary' with the expenses incurred there, 'bothe in lones of money' and 'in waging of men bothe by land and sea' (Unton, 319-20).

Even I.A.A. Thompson, who begins his study of 'The Impact of War' in the 1590s with the flat assertion that war 'was not a defining characteristic' for Europe as a whole, acknowledges that England was something of an exception (261). He notes the 'overpowering fear of invasion ... which magnified and distorted the psychological impact of war' (262), felt in a community to whom the 'open war' to which it sent increasing numbers of men was a 'relatively new experience' (261). Thompson de-emphasizes the statistical scale of the numbers thus annually dispatched – 0.13% of the population between 1585 and 1603, from a country where overpopulation was considered a problem (266) – but the evidence of MacCaffrey's more recently researched figures (11-12% of eligible men) (47), the fact that the burden was spread over every parish, and the blunt total of 100,000 men conscripted (Cruickshank, 290) argue for a heavy and direct impact on the community. These figures, furthermore, only account for the men actually sent abroad; many others were systematically drilled for the Trained Bands (introduced in 1573), to be held in readiness to withstand imminent invasion (Boynton, 90-125). Musters and drill-parades were held in London fields, and in the churchyards of the counties (Holmes, 45-51; Boynton, 26; Chadwick, 227-31). Meanwhile, enlistment to foreign service from agrarian workers aggravated the problem of poor harvests, leading to widespread discontent. To choose just two examples: in 1586 a crowd in Ipswich demonstrated against the shipping of meat to a Dutch garrison, and in 1595 the Mayor of Chester complained that food-purchases for Irish garrisons had increased prices (Pearce, 40-45). In London, the large numbers of European Protestant refugees provoked race riots in 1593 (Scouloudi, 31). In addition, the weaknesses of the as yet rudimentary welfare system for veterans led to increasing social unrest. After the wasteful Portugal expedition in 1589, 500 unpaid soldiers threatened to loot Bartholomew Fair and were scattered by 2000 militiamen (Judges, xvii-xviii). 'No occupational groups increased as much as soldiers and sailors among vagrants from 1560 to 1640' (Beier, 93).[4]

This volatile social circumstance was eventually eased by James I's accession. In 1604, as Stow's *Annales* records, 'the true Merchant, and honest Citizen, was exceeding glad and right joyfull of this peace, hoping thereby to have free trade with all nations, prevention of bloodshed, [and] quiet enjoying of their sonnes and servants, which yearely were prest for forraine services' (1631, 845). The parameters of my enquiry are thus set by the war-years: from the Queen's declaration of aid to the Dutch in 1585, to the King's declaration of peace in 1604. One of the first legislative acts of James's government was the repeal of the 1558 statute concerning the military obligations of his subjects (Boynton, 209). For the purposes of this study, the context within which it considers the drama may be said to have changed at that moment.

This book will read the Elizabethan plays of Shakespeare and his contemporaries in the light of contemporary writings which deal overtly with the waging, reporting, and social context of war. As Cockle's *Bibliography of Military Books* (3rd edn, 1978) records, the period saw the publication of a spate of military treatises, works which deal with a broad range of subject matter. *The Theorike and Practike of Moderne Warres* (as

Barret's 1598 title has it) was considered from a variety of perspectives, whether philosophical, religious, technological, logistical, mathematical, legal, or (more commonly) a blend of each. Other printed works variously related the situation in Europe. The period's well-known vogue for cartography was in part encouraged by the utility in war furnished by maps, and their capacity to render vivid the recent episodes of conflict. The geometric calculus of the surveyor was also essential to the innovative technologies of early modern combat. As well as news-maps, the war-years witnessed the unprecedented proliferation of news-letters from the continental campaigns, the origin of modern journalism, in pieces that were often versified into popular ballads, and (on at least one documented occasion) dramatized on a London stage.

My title, *Shakespeare's Theatre of War*, at once refers to the milieu in which Shakespeare worked, to the European campaigns with which he and his audiences were variously and consistently familiar, and to their many points of intersection. My chief aim has been to allow a series of the period's non-'literary' texts both generally and in detail to further the interpretation of its drama. Precedents for such an approach are available from the critical procedures of 'old' and New Historicism, but a series of qualifications should be registered. It was a damaging weakness of earlier traditions of literary historical scholarship that contextual documentation was thought capable of providing a set of factual 'keys' with which topical particularities in (generically privileged) artistic works could be unlocked and 'explained'. By contrast, 'New Historicism', while usefully demonstrating the rewards of a common scrutiny of printed playhouse-scripts and non-'literary' texts, has laboured too hard to deny (at least in theory) the retrospectively evident cultural centrality of the works of authors like Marlowe and Shakespeare. This study has been written with an eye to avoiding the faults of both kinds of enquiry. Certainly it has been indirectly encouraged by the New Historicist discovery of parallel coalitions of meaning in generically distinct texts (within a clearly defined social circumstance of literary production), but such an approach is prompted by the play-texts themselves (Marlowe's verse paraphrase from Ive's *Practise of Fortification*, for example) rather than by any direct ideological or theoretical influence. (It is a striking fact that, despite its obsession with violence and power, New Historicism has neglected the subject of early modern war.) Above all, this study, while displaying some of the range of reference typical of New Historicist work, makes no apology for placing literary texts at the heart of its enquiry, and Shakespearean plays at its heart of heart. Although *Hamlet* is as surely caught up in negotiations between the contemporary historical and the fictive as, say, *The Oppugnation and Fierce Siege of Ostend* (1601), I assume as self-evident the fertile sophistication with which the play addresses the enduring subject of war.

Wartime imposed itself on London's Elizabethan stages in a variety of ways. Henslowe's Diary, for example, provides evidence that plays could perform the function of news-letter or news-ballad: he commissioned a four-part drama on the 'syvell wares of fraunce' at the end of 1598, a few months after they ended (98-103). Another source records how Vere's 1598 victory at Turnhout was 'acted upon a Stage' in October 1599 (Collins, 1746, 2, 136). Nashe noted that 'Captaines and Souldiers about *London*' were a common constituent of audiences at playhouses which themselves stood in close proximity to the sites of London's musters of its citizen militia (1, 212). On at least one occasion, civilian audiences were forcibly conscripted 'for fflaunders' from the theatres themselves (Gawdy, *Letters*, 121). Such proximity to current affairs is often registered in the play-texts. Gascoigne's eye-witness account of *The Spoyle of Antwerp* (1576) provided the source for the anonymous *A Larum for London* (*c.*1600), a play performed by Shakespeare's company. Marlowe's second *Tamburlaine* incorporates a lengthily technical passage from Ive's fortification manual, and features a geography drawn from a contemporary atlas. Kyd's *Spanish Tragedy* draws details of the war with which it opens from contemporary news-pamphlets (A. Freeman, 52-4). Sometimes, furthermore, the influence was reversed: G.K. Hunter notes that Greene's 1587 *Euphues His Censure to Philautus* includes a debate about the 'perfect martialist' (1962, 259), but neglects to mention that several of its aphorisms reappeared *verbatim* in an anonymous military pamphlet, *A Myrrour for English Souldiers*, published in 1595.[5]

Elizabethan writers often regarded the literature of war as having a practical application. Thomas Proctor, in common with many martial authors, advocated the usefulness of 'reportes, historyes, & Chronicles written of warres' to their present waging (1578, [Preface] iiii v), and it is to this tradition that Nashe turned his defence of drama in 1592, praising the 'hopes of eternitie' inspired in audiences of history plays, 'to encourage them forward' (1, 213), adding that 'In Playes ... all stratagems of warre ... are most lively anatomiz'd'. It seems likely that the play Nashe had in mind was Shakespeare's *1 Henry VI*, and it is significant that one of the dominant genres of Elizabethan drama between 1585 and 1604 was the chronicle history play. If, as Ralegh stated, 'The ordinary Theme and Argument of History is War' (1650, C7r), it should not surprise us to find dramatic representations not only of English victories in the genre (Agincourt, Crécy) but of Roman and Greek battles (Philippi, Troy) as well as the more exotic campaigns of Tamburlaine and Selimus. Elizabethan distinctions between History and Tragedy were never pronounced, but while Anne Barton writes that 'the chronicle history seems to have died with Elizabeth' (1994, 234) it is perhaps more accurate to assert that the form died with the wars that the accession of the Peacemaker James dispelled. It is not, however, only in Tragical Histories that war cast its shadow, as reference to Shakespeare's Comedies confirms. Whether reflected in the military societies in which they are set (*Much Ado About Nothing, All's Well That Ends Well*); in the intrusions on to conventionally comedic, domestic settings (the Prince of

Morocco in *The Merchant of Venice*, Falstaff's band in Windsor); or in the flickerings of contemporary allusion in a name (Berowne, Dumaine, Navarre in *Love's Labour's Lost*, Don John in *Much Ado*), the 'smoake of warre' is never far away (*Twelfth Night*, 5.1.49).

The work of Paul A. Jorgensen is the most substantial precedent to my own. His many articles and his major study of the theme, *Shakespeare's Military World* (1956a), remain useful, though the meticulous parallels they establish between Shakespearean drama and prescriptive martial pamphlets tend to overshadow the essentially theatrical auspices of the literature he discusses. It is the aptness of the stage to the representation of war that Jorgensen overlooks and with which this book is concerned. Sir John Hale's predominantly historical research has been invaluable in providing scholars with a European framework for understanding the military revolution of the times. His 1985 essay on 'Shakespeare and Warfare' is a helpful summary of material, but once again my own work seeks to expand the literary focus beyond Shakespeare, and beyond the construction of a 'notable gallery of military character studies' (85) that typifies both Hale's and Jorgensen's approach. Two works from 1980, Terry Jones's *Chaucer's Knight: A Portrait of a Medieval Mercenary*, and James A. Freeman's *Milton and the Martial Muse: 'Paradise Lost' and European Traditions of War*, at once attest to the insights that can be produced from the more contextual yet critical approach which I have favoured, and alert us, by their medieval and seventeenth-century emphases, to the relative neglect of the theme in the Shakespearean period. *War, Literature and the Arts in Sixteenth Century Europe*, ed. Mulryne and Shewring (1989) and *Shakespeare et la Guerre*, ed. Jones-Davies (1990) do something to amend that neglect, but their status as composite collections means that they do not present a systematic overview of the sort I have attempted to provide.

Citing John Keegan's *The Face of Battle* (1976) as a precedent, the editor of another recent collection of essays on *Hoplites: The Classical Greek Battle Experience*, declares that its aim is 'one that eschews the traditional triad of strategy, tactics, and logistics to concentrate more on the experience of fighting' (Hanson, 253). That emphasis resembles my own, though the literary critical triad that I hope to avoid involves authorial biography, perceived allegories of political and military careers in dramatic characters, and the centrality of the 1588 Armada. It is to the experience of war on the battlefield, and to the effects of wartime at home, that my readings are addressed – in short, to the currency of war among the audiences and players of London between 1585 and 1604.

Perhaps the strongest anticipation of my work, in form if not in subject, is Paul Fussell's *The Great War and Modern Memory* (1975), which also concerns the 'experience' of war, focuses on 'places and situations where literary tradition and real life notably transect', and reads the works of great poets as well as 'what the ordinary man has to say about it all' (ix). Mention of this work prompts two related explanations of my own. First, both

Fussell and Keegan demonstrate a continuity in experience of war from early to modern times, and where apposite I have not hesitated to draw parallels between Elizabethan and more recent theatres of war, as the various epigraphs to my chapters demonstrate. Certainly, later episodes of wartime have forced the re-appraisal of Shakespeare's plays both in performance and criticism.[6] Second, this thesis is structured, as Fussell's work is, about a *thematic sequence* rather than a strictly chronological one. Although, broadly speaking, it moves from discussion of *Tamburlaine* (performed *c*.1587) to *Hamlet* (published 1603-05), consideration (for example) of *The Spanish Tragedy* (*c*.1585-87) is reserved until Chapter Five since that play begins with the ending of a war. My chapters are organized as follows.

'Casualties of War' reviews the range of sixteenth-century theories accounting for war. Taking its cue from the multiplicity of one-legged veterans represented on the late Elizabethan stage, it seeks to demonstrate the emblematic force of this handicap and its iconographic pertinence both to the ambiguities of those theoretical accounts and to the social grievances of crippled veterans. *The Trial of Chivalry* and *A Larum for London*, and their limping heroes, Captain Bowyer and Lieutenant Stump, are revealed as the sites of an emblematic accommodation of the contending systems of war-theory. I focus on these plays because, though all but ignored elsewhere, they offer remarkably direct treatments of contemporary campaigns. In particular, *A Larum*'s narrative is compared with the explication of the central Elizabethan doctrine of the just war provided by C.G.'s contemporary treatise, *A Watch-worde for Warre*. An argument is advanced that links Lieutenant Stump to the instrumental role essential to it (figured in his representative rank). The chapter closes by considering a contrary symbolism of the lame, and claims that the troubling symmetry between Stump and Shakespeare's Richard III reveals an inherent instability in contemporary definitions of war.

Throughout my second chapter, 'The Art of War', the orthodoxies of the divinely sanctioned just war are implicitly contrasted with Marlowe's Tamburlaine, as the embodiment of an autonomous, secular and above all technological militarism. Editors and critics have uniformly sought to apologize for Marlowe's debt to Ive's treatise on fortification in Part Two as evidence of the waning imaginative engagement typical of sequels. This chapter seeks to discredit that consensus. The geometric basis of the art of war, as explicated in a series of military text-books, is seen there as characteristic of the aspiring methods of Marlowe's heroes. Faustus and Tamburlaine are read as versions of the military epitome of the Soldier-Scholar, an ideal sponsored by the technological advances of sixteenth-century warfare and promoted in military books like Ive's. A connection is suggested between the map that *Tamburlaine* features at its close, and the lecture on the 'rudiments of war' its hero delivers, since Tamburlaine's multinational belligerence mirrors the technical vocabulary of sixteenth-century warfare, a vocabulary of generally foreign extraction. What I call the Esperanto of war, and the multinational groupings of the armies ranged against each other in 1590s Europe, are both staged in Marlowe's theatre of war.

'Theatres of War', my third chapter, investigates the broad and specific implications of its title. An equation is argued for between the tactics of dissimulation recommended in military treatises and described in contemporary news-letters, and the technique of theatrical performance. This is shown to be acknowledged in a number of stage-depictions of war, including Shakespeare's early history-plays. The chapter further remarks on the proximity, actual and notional, of the playhouse to the musters of London's citizen militia, and makes this the basis of an understanding of the sense of solidarity explored in *Henry V*. The first three chapters move from the theoretical (what is war?) to the technological (how is war fought?) to the pragmatic (what is it like to fight in a war?) before returning from the battlefield to what we might call the home front.

In 'Rumours of War' I concentrate on soldiers returning home, and identify a newly emergent comic equivalent to the Soldier-Scholar in the Braggart-Pedant. A pedigree is established for the Elizabethan *miles gloriosus* which incorporates contemporary anxieties over the social problems engendered by veterans, the volatility of their news from the front, and the modern language of war they paraded. This pedigree stretches from Munday's Captain Crackstone and Lyly's Sir Tophas, via Kyd's Basilisco, Strumbo in *Locrine*, and Jonson's Bobadilla, to Shakespeare's Armado, Pistol, Falstaff and Parolles. The discrepancy between word and deed that renders the Braggart comic is also the basis, as I also argue, of his kinship with Rumour, and the far from comic part that rumour plays in war. This chapter seeks to restore to characters hitherto considered merely laughable the trauma and solemnity originally associated with them.

Chapter Five, 'Ghosts of War', darkens the tone still further by considering another sort of revenant soldier. It reads *The Spanish Tragedy* and *Henry V* in the context of a specifically military folklore of the supernatural. Part Senecan spirit of revenge, part figure of military exhortation, Andrea's Ghost presides over the uneasy boundaries between private and public vengeance. The same borderlines are explored in *Henry V*, and a case is made for rooting the play's often troubling and uncanny atmosphere in the popular superstitions of its day. Both plays, for different reasons, are shown to anticipate *Hamlet*.

My final chapter, 'The Question of These Wars', gathers the evidence of earlier sections into a sustained account of that single – but textually plural – play, *Hamlet*, and views it in the context of a theatre increasingly devoted to propagandist appeals to patriotism. It argues that the play's Ghost would have been recognized as a figure of patriotic martialism, and that its Braggart (the critically misunderstood Osric) belongs in the tradition of the sombrely re-imagined *miles gloriosus*. It notes the play's preoccupation with military technology as well as the tendency of that technology to fail. It argues that the perceived similarity between player and soldier offers the basis of a structural and thematic understanding of the play, and further suggests that in addition to reflecting the anxieties of the time, the military auspices of *Hamlet*'s composition and performance help account for the disparity between its three texts. It is proposed that variations between the first and second Quarto and first Folio texts are the result of a judicious process of self-censorship involving widespread revision which centred, most decisively, on the removal of Hamlet's Fourth-Act soliloquy concerning Fortinbras.

The range of my enquiry extends from undisputed masterpieces to rather more mediocre literary efforts because the latter often serve to define the expectations and assumptions against which plays like *Hamlet* first achieved their effect. The stage was above all eclectic in the source materials it drew on and the cultural influences it refracted, and my range of contextual reference accordingly extends from erudite algebraic treatises, or disquisitions on Augustine and Aquinas, to popular ballads and accounts of popular superstitions. My treatment of iconography likewise derives from both scholarly digests such as Ripa's *Iconologia* and less rigorous works like Batman's *Golden Booke of the Leaden Goddes* because, as Noel Purdon points out, 'as a dramatist Shakespeare had working on him an unusually various assembly of [mythographic] material' from inn-signs to dictionaries (205). 'There is no distinct, mathematically conceived system of correspondence', agrees Malcolm Evans, and the 'commonly identifiable pool of symbolism' which he argues for is one which I seek to establish and exploit (114). It should finally be noted that a measure of familiarity with the better known plays of the period is assumed, so that more space may be devoted to a fuller explication of less familiar but influential military texts. In a sense the clearest justification of my method lies in the scope it shares with my subject: for the effects of war were felt in pubs as well as palaces and represented most richly in the playhouses that dramatized both.

## Notes

1. *The Atheist's Tragedy*, eds Morris and Gill (1976), vii.
2. See also Burelbach (1968), 100, and Marcus (1988), xiii.
3. See also MacCaffrey (1992), 95, 131, 137, 168, 296, and 571.
4. See also Aydelotte (1913), 72.
5. Compare *A Myrrour*, B1v-B2r and Greene, *Works*, ed. Grosart (1964), 6, 206-8.
6. See for example G. Gould (1919) and O.B. Campbell (1921).

CHAPTER ONE

# Casualties of War

*'Does it matter? — losing your legs?'* [1]

The tall story is told of a conscientious theatre-critic, whose diffidence towards definitive judgement was at last relieved by an assignment to review the latest touring Shakespeare production. Now he was 'prepared to assert unequivocally that Sarah Bernhardt was the greatest one-legged female Hamlet of her generation'.[2] The leg-pull is quickly revealed: Bernhardt opened in *Hamlet* in Paris in May 1899, and in London the following month; her leg was not amputated until after the outbreak of the First World War, and there were no revivals (Richardson, 141, 170). But the comedy of the anecdote, the exaggerated taxonomy of its critic's hedged bets, in fact disguises as absurd two distinct theatrical traditions.

The first is plain. Historians of the nineteenth-century stage agree that 'female Hamlets were by no means rare', that Bernhardt's assumption of the role belongs in a 'distinct tradition' of mature actresses playing youths, and 'should not be regarded as entirely untoward' (Trewin, 120; C. Smith, 223). As unremarkable, perhaps, as the first (male) Ophelia, though *Punch* overlooked that far older tradition too, in its sarcastic suggestion that Bernhardt's cast be supplemented by Henry Irving in that role.

The second is less apparent. A one-legged Hamlet, female or not, seems to prompt the same laughter as attended Peter Cook's sketch in which a diplomatic theatrical agent attempts to dissuade a one-legged actor from the part of Tarzan, 'a role for which two legs would seem to be the minimum requirement' (H. Thompson, 83). Such laughter meets rebuke in the circumstances of Bernhardt's disability. One of the first roles she played after losing her leg was that of a front-line nurse in a patriotic film; in 1916 she toured the front in person, performing inspiriting recitals to the *poilus*. 'She continued like a soldier of the theatre' (Richardson, 179): her biographer's remark gains poignancy when one considers that she shared her handicap with so many casualties of the First World War; and that Bernhardt herself seems to have recognized the bitter parallel between player and soldier. She composed the monologue she performed in London in 1916, in which (as one young member of the audience recalled) 'she played the part of a young French *poilu* lying mortally wounded on a bank in the wood near the battlefield ... she recited some patriotic verses, after which she fell back dead', and was carried off by stretcher-bearers (Trewin, 129). Like a soldier to and from the stage: it is entirely fitting that the author of that eye-witness account is Sir John Gielgud, unequivocally the greatest Hamlet of his generation.

The maimed rites Gielgud witnessed sound echoes to the circumstances of the stage for which *Hamlet* was composed. The recital of 'patriotic verses' by a 'mortally wounded' veteran finds perhaps its closest precedent in Talbot's dying speech to his dead son, in *1 Henry VI* (4.7.18-32). It is probably the passage Nashe bore in mind in his 'Defence of Plays' in *Piers Penilesse* (1592), recommending the reproof and encouragement such spectacles presented to their wartime audiences, 'who, in the Tragedian that represents his person, imagine they behold him fresh bleeding' (1, 212). As I shall argue in my final chapter, later audiences would have carried similarly inspiriting expectations of Old Hamlet's posthumous apparition through the opening scenes of that play. Furthermore, far from being incongruously comic, had Hamlet first limped on stage around 1601, he would have joined a gallery of one-legged military roles constituting a 'distinct tradition' of Elizabethan theatre. The humble *mutilé de guerre* of Elizabethan theatres of war was often made the spokesman for propagandist encouragement in wartime theatres; and unlike Bernhardt's, the 'lower half' of whose body was 'covered with a rug' (Trewin, 129), such characters drew attention to their singular disability.

When the wars were over, the likes of Othello (1604), Bussy d'Ambois (1604), and Coriolanus (1608) underwent an uneasy transition from casque to cushion, while the neglected plight of their disabled P.B.I. haunted the fringes of their stage as the occasion of a bitter comedy. 'What wold you have me do?', asks the pandar Boult in *Pericles* (1607), 'go to the wars, wold you? wher a man may serve 7. yeers for the losse of a leg, & have not money enough in the end to buy him a woodden one?' (4.6.170-2). Webster has Bosola calculate the same meagre returns from military apprenticeship in *The Duchess of Malfi* (1613). In a period when '*Mathematicall Muses*' were deployed 'upon this *Militare Argument*',[3] the 'Geometry' awaiting 'a Souldier, that hazards his limbes in a battaile' is caustic: 'to hang in a faire paire of slings ... upon an honorable pare of Crowtches, from hospitall to hospitall' (1.1.57-62). One such veteran with a 'Stump of wood' volunteers his expertise in 'the rules i'th Schoole of warre' in Dekker's *If This Be Not a Good Play, The Devil Is In It* (1611), only to be 'baffuld | For my limbes lost in service'. 'Ile stand toot, I', he says. 'With one leg', comes the scornful reply (2.1.105-24). While drawing attention to a welfare system that remained rudimentary through the reigns of both Elizabeth and James (Cruickshank, 182-88; Gasper, 116), abrasive jokes like these were limited to the stuff of isolated walk-ons and asides. Such distinguished portrayals of the plight of veterans as postwar Hollywood's *The Best Years of Our Lives* (1946) find no precedent on the Jacobean stage.

While the wars continued, their Elizabethan victims were not excluded from the stage in the way their descendants were to be from the screen. Limping casualties of war populated the Elizabethan theatre – on occasion holding centre-stage – because the range of their signification was made broader by wartime. Criticism of the neglect of disabled veterans was tempered there by an imperative tendency to enlist their status to the patriotic demands made on their audiences. As we shall see, London playhouses were the site of both notional and actual recruitment, and the Old Soldier was made the focus of a series of responses to the pressing circumstances of war. One play, *A Larum for London*, contrived a crippled hero in order to demonstrate the principles of the Just War his audiences were then being expected to wage. The construction of that play's hero was balanced by a similarly counterfactual villain, whose dramatic pedigree involved the vexed iconological status of the one-legged soldier.

Scholars from previous centuries have notably fixed upon unidexterity as evidence of the singularity of their subjects. So Capell's *Notes ... to Shakespeare* (1779) includes an account of the Bard's 'accidental lameness', evidenced by two references from *The Sonnets* (Schoenbaum, 202-3); and according to Collier, Marlowe 'brake his leg in one lewd scene | When in his earlie age' (Dabbs, 65) – a forgery usefully corroborative to his ascription to Marlowe of *A Larum for London*. Yet both the on-stage injury Collier contrives for Marlowe (break a leg!), and the mystery Capell weaves about Shakespeare's injury ('without saying how, or when, of what sort, or in what degree') overlook the theatres of war in which so many of the playwrights' countrymen lost their limbs.

'I am a Souldier', says Dekker's veteran; 'We know that by your legges', comes the retort (2.1.100-101). This chapter seeks to explore the range of meaning attached by Elizabethan playwrights to a figure already revealed here as a site of conflicting emotion. We may find a one-legged actor comic, with Peter Cook ('I've got nothing against your right leg. The trouble is – neither have you') or poignant, with John Gielgud ('The curtain fell, but rose again ... to reveal her standing proudly upright on one leg, leaning her hand on the shoulder of her fellow-actors'). Elizabethan dramatists erected about the damaged figure of the returning soldier an ideological scaffolding that enhanced both roles, and which sought comparison and contrast between war and revenge, valour and villainy, hero and braggart.

### 'Her privates we' [4]

'We know that by your legges': if a soldier was known by the halting gait he managed, it was a badge of office shared by all ranks of Elizabeth's army, from the limping General Mountjoy (Falls, 1955, 233) to the 'souldiour with one legge' celebrated in Churchyard's *General Rehearsall of Warres*, 'whose name was haltyng Dick' (1579, E4r). But veterans like Churchyard or Riche made no bones about the 'colde reward' in store for the rank and file, the 'lacke of limmes', the 'Lame lims and legs, and mangled bones' ventured in a soldier's service (Riche, 1578, E2r, E2v; Churchyard, 1596 B4v). Contemporary playwrights variously testify to how unremarkable were such casualties.

Robert Wilson's *The Cobbler's* Prophecy (printed 1594), for example, narrates Ralph's embassy to the Court of Mars, sent by Mercury, to warn of the dangers of neglecting military expertise. 'Art thou one of God Mars his traine?' he asks at the gates, 'Alas good father thou art lame'; 'My lamenes comes by warre, | My armours rustines comes by peace', comes the reply, 'A maimed souldier made Mars his Porter | Lo thus I am'.[5] Shakespeare too contrives a casual reminder to Orsino of a recent battle in *Twelfth Night* (1602), 'When your yong Nephew *Titus* lost his legge' (5.1.59). Dekker builds the evident familiarity of such asides into an entire subplot, when he allows the 'smoake of Warre' (49) to drift across his own comic stage in *The Shoemakers' Holiday* (1599). '*Enter Rafe being lame*', read Dekker's stage-directions there (3.2.54), his choice of name for a cobbler-turned-soldier, suggestive of Wilson's influence on his play.

In contrast to his Jacobean descendant (the spurned soldier in Dekker's *If This Be Not a Good Play*), the harsh realism of Ralph's predicament is tempered by the accommodation it receives within the solidarity of the 'Gentle Craft' the play celebrates. 'Limbs?', exclaims Hodge, 'hast thou not hands man? thou shalt never see a shoomaker want bread, though he have but three fingers on a hand' (76-7). The painful ironies of Ralph's status as a one-legged shoemaker are not shirked, but transcended: 'since I want lims and lands', says Ralph, 'Ile to God, my good friends, and to these my hands' (101-2). At the same time as cementing wartime 'Anglo-Dutch solidarity' (Gasper, 21), the play is careful to reward Ralph's humble resignation. Not only does his wife recognize the error of her ways in dallying with another, but he receives 'twentie pound' (5.2.90) from his shamed rival, double the private's pension proposed in 1597 (Cruickshank, 185). To 'the number of Captaines and Souldiers about *London*' that Nashe recorded among theatre-audiences (1, 212), Ralph's progress through *The Shoemakers' Holiday* must have offered reassurance, the more effective (however spurious) for its steady contemplation of hands without fingers, men without limbs. The play's measuredly wishful thinking extends as far as to transform the apparatus of Ralph's disability into a 'brave sport': 'the prowdest of you that laies hands on her first, Ile lay my crutch crosse his pate' (5.2.132-4). The same reassurances were elsewhere repeatedly pressed home.

'For lims, you shall have living, lordships, lands', announces the king in Peele's *Edward I* (1593) to a group of 'maimed Souldiers'.[6] In today's currency, Ralph's gift of twenty pounds is relatively modest – some £12,500 (Nicholl, 1992, [xiv]); Longshanks presents the equivalent of five million to certain of his 'Countrimen' whose 'lims are lost in service of the Lord' (111). Yet in an escalating auction, his queen trumps even this bounty by adding a nought ('*shee makes a Cipher*') to the pension he proposes (193). 'To a souldier sir', comments Sir David of Brecknock, one 'cannot be too liberall' (167). The scene is replayed in allegorical mode at the climactic trial of *The Contention Between Liberality and Prodigality* (printed 1602):

| 3 SUITER | Now, good my Lord, vouchsafe of your charitie, |
| | To cast here aside your pittifull eye, |
| | Upon a poore souldier, naked and needy, |
| | That in the Queenes Warres was maimed, as you see. |
| LIBERALITY | Where have you served? |
| 3 SUITER | In Fraunce, in Flaunders, but in Ireland most.[7] |

'He was my souldier, indeed sir, untill he lost his legge', confirms Captain Wel-Don (1226). The bulk of this play perhaps dates from the 1560s, but (as Greg noticed) seems to have been revised to include reference to the specific campaigns of 'the Queenes Warres' in time for its intended performance before her, dated in the text itself as 4 February 1600/01. *Edward I* also sounded topical that year – or so we may infer from the price Henslowe paid for it in August (*Henslowe's Diary*, 204). In any case, the theatrical profile of crippled veterans increased substantially during the last few years of Elizabeth's life and wars – years that included the largest invasion-scare since 1588, a disastrous campaign in Ireland, and increasingly urgent recruitments to military service from among London's inhabitants.

Fantasies of Liberality like these were predicated upon the twin circumstances of a converse reality: that after fifteen years of war, large numbers of men were still being (more or less forcibly) enlisted to fight; and that for such men, the end of campaigning was, as the military author Matthew Sutcliffe had commented, 'the beginning of beggarie and calamitie to many poore souldiers' (1593, 298-9). Dramatists seem accordingly to have realized that a conspicuous gratitude to veterans was useful in garnering sympathy for their heroes. So Heywood contrives the reading of Bess Bridges's will in *The Fair Maid of the West* (c.1600): 'To relieve maimed Souldiers, by the yeare ten pound'.[8] And '*Some souldiers*' with 'maimed limbs' are among those who petition the protagonist of *The Life of Sir John Oldcastle* (1599, printed 1600).[9] 'There be more stockes to set poore soldiers in', complains one, 'Than there be houses to releeve them at' (327-8). Oldcastle shrugs off his steward's distaste and offers them 'such alms as there is to be had' (405-6). The speech-prefix specifies that it is a '*Souldier*' who is first to thank him (407). The contrast with the character originally named Sir John Oldcastle in *1 Henry IV* (Q 1598) could not be more explicit: 'I have led my rag of Muffins where they are pepper'd, theres not three of my 150. left alive, and they are for the townes ende, to beg during life' (5.3.35-8).[10] Each addresses, from opposite corners, the 'beggarie' endured by veterans. 'And yet lame as I am, Ile with the king into France, if I can crawle but a ship-boorde' (341-2): in common with all the lame soldiers in these plays, Oldcastle's supplicant suborns his social grievances to an unquestioned patriotic duty, acidly though they are voiced: 'I hadde rather be slaine in France, than starve in England' (343).

The popularity and sympathy evoked by characters like these among audiences swelled by 'Captaines and Souldiers' is evinced by two further plays of the period, each of which affords them starring roles. Captain Bowyer and Lieutenant Vaughan, the soldier-heroes of *The Trial of Chivalry* and *A Larum for London* respectively, are each advertised on the title-page of their plays' first editions. Bowyer, slightingly addressed as 'Stumps' (C2v), has 'halfe the nature of a Badger, for one leg is shorter than another' (C1v). 'And still my olde rotten stump and I, | Trot up and downe as long as we can wag', declares Vaughan, referred to throughout his play's stage-directions and speech-prefixes as Stump (746-7).[11] Probably performed around 1600-02, the roles of both protagonists speak at large to their wartime contexts, Bowyer to the recent campaigns in France, Stump to those persisting in the Low Countries.

Bowyer and Stump variously embody an iconography of what, in 1598, Robert Barret called *The Theorike and Practike of Modern Warres*. Before concentrating attention on their emblematic status as *mutilés de guerre*, however, it is necessary to provide an overview of the theoretical and practical modernity they inhabit. Elizabethan doctrines of war, as Jorgensen summarizes, 'suggest the fitting of pagan theory, historical fact, or socio-economic necessity into a framework of Christian ideals' (1952, 479). While a range of (often contradictory) authority was cited to explain the fact of Elizabethan war, contemporaries perceived the techniques of its waging to be quite without precedent. Henry Barret observed in 1562 'how throughe mutacion of tymes and invencions of menns wittes the practises of the wares dothe daylie alter and chaunge' (Hale, 1983, 271), and Thomas Lodge's *A Fig for Momus* (1595) agreed that 'All things are chang'd, the meanes, the men and armes, | Our stratagems now differ from the old' (E1r). Taking its cue from the play's title, the remainder of this section will call *The Trial of Chivalry* as witness to the range of doctrine and 'mutacion of tymes' that animate its main plot and Captain Bowyer's role within it. Discussion is then focused, via the iconographic pertinence of their shared handicap, on to Lieutenant Stump and his representation of the central Elizabethan doctrine of the just war.

*The Trial of Chivalry* has been called a 'pseudo-history' (Harbage and Schoenbaum, 81), but its fictional occasion – a truce between contending claimants to the French throne – was real enough. The Franco-Spanish peace of Vervins was an 'accomplished fact' by May 1598 (MacCaffrey, 515), and the King of Navarre, now Henry IV, 'settle[d] ... into a quiet government' (Riche, 1598, E2r). The play's King of Navarre is likewise assisted in his claim by 'Englishmen | Squadron'd with ours' (A2r), and the novel freedom of references like these suggests contemporary affinities with the four-part 'syvell wares of france' Henslowe commissioned for the Rose in 1598-99. The extreme symmetries of the play's construction enable its love-plots (so that each king's son and daughter are matched with their counterparts), but they offer too a usefully schematic account, to audiences still preoccupied by war in Ireland and the Low Countries, of what Dick Bowyer calls 'the difference betweene these French Curres, and our English

Cavaliers' (E1r). In particular, the chivalric peace-keeping role of the play's Earl of Pembroke is formally contrasted with the scheming belligerence of Rodorick, 'a perfect villayne' (H4r). Pembroke and Rodorick are the opposing counsels of *The Trial of Chivalry*, and comprise exempla of the contradictory views expounded in contemporary military pamphlets. Briefly put, Pembroke represents the theory of the 'just war' (A3r), Rodorick the practice of the 'wily stratageme' (A3v).

Nicholas Breton's 'Character' of war begins with the common Elizabethan doctrine, after St Augustine, that 'Warre is a scourge of the wrath of God, which by famine, fire, or sword, humbleth the spirits of the Repentant, tryeth the patience of the Faithfull, and hardneth the hearts of the ungodly' (1615, 23). Augustine 'accepted the scourge of war as a consequence of sin ... and also, on certain conditions, a remedy for it' (Russell, 5). The central issue of his break with the robust pacifism of the early Church lay in those conditions, the circumstances by which war might be justified, a stance best characterized as extreme reluctance. War was a 'sad necessity', but sadder still would be the domination of just men by wrongdoers (I. Clark, 33). So de Loque's *Discourse of Warre* (1590) prescribes the 'greate neede, and ... case of extremity' which can only justifiy resort to arms, 'and then to use it as a remedy very dangerous and mortall' (16), the same 'last refuge' Thomas Beard's *Theatre of Gods Judgements* allows, 'when all other meanes of maintaining our estate against the assaults of the enemy faile' (1597, 294). These are the terms by which C.G., in *A Watch-worde for Warre* (1596), distinguishes between Spain's 'injurious' belligerence and the 'just' cause of England's self-defence (F4r). Christian soldiers were the instruments of a 'divine police action' (van Elbe, 668), their mandate, following Aquinas, 'the conservation of peace' (Russell, 5): 'The End, which ought to be aymed at in war, is not victory but peace' (C.G., G2v). The third of Aquinas's refinements of the requisite conditions for war (right authority as a minister of God, just cause in punishing a fault, and right intention in doing so) insisted on the restriction of the methods by which such a war may be prosecuted (J. Johnson, 38-43).

By the sixteenth century, a series of new interpretations had come to be placed upon this classic formula. Firstly, 'proper authority had come largely to mean the authority of the secular sovereign prince', who in the decline of the Church's role in war became plaintiff, prosecutor and judge of his own cause (J. Johnson, 76-7). Secondly, just cause (divine punishment of sin) had 'been reduced to worldly size', and the notion of 'invincible ignorance' by which God alone knows the justice of a war, allowed an honourable fight to both sides (188-95). Thirdly, right intention had shifted its once exclusive concern of the belligerent prince to that of each individual soldier, to banish from his heart the 'real evils in war' (78) Augustine had censured: 'love of violence, revengeful cruelty, fierce and implacable enmity' (Hartigan, 198). 'How can Mercie and Revenge draw both in one yoke?', asks the ignorant Captain Pill in Riche's *Souldiers Wishe*, to whom Captain Skill explains that 'as the pleasure of Revenge, doth sudainlie passe away so the contentment of Mercie doth for evermore indure' (1604, 49). The classic just war theory that was bequeathed to the Elizabethan period comprised a synthesis of traditions, or 'confluence of various streams – religious, chivalric, and secular' (I. Clark, 38). The *jus ad bellum* (governing the rights of under-taking war) was mainly derived from ecclesiastical sources, the *jus in bello* (the proper conduct of war, by which its outcome could be affected) principally from secular chivalric sources – 'the remnants of the decaying chivalric code' (J. Johnson, 75).

The extent of that decay in the Elizabethan period remains a matter of debate.[12] Richard McCoy has insisted on the enduring political importance of what he calls *The Rites of Knighthood*, dismissing previous accounts of chivalry as an outdated, self-conscious delusion (1989, 15-16). While his own definition of it as a 'cultural resolution' (2) of the Elizabethan political dichotomy between knightly independence and duty to the state is convincing, a shift is conceded in chivalry's arena from 'actual warfare' (50) to its courtly symbolism. The decline of its military relevance coincides with the emergence of a professional soldiery. During the war-years of the 1590s, 'only a minority [of the nobility] took an active part in military campaigns' (Stone, 239); 'humanism intellectualised [chivalry], focussing on strategy rather than on valor' (Whigham, 1984, 75). The prominence of a medieval knight's military role, the mounted battle, waned as 'war reverted to its earlier pattern of siege and countersiege', assisted by technological advances in ballistics and fortification (Vale, 171). Such wars were infantry-based, and as the sixteenth century advanced, recruitment in England was increasingly made in the form of shire levies, as opposed to the quasi-feudal system by which men were enlisted from among the retinue of noblemen (Goring, 185-97). With the implementation of strategies culled from Roman military treatises, the hierarchical retinue of the chivalrous knight was supplanted by a greater insistence on the solidarity of all soldiers. The reorientation of chivalry's medieval orders to the services of the state, and the conditions of modern warfare, reduced the trappings of chivalry to a 'picturesque appearance' on the battlefield (Hale, 1961, 1) though its sym-bolism still housed crucial political issues at home.

Certain components of Just War theory find dramatic expression in the presentation of the Earl of Pembroke in *The Trial of Chivalry*. De Loque's *Discourse of Warre* (1590) sets out a list of 'rules and lawes to be practised of those that undertake to wage warre', chief among which is the iteration of Augustine's necessary reluctance (17). Since 'warre traineth after it so many and infinite mischeifes, that worthily it is called *the scourge of God*'; and since 'the end of war be to seeke to conclude peace againe', the warrior should be careful 'before hee make warre, that hee assay by all meanes possible to maintaine peace and concord' (16-17). In the play, Pembroke repeatedly intercedes between its contending factions, appealing to them to 'sheathe your weapons: by our martiall law' (C2v), to 'cease the fight' (I1r), and seeking (as de Loque prescribes) 'to pacify and accord all differences, before he proceede to armes' (17). This exemplary reluctance is dramatized when, challenged by the 'misse-inform'd' Prince Ferdinand of Navarre (E2r), Pembroke is forced into combat only when wounded:

> Wound me so desperately? nay then ile draw,
> Not to offend, but to defend my selfe.
> Now I perceyve it is my bloud thou seekst:
> Witnesse you heavens, and all you gracious powers,
> That stand auspicious to this enterprise,
> That Pembrooke drawes forth an unwilling sword.
> (E2v)

When both combatants are felled, Ferdinand's response is characterized by what Augustine censured as 'fierce and implacable enmity' ('I hope I have slayne thee') while Pembroke's demonstrates the appropriate regret resort to arms brings with it ('Oh, I feare thy life') (E2r). Believing Ferdinand dead, Pembroke erects a tomb to him and once more intervenes between the armies of France and Navarre (G2v), successfully challenging the knights of either retinue to single combat in his honour. The 'picturesque' redundancy of such gestures in the actual campaigns in France in the 1590s are made indistinguishable from the theoretical justice of English involvement, as a divine police force, in the continuing European campaigns.[13]

Pembroke's romanticized tournament is succeeded by its most vivid scenic counterpart, the double-betrayal effected by Rodorick on the turncoat Burbon, to whom he leads the vengeful Prince Philip of France, and on Philip himself, whose killing of Burbon (though 'In knightly maner') Rodorick denounces as murder (H3v). Rodorick is systematically contrasted with Pembroke throughout the play. Where Pembroke 'drawes forth an unwilling sword' in the name of a higher power, Rodorick 'builds his hopes' on 'mutuall strife' and 'civill discord', 'laugh[ing] to see these Kings at jarre' (F2v). Where Pembroke insists on reluctant limitation in the practice of arms through chivalric single combat, Rodorick urges 'Ruthelesse and bloudy slaughters' (I1r), revealing what C.G. proscribed as the soldier's 'Sinister Joy' (C4v).

Crucially, where Pembroke subscribes to de Loque's second rule that 'the end of war be to seeke to conclude peace' (17), Rodorick flouts the third, 'That no man warre to the ende to usurpe the goods and inheritances of other men' (18). 'Burbon is thine', he gloats after assisting in the poisonous disfigurement of Prince Philip's betrothed,

> the Dukedome is thine owne:
> For onely he in the Inheritance
> Stood as an obstacle, to let my clayme.
> This deed of his will take away his life:

> And then let me alone to injoy his land.
> (D2r)

His declared motive draws on a long-standing tradition of war theory substantially distinct from that of the Just War, and one again touched upon by C.G. 'The Phylosophers', he writes, 'define war to be the pride of Princes; We reade of *Alexander*, that hee was so aspyring minded, that he thought the whole world too little to satisfie his lust' (C1v). Whetstone's *Honourable Reputation of a Souldier* (1586) begins by evoking the time that '*Ambition*, the Impe of miscreate *Envy*, upon desire of Soveraigntie, begat *Warre*' (25). 'Secularized interpretations of war's inevitability', comments Hale, 'given rulers' ambition and the nature of man as a political animal, led to cyclical theories on the lines of Luigi da Porto's "peace brings riches, riches pride, pride wrath, wrath war, war poverty, poverty mildness, mildness peace, peace riches", and so on and on' (1985, 39).

George Gascoigne's 1575 poem *The Fruites of Warre*, with its preliminary survey of 'What thing warre is, and wherof it proceeds', demonstrates the currency of such a view in Elizabethan England.[14] 'What sayth the common voice'? it asks:

> That Princes pryde is cause of warre alway:
> Plentie brings pryde, pryde plea, plea pine, pine peace,
> Peace plentie, and so (say they) they never cease.
> (9)

The lessons of this secular view of war's perpetual cycle, dependent not upon a periodically indignant God, but upon the political nature of man, were covertly accepted and publicly denounced (J. Johnson, 63-4, n.42). Gascoigne for example could 'never ... thinke *Vox populi vox Dei est*' (10) since 'If pryde make warre (as common people prate) | Then is it good (no doubt) as good may bee' (16), whereas war is a divinely appointed evil to be shunned by repentance in all strata of society (19-25); Thomas Fenne's treatise on war terms this chain of natural causation (war, ruin, poverty, peace, riches, envy, malice, war) a 'sophisticall argument' (1590, P1v); and to C.G., succinctly, 'War is nothing else but a divine scourge for sinne' (C2r).

Yet, as Hale continues, the reasoning behind this Livyan model of a self-regulating political system led to the commonplace espousal of a variety of its implications. That in the midst of peace one should prepare for war, for example, especially necessary given England's relative military backwardness at the time of Elizabeth's accession (see *Henry V*, 2.3.16-20). Or that war might actually improve a national community, by diverting potential dissent abroad, 'to busie giddie mindes | With forraine quarrells' (*2 Henry IV*, 4.5.342-3), or providing the hygienic disposal of 'social dross' (Hale, 40), the 'meanes to vent | Our mustie superfluity' (*Coriolanus*,

1.1.225-6). That last image finds a parallel in many contemporary instances. Riche's 1604 tract, for example, after characterizing war as 'the scourge of God to punish sinnes', proceeds to reason that war is the

> oyle in the stomacke that hath disgested poyson, as a medecine to a body that is choaked up with corrupt humours, as a Fyre to the mettall that wants refining, as exercise to the body growne pursie with ydlenesse.
> (4)

Dudley Digges likened war to a dose of mercury (1604, 105); Walter Ralegh, in his *Discourse of Warre*, to a 'potion of *Rubarbe*, to wash away Choler from the body of the Realme' (1650, D5r); and John Marston used the cyclic sequence of Peace to Peace via Plenty, Pride, War, and Poverty, as the basis of the six-act structure of *Histrio-Mastix* (performed *c*.1598), in which it is War's role to 'purge the aire of these grosse foggy clouds' of luxury (1610, E4r).

The rigid personifications of Marston's play allow his Chrisoganus to moralize that 'Justice hath whips to scourge impiety' (F4r). In effect and at root, however, the two systems of thought – war as a divine scourge of sin, and war as a political instrument of will – were incompatible, as Fenne, Gascoigne and C.G. all variously agreed. Other writers made a virtue of necessity by accommodating such conflicting views to an admission of war's 'impossible infinit', 'neyther hath arte ever sought out a subject more ambiguous' (Riche, 1604, 4). Breton called war 'Reasons trouble' after opening his Character of War with a sentence including both theories: 'Warre is a scourge of the wrath of God ... it is the misery of Time, and the terror of Nature, the dispeopling of the Earth' (1615, 23). The difficulties of squaring the latter, secular views with the demands of Christian orthodoxy were further compounded by the fact that Machiavelli was the most infamous exponent of them, his *Discorsi* an influential source of both Ralegh's *Discourse of Warre* (1650) (Luciani, 1948) and Shakespeare's *Coriolanus* (Barton, 1994, 136-60).

Machiavelli's philosophy of war are a sort of exact negative-image of those of his contemporary, Erasmus. In his *Querela Pacis* (1516), and his 1515 Adage, *Dulce Bellum Inexpertis*, Erasmus interpreted the militant language of Old Testament prophecy strictly metaphorically, insisting that 'he that dyvulgath warre, divulgath hym that is mooste unlyke Chryste' (1559, B7r). The innocents so outnumber the sinful in war, he argued, that the notion of its punitive remedy as the scourge of God was untenable: on the contrary, sins are 'learnt in war' (1559, E8r), itself the 'sede of all evylles' (A5r). Most importantly, Erasmus challenged the notion of the just war, since 'this means any war declared in any way against anybody by any prince' (*Adages*, tr. Phillips, 337). In later life, he came to admit the use of war 'when reduced to extreme need, and if all other means have failed' – to admit, in other words, one of the basic premises of the just war (Fernández, 224); but his influence over Elizabethan military thought renewed the relevance of Augustine's doctrine. So in the first essay of *Allarme to England* (1578), Riche cited Old Testament scripture 'to proove that warres have byn acceptable before ... God', before rehearsing Christ's turning of the other cheek (A2v): 'But I trust they wyll not mainteyne by this that a Prince should surrender up his crowne' to an aggressor (A3v). While Erasmus disputed war's divine provenance, claiming its manmade status as an affront to his creator, Machiavelli denied this orthodoxy for the purposes of military reform.

Machiavelli's sardonic remark in *The Prince* refutes the causation of war from sin as uncompromisingly as Erasmus:

> Whereupon *Charles* the King of *France*, without oppos-
> ing made himself master of all *Italy*: and he that said, that
> the cause thereof were our faults [*peccati*], said true; but
> these were not those they beleevd, but what I have told;
> and because they were the Princes faults, they also have
> suffered the punishment.
> (tr. Dacres, 1640, 93-4)

War is a punishment dispensed by men not God; the 'faults' castigated those of ignorance rather than sin. To Machiavelli, a prince must be a soldier, because war is 'part and parcel of his general philosophy of politics' (Earle et al., 22), 'the foundation of all states is in "good arms"' (I. Clark, 14), and war is both natural and expedient. His challenge to the pious reluctance Augustine prescribed (*jus ad bellum*) was accompanied by an equally dismissive stance regarding *jus in bello*. It is victory rather than method that is important (Earle et al., 14), the 'extremity of the contrast' succinctly demonstrated by Ian Clark's quotation: 'Where the very safety of the country depends upon the resolution to be taken, no considerations of justice or injustice, humanity or cruelty, nor of glory or shame, should be allowed to prevail' (51).

The lessons of such pragmatism were soon learned in Elizabethan England: Machiavelli's *Arte of Warre*, in Whitehorne's translation, 'thrice issued, in 1562, 1574 and 1588 – remained the only published translation of any work by Machiavelli till 1595' (Anglo, 1969, 129-30). But his opinions as to the enfeebling effects on soldiers by Christianity were impossible to align with the notion of war as the scourge of God. Barnaby Riche carefully distinguished between 'true Christian valiance' ('that fighteth for equitie and justice') and the 'knowledge, skil or policie, that is severed from justice' which 'is rather called subtiltie then wisedome'. It is no wonder, he claimed, that Machiavelli thought it 'not convenient for a Captaine, to be overmuch inclined to religion' since the true religious conscience would balk at the methods of 'fraude, deceit, and injurie' he counselled, and prove 'an abatement of their hairebraind rashnesse, which by them is called courage and valiance' (1598, C4v-D1r). Such distinctions (as James Freeman puts it in his study of *Milton's Martial Muse*) 'polarize about the time-battered axes of a human commander', force or guile, *bia* or *dolos*, the lion or the fox (156). Riche may call Machiavelli 'the divells politician', but the 'ethics of expedience' (J. Freeman, 163) he advanced were commonly promoted in contemporary military treatises, though often held at arm's length. For all Sutcliffe's derision for Machiavelli as an armchair soldier (1593, A4v), he still maintained that 'whatsoever tendeth to deceive, and abuse the enemy ... the same ought wise leaders to devise, & practice', 'Provided alway, that they neither breake othe, nor promise nor offend against piety, or the lawes of nations. Let such vile facts be practiced of Turks, & Spaniards'(196). This tacit consensus prompted John Udall's complaint in *The True Remedie Against Famine and Warres* (1586) at 'these our daies, wherein the moste blasphemous conclusions, and pestiferous platformes of that Italian hel-hound *Machiavell*, are so reputed of and esteemed, that he onely is reckoned a right politist, that frameth his course after his rules ... and yet doth he esteeme as much of religion, as of *Aesopes* fables' (65r-v).

Jorgensen has absorbingly described how the 'cosmopolitan stream of military science' met resistance in 'English military provincialism', and how its dissembling techniques are 'of the sort usually practised by villains in Elizabethan drama' (1956b, 46-9). That observation is borne out by *The Trial of Chivalry*, most amply by the scene in which Rodorick the 'perfect villayne' (H4r) stages his double-betrayal. Swiftly succeeding the chivalric combat of Pembroke's tournament, the scene presents vivid testimony as to how 'Our stratagems now differ from the old' (Lodge, 1595, E1r).

The familiar language of Machiavellian stage-villainy (Praz, 1928) and 'policy' (Orsini, 1946) surrounds Rodorick's progress through the play. Dispensing villainous asides, he conspires with, then betrays Burbon's 'wily stratageme' and 'plot' (A3v), poisons Bellamira, and seduces Prince Philip to the 'complot' of his methods (H2v). But the scene in which, Iago-like, he contrives Philip's murder of Burbon only to betray him as a murderer, takes place within a context that emphasizes the military aspects of his plotting: 'Go to your Tent', he tells Burbon, 'There draw your battels modell'. 'Ha Rodoricke', exclaims Burbon, 'are not we fine Polyticians', before being urged to 'Sit downe, sit downe and make your warlike plot'. Burbon's strategic mapping of the new military science ('Some paper, pen, and incke ... Post to the Master Gunner, | And bid him plant his demy culverings | Against the kings pavilion ... I will to my plot') provides the apt occasion for his betrayal by Rodorick. Udall's 'pestiferous platformes' are elided into a compact image that equates the plotting of military science with the plots of murderous villainy:

> BURBON  The Incke that's in the Standage doth looke blacke,
> This in my pen is turnd as red as blood.

PHILIP    The reason that the platforme you would make,
              Must by this hand be written with thy bloud.

(H3r)

*The Trial of Chivalry* is itself mapped out by the co-ordinates of contemporary debate. Just as military theorists demonized the sources of the political expedience they tacitly promoted, so the play rewards Rodorick's 'trecheries ... with death' (I3r), but dramatizes the accommodation of his 'policy' to native belligerent traditions. For the 'Model of vertue, honord Pembroks Earle' (K1r), finally resolves a lasting peace by deploying the hitherto questionable resources of strategic deception:

Princes, agree: force cannot end this war, but policy.
Therefore dispearse your selves, and let our Squires,
With Trumpets in their mouthes sound lowd retreat,
Where you perceive the fight most violent.
The strangeness of which act will straight amaze,
When they shall heare both peace and war denounc'd,
And one selfe instant, they will soone retire.
(I2r)

One of Frontinus's *Stratagemes, Sleyghtes, and Policies of Warre* was (in Morysine's translation) 'To dissemble retreate' (1539, K2r). Despite the chivalric trappings of his 'Squires', Pembroke's dissimulation clearly owes a debt to what Sutcliffe called the 'speciall and yet common stratageme ... to cover our counsels and enterprises by contrary pretenses' (1593, 192); 'And furthermore, a Generall may sometimes use dissimulation in his enterprises' (du Bellay, 1589, 219). 'Strength stryketh', Morysine's Frontinus reads, 'but Policie provydeth, that the stronge be not overmatched' (1539, A4r). *The Trial of Chivalry* provides a test-case for this compromise, yoking the limited mandate of one tradition ('The End ... aymed at in war, is not victory but peace') to the methods of another ('no considerations of ... glory or shame, should be allowed to prevail'). With de Loque, the play 'must put a distinction betwixt subtilty and treachery' (1590, 33), for ''Tis worke of charity ... If we could end this battell without bloud' (I2r).

Published soon after Riche's assertion that war was the most 'ambiguous' subject art could address, *The Trial of Chivalry* schematizes the Elizabethan variety of that ambivalence. For the defence stands Pembroke whose 'unwilling sword' is drawn in a chivalric intercession restricted to the ends of procuring peace, under God. For the prosecution stands Rodorick, impelled by his usurping ambition, whose military command substitutes for the model soldier's sword the artillery of the 'battels modell' (H2v). The figure celebrated on its title-page, however, is neither its chivalric hero nor its politic villain. The subplot, containing 'the life and death of Cavaliero Dicke Bowyer' it advertises,[15] presents, as I shall now argue, an exemplary amalgam of the traditions Pembroke comes to unify, and demonstrates, via a judicious system of selective allusion, the contemporary compromise that 'force cannot end this war, but policy'.

Bowyer's name reverberates with what a 1599 ballad called 'the noble conquestes' of England's military past, 'Obtainèd by the gray goose winge'.[16] More than a symbol of Agincourt, however, bowmen were also the subject of a contemporary debate *Concerning* (as the title of Barwick's 1594 contribution reads) *the Force and Effect of all Manuall Weapons of Fire, and the Disability of the Long Bowe*. There were still voices in the 1590s reluctant to cede dominance on the Elizabethan battlefield from bowyers to musketeers (Cruickshank, 114-15). Barwick's work sought to refute Sir John Smythe's ridicule of those who would 'subvert all our ancient proceedings in matters Militarie' (1590, B2r), in a spirit of pragmatism closely allied to England's accommodation of strategy by valour: 'Why should not Spaniards', counters Barwick, 'being owners of that pleasant wood the Yewe, become Bowmen and Archers?'(B2r).

The myth of Agincourt, reinvested in by *The Famous Victories of Henry the Fift* (printed 1598), *Sir John Oldcastle* (1599), *The Shoemakers' Holiday* (1599) and *Henry V* (1599), informs the main plot of *The Trial of Chivalry*. Countering the French king's scorn ('Their single force against our multitudes'), the cadence of Pembroke's words is familar from those famous victories: 'Nay, smile not, though our number's few | Our great hearts tell us, we shall conquere you' (I1v). Familiar too are both the romantic conquest Bowyer achieves and the halting French with which he manages it. 'He came over with the Earle of Pembrooke', complains Peter de Lions (Rodorick's servant to Rodorick, and Bowyer's rival for the hand of Thomasine): 'and he limps, and he limps, & he devoures more French ground at two paces, then will serve *Thomasin* at nineteen ... If ever he speake French he wil murder the toung' (C4v). Militarily disadvantaged and linguistically challenged, Dick Bowyer's 'lame legs' and 'lisping tongue' (C4v) offer a peculiarly enduring model of English soldiery: 'my heart is as sound as a bell, heart of Oake, spirit, spirit' (C1v).

Despite the Agincourt echoes of his name, the duties 'Captayne Bowyer' performs (C3r) are discernibly Elizabethan. First introduced setting the sentries' watch – 'Stand, give the word along, stand' (C1r) – he next announces that 'Ile to the trenches' (C3r), and we later see him 'walking of the Round', which is when he challenges Prince Ferdinand: 'but soft, *qui vou la?*' (D4r):

| | |
|---|---|
| FERDINAND | My name is Ferdinand. |
| BOWYER | Stand. |
| FERDINAND | Why, Captayne, thou dost know me well inough. |
| BOWYER | Know, or not know, without the word you passe not. |
| FERDINAND | Soliman. |
| BOWYER | So, *allie, allie, Monseur*. |

This is up-to-the-minute text-book soldiering, summarized, for example, in Robert Barret's marginal gloss to his detailed account of the 'severall duties' of sentries (1598, 103-9): 'The officer or Rounde; ought to give the word unto the Sentinell first. The souldier set at Sentinell, not bound to re-knowledge any person, without giving the word' (107). Not only does Bowyer follow Barret's *Practike of Moderne Warres*, but the language of its procedure is conspicuously continental. Barret's text included the word '*Trench*' ('a French word') in his glossary of 'sundry forraine words, used in these discourses' (1598, 248-52), and according to Garrard's *Arte of Warre*, the sentry must demand '*Qui vala?* Who goes there?' (1590, 12). Smythe supported his advocacy of the  longbow with a virulent condemnation of men (like Barret and Garrard) who 'will not vouchsafe in their speeches or writings to use our ancient termes belonging to matters of warre' (1590, B2v). Dick Bowyer's 'lisping tongue', forking between ancient and modern, accommodates both Smythe's distaste for, and Barret's embrace of, the jargon of war. 'I am an *Onyon*', he announces, 'if I had not rather serve formost in the forlorne hoope of a battell, or runne poynt blancke against the mouth of a double charged Cannon' (C1r).[17]

Shakespeare's *1 Henry IV*, thrice printed in 1598-99, casts a long shadow over *The Trial of Chivalry*. Sharing with Bowyer both a name bespeaking an earlier military age, and a tongue familiar with the currency of modern war,[18] it is Hotspur whose valour underpins Bowyer's final challenge to Peter: 'We must have bloudy noses: stand on your gard' (I3r; compare *1 Henry IV*, 2.4.90). 'Anon sir' replies Bowyer's sergeant as he sets the watch: 'Anon sir!', exclaims Bowyer, in a marked allusion to the comic mileage spun out by the earlier play (2.5), 's'hart, the Rogue answers like a Drawer' (C1r). But as his previous allusion shows ('I am an *Onyon*'), it is Falstaff with whom Bowyer most seeks comparison. 'If I do not teare out his heart and eate it with mustard', he vows, 'let him say Dick Bowyer's a Mackarell' (C2r). 'If I be not ashamed of my soldiours', says the fat knight, 'I am a souct gurnet' (4.2.12-13). The 'grinning honour' shunned by the evasive Falstaff on Shrewsbury field (5.3.58-9) finds its remorseful echo when Peter is killed: 'ah, sirra, never gryn for the matter, tis Captayne Bowyer that speakes it' (I3v). Such borrowings emphasize as well Bowyer's distance from his fellow-captain as his bid for a share in his robust popularity. Angling for the reflected glory of Jack Falstaff, Dick Bowyer carefully filters out the more troubling tones of his model.

Falstaff denounces his company as mere 'foode for powder' (4.2.66), while Bowyer tells his men they are 'are all dead men, all dust and ashes, all wormes meat' (C1v). But Bowyer is properly solicitous in his warning to 'follow my discipline' and not post 'a very Dormouse' as a sentry: 'if he shall find any negligence or carelessnesse in such officers, he is to reprehend and chasten them with such severity as the case and cause shall require' (Barret, 105). Falstaff, having 'misused the kinges presse damnablie', instead calculates how many 'dead-pays' he can afford to spend.[19] Indeed, it is Bowyer's rival Peter who is shown to display Falstaff's callous coward-ice: 'You that have nine lives', he instructs his '*2. or 3. souldiers*', when Rodorick orders the arrest of Prince Philip, 'assault the gentleman' (H4r).

If the play's Earl of Pembroke demonstrates the theoretical premise of the Just War, its Captain Bowyer dramatizes an idealized portrait of its practice, which, by systematic allusion, presents the impression of a loyalist Hotspur and a valiant Falstaff. Proficient in 'the discipline of warre' (D4v), Bowyer's equal custody of 'the law of armes' (E1v) rescues his expertise from the dastardly taint of Rodorick's 'warlike plot'. A veteran of the military past his name embodies, the limping Bowyer is a sympathetic model of contemporary soldiery. Yet, as the play's development of his role implies (and as a counterpart to its main plot) Bowyer comes to personify the punitive nature of war itself. Immediately after Pembroke's announcement of the alliance of force by policy, Peter enters, '*leading Thomasin*'(I2r). Her cries for help prompt in her oppressor a sarcastic challenge: 'And the God of warre come in thy defence, my humour is to kill him'. '*Enter Bowyer*' reads the immediate stage-direction. The invocation cues Bowyer's entrance on his 'lame legge' (G3r) to punish Peter's villainy. The texture of Bowyer's portrait is such, however, as to warrant contemplation as to which precise 'God of warre' Peter and his audiences might have held in mind.

'The Poets olde', begins Gascoigne's *Fruites of Warre*, 'in their fonde fables faine, | That mightie Mars is god of Warre and Strife' (5). *The Trial of Chivalry* also refers in its opening scene to 'the warlike brood of *Mars*' (A2r), but, as Gascoigne continues,

> Some thinke *Bellona* goddesse of that life:
> So that some one, and some another judge,
> To be the cause of every greevous grudge.

'Some one, and some another judge': the lines reflect the proliferation of military deities in the period. In fifteenth-century depictions, Mars increas-ingly resembled a chivalric knight, more the lover of Venus than the bloodthirsty warrior, a trend that prompted the 'disinterment' of Bellona to represent the harsher side of war (Hale, 1983, 372). With the 'mutacion' of Renaissance times, the classical pantheon was further 'ransacked' (Hale, 1962, 23). The rise in importance of scholarship and arithmetical learning to the technologies of war, for example, led to Mercury's recruitment to military iconography. 'Mars and Mercurie are both of a broode', asserts *A Myrrour for English Souldiers* (1595, B2r): indeed in Riche's first work, it is Mercury who instructs his *English Souldier* 'in the knowledge of martiall [*sic*] feates' (1574, G2r).

The increasing dominance of gunpowder in combat, furthermore, reanimated the classical mythology both of Jupiter's thunderbolt (Langer, 97), and Vulcan's smithy – 'horned Vulcan forger of heavens fire', as Wilson calls him in *The Cobbler's Prophecy* (27). Vulcan appears beside

Minerva on the title-page of a *Treatise of Artificial Fireworks* in 1629 (Hale, 1961, 17); and Jonson's 'Execration' (1623) wishes Vulcan had 'fixt in the *Low-Countrey's*', making 'Petards, and Granats, all your fine | Engines of Murder' (203-7). Fowler notes a further recruitment: Spenser's 'presentation of war in terms of a House of Ate', he writes, 'implicitly rejects the medieval tradition [of the Chaucerian Temple of Mars]'; the poet, 'as concerned ... with the causes as the effects of war', turns to the Homeric Ate, or Discord, the personification of 'originating mischief' (153-4). Erasmus's *Complaint of Peace* had criticized those who 'laye the causes of dissention ... (as Homere doth write) to the Godes Aten, so [they] let those thinges that at no tyme can be excused, be imputyd to desteny, or yf ye will, to some evyl God, and let hatred be translatyd from men into these thinges' (1559, E7r). Peter de Loier included the same 'evyl God' in his *Treatise of Specters* (1586, 'Done out of French' in 1605), in a clear reference to the civil war then being waged, 'the same *Ate* which at this day doth range up & down marching & wandring in the Heads of men' (D3v).

'And the God of warre come in thy defence': the force of Bowyer's vivid entrance to his rival's cue begins to emerge from these latter arrivals to the Elizabethan military pantheon: for as well as each being a 'God of warre', Vulcan and Ate both limp. Linche's *Fountaine of Ancient Fiction* (1599) describes Vulcan as 'lame of one leg, and of a very blacke and swart complexion' (V2r); and Discord/Ate's legs as 'wondrous crooked, and little, as scarce able to support the burthen of her withered bodie' (X1r). Spenser builds this aspect of Ate's iconography into his halting lines from *The Faerie Queene*: 'so eke her feete were odde',

> And much unlike, th'one long, the other short,
> And both misplast; that when th'one forward yode,
> The other backe retir'd, and contrarie trode.
> (4.1.28)

The familiarity of Vulcan and Ate's gait was not restricted to learned poems like Spenser's, or Jonson's 'Execration' to the 'lame Lord of fire', but seems to have been assumed too in popular plays. The Olympian tableau that opens *The Cobbler's Prophecy* includes 'Vulcan *limping*', while 'Atey' acts as Chorus to *Locrine* (c.1591), 'all in black, with a burning torch in one hand, and a bloodie swoord in the other'.[20] True, Ate's limp is not specified there, but, as Jackson Cope has shown, Jonson makes its familiarity the basis of a joke in *Bartholomew Fair* (1614), when he identifies Ursula (the fair's presiding spirit of misrule) with Ate the goddess of Discord (1965, 143-5): 'Curse of hell, that ever I saw these Feinds', she exclaims after a brawl, 'oh! I ha' scalded my leg, my leg, my leg, my leg. I ha' lost a limb in the service!' (2.5.161-4).

That parting shot, with its knowing reference to limbless veterans, provides access to the same equation made at large in *The Trial of Chivalry*.

Bowyer, we are repeatedly told, 'limps, and he limps' (C4v), having 'halfe the nature of a Badger, for one leg is shorter than another' (C1v): Spenser's Ate has 'th'one long, the other short'. Ate's 'tongue was in two parts divided' (4.1.27) while Bowyer 'wants a piece of his toung, and that makes him come lisping home' (A4r). This lisping, limping 'God of warre' seems to originate in the same 'darksome delve farre underground' as Spenser's 'mother of debate' (4.1.19-20). And like Ate, Bowyer is sent to Thomasine's aid (one of Spenser's rare jokes, this) to 'punish wicked men, that walke amisse'. Like Ate and Vulcan, Bowyer prides himself on being 'writ a bountifull benefactor in hell' (I3v), and it is in the flames of Hell that the iconography of Elizabethan war meets the technology of its waging.

We have seen how Vulcan's fiery armourer found renewed relevance in contemporary ballistics – so that, for example, the translation of Ocland's *Anglorum Praelia*, a set-text in Elizabethan schools (Hale, 1961, 10), described Leith 'ransact, to the ground by *Vulcans* blasing brandes' (1585, G3r). By the same token, the myth of the Golden Age was reanimated by the praxis of the military revolution. In former times, as Robert Greene paraphrased in *Selimus* (printed 1594),

> The plough-man with a furrow did not marke
> How farre his great possessions did reach:
> The earth knew not the share, nor seas the barke.
> The souldiers entred not the battred breach,
> Nor Trumpets the tantara loud did teach.[21]

That myth remained current since it matched Christian prophecies of the return of a universal peace, linking the Virgin Queen with its virgin Justice Astraea (Yates, 1973, 29-87). It also did so for the purely practical reasons, adumbrated by Chaucer's poem on this 'Former Age', which curses the time 'That men first dide hir swety bysynesse | To grobbe up metal, lurkinge in derkenesse', since beforehand 'Unforged was the hauberk and the plate' (*Works*, ed. Robinson, 534, ll. 29-49). Golding's Ovid cites the excavation of iron and gold from the 'bowels of the ground ... in places nere to Hell' as the advent of 'battle bolde, that feightes with bothe'.[22] In the years separating Chaucer's from Golding's Ovidian accounts, such mythology received vivid affirmation in the sieges and stalemates of sixteenth-century war, where the 'myne, and countermyne' of Jonson's Vulcan replaced pitched battle. The reason for that strategic shift – the increasing dominance of gunpowder – sounded still further resonance to the military resources 'lurkinge in derkenesse'. Agricola's *De Re Metallica* (1556) attributes the cause and origin of war to the excavation of iron and saltpetre (G.C. Taylor, 26-7), and it is this tradition which prompts Hotspur's scorn for the 'certaine Lord' who regrets 'This villanous saltpeeter should be digd | Out of the bowels of the harmeles earth' (*1 Henry IV*, 1.3.32-60). Breton rooted war's elemental force in the same myth: 'shee thunders in the Aire, rips up the Earth, cuts thorough the Seas, and consumes with the fire ... Shee is indeed the musique of Hell, and the daunce of the Devill' (1615, 24).

The fiery attributes of the re-emergent Pantheon (Mars, Bellona, Jupiter, Vulcan, Ate) and the sulphurous flames of 'villanous saltpeeter', reinforced Virgil's placing of war 'within the very jaws of hell' (*Aeneid* 6, 273). This is where Spenser locates his House of Ate, 'Hard by the gates', and it is 'in deepest Hell', he relates, where 'that divelish yron Engin' is wrought (4.1.20), 'with windy Nitre and quick Sulphur' (1.7.13). The provenance of gunpowder was variously attributed to a German alchemist's pact with the Devil (Hale, 1983, 395), and to Roger Bacon, 'who', as Jonson's 'Execration' puts it, 'from the Divels-Arse did Guns beget' (202). An early compound of gunpowder was known as 'serpentine' (Bourne, 1587, 6), and the same name was used to describe that part of a handgun that 'brought the burning match held in its jaws into contact with the priming' (Clephan, 111). The earthworks and mining of modern combat, and the *Manuall Weapons of Fire* that demonstrated *the Disability of the Long Bowe*, maintained a continuity from the symbolism of war furnished by classical antiquity.

Further, this hellish presidency of war found ironic renewal in the very name of late sixteenth-century English troops' most conspicuous field of action: the Netherlands. So Nashe prefaces Pierce Penniless's *Supplication to the Devil* (1592) with an address by an infernal postman: 'there is not a cormorant that dies, or Cut-purse that is hanged, but I dispatch letters by his soule to him, and to all my friends in the Low-cuntries' (1, 164). Dekker's reply, *Newes from Hell* (1606), likewise jestingly refers to Charon's ferry as the 'Flemmish Hoy of Hell' (*Non-Dramatic Works*, 2, 78). Pamphlets like these parodied the news-letters from European theatres of war that were beginning to proliferate in the period. The enduring equation of war with hell was perhaps consolidated in the Elizabethan imagination by the coincidence of folklore portrayals of the Devil's limp, sustained in 'his fall from heaven' (Rudwin, 50), with the injuries of veterans maimed while serving in Dekker's 'low countries of blacke hell' (*1 Honest Whore*, 4.4.90). Such men – increasingly conspicuously – haunted London's streets; the Esperanto language of war they paraded, familiar too from news-letter and play-text, must have chimed with the equally widespread superstition of Satan's multilingualism (Rudwin, 66).[23]

Such blends of military topicality and supernatural topography lend depth to the portrait *The Trial of Chivalry* provides of Dick Bowyer. The text-book undertaking of his duties, his knowledge of the tactics of 'double Cannon' (D4r-v), his command of foreign jargon, and his crippled gait (the *Disability of the Long Bowe* indeed), all bespeak the naturalism of his veteran status. While swelling the ranks of those maimed soldiers we have seen marching on the late Elizabethan stage, however, this particular 'haltyng Dicke' also displays a marked familiarity with the supernatural apparatus of the underworld. 'Zounds', he exclaims in his first scene, 'tis hotter a great deale, then hell mouth, & *Dives* burning in Sulphur' (C1r).

Having set the watch, and 'stumbling up and downe all this night', he confesses he 'can resemble our campe to nothing better then hell, save that in hell they are alwayes waking, and heere the villaynes are as drowsie as swyne' (D4r). And when he dispatches Peter, he addresses the corpse in terms reminiscent of Nashe's 'Knight of the post':

> When thou meetst the great Devill, commend me to him, and say, I sent thee for a new yeres gift ... if Dicke Bowyer be not writ a bountifull benefactor in hell for my good deeds, in sending thither such Canibals, I am a Rabbit-sucker.
>
> (I3v)

Earlier in the play, Bowyer takes his turn and is bested in single combat by the disguised Pembroke. Ascribing his defeat to Pembroke being 'a witch or some Devill', Bowyer lays odds 'this fellow has a familiar: but howsoever, thou mayst thank my lame legge' (G3r-v). Within the systematic symmetries of *The Trial of Chivalry*, however, it may surely be argued that Pembroke's familiar throughout is Bowyer himself. His 'lame legge' provides the iconic focus for the contending voices of Elizabethan war: a pagan 'God of warre' in both theory (Ate the 'witch' of discord) and practice (Vulcan the lame lord of fire); an old English bowyer proficient in the modern arts of ballistics and mining, and likened to those burrowing creatures the badger (C1v) and the mole (E2r);[24] a disabled veteran who allies force with policy; and a minister of divine punishment whose habitat is 'hell mouth'. Bowyer's feet are firmly planted in the opposing camps of Elizabethan war, straddling the span of its abstract theory and concrete practice.

'Pseudo-history' though it be, *The Trial of Chivalry*'s negotiation of myth and doctrine, naturalism and iconography, is rooted in the recognizable context of the Civil Wars of France (1562-1598). It is a striking fact that the surviving Elizabethan play most directly engaged with its neighbouring theatre of war, the Low Countries campaign, also features as its hero a crippled veteran. The 'lame lieutenant' of *A Larum for London* dramatizes the central components of Elizabethan war-theory: the Just War and the Scourge of God.

## 'Now art thou my lieutenant' [25]

Despite G.K. Hunter's admission that he 'cannot think of a single play ... set in contemporary Holland or Belgium' (1964, 45), at some point between 1597 and 1600, Shakespeare's company performed a play that, if not precisely contemporary, at least enacted scenes immediately relevant to the Dutch wars. *A Larum for London, or The Siedge of Antwerpe* dramatizes George Gascoigne's eye-witness account of *The Spoyle of Antwerp*, the so-called Spanish Fury of 1576, when a band of Spanish troops, mutinous for want of pay, massacred 8000 civilians (Parker, 1990, 118-19).

The atrocity provided many writers with the grounds to reinforce their calls for military reform. Riche's *Allarme to England* (1578), for example, stated that Antwerp's 'spoyle hath proved plaine | Where martiall mindes do want, no state in safety may remaine' (** iii r-v), and Gates's *Defence of Militarie Profession* (1579) rehearsed recent events in 'low *Duchland*' (23) to demonstrate the need for military readiness: 'Then should *London* be martial against the day of war' (54). When that day came with the Queen's 1585 declaration, she counted among her 'just and reasonable grounds' the need 'to aid the natural people of these countries to defend their towns from sacking and desolation' (Strong and van Dorsten, 26).

As its title suggests, *A Larum for London* is intimate with both the tone and vocabulary of such works. Riche began his *Allarme to England* by explaining the military jargon of his title (a '*Caveat* ... a friendly warning the which I have termed by the name of an *Allarme*'), and cast himself in 'the part of some poore belringer' who 'hath rong the larum bell, or hath runne through the campe in great haste, crying Arme, arme, arme', only to be revealed as a 'poore man ... afraid of some shadow in the Moonshine' (* iii v). By the time of *A Larum*'s first performances, that bell had rung in earnest through London's streets, 'the alarme wherof', as John Chamberlain wrote in August 1599, 'begins to ringe in our eares here at home as shrill as in your besieged town' (*Letters*, ed. McLure, 1, 78). By the time of the play's 1602 publication, it had found renewed relevance, as its misleading subtitle, *The Siedge of Antwerp*, indicates. For as the Spaniard Danila says there, Antwerp is won 'Not by a lingering siedge, of monthes or yeares, | But in a moment' (816-17). From 1601, just such a 'lingering siedge', at Ostend, increasingly commanded the attention of London's populus, a campaign that was seen as just the latest in a series of 'continuall troubles' that had 'vexed' Flanders since the 1570s (Grimeston, 1604, A2v).

The example of Antwerp prompted three related morals from the authors of the military tracts published in its immediate aftermath, each of which finds expression in the play later made of it: moral reform, military readiness, and the justice of a self-defensive war. Otherwise slavish in its rendering of Gascoigne's source, the play's author makes two significant additions, by which those lessons are translated into dramatic form. Firstly, the direct responsibility for the massacre is transferred from Gascoigne's mutinous 'common Souldiers' (A1v) to the Duke of Alva, unhistorically introduced. Secondly, he presents a one-legged soldier, Lieutenant Stump, whose 'ventrous actes and valorous deeds' are proclaimed on the play's title-page. In short, he invents a villain and a hero: the Scourge of God and the Just Warrior.

Gascoigne had cast his own reportage as a 'rewfull tragedie', from which to learn 'to detest & avoyde those synnes, and prowde enormyties, which caused the wrath of God to be so furiouslye kindled and bent against the

Towne of Antwerpe' (C7r-v). Churchyard's *Warres in Flaunders* (1578) reiterated its 'warning to all wanton Cities ... that they come not into the indignation of the highest' (60), and this is also the play's stated purpose, 'a meane all Cittyes to affright | How they in sinne and pleasure take delight' (1677-8). 'When the Lord meaneth to plague a wicked natione for sinne', explains Gates, 'then he filleth them with the fatnesse of the earth and geeveth them peace that they may wax rotten in idlenesse' (1579, 20). In sixteenth-century Christian tradition, Satan was cast as the instrument of that divine indignation, the 'whippe of God', but 'the most consistent invocation of the traditional theory was made in connection with the Ottoman empire' (Patrides, 130). 'Solimanne', wrote Theodor Buchmann in 1542, 'is onely the whippe with the whych the holy and ryghteous Lorde doth beate and scourge us for owre vicious lyvinge' (Patrides, 133); in the following year, Thomas Becon denounced the 'Nero-like tyrant the great Turk', concluding that 'the cause of wars is idolatry, strange worshipping of God, despising of his word, killing of the true preachers, and wicked living'.[26] But though the Turkish threat sporadically induced a pan-Christian defence (notably at Lepanto), as the ramifications of the Reformation widened, it was the Catholic empire which replaced the Turk as the new scourge of God. Sidney referred to Philip II as 'this Spanish Ottoman' (Howell, 40), and an early news-letter prefaced its *Certayne Newes of the ... low Countries* with a quotation from Revelation, and an account of the 'hellishe Dragon' that had tyrannized Europe for the last decade (1574, 2).

A *Larum for London* embodies in Alva, the instrument of 'royall *Phillip*' (903), 'the sharpe scourge, that fond securitie, | Hath justlie throwne on *Antwerpes* wilfulnes' (657-8). His Captain Danila wields the 'sharpe point' of an Ottoman 'Semiter' (949), and champions, like Burbon in *The Trial of Chivalry*, the hellish technology of gunpowder.

> Goe light thy Linckstocke at some hellish brand,
> To send blacke vengeance to that hated towne;
> Let every corne of powder be a spirit ...
> To vomit horred plagues upon them all.
> (195-202)

Like Rodorick's betrayal of Burbon in that play, Alva's role allies military tactics with theatrical villainy: he has caused it 'to be publisht he is dead ... to delude | These credulous inhabitants' by disguising his army as a funeral cortège, 'Which well may serve to shaddow his approach' (107-12). This 'better cullour' of policy (107) allows his histrionic entrance from a coffin:

> Zwounds the dogs barke at me, a plague upon them all,
> I thinke they doe not hate the Devill so ...
> Well, I am dead, but *Alvas* spirit (ere long)
> Shall haunt your ghostes, and with a fatall troope,

> Come in the dreadfull night about your walles.
> (306-13)

The sequence may owe a debt to Marlowe's Barabas, who also pretends death to be 'reveng'd on this accursed Towne' (5.1.62), and to that play's resurrected Chorus ('Albeit the world thinke *Machevill* is dead ...'). While Malta is betrayed to the Turk by a Machiavellian Jew, however, Antwerp is exposed in Alva to a compendium of Elizabethan villainy – another 'hellishe Dragon' poised on the walls of its 'bower of earthly blisse' (90).[27] 'These Spaniards, they are devils I think', shudders a fat Burger later in the play, 'Nay farre more covetous than devils of hell' (1518-19). The words are spoken to the lame soldier Lieutenant Vaughan, known throughout the play as Stump. Lieutenant Stump, himself likened to 'a devil of hell' by a Spanish soldier (1060), forms a structural and moral counterweight to Alva, acting as a fellow-spokesman for the play's admonitory title, but furthermore and crucially, as an agent of just war in self-defence as a last resort against Spanish excess.

Both components of Lieutenant Stump's name are to the purpose. It is notable that, though his immediate superior in rank, the role of the unnamed Captain who accompanies Stump through part of the play is markedly inferior to that of the 'olde Lieuetenant' (1370), whose rank is continually stressed. Attention would have been drawn to his rank because, as Michael Neill explains, 'while captain was a long-established military rank, lieutenant was still something of a novelty' (120). That novelty extended to its double-use in the newly emerging military hierarchy. Whetstone placed it between General and Coronel (1586b, 25), but more commonly it represented the office immediately below Captain, who 'in his Captaines absence hath authority to directe all', as Riche prescribes (1587, G1v), and who 'carieth his roome', as Robert Barret agrees, though 'he must use it with such discretion and moderation, that he arrogate not too much unto himselfe' (1598, 22). *A Larum*'s first lines have Danila issue orders to '*two other Captaines*' to be carried out 'in mine absence' (1-2). Rather later in the day, Stump's captain demands, 'Leivetenant what newes?'; 'What newes quoth our Captaine!', exclaims Stump, 'where have you been?' (1444-7). What Thomas Styward described as the Lieutenant's 'authoritie in the absence of the Captaine' (1581, 36) finds pointed expression in Stump's subordinate rebuke.

Neill illuminates the force of the word's etymon (place-taking) on the lips of the status-obsessed Iago; but that notion of place, and of the position of delegated responsibility the Lieutenant accommodates, is also crucial to Elizabethan theories of war. Ideally a 'friendly mediator between captain and men' (Cruickshank, 57), the word itself mediated between divine and earthly authority. So Camden described Leicester's status as the 'highest authority of Lieutenancy under the Queene' (1635, 3, 145), while the title-page of Leicester's own *Lawes and Ordinaunces Militarie* (1586) distinguishes between his literal and military lieutenancy: 'her Highenes Lieutenant and Captaine General of her *Majest.* Armie'. As the 1559 *Mirror for Magistrates* notes, the Queen too was a lieutenant: 'God hath ordayned the power, all princes be | His Lieutenauntes, or debities in realmes', and it is in this sense that Donne refers to 'Lieutenant Nature' in 'Goodfriday, 1613'.[28] Theological and military terms were in any case often elided in the period. Geoffrey Gates terms God the 'High generall of all warres' (1579, 16), and Robert Prickett appealed to the new King James to 'Be then ... under your captaine Christ, a glorious instrument' (1603, D4r).

Given that the central premise of the just war hinged about the selfless pursuance of duties dictated by an absent authority, and in His name, the fitness of Stump's rank becomes clear. Its representative resonance extends to the suggestion that Stump takes the place of Gascoigne's own first-person narrator in the source, like him an old soldier who lends his help against the Spanish as a 'glorious instrument' under God: 'I wyll not boast of any helpe afforded by me in that distresse', it reads, 'but I thanke the Lord God, who made mee an instrument to appease their devillish furies' (C4v-C5r). It is worth illustrating the finesse with which the play enacts for populist consumption the abstrusities of the Just War, by referring to C.G.'s contemporary treatise. *A Larum for London* and *A Watch-worde for Warre* invite such comparison by dint of the modern vocabulary of war their titles employ: 'Al'arma' and 'watch Word' both appear in Barret's glossary of 'war termes, and words, as we do borrow from straungers' (1598, 248-53).

'It is better to live in feare then securitie', writes C.G. (A3r), 'for outward warres are sent to intimate Gods indignation for our securitie' (B2v), 'to reforme and amend us' (E1r). Like the Turk of earlier formulations, the Spanish are instruments of God's wrath:

> the Lord useth the Spaniard as a spur to provoke us to amendment but it may be sayd of him [:] ... but he thinketh not so, neyther doth hys heart esteeme it so, but he imagineth to destroy ... Yet this is our comfort, he is but Gods Servant, and therefore he can doe no more then God will permit & appoint him.
> (D4r)

The same argument informs the Spaniards' carping admonition throughout the play, and helps explain why it shifts responsibility for the massacre from the mutineers to Alva's explicitly contrived policy of war. This is the 'great ... cause' (13) of the Spanish actions: the Dutch 'are remisse and negligent',

> Their bodies us'd to soft effeminate silkes,
> And their nice mindes set all on dalliance;
> Which makes them fat for slaughter, fit for spoile.
> (47-50)

But the Spaniards' moral censure is incidental: 'he thynketh not so'; rather it is the 'dalliance' they describe that make Antwerp vulnerable. To them, the Dutch are defenceless rather than wicked, and their actions proceed from envy and covetousness, allowing the true Christian, as C.G. insists, to act in self-defence:

> The Spanyard he offereth injury, wee defend it, hee assaulteth us, we withstand him, he urgeth war voluntarily, we are provoked of necessity; hee sinneth in offering injury, and not we in defending it ... therefore thys is our comfort, if the Spaniard commeth, hys cause is not just, but injurious, which may make us the more bold to buckle with him, and hope to have the better successe.
> (F4r-F4v)

With the scourge explicitly equated with the Spanish, in particular with Alva, it is Lieutenant Stump's delegated role to enact these reassurances.

'Spare neither widdow, matron, nor young maide', orders Alva, 'Gray-bearded Fathers, nor the babe that suckes' (833-4). The play remorselessly stages that explicitly Machiavellian disavowel of the *jus in bello* regarding non-combatants: 'For this sentence, *that the lawes cease, & are of no force in warre*, is not of God but of the Devill' (de Loque, 1591, 22). Stump repeatedly appears in specific response to such offences. 'Have mercie on a woman I beseech you', cries Champaigne's wife, '*hurried by two rascall Soldiers*', 'If you be christians doe not doe me shame' (730-3). Stump's subsequent entrance prevents them from 'ransacking a woman' (754), and draws a clear distinction between punitive reprisal and injurious assault: 'Take that she has', he commands, 'it is sufficient, | But goe no further, it is inhumaine to abuse a woman' (769-70). And later, when Danila murders a virgin and her elderly father, Stump spells out to his captain the expiry of God's permit:

> Yet is not Antwerpe quite bereft of life,
> So long as we two breath, to stand for her,
> Nor shall her ransacke passe, without some right
> Of just revenge.
> (1083-86)

'The Scales of Justice' (1087) at last begin to turn. When, towards the end of the play, he enters 'bloudy and wounded' (1570), Stump's last breath reiterates C.G.'s 'comfort':

> The bloud that I have spilt (the Massacres
> Procur'd and practis'd by this hand of mine)
> Heaven lay not to my charge; for though my sword

Was never drawne but in a rightfull cause,
Yet much misprision hath attended it.
(1599-1603)

Like Pembroke in *The Trial of Chivalry*, Stump 'drawes forth an unwilling sword' (E2v) to counter the excesses of Alva's firearms. Both plays dramatize the doctrinal necessity of conscience, and the limitation of prosecuting arms essential to Christian punitive war. Unlike the Spanish who revel in the destruction they wreak, Stump is conscious of the 'misprision' that must accompany his profession, abjuring what C.G. called the 'sinister Joy' (C4v) of those who 'laugh when they see others lament' (D1v). The character of Stump pulls together the model behaviour of the just warrior, as defined by contemporary treatises, a 'glorious instrument' (in Prickett's words) whose 'dutie is (when just cause requires) to fight for God' (1603, D4r). Stump's rank, his lieutenancy 'to stand for' Antwerp (1084), is a stroke of considerable intelligence. For it acknowledges the translation from first-person journalism to popular drama; spells out the instrumental role of Christian warfare; and elides this with the organizing principles of the emergent modern army, blending Pembroke's chivalrous conduct with Bowyer's professional expertise. Like Bowyer too, Stump's crippled status lies at the heart of the play's dynamic.

I have said that the Sack of Antwerp illustrated three related truths to its first commentators: repentance from sin; the justice of a self-defensive war; and the need for military readiness. Stump graphically unites the dangers of neglecting peacetime defence with the didactic aims of the many old soldiers who warned against the 'effeminacies and superfluities' of a 'long peace' (Smythe, 1590, * 4r).[29] Like his rank, Stump's handicap mediates between a naturalist portrayal of the casualties of modern war, and a symbolic emblematizing of the supernatural apparatus of war-theory.

In common with the many maimed soldiers we have seen to congregate on the late Elizabethan stage, this 'lame fellow that doth want a legge' (1060) gives stringent voice to their grievance. Unlike those plays, however, and perhaps because it is not set in England, *A Larum for London* can afford to dramatize the consequences of their neglect, rather than palliate the issue with the usual fantasies of financial reward. When we first hear from him, Stump repeats the charge of Antwerp's complacent 'sloath' (572), but his rebuke is animated by contemporary complaint, and shares with Wilson's cobbler and Dekker's shoemaker their pointed contrast with legless veterans:

A swettie Cobler, whose best industrie,
Is but to cloute a Shoe, shall have his fee;
But let a Soldier, that hath spent his bloud,
Is lame'd, diseas'd, or any way distrest,
Appeale for succour, then you looke a sconce

> As if you knew him not.
> (611-14)

'It is thy Countrie that doth binde thee' to fight, he is told, a command he counters by promising to 'measure my desert | According to the rate', and agreeing to fight only to the extent to which he has been paid: 'a poore groates-worth of effection' – 'a groate, | To be infeebled, or to loose a limb' (617-24).

Stump's scornful rebuke fittingly roots Augustine's doctrine of a soldier's necessary reluctance in the social grievances attendant on his profession's peacetime neglect. When presented by a 'case of extremity' (de Loque, 1591, 16), the 'ransacking' of Madame Champaigne, he draws the moral pressed home by earlier writers:

> Heere is she, that would not have been seene
> with a moath upon her, for a thousand pound;
> That spent as much on Munkeys, Dogs and Parrets,
> As would have kept ten Soldiers all the yeere.
> (756-9)

The lines precisely echo complaints in Riche's *Allarme to England* (1578, B iii r) and Gates's *Defence of Militarie Profession* (1579, 46). Gates's work in particular suggests a direct influence on the play, with its vivid contrasts between spending 'a shilling on a destitute soldier' and 'five poundes on a superfluous banket'; 'a Testone' on a veteran 'distressed with nakednes, & hunger, begging his relief' and 'five pounds on the lining of a sommer gowne'; or 'a hundreth shillings in a subsidie' and 'a hundreth pounds on building of a banketting house in his garden' (46). 'Your closet will not serve your turne', says Stump to Madame Champaigne, 'You cannot walke to your garden-house' (792-3). His exchange with the Spaniards he fights in her rescue, however, held greater topicality still for his original audiences. 'What roague art thou', asks one:

> No roague Sir, but a Soldier as you are,
> And have had one leg more then I have now.
> > *Pointing to his leg.*
> Sir, heer's my Pasport, I have knowne the warres.
> (771-7)

These lines suggest an anterior limit to the play's composition. For on 5 November 1597 there was issued an Act 'for Punyshment of Rogues, Vagabondes and Sturdy Beggars', compelling veteran soldiers to carry 'lawfull pasportes' of their service, in an effort to reduce the potential unrest of their enforced vagrancy. *Sir John Oldcastle*'s petitioners complain of the effects of its maladministration:

> — If a poore man come to a doore to aske for Gods
> sake, they aske him for a licence, or a certificate from a
> Justice.
> — Faith we have none, but what we beare uppon our
> bodies, our maimed limbs, God help us.
> (337-40)

Stump explicitly equates his 'wodden legge' (1402) and 'notch'd limmes' (1364) with the passport of his military service, and when he and his Captain enter their final scene, the image of the passport returns, now invested with the broader symbolism of a larger 'Justice'. Mortally wounded, Stump anticipates the 'blessed haven of eternity' (1579), where 'our travell shall be recompenc'd, | Our love requited, and our wounds repayde | With double merit' (1563-5). 'My pasport (I doe thinke)', replies the Captain, 'the Spaniards | Has seal'd as deeply' (1581-2).

The 'double merit' of Stump's reward recasts in spiritual form the inflated financial dividends dispensed to veterans in other plays of the period. It underlines too the inklings of his supernatural status provided throughout the play. When '*olde blinde* Harman' is slaughtered with his wife and children, his protest at 'this foule injurie to armes' echoes Stump's earlier encounter. 'My selfe have bin a Soldier as you are', he says, 'Now blinde with age'. Harman's disability is significantly imbued with an unearthly compensation: 'I have tolde this towne, | That you should sacke it, I did prophesie' (1147-78). A Blind Pew to Stump's Long John Silver, both veterans possess the paradoxically 'maimed strength' that was Stevenson's inspiration.[30] Like Silver, who has 'still a foot in either camp' (170), Stump's wooden leg itself forms a passport between two significations: his practical peacetime neglect and his theoretical wartime role.

For insofar as Stump declares his 'right | Of just revenge', his disfigurement emulates the lame gods of war we have considered, sent like Ate to 'punish wicked men, that walke amisse'. It seems possible even to equate the 'burning torch' which the choric Atey carries in *Locrine* (1595) with the Lieutenant's own stump:

> heere is my poore stumpe and I have stumbled through a
> thousand shot, & yet we halt together; there was never
> one poore peece of Timber has been so sindg'd as it has
> been: zbloud it has been foure times a fire under me, and
> yet we scramble together trotting, trotting.
> (1381-86)

'Trotting, trotting'; 'and he limps, and he limps': Stump and Bowyer's halting gait, shared by a series of roles on the late Elizabethan stage, receives repeated emphasis in their respective plays. That this aspect of their construction intends to convey iconographic as well as sociological weight is suggested by the Chorus devised for *A Larum for London*: Time.

Sharing his 'feathers' (10) with the 'wings' of a later Chorus (*The Winter's Tale*, 4.1.4), and his 'hoary scalpe' (5) with 'the plaine bald pate of Father time' (*Comedy of Errors*, 2.2.69-70), *A Larum*'s chorus appropriately introduces 'actions long since cast behinde his backe' (1665). Shakespeare characterized Time as both Revealer and Destroyer in *Lucrece* (1594), 'To unmaske falshood, and bring truth to light', as 'To ruinate proud buildings with thy howres' (940-55). By contrast, *A Larum*'s Time reveals the sack of Antwerp in order to prevent the destruction of London: he has 'searcht the worlds corrupt enormities' (4) so as to 'Reforme the mischiefe of degenerate mindes' (21). Indeed, while its catalogue of 'streetes besmear'd with bloud ... totter'd walls ... building's overthrowne' (1674-5) elsewhere describes the inevitable ruins of time (notably in Shakespeare's Sonnet 55), it here presents the reassurance that 'No heavy or disastrous chaunce befall | The sonnes of men, if they will warned be' (1677-8). If 'the roots of Time's symbolism lie ... in the springs, coils, and pendula of renaissance machinery', the play's chorus may be likened to an Elizabethan alarm-clock,[31] a function served by Lieutenant Stump's first words: 'Are yet your eye-lids open, are you yet | Awakt out of the slumber you were in?' (570-71). The roles of Stump and his Chorus certainly invite comparison (might resonantly have been doubled) since both are lame.

'You will scorne my wants', says Time,

> Laugh at my lamenes, looke basely, fume and frowne:
> But doe so, doe so, your proude eyes shall see
> The punishment of Citty cruelty.
> (16-19)

That Time is both 'fleeting' (3) and lame is true both to contemporary iconography – Father Time has wings, Saturn a wooden leg (Davis, 1983, 156, n.11) – and common experience – time can both fly and drag its feet. Shakespeare calls Time 'Misshapen' in *Lucrece*, the 'copesmate of ugly night' (925), and the association recurs in 'the creeple-tardy-gated Night' before Agincourt, 'Who like a foule and ougly Witch doth limpe | So tediously away' (*Henry V*, 4.Ch.20-23). The lines suggest affinities with Ate, 'that hag ... old and crooked' (*Faerie Queene*, 4.1.31); if so the 'punishment of Citty cruelty' *A Larum*'s Chorus reveals shares Ate's punitive presidency over 'Great cities ransackt, and strong castles rast' (4.1.21). War, as Breton later wrote, 'is the misery of Time' (1615, 23).

The admonitory role performed by Time and Stump features in the handicap they share. Truth will out, however Time may drag its feet: that is the allegorical force of the play's admonition to 'this froward age' (3). Justice will out, though neglect of its veteran ministers may imperil their 'right | Of just revenge': that is the literal force of the play's alarum for Elizabethan London. Their joint symbolism is enlivened by reference to the *locus classicus* of Stump's rallying exhortation to 'Dye like men' (1391). Wilfred Owen called Horace's Ode 3.2 'the old Lie: Dulce et decorum est | Pro patria mori' (1985, 117), and his description of men who 'lost their boots | But limped on, blood-shod' gains its force from the turn it effects to Horace's closing reassurance:

> for, slighted, often God confuses
> The innocent with the evil-doer's fate.
> Yet Vengeance, with one lame foot, seldom loses
> Track of the outlaw, though she sets off late.
> (Stallworthy, 14)

Punishment may be tardy, but it eventually arrives: that moral informs the play's choric purpose and the progress of its hero's reluctant resort to arms.

The realist and symbolist components of Stump's character come together in the curiously brutal scene featuring the trapping of Van End, the traitor who betrayed his town to the Spanish, lured by a Burger's wife to her 'vault' or cellar (1307) with the promise of more plunder:

> *She pushes him downe.*
>
> WIFE    That is the cursed way,
>               Goe thou accurst into that shade of hell,
>               The Image of that everlasting night,
>               Where thy damn'd ghoast must dwel exempt from light.
>                                   *Enter* Stumpe
> STUMP   What stirre is heere? what discontented rumor
>               Sendes second message to my dull strucke dayes
>               Accustom'd the screeching yell of death?
> (1311-19)

We have noted the play's structural kinship between Stump and Alva. While Alva's supernatural, satanic agency is suggested by the staging of his own resurrection '*from under the hearse*' (303), Stump, like a later (flying) Dutchman, declares that 'I that am a wearie of my life, | And would faine dye I cannot' (740-1). Neglected even by Death, whose 'foote-steps' he haunts (1552), his uncanny presence is constantly related to his loping tread: 'And still my olde rotten stump and I | Trot up and downe' (746-7).

The modern playwright Wole Soyinka has one of his characters remark that 'When a man has one leg in each world, his legs are never the same' (45). The sentiment betrays the conceit of Flann O'Brien's *The Third Policeman* (1967), whose one-legged narrator is 'dead and alive, "real" yet illusory', and inhabits (according to a recent critic) a 'borderland between reality and fiction' (Hopper, 110; 140).[32] It also testifies to the mystique so long associated with the lame, on whom, from Saga to Film, having one foot in the grave has bestowed an eerie power.[33] In a recently staged reading of *A Larum for London*, the actor playing Stump paced his lines with an authoritatively slow gravitas naturally synchronized to his dogged gait.[34] Dick Bowyer's entrance to Peter de Lion in *The Trial of Chivalry* partakes of the same elemental force.

Cued on a providential rhyme, Stump's entrance here shares Bowyer's familiarity with the underworld of war, as he presides over the vault that figures the 'shade of hell' (presumably the trap-door on the stage of the Theater or Globe). Like Bowyer, too, Stump presents Van End 'for a new yeres gift' to 'the great Devill' (I3v), in a startling elision of the 'despis'd ingratitude' shown to soldiers in peacetime with the punishment of God on the luxuries of peace:

> For Gods sake let me come plague the dog,
> Ile stone the Jew to death, and paint this Vault
> With the unhallowed bloud of wicked treason:
> Heere, weare this waightie Jewell in thy hat,
> The towne hath sent it for a token slave;          *Throw stones*
> I bought this with the groate you gave me sir;          *Another sto.*
> Soldiers must loath despis'd ingratitude.
> This woman for her ransome sends you this;          *another*
> Give these two unto Charon for your passing.          *another*
> And with this last, present grim *Belzebub*.          *another*
> (1325-34)

The 'waightie Jewell' is turned into a weapon to scourge the peace it exemplifies, and of the Dutchmen's pleasant vices makes instruments to plague them. The scene answers, in another theatre of war, Norden's contemporary *Prayer for the ... Earle of Essex and his Companies in their present expedition in Ireland* (1599), which takes for text Psalms 7, 16: 'His mischiefe shall returne upon his owne head, and his crueltie shall fall upon his own pate'. 'Are there no stones in heaven', asks Othello, 'But what serves for the thunder?' (5.2.235-6): the lame lieutenant's 'stones of sulphur' (*Cymbeline*, 5.5.240), cast by one without sin, insist on Stump's delegated administration of divine wrath, a 'bountifull benefactor' of hell, voicing urgent social complaint, yet restricted, as every just warrior should be, by the 'misprision' of conscience that accompanies every blow.

## 'You a captain?' [35]

> 'I've got a false leg, but that's different. Boys respect that. Think I lost it in the war. Actually,' said the Captain, 'and strictly between ourselves, mind, I was run over by a tram in Stoke-on-Trent when I was one-over-the-eight. Still, it doesn't do to let that out to everyone'.[36]

The discreet fraudulence of Captain Grimes in Waugh's *Decline and Fall* (published in 1928, a year before Graves's *Goodbye To All That*) belongs in a tradition of military opportunism at least as old as Captain Falstaff:

> a pox of this gowt, or a gowt of this pox: for the one or the other playes the rogue with my great toe. Tis no matter if I do hault, I have the warres for my color, and my pension shal seeme the more reasonable: a good wit will make use of any thing; I will turn diseases to commoditie.
> (*2 Henry IV*, 1.2.245-50)

Falstaff's 'good wit' seems to have been unique neither among Elizabethan soldiers, nor those (in the words of a contemporary proclamation) who have 'neither bene maymed nor hurt, nor yet served at all in the warres, but take that cloak and colour, to bee the more pitied' (Hughes and Larkin, 3, 105). The acts passed in 1593, 1597 and 1601, for the relief of veterans who had 'lost their limbs or disabled their bodies' (Cruickshank, 184-5), alternate with proclamations, in 1591/92, 1596 and 1598, against their widespread and longstanding exploitation by impostors (Aydelotte, 72). John Awdeley's catalogue of the *Fraternity of Vagabonds* (1561) includes the 'ruffler ... saying he hath been a servitor in the wars' (Judges, 53); and among the *Common Cursitors* listed by Thomas Harman in 1566 is a certain 'John Donne (with one leg)' (Judges, 67). The other John Donne (a genuine veteran despite his two legs) testifies to the ambivalence provoked by such figures in 1590s London in his pithy epigram, 'A lame begger': 'I am unable, yonder begger cries, | To stand, or move; if he say true, hee *lies*'.[37]

In his first published history, Shakespeare lets Donne's joke play beneath the surface in the scene he embellished from Foxe's *Actes and Monuments*. 'Sit there, | The lyingest knave in Christendom', says Duke Humphrey in *The First Part of the Contention* to the false beggar Saunder Simpcox (*2 Henry VI*, 2.1.130-1); 'I am not able to stand', he complains in reply (154). Foxe merely described 'a certayne begger ... walkyng about the towne ... saying he was borne blind' (Bullough, 3, 127), but Shakespeare added to the disabilities he claims: 'would you not thinke his cunning to be great, that could restore this Cripple to his legges againe'? (2.1.137-8). The refinement provides an opportunity for the vivid stage-business of his exposure ('he leapes over the stoole and runnes away'), but also gains the resonance of a topical symbolism. For although Simpcox makes no claim to military service, his trial appears to burlesque the special sessions designed to distinguish veteran from impostor that were ordered in February 1591/92 (Aydelotte, 72) – midway within the probable parameters of the play's composition (Harbage and Schoenbaum, 56).

The relationship between pretended veterans, the braggart warrior and Rumour is the subject of my fourth chapter: suffice it to remark here that the uneasy likeness between true veterans of just war-service ('We know that by your legges') and false impostors ('Tis no matter if I do hault') was strengthened by the contrary iconography detailed in Ripa's *Iconologia*, that Lying 'limps upon a wooden leg ... her lameness relates to the vulgar notion that falsehood has short legs'.[38] 'Lies come on a limping leg', glosses Natalie Davis, 'for you can't go very far with them' (122). Thomas Dekker, whose *O Per Se O* (1612) includes the recipes used by 'counterfeit soldiers' for 'making of their sores' (Judges, 374), was certainly aware of such a double symbolism: '*Oathes* are *Crutches*', he writes in *The Seven Deadly Sinnes of London* (1606) 'upon which *Lyes* (like lame soldiers) go, & neede no other pasport' (*Non-Dramatic Works*, 2, 34-5).[39] 'The lameness [of Simpcox] is added by Shakespeare', comments the Arden editor of *2 Henry VI* (1962, 41);[40] the same is true of the figure who limps his way into its final scenes, and claims, in its sequels, centre stage.

To modern readers, Richard III is all but inextricable from Olivier's 'politely crippled' (Sher, 21), provocatively stagey limping tread; and indeed it is a trait upon which Shakespeare takes care to insist. As the role of this 'Foule Stigmaticke' grows (5.1.213), attention is repeatedly drawn to the legs that 'came into the world ... forward' (*3 Henry VI*, 5.6.71). Nature was bribed, claims Richard, 'To make my legges of an unequall size' (3.2.159); he is 'made up ... so lamely and unfashionable, | That dogs barke at me as I halt by them' (*Richard III*, 1.1.21-23); he wonders that Ann can look kindly 'On me that halt, and am unshapen thus' (1.2.255); and sardonically casts himself as the 'tardy cripple' who 'bore the countermaund, | That came too lag' to prevent Clarence's murder (2.1.90-91). The details amount to a pronounced enhancement of the sources, where Richard is 'lamed armed', or more vaguely 'eivell featured of limnes'.[41]

Of course, Shakespeare's Richard doesn't limp because of injuries received in battle, but he is no less a veteran. Indeed, the soliloquy which opens his own play apes a convention of soldierly admonition to the complacences of peace which was to find dramatic example in *A Larum to London*. Riche had sensed his own *Allarme to England* (1578) falling on deaf ears, and the preface to his next work, *His Farewell to Militarie Profession* (1581), repeated the 'slender estimation' (B ii v) and 'small recompence' (B iii v) bestowed on soldiers. This work is best known for providing Shakespeare with a direct source for *Twelfth Night*, but it begins where *Richard III* does. 'I see now it is lesse painfull to followe a Fiddle in a gentlewomans chamber', reads Riche's address to his female readership, 'then to marche after a Drumme in the feeld' (A ii r); 'if you will followe myne advise', he writes to 'noble Souldiours', 'laie aside your weapons, hang up your armours by the walles, and learne an other while ... to Pipe, to Feddle, to Syng, to Daunce, to lye, to forge, to flatter' (B iii v; compare 1.1.6-13).

'This weake piping time of peace' (1.1.25) was conventionally a source of grievance to veterans like Riche or Stump, and Richard duplicates his loping stance as surely as Simpcox. The exposure of that 'lyingest knave in Christendom' leaves the field clear for Richard to inherit the title. Like the gout-ridden Falstaff, the lame king embraces the opportunity peace provides 'to lye, to forge, to flatter': his lies, 'well steeld with weighty arguments' (1.1.147; see also 1.1.115), in Dekker's words '(like lame soldiers) go, & neede no other pasport'. Dekker's own *Whore of Babylon* (1607) later instructed her satanic agents to 'halt with soldiers' and 'take all shapes | To escape taking' (3.1.177-9).[42] In his last scene in *1 Henry IV*, Falstaff carries off Hotspur's body 'just as Satan carries off Worldly Man to hell in Wager's *Enough is as Good as a Feast*' (5.4.126).[43] The limp with which he enters his first scene in the sequel seems to sustain that satanic equation with the Father of Lies, and his 'broken or crooked leg' (Rudwin, 50). So while Stump's handicap emblematizes honourable Christian service in a Just War (what Riche called the 'vertue that fighteth for equitie and justice'), Richard, repeatedly called a devil in his play, champions the lying strategies of 'the divells politician' (Riche, 1598, D1r). He will

> Deceive more slyly then *Vlisses* could,
> And like a *Synon* take another Troy.
> I can adde Colours to the Camelion,
> Change shapes with *Proteus*, for advantages,
> And set the murtherous *Machevill* to Schoole.
> (F *3 Henry VI*, 3.2.189-93)

Stump and Richard mirror one another across a moral divide at the heart of Elizabethan war-theory between force and fraud, chivalry and policy, the 'right | Of just revenge' and the Scourge of God. The extent of their symmetry can be gauged by the fact that each resembles the other's enemy. So Richmond's prayer before Bosworth invokes what Stump's punishment of van End enacts, ('Put in [my army's] hands thy brusing Irons of wrath | That they may crush ... The usurping helmets of our adversaries, | Make us thy ministers of chastisement', 5.3.109-14); while Alva's curse on Antwerp ('Zwounds the dogs barke at me') echoes Richard's plaintive half-boast that 'dogs barke at me as I halt by them'. The vivid resemblance between their limping opponents reveals an inherent precariousness in contemporary definitions of war, and one mediated by the comparably contradictory symbolism of the lame.

In his preface to *Miss Julie* (1888), Strindberg described its *dramatis personae* as 'characterless': they are 'hard to grasp, classify and pin down', in strict contrast to the prevailing 'bourgeois notion' by which 'in order to characterise [an individual] it was only necessary to give him a physical disability such as ... a wooden leg or a red nose' (xiv). Yet just as a recent 'Complete History of Comic Noses' demonstrates how 'highly ambivalent' is that organ's comic profile (Kerrigan, 1994, 242), so the ostensible subject of Montaigne's essay 'Of the Lame or Cripple' yields to a disquisition on the 'flexibilitie of our invention'. Surveying a range of proverbial wisdom regarding the sexuality of 'the crooked-backt or halting-lame', he concludes with a simile apt to his (and our) theme: '*There is nothing so supple and wandering, as our understanding*. It is like *Theramenez* shooe, fit for all feet. It is double and divers and so are matters diverse and double'; 'Our reasons doe often anticipate the effect, and have extension of their jurisdiction so infinite, that they judge and exerciseth themselves in inanitie, and to a not being' (1603, 616-17).

In the year after Montaigne's essay was first published in English, Riche found a subject likewise 'diverse and double', and equally vexatious of reason:

> Nothing waxeth young in this world but warre, neyther hath arte ever sought out a subject more ambiguous, for with the Camelion it changeth according to the object, and like an imposible infinit in nature, carrieth his events beyond the reach of conjecture.
> (1604, 4-5)

Contemporary accounts of 'what thing warre is' had constant recourse to similar negotiations of contradiction. War was an 'impious good, and good impietie', an 'unjust-just scourge of mens iniquitie' (Daniel, *Works*, ed. Grosart, 2, 152-3); simultaneously a plague and a medicine, 'Shee is the seasoner of the body', yet 'the grave of the flesh': 'her cures' are 'mortall' (Breton, 1615, 23). The 'new warlike Discipline' is one 'man both loves & hates' (Dekker, 1616, D1v); it is 'the worst and best that ever Fortune could promise her favourites' (Riche, 1604, 5).

This 'Camelion' of war, and the sliding scale of its 'impossible infinit', inform the dynamic of the apostrophe to war spoken by Young Clifford in the Folio text of *2 Henry VI*. The first part of the speech gathers together the components we have traced of the just war:

> O Warre, thou sonne of hell,
> Whom angry heavens do make their minister,
> Throw in the frozen bosomes of our part,
> Hot Coales of Vengeance. Let no Souldier flye.
> He that is truly dedicate to Warre,
> Hath no self-love: nor he that loves himselfe,
> Hath not essentially, but by circumstance
> The name of Valour.
> (F 5.2.33-40)

War is here the scourge of God, 'Whom angry heavens do make their minister', the 'sonne of hell' by dint of Satan's role as the whip of human sin. Their flicker of medieval scholasticism (39) is expressive of the lines' theoretical, discursive rationale, Clifford's 'frozen bosomes' appropriate to the proper reluctance of resort to arms. Editorial procedure since Theobald has been to punctuate the radical shift in moral gear that follows, by having Clifford notice his father's body before continuing:

> O let the vile world end,
> And the premised Flames of the Last day,
> Knit earth and heaven together.
> Now let the generall Trumpet blow his blast,
> Particularities and pettie sounds
> To cease ...
>           Even at this sight,
> My heart is turn'd to stone: and while 'tis mine,
> It shall be stony. Yorke, not our old men spares:
> No more will I their Babes, Teares Virginall,
> Shall be to me, even as the Dew to Fire,
> And Beautie, that the Tyrant oft reclaimes,
> Shall to my flaming wrath, be Oyle and Flax:
> Henceforth, I will not have to do with pitty.
> (40-56)

From defining war as a divinely sanctioned duty, Clifford's personal grief impels a raise in the stakes to an absolute view of the 'premised Flames' of Apocalypse, specifically at odds with the 'frozen bosomes of our part'. Selfless, instrumental moderation dissolves and in its place flares the 'flaming wrath' of private animosity. Resembling the instrumental Lieutenant Stump when it begins, Clifford's speech comes to match Stump's own description of the Spanish force he counters: 'Faire words will be as oyle to burning pitch; | And golde as Sulpher to inkindled flames' (583-4). 'My hart for malyce fryed', confesses Clifford in *The Mirror for Magistrates* (193), an image to which Churchyard's account of *The Warres in Flaunders* adds a gloss: 'And commonly malice is never quenched, till revenge hathe produced some notable mischiefe, and so ye person yt striketh, and body that is striken ... end in short season, their lives' (62). Robert Ward's *Anatomy of Warre* later observed that war 'is not to be moved, but repelled: not kindled, but quenched' (1): 'for although a man may kill his enemy in battell, yet he should not delight in using cruelty towards him, by devising new or strange torments to make him die' (7). Clifford veritably relishes the prospect of such torments, marking down for punishment the non-combatants of the *jus in bello* tradition, as the Christian imagery of his language turns to pagan myth:

> Meet I an infant of the house of Yorke,
> Into as many gobbits will I cut it
> As wilde *Medea* yong *Absirtis* did.

In cruelty, will I seeke out my Fame.
(57-61)

War is successively stripped of the appurtenances of Christian limitation, 'for with the Camelion it changeth according to the object'. The shoe is shuffled on to the other foot.

The pattern of Clifford's apostrophe was later repeated in a sermon preached in May 1598 by Stephen Gosson, and printed as *The Trumpet of Warre*. Warning his soldier-audience that 'they must remember that in this case they are inferior instruments unto God to punish the offences of the wicked' (C1v), Gosson turns from the limitations and restraints of Augustinian orthodoxy to an absolutist 'exhortation to the action of warre' (C8r), claiming that 'al the meanes are lawful that are requisite to the attaining of the victory, sleights, shifts, stratagems, burning, wasting, spoiling, undermining, battery, blows and bloud' (C5r). 'Such warfare', comments James T. Johnson of the passage (99),

> is 'just' in a sense quite different from that intended in just war doctrine. There 'just' means principally 'justifiable', with the emphasis equally on *permission* for Christians to participate in certain kinds of war and on *limitation* of their participation in even such a war. There the soldier could still be called upon to do penance for the killing and other uncharitable acts he had performed, even though they had been done in the course of a 'just' war. But for Gosson the term 'just' has taken on a new meaning ... a 'just' war is not merely 'justifiable'; it is 'justified'.

Clifford's descent into what the 1559 *Mirror* calls 'his straunge and abhominable cruelty' (193) presents a perturbing counterpart to the queasy accommodation of policy by force in so much Elizabethan martial literature. The urgent pragmatism of such compromise is acknowledged by Bowyer and Pembroke in *The Trial of Chivalry*, and strenuously distinguished in Stump and Alva by *A Larum for London*. The sliding-scale of Clifford's shift of moral ground is unique to the Folio text of *2 Henry VI*; the 1594 Quarto of *The First Part of the Contention* substitutes in its place a sequence of extraordinary theatrical force.

Poetically inferior and (it seems) textually corrupt, Q contracts F's first ten lines into a single line of explication and blunts F's sophisticated structure into a tired Senecan exclamation: 'O! dismall sight ... to thy murthred ghoast I sweare, | Immortall hate' (H3r). To this extent modern editors can hardly do otherwise than base their texts on F. But to dispense with Q is to sacrifice a stark dramatic emblem of the incremental animosity of the Folio speech. F ends the speech with the stage-direction, 'Enter Richard and Somerset to fight' (5.2.65), and leaves Clifford to exit 'bearing off his father' (as Pope first specified). In Q Richard has already killed Somerset, and it is his solo entrance that is cued by Clifford picking up his father's body:

> But staie, heres one of them
> To whom my soule hath sworne immortall hate.
>> Enter *Richard*, and then *Clifford* laies downe his father
>> fights with him, and *Richard* flies awaie againe.
> Out crooktbacke villaine, get thee from my sight.
> (H3r)

However prosaic the verse, the force of the resulting tableau is worth stressing. Visually, the encounter is unusually vivid and troubling. On one side of the stage Clifford hoists his father on to his 'manly backe' (H3r) in what, we may presume, children call a piggyback. The two Cliffords – in this sequence of plays so preoccupied by sons and fathers – reassemble before our eyes into an eight-limbed embodiment of 'Comberlands true house' (H3r). To them, on the other side of the stage, there enters a limping 'crooktbacke villaine', with 'an envious mountaine on my backe' (*3 Henry VI*, 3.2.157), the scuttling 'bottled spider' that is Richard (*Richard III*, 1.3.242).

The symmetries of such stagecraft visit on the sons the verbal impasse into which their fathers had wrangled at the outset of the play's collapse into bloodshed. 'Why what a brood of Traitors have we heere?', Clifford *père* had asked (in the Folio) some few minutes before; 'Looke in a Glasse, and call thy Image so', replied York (F 5.1.143-4). The Quarto's dramaturgy enacts a perfectly mirrored emblem of the incremental animosity contained in the Folio's poetry. For while F anticipates the likeness Riche was later to seek between war and 'the Camelion [which] changeth according to the object', Q embodies that ethical mutation in the entrance of a figure who (as he later boasts) 'can adde Colours to the Camelion' (*3 Henry VI*, 3.2.191). Clifford, the 'minister' of 'angry heavens' and their instrumental lieutenant, meets his limping double, Richard, a usurping scourge of God.

The figure of the lame soldier provided a vivid focus for the bewildering varieties of Elizabethan military theory and practice. If 'one-legged gods are suggested variously as axis symbols' (J. Cooper, 96), the brute fact of their many counterparts as casualties of war aptly represented the contradictions of the 'unjust-just scourge of mens iniquitie'. Indigent veterans like Dekker's Ralph were known by their legs, but limps were readily faked, as Shakespeare's Simpcox well knew. Both his Falstaff and Richard III turn such diseases to commodity. Lies go on a wooden leg because they are soon found out, but Vengeance limps because it gets there in the end, which is (as Montaigne affirmed of the examples he gathered 'Of the Lame or Cripple') 'another cleane contrary conclusion' (1603, 617). David Riggs has well described how the escalation of hostilities it traces makes *3 Henry VI* 'probe the uncertain boundaries that divide acts of war from crimes of blood' (128). Such distinctions preoccupied Elizabethan appraisals of 'what thing warre is, and wherof it proceeds' (Gascoigne, 1575, h i r). The boundaries between *The Theorike and Practike of Modern Warres*; between force and fraud, chivalry and policy, bow and musket; between past victories and present neglect; between public retribution and private revenge, divine punishment and Christian self-defence – the boundaries between all these were patrolled in the Elizabethan playhouse by a veritable platoon of *mutilés de guerre*.

On one side march the lame veterans whose rich reward for loyal service is repeatedly dramatized; the consequences of their neglect are explored by Lieutenant Stump, whose 'right | Of just revenge' also enacts the spiritual reassurances of war's divine sanction. 'In the heavens [war] worketh harmony' (Riche, 1604, 4), but Captain Bowyer's tour of duty takes him closer to the front line by demonstrating the necessity of chivalry's compromise with 'the musique of Hell, and the daunce of the Devill' (Breton, 1615, 24). On the other side is grouped a band of rufflers, whose range of military imposture extends from false claims of pension to the diabolic incarnation of all that is 'double and divers': Richard III.

A one-legged Hamlet seems not to have first limped on stage. Yet the final scene of Shakespeare's first postwar tragedy gains part of its force from the vestigial remnants of this richly ambivalent symbolism. 'I look down towards his feet', bemoans Othello of Iago, 'but that's a fable' (5.2.292). Shakespeare's well-known allusion to the devil's cloven-footed gait emphasizes Ancient Iago's descent from the same Vicious stock as his Captain Falstaff and King Richard. Less noticeable perhaps is the contrast it effects with Cassio, who enters with the guarded Iago just three lines before. Unlike the Folio, the 1622 Quarto specifies his entrance '*in a Chaire*', presumably the one called for in the previous scene (5.1.96) when he is 'maym'd for ever' by Iago (F 27), since his 'leg is cut in two' (71). The culmination of the story Shakespeare adapted, Cinthio's *Hecatommithi*, hinges about the wooden leg 'Cassio' is forced to wear, maimed by the Ensign who successfully persuades him ('It is time you got your revenge for the leg you lost') to accuse the Moor 'both of cutting off his leg and of causing the Lady's death' (Bullough, 7, 251). The two soldiers who at last converge on *Othello*'s stage, the loyal Lieutenant Cassio and the usurping Ancient who takes his place, each wields the phantom limb of their wartime symbolism. Yet, in a pattern of frustrated justice characteristic of the play, this lame lieutenant is denied his right of just revenge; and as to Iago's limp, 'that's a fable'.

'Deformed Persons ... are *Envious*', claimed Bacon, 'for he that cannot possibly mend his own case will do what he can to impair another's'.[44] The Stationers' Register of 1600 records a work devoted to the 'famous

Tragicall history, of ye Tartarian Crippell Emperour of Constantinople'. If a lost play, the 'Crippell Emperour' was a military role with many precedents. Chief among these was the figure included by Bacon among the 'Lame men' he cited; whose story was told in George Whetstone's 1586 *English Myrror, A Regard Wherein Al Estates May Behold the Conquests of Envy* (1586); and whose exemplary soldiership was dramatized by Christopher Marlowe: Tamburlaine, the Scourge of God – known to history as Timur the Lame.

## Notes

1.  Sassoon, 76.
2.  Attributed to Flann O'Brien by John Lanchester (*Daily Telegraph*, 26 July 1997, A7) to whom I am grateful for his correspondence.
3.  L. Digges (1579), A2v; see below p. 56.
4.  *Hamlet*, 2.2.235.
5.  *The Cobbler's Prophecy*, MSR, lines 737-46.
6.  *Edward the First*, MSR, lines 113; 46-7.
7.  *Liberality and Prodigality*, MSR, lines 1218-23.
8.  T. Heywood (1631), G2r.
9.  *Sir John Oldcastle*, MSR, lines 324; 340.
10. On Falstaff/Oldcastle see *1 Henry IV* ed. Bevington (1987) 3-10; on the contemporary scandal of such abuse see *1 Henry IV*, ed. Humphreys (1960) 153 (5.3.36.n) and Jorgensen (1956a) 68-9.
11. Reference is to the 1605 quarto of *The Trial of Chivalry*, and to *A Larum for London*, MSR. Modern-spelling editions of both plays, edited by the present author, are forthcoming from Globe Quartos.
12. See for example Huizinga (1955); Ferguson (1960); R. Barber (1970), 337-9; Vale (1981); Keen (1984), 238-53; Contamine (1986), 270-80; Ferguson (1986); and Anglo (1990).
13. Before Rouen, the Earl of Essex challenged Chevalier Pickard 'that the king's cause was more juste and honest than that he upheld of the league; that he himselfe was a better man than he, and his mistress fayrer than his' (Coningsby, 38).
14. *The Posies of George Gascoigne* (1575), fo. 113 (h i r), stanza 4. Subseqent reference is to Gascoigne's numbered stanzas.
15. Inaccurately, since Bowyer is last mentioned entering with Navarre in the play's final scene (I3v).
16. 'A new ballade of the tryumphes kept in *Ireland* upon Saint *George*'s day last, by the noble Earle of *Essex*', *Shirburn Ballads*, ed. Clark, 322-5. Hale notes the further association with the folk-hero Robin Hood: 'on historical and legendary grounds the bow was par excellence the Englishman's weapon' (Smythe, *Discourses*, ed. Hale, 1964, xliv).
17. On the 'Forlorn hope' (from the Dutch *verloren hoop*, or lost troop)

see Digges (1579), 102; on the French 'point blank' see Hale (1983) 428, and below, p. 89 n. 44.

18. *1 Henry IV*, 2.3.51-6; and see below, pp. 160-61.

19. On the scam of Elizabethan captains' exploitation of 'dead-pays' see Cruickshank (1966), 153-8.

20. *The Lamentable Tragedy of Locrine*, MSR, lines 2-4.

21. *Selimus*, MSR, lines 312-16.

22. *The .xv. Bookes*, tr. Golding (1567), B3r. See also H. Levin, 22-4.

23. See Marston, *The Malcontent* (1604), ed. Wine (1965), 1.3.29-32.n; and Jonson, *The Devil is an Ass* (1616): 'It is the *divell*, by his severall languages' (5.8.121). 'Your shoo's not cloven, Sir, you are whole hoof'd', comments Fitzdottrell in that play; 'Sir', replies the eponymous Pug, 'that's a popular error, deceives many' (1.3.29-30). On the Esperanto of War, see below, pp. 75-9.

24. On military moles see below, pp. 231-2.

25. *Othello*, 3.3.481.

26. *The Policy of War*, *Early Works*, ed. Ayre (1843), 239-40.

27. The lines may share Milton's scriptural allusion: see *Paradise Lost*, ed. Fowler (1971), 4.181-93. Fowler cites John 10, 1, and Joel 2, 3-9.

28. *The Mirror for Magistrates*, ed. Campbell (1935), 177; Donne, *Works*, ed. Grierson, 307, line 19.

29. See also Riche (1587), A5r and Barret (1598), 2.

30. *Treasure Island*, ed. Letley (1985), 203. The phrase is Stevenson's description of his friend, the disabled W.E. Henley, in a letter to him of May 1883.

31. *The Sonnets and A Lover's Complaint*, ed. Kerrigan (1986), 34. The *OED* gives 1683 as the earliest occurence of 'larum-clock', though one such device provides the climax to Middleton's *A Mad World, My Masters* (c.1604): 'the watch rings alarum in his pocket' (1608, I1r).

32. 'Legs being an important motif in the text as a whole' (Hopper [*sic*], 163), John Lanchester's attribution to O'Brien of the gag about Bernhardt's one-legged Hamlet begins to stand up. Hopper draws some suggestive parallels between *The Third Policeman*'s narrator and both Hamlet (119) and Faustus, whose leg is pulled off by the horsecourser, the relevance of which, he claims, lies in 'the way the wooden leg foregrounds the artificiality of physical description' (213).

33. When, in *The Saga of Grettir the Strong* (c.1300), Onund Treefoot ('the boldest and most active one-legged man that ever came to Iceland') meets his fellow-veterans, 'each thought the other risen from the dead' (ed. Foote [*sic*], 1965, 5, 19); Orson Welles's *Touch of Evil* (1958), artfully set within a geographic and ethical borderland, locates its policeman's detective intuition in the bullet lodged in his limping leg. On the relationship between the wooden leg and revenge, see also Kerrigan (1996), 279-89. For a modern example of the association between unidexterity and uncanny providence, see the *Evening*

*Standard*, 3 December 1997 ('Slip-up in a greasy plot to kill the one-legged lover').

34. Globe Education Centre, 16 March 1997. Colin Mace played Stump and the reading was co-ordinated by Francis Stirling.

35. *2 Henry IV*, 2.4.139.

36. Waugh (1928), 25-6.

37. *Works*, ed. Grierson, 68.

38. 'Bugia ... sarà zoppa, cioè con una gamba di legno ... L'esser zoppa da notitia di quel che si dice trivialmente, che la bugia ha la gambe corte' (Ripa, 1610, 53-4). I am grateful to Hetty Meyric Hughes for her help with the translation.

39. The same association informs John Collier's poetic exchange between 'The Pluralist and Old Soldier' (1763). To the veteran 'Timber-toe' who begs alms, the clergyman replies: 'Heav'n pay me double! Vagrant – know that I | Ne'er give to strollers, they're so apt to lie' (Lonsdale, 511).

40. *2 Henry VI*, ed. Cairncross (1957), 41 (2.1.60.n).

41. *The True Tragedy of Richard the Third*, MSR, line 57; Hall (More) in Bullough, 3, 253.

42. The pretended veteran Lieutenant Bots in Dekker's *The Honest Whore, Part Two* (*c.*1605) likewise claims to have been 'wounded in this thigh, and halted upon't, but 'tis now sound' (5.2.228-9).

43. *1 Henry IV*, ed. Bevington (1987), 26.

44. *The Essayes*, ed. Kiernan (1985), 28.

# CHAPTER TWO

# The Art of War

*'I am the very model of a modern major-general'* [1]

'The worlde was merier, before mesurings were used then it hath beene since', remarks a clothier in Edward Worsop's *Discoverie of Sundrie Errours and Faults Daily Committed by Landemeaters, Ignorant of Arithmetike and Geometrie* (1582). 'A tenant in these daies must pay for every foote', he complains, but is then reassured that while 'common measurings' discriminate against tenants, the new 'true measure' allows him to 'live meryer' (I2v). Worsop's work belongs to a period which saw the widespread dissemination of the mathematical art of mensuration, both locally 'betweene Lord, and tenant', and more broadly in the cartographic achievements that were newly depicting the 'whole worlde' (K2v).[2]

'Al studies have theyr speciall tymes', claimed Richard Willes's preface to Eden's *History of Travayl* (1577), and while grammar, logic or philosophy have each waned in 'theyr singuler seasons', 'of late who taketh not uppon him to discourse of the whole worlde, and eche province thereof particulerly'? (* ii r-v) – apparently even the humble tradesmen featured in Worsop's treatise. John Dee had noted in 1570 'how manifolde commodities do come unto us, daily and hourely' from the advances in geographic technique, in his preface to Billingsley's translation of Euclid: 'some, for one purpose: and some for an other, liketh, loveth, getteth, and useth, Mappes, Chartes, & Geographicall Globes' (a iiii r). It was also in 1570 that one of the most prominent of such 'commodities' first appeared in Antwerp: Abraham Ortelius's world atlas, *Theatrum Orbis Terrarum*.[3]

The shift from woodcut to copper engraving around 1550 allowed an unprecedented detail and compactness to maps, and the Netherlands became the centre of cartographic expertise since it boasted the best engravers (L. Brown, 158). With this shift in method came a decisive break with medieval representations of the world. Four continental maps begin Ortelius's collection, rather than the three partitions of the so-called T-in-O maps (Thrower, 31), reflecting the increasing accuracy in charting lands discovered in the maritime enterprises of the century. Though the two world-views 'showed remarkable powers of co-existence' (Hunter, 1964, 39), Ortelius's *Theatrum* promulgated the ascendance of the physical over the spiritual world, ousting Jerusalem from the symbolic centre of the older *mappae mundi* (L. Brown, 96-8). A comparable break with the past attended Braun and Hogenberg's serially published cityscapes, *Civitates Orbis Terrarum*, first published (again in Antwerp) in 1572. Advances in surveying methods meant that while medieval cities were uniformly shown in profile (and in some cases were represented by interchangeable or fictitious portraits), the *Civitates* displayed their towns from an aerial perspective (Keuning, 41). Immediately successful, both works were regularly reprinted, translated, and augmented into the seventeenth century.[4]

It was in the 1570s too that Christopher Saxton was commissioned to prepare the first systematic survey of England, by which mayors were instructed to 'see him conducted unto any towre, castle, high place or hill, to view that country', and which was published in 1579 (L. Brown, 168). Willes's invocation of the widespread vogue for geography in his prefatory advertisement has been described as 'chronological intimidation' (Lewis, 308), and the vogue is certainly confirmed by the several reprints achieved by Valentine Leigh's *Commendable Science of Surveying* between 1562 and 1596.[5] 'One of the first, that attempted the collectyng of the same Arte into a volume' (A3r), Leigh addressed his readership as 'all men (inasmuche, as the thyng it self, appertaineth to every manne)' (A2r).

The anxiety related by Worsop's clothier about the 'merier' world 'before measurings' indicates the ubiquitous extent of the arts which in Elyot's *Boke Named the Governour* (ed. Croft, 1, 45) 'call[s] in englisshe the discription of the worlde'; but they also resonate with the broader fable of the Golden Age. In those peaceful days, according to Golding's Ovid, 'Men knew none other countries yet, than where themselves did keepe' (B2v), but then came war, 'and men began to bound, | With dowles and diches drawen in length the free and fertile ground' (B3r). 'So twice five miles of fertile ground | With walls and towers were girdled round': the 'Ancestral voices prophesying war' that Coleridge's Kubla Khan 'heard from far' illustrates the longevity of the perceived link between the genesis of war and the demarcation of land.[6] That mythic equation was rendered graphic in the sixteenth century by the crucial military applications of surveyance: Worsop, for example, proceeds to recommend the calculus requisite to determine the strength of an approaching army, the 'chiefe pointes in undermining', or 'how farre any peece beareth point blank' (C1v). It was further compounded by the singular historical coincidence by which the centre of the period's cartographic expertise was also the cockpit of its wars. This chapter seeks to reveal that the common ground between those two Elizabethan archetypes, the geographer and the playwright, extended beyond any shared authorship of a 'discription of the worlde'. The worldly definition each represented (in *Theatrum* or Theater, Globe or *Atlas*) was furthered by the scientific advances of its wars.

## Matters mathematical

Robert Greene placed an account of the Golden Age in the mouth of his warrior-king Selimus: the 'earth knew not the share, nor seas the barke. | The souldiers entred not the battred breach' (see above, p. 29). Greene's contemporary authority on military affairs, Helenus in *Euphues his Censure* (1587), lists the benefits of the modern arts of mensuration to the circumstance of the renewed Iron Age:

> How necessary the knowledge of the lyberall Sciences is for a Souldier, let experience manifest: for what captayne shall bee able to make choice of his ground to fight with his enemy to intrench to imbattayle, to leguer, to pitch his Pavilions at advantage, unlesse skilfull in Geography, to know the Nature and plott of the Countrey so lately discovered. How shall he order his men, or devide them in companyes: how shall hee bring them into square, rounde, triangle, cornet, or any other forme, unlesse instructed in Arithmetike and Geometry.
> (*Works*, ed. Grosart, 6, 207)

'Geography ... so lately discovered': Thomas Digges had indeed lately revealed such expertise in his *Arithmeticall Militare Treatise, Named STRATIOTICOS* in 1579, a work whose 'chiefe intention' he defined as 'to shewe how *Arithmetike* maye stande a Souldioure in steade' (31). This work had been started by Thomas's father Leonard, himself the author of a series of influential texts that had detailed 'the exacte measurynge and speady reckenynge all maner Lande'.[7]

*STRATIOTICOS* fulfils its promise to 'employ ... *Mathematicall Muses* upon this *Militare Argument*' (A2v) by couching a course of Euclidean problems in terms of the calculations necessary to determine, for example, the rate of soldiers' pay to the length of a campaign (67), the supply of victuals to an army's demand (67), the proportion of gunpowder to a cannon's firing-rate (31), of halberdiers to pikemen to shot in an optimum formation (48), or of ground required to encamp an army (57). Although it has been observed that in one of these equations, 9,416 and two thirds of a pioneer were required (Cruickshank, 197), the model provided by the work was emulated by a flood of military treatises that followed it.[8] Digges himself was appointed supervisor of the fortifications built around Dover Harbour in 1582, since the angular defences of the 'many fortyficacions beyond the seas' (Summerson, 206) – the *trace italienne* – demanded the application of arithmetical calculus. Such expertise was likewise essential to the converse art of siege. When Sir Thomas Coningsby arrived at Rouen in 1591, he records, he and his men immediately 'wente to the hill, where we mighte verie playnely discerne the scytuation of it' (22), much as Saxton had been conveyed to any 'high place or hill, to view' the country he surveyed (L. Brown, 167). The mathematics of surveying a town in order to draft its map are recognizably of the same order as the calculus required for the purposes of its assault. The trajectories traced in contemporary diagrams illustrating the principles of a town's geometric construction, and of its ballistic destruction, coalesce.[9]

'*The Generall,*' reads *STRATIOTICOS*, 'is by good, especial, and perfite *Plattes, Mappes,* and *Models,* to know the *Scituation,* Nature, and propertie of the Countrey'(143). Later citing Suetonius's praise for Caesar's use of maps (148), Digges presents a modern analogue that alerts us to the singular coincidence of the centre of the period's cartographic excellence also being the cockpit of its wars:

> hereby also hath the *Prince* of *Orenge* in these late *Flemishe* warres greatly aided himselfe: For havyng of *Hollande, Zelande,* and all other partes of the lowe Countries verie perfite and exquisite *Mappes & Plattes,* he was able at one time in sundrie partes to give *Direction* whiche *Straites* shoulde be garded.

It seems likely that these 'perfite' maps were taken from Ortelius's collection: certainly there is evidence of a Dutch soldier requesting from a friend a 'cheap set of Ortelius's maps for the summer campaign' in May 1586 (van Dorsten, 131). The military potential of the *Theatrum*'s sister-publication, the *Civitates,* is signalled in its preface to the 1572 volume. Some of the maps feature human figures, it claims, to illustrate native customs, 'but also in order to prevent the Turks from being able to use the pictures in their wars of conquest, since their religion prohibits the portrayal of human beings' (Keuning, 42). A copy of Saxton's atlas is likewise extant, with detailed annotations prepared for Burghley concerning the likely landing places for a Spanish attempt on the coast (Boynton, 129).

Dee had commended the aesthetic qualities of maps as a useful way 'to beautifie ... Galeries, Studies, or Libraries' (a4r), but their military utility was also fully recognized; on the other hand, 'the development of rapid survey methods owed much to military requirements' (E. Taylor, 1930, 26). Furthermore, 'while in another country a battle would be accounted for in a large history painting ... the Dutch issue a popular news map' (Alpers, xxvi). Geographic methods not only proved essential to waging war, and were themselves in part the product of those exigencies, but the details of those campaigns were narrated in 'exquisite *Mappes & Plattes*'. The Dutch influence in England is clearly visible in George Gascoigne's poem on his 'voyage into *Holland.* An. 1572', which closes with the promise to supplement his 'riming sporte' with news 'of *Hollandes* state, the which I will present, | In Cartes, in Mappes, and eke in Models made' (1575, 173). Barnaby Riche intended to include 'many plattes of fortifications' in his account, never published, of the Dutch wars (1581, B ii v). And Gascoigne's eye-witness report of *The Spoyle of Antwerp* (1576) originally included a 'Model of the whole place ... annexed to thend' (A7v), apparently thumbed out of existence from all extant copies.[10] The missing map nonetheless seems to have found its way into the play made of Gascoigne's journalism, *A Larum for London*, transmuted into a graphic image of military conquest. 'This Cittie ... now remaines the Map, | Of sad destruction and perpetuall ruyne', gloats Danila, 'Her streetes lie thwackt with slaughtered carkasses' (1614-17).

From around the middle of the sixteenth century, then, the mathematical arts 'called in englisshe the discription of the worlde' achieved increasingly conspicious results. Maritime enterprise opened up the world to trade and imperial ambition, while techniques of engraving ensured that this physical world was realized in remarkably vivid form for a public voracious in its appetite for such depictions. Closer to home, the art of surveyance exactly defined 'what is indifferent betweene Lord, and tenant'. And while cities for the first time achieved a graphically distinct representation, one from another, those cities themselves were girdled by fortifications derived from the military applications of that science. It was in war that the full extent of the mathematical revolution was both felt and furthered. The finest examples of cartography derived from a group of states racked by war, the focus of the ideological confrontation of the age. It has been claimed that these wars deserve to be considered the first First World War (Parker, 1975, 57): it was certainly the first time that war had been both waged and envisaged in terms of an accurate description of the world.

The mutually informative nature of war and cartography is demonstrated by the fact that Mercator's *Atlas, or a Geographicke Description of the ... World* was first translated into English in 1636 by Henry Hexham, who had served as page under Sir Francis Vere at the Siege of Ostend, and had published several accounts of campaigns as well as an Anglo-Dutch dictionary.[11] His preface attributes the victories of Caesar, the Black Prince, and William of Nassau to a knowledge of what he calls 'these two *Gemini Geographie* and *Historie*' (**1r):

> Here then the great Monarches, Kings and Princes of this
> Universe, may representively in their Cabinets take a view
> of the extention, and limits of their owne Kingdomes, and
> Dominions ... Here the Noble-man and Gentle-man by
> speculation in his closset, may travell through every
> Province of the whole world ... Here the Souldier hath
> matter of delight ministred unto him, in beholding the
> place, & reading the storie, where many bloodie Battles
> have beene fought, and many famous seiges performed ...
> Here the Marchant sitting in his counting-house, may
> know what Marchandises every Countrie affordeth, what
> commodities it wanteth, and whither he may transport,
> and vent those which are most vendible, to returne gaine
> and profite into his purse.
> (**1v - **2r)

The customers solicited by Hexham's advertisement, indeed the very terms of its meditation on the powers of a map, strongly recall the points of departure Marlowe provides for the heroes of *The Jew of Malta, Doctor Faustus* and *Tamburlaine*.

'Here the Marchant sitting in his counting-house': part of the effect of Barabas's opening soliloquy, delivered 'in his Counting-house' (1.1.SD), resides in his precise knowledge of 'what Marchandises every Countrie affordeth ... and whither he may transport, and vent' them. Hexham's gentleman 'by speculation in his closset, may travell through every Province of the whole world': Faustus's darker speculations originate 'in his study' (A 29-30) and come to 'proove *Cosmography*' (A 816).[12] From his 'stately tent of War' (*One*, Prol. 3), the 'extention, and limits' of Tamburlaine's conquests culminate in the soldier-king 'reading the storie' of his own 'bloodie Battles' from the map he has made of them. The scholar, merchant and soldier of Marlowe's plays sustain Richard Willes's view that 'all Christians, Jewes, Turkes, Moores, Infidels, & Barbares be this day in love with Geographie' (Eden, 1577, * iii r).

When the surveyor in Worsop's *Discoverie* explains why his procedures are conducted in Greek, the serving-man Steven is greatly relieved. He 'would have thought them, words of conjuration', he confesses, relating how he had once caught a glimpse of a surveyance-manual, 'a booke that had many crosses in it, & a great number of like figures, and circles':

> one of our company did reade such strange wordes, one other saide: my friend, you were not best to reade too farre in that booke, least you fetche one up, that will aske what he shall doe, and if you can appoint him nothing, neither know howe to laye him downe againe, he will doe much hurt.
> (1582, C1r)

Such fears were both topical and longstanding. According to the antiquarian Anthony à Wood, when Oxford's libraries were rifled in 1550, and 'such books wherein appeared Angles or Mathematical Diagrams, were thought sufficient to be destroyed because accounted Popish, or diabolical, or both' (Yates, 1969, 15). In May 1583, Dee's house was attacked by an angry mob convinced of his satanic powers (E. Taylor, 1930, 138). 'The common people are in great fear', wrote Worsop himself that year, 'when survey is to be made of their land' (E. Taylor, 1947, 131 n.1). The fearful anecdote Steven relates might almost be a précis of the later comic scene in which Robin, having 'stolne one of doctor Faustus conjuring books', endeavours to 'search some circles for my owne use' (949-51), and summons Mephostophilis, who irascibly turns him into a monkey.

Such superstitions prevailed independently of the particularities of Euclidean maths: but whispers of these concerns can be discerned, I think, in what Greg called the 'pure gibberish' (359) of Robin's spell. '*Sancto-bulorum Periphrasticon*', he reads from Faustus's book, '*Polypragmos Belseborams*' (1009-10). The line is garbled, perhaps for comic effect, almost certainly because textually corrupt, but '*Periphrasticon*' nevertheless seems cognate with geometric terms to do with boundaries and circumferences,[13] while the common fears Worsop relates derive, he says, from the suspicion that surveyors sent spirits to circumscribe lands 'before they were measured' (C1v) – how else explain the accuracy of calculus? The manifold practical applications of mensuration, furthermore, is the very theme of works by Worsop, Digges, Dee and so on – the *polypragmatism* of mathematics. Such limited conjectures find at least a shred of support in Mephostophilis's subsequent appeal to the 'Monarke of hel, under whose blacke survey | Great Potentates do kneele' (1023-4). 'Ile never rob thy Library more', promises Robin (1019).

Whatever the true relationship between *Doctor Faustus* and *Friar Bacon and Friar Bungay*, the accounting of 'Mathematical Diagrams ... diabolical' informs Greene's play. 'No doubt but magicke may doe much in this', comments Doctor Mason there,

> For he that reades but Mathematicke rules,
> Shall finde conclusions that availe to worke,
> Wonders that passe the common sense of men.[14]

Bacon's command of 'Mathematicke rules' are repeatedly linked by Greene to his mastery of 'magicke spels' (506; see also 497-8), yet 'the flowers of the Sciences Mathematical', as Leonard Digges called them (1562, A2r), find no place in Faustus's dispute with 'every Art' (34).

In that celebrated passage, Faustus settles his studies, and begins to 'sound the deapth' of his learning (32). Logic, medicine, law, divinity are each restlessly dispatched as 'paltry' (60), and 'Negromantike bookes' instead embraced (80). In 1577, Willes's eulogy of geography had similarly consigned grammar, logic, and astrology to the past, instead celebrating the 'Mappes, Globes, tables, and Cardes', whose 'tyme is now' (Eden,* ii v). How singular that the 'chronological intimidation' exerted by geography, so pervasive in 1577, should nowhere feature in the doctor's speech. Such rules and sciences in fact provide, by their ostentatious absence, a resonant context to the black arts to which he there turns. Consider, for example, the terms with which he describes his 'Negromantike bookes':

> Lines, circles, sceanes, letters and characters:
> I, these are those that *Faustus* most desires.
> O what a world of profit and delight,
> Of power, of honor, of omnipotence
> Is promised to the studious Artizan?
> (81-85)

Where the English Faust Book describes an expertise 'in using his *Vocabula*, Figures, Characters, Conjurations, and other Ceremoniall actions',[15] Marlowe seems preoccupied by the various calligraphy of his books, especially if Greg's emendation of the unintelligible 'sceanes' to 'Signes' is accepted (301). The passage has been called the 'hellish signifying nonsense of magic' (Belsey, 73), and, more particularly, compared to the 'technical and specialized business of ... magic' detailed in Cornelius Agrippa's *De Occulta* (1533) (G. Roberts, 154-5). Faustus's 'Lines, circles, Signes, letters and characters', however, were neither unique to necromantic books, nor *per se* nonsensical scribbles, as the 'crosses ... figures, and circles' of Steven's surveyance-manual testify.

It is certainly notable that Faustus's speculations on a 'world of profit and delight' involve only slightly grandiose variations on the 'mathematicall knowledges' (F4v) Worsop commends from Euclid, including 'Astronomie, Perspective, Cosmographie, Geographie, Navigation, Martiall exploits, survey of lands ... architecture, Ingins, dreinings or mountings of water, and many other faculties' (G2v):

> Ile have them flye to *India* for gold,
> Ransacke the Ocean for orient pearle,
> And search all corners of the new found world
> For pleasant fruites and princely delicates ...
> Ile have them wall all *Jermany* with brasse,
> And make swift *Rhine* circle faire *Wertenberge*.
> (114-21)

Instruments of surveyance, Worsop notes, are 'thinges in navigation of greate necessitie' (C1v), and Humphrey Gilbert's *Discourse of a Discoverie for a New Passage to Cataia* (1576) includes a 'General Map' illustrating 'what commodities woulde ensue', 'the onely way for our princes, to possesse ye welth of all the *East* partes ... of the worlde, which is infinite' (H1r). Faustus too looks east for the gold and 'princely delicates' of the 'new found world'. The extravagant 'dreinings or mountings of water' he plans stem from the same expertise – Dee calls it 'Hydrographie' (1570, A4r) – but characteristically of its time, the speech turns to consider how '*Geographie* [is] for a Souldior requisite' (Digges, 1579, 148).

Faustus's diversion of the Rhine and his fortification of 'all *Jermany*', find a precedent in Aeneas's plan to 'build a statelier *Troy*' in *Dido, Queen of Carthage* (5.1.2). He will grace Carthage 'with a fairer frame, | And clad her in a Christall liverie'; and have the River Ganges 'triple wise intrench her round about' (5-10). He enters Act Five 'with a paper in his hand, drawing the platforme of the citie'. Described as a 'perfite souldier' in the 1595 *Myrrour for English Souldiers* (A2r), Aeneas is carefully, anachronistically, introduced as a perfect practitioner of the Elizabethan *Arte of Warre*. An officer, reads Garrard's treatise of that name, 'must indevour himselfe to be perfect in drawing platformes, in the Mathematickes, in the martiall Lawes, in besieging of townes, batteries, mynes' (1591, 78). The crystalline and brass fortifications each of Marlowe's heroes intend to build opulently reflect the geometric methods by which European cities were being girdled at the time of their plays. The 'Mathematicke rules' and 'magicke spels' of Greene's Friar Bacon repeatedly aspire 'by the helpe of Divels and ghastly fiends ... To compasse England with a wall of brass' (202-4; see also 351; 1583; 1668). Faustus's 'servile spirits' are charged with still more overt military service, the 'Martiall exploits' and 'Ingins' Worsop lists, in the lines that follow:

> Ile levy souldiers with the coyne they bring,
> And chase the Prince of *Parma* from our land,
> And raigne sole king of all our provinces:
> Yea stranger engines for the brunt of warre,
> Then was the fiery keele at *Antwarpes* bridge,
> Ile make my servile spirits to invent.
> (124-9)

If the real-life counterpart to Friar Bacon, and the 'brazen walles' he vows to erect about 'the English strond: | From Dover to the market place of Rie' (237-40), was Thomas Digges, the surveyor of Dover Harbour's fortifications in 1582, Faustus too finds anachronistic inspiration in contemporary military science. For despite the patronage of '*Carolus* the fift' (944), in February 1585/86, within months of Elizabeth's declaration of aid to the Low Countries, Sir Philip Sidney entertained Gianbelli, the engineer responsible for the 'fiery keele at *Antwarpes* bridge', the explosive fire-ship which had killed five hundred of the town's besiegers the previous April (M. Wilson, 255).

'Our land', 'our provinces': Faustus squarely identifies himself with the Anglo-Dutch war-effort in which his audiences were engaged, from the play's '*terminus a quo*' provided by the allusion (Greg, 7), to the year of its publication in 1604. But he also declares himself a fellow-countryman to the great exponents of geographic technique – Mercator, Ortelius, Braun and Hogenberg – their home the centre of cartographic endeavour.[16] 'How wonderful a good map is', wrote the later connoisseur, Samuel van Hoogstraten in 1678, 'in which one views the world as from another world' (Alpers, 141). Faustus's astronautical flight aboard his dragon's back, 'to know the secrets of *Astronomy*' and 'proove *Cosmography*' (811-16), is infused with a comparable wonder. With an atlas before him, Hexham was to claim, a 'Gentle-man by speculation in his closset, may travell through every Province of the whole world'. By speculation in his theatre – at once the forum for thaumaturgic illusion (Palmer, 56-67) and the geographic description of the world – Marlowe's play does similar work:

So high our Dragons soar'd into the aire,
That looking downe the earth appear'd to me,
No bigger then my hand in quantity.
(B 872-74)

The results of this airborne survey (822-61) provide a sort of chorographical verse-equivalent to the cityscapes of the *Civitates Orbis Terrarum* – indeed the cities detailed there (Trier, Paris, Naples, Venice and Rome), while mentioned in the source, also feature in the first volume of the *Civitates* (issued six times between 1572 and 1593). 'I do long to see the monuments | And scituation of bright splendant *Rome*' (865-6), says Faustus. Comments Greg, '*situation* properly means site or location, but here the notion seems to be rather that of internal disposition (of parts)' (350); its occurrence has been advanced as evidence of Rowley's co-authorship, since *When You See Me You Know Me* (1605) deploys it in the same 'rare' sense.[17] On the contrary, however, and as Aeneas's 'platforme of the citie' suggests, the word rings with its specialist currency. One of the period's most frequently cited military texts, for example, *STRATIOTICOS*, cites the Prince of Orange's 'excellente knowledge in *Fortification*' as exemplary of the military need 'by good Plattes to consider the *Scituation* of the Countrey' (1579, 144; 147-8); Sir Thomas Coningsby, putting the theory into practice, knowingly deployed the word in his *Journal of the Siege of Rouen* (22).

The telescoping of space *Doctor Faustus* achieves, at any rate, is the very principle by which Mercator's *Atlas* was subsequently presented to its readership, by which counting-house, closet and cabinet would contain 'the whole world'. Barabas's cartographic survey of his fleet famously turns 'to inclose | Infinite riches in a little roome' (1.1.36-7), a phrase that came to be echoed in Francis Bacon's essay 'Of Travaile'.

If you will have a Young Man, to put his Travaile, into a little Roome, and in short time, to gather much, this you must doe. First ... he must have some Entrance into the language ... Then ... Let him carry with him also some Card or Booke describing the Country, where he travelleth.[18]

Paul Ive's *Practice of Fortification* passingly calls the cannon 'an Engine of much more force than any before invented' (1589, 35). Doctor Faustus promises 'stranger engines' still, and Barabas too 'was an Engineere, | And in the warres 'twixt *France* and *Germanie*, | Under pretence of helping *Charles* the fifth, | Slew friend and enemy with my stratagems' (2.3.186-9). The 'extention, and limits' of Tamburlaine's 'Kingdomes, and Dominions' are explicitly furthered and defined by the thoroughly contemporary military technologies he champions. 'I will with Engines, never exercisde, | Conquer ... Your cities' (*Two*, 4.1.191): the 'Language' and 'Card' of Tamburlaine's military progress – in siege, ballistics, surveyance, fortification and cartography – is the subject of the remainder of this chapter.

## Model soldiers

'This day there is a platforme laied for the better increace of the Mathemeticall science', announced Thomas Hood on 4 November 1588, in his inaugural address as mathematical lecturer of the City of London, a post sponsored by a Privy Council prompted by the invasion-scare that summer.[19] Aimed at the as yet untested captains of the Trained Bands, Hood's lecture was intended as a bridge between 'noble Captaines and loving Schollers' (105). Of all disciplines, 'the mathematicks surpasse them all', he declared, not least because it is a 'Knowledge most convenient for militarie men' (100-101):

> Let Geographie witnesse in universall Mappes, let Topographie witnesse in several Cardes, let Hydrographie witnesse in the Mariners plat, you your selves may witness in Martiall affaires, let the Gunner witnesse in planting his shot, witnesse the Surveior in measuring land, witnesse all those, that labor in mines, and those that practise conveying of water, whose skill being tolde us, we would scarsely beleeve it, were it not lying at our doores.
> (105)

Let the playwright witness (we might add) in the scarcely believable feats he represented on stage: for if the audience assembled to hear Hood's lecture in Gracechurch Street that day had wandered south, and crossed the Thames to Bankside, it is possible they might have witnessed another mathematical lecture on the 'rudiments of war', and allowed geography to witness in a universal map the martial applications of the 'discription of the worlde'. For certainly within a mile, and probably within a year of Hood's lecture, Marlowe's Tamburlaine first emerged from his stately tent of war.

Before Marlowe dramatized his life, Timur the Lame, Tamburlaine the Great, exemplified two distinct ideological traditions. He was glorified by the Italian humanists as a perfect prince of *virtú*, pre-eminent through deeds rather than birth; second, his victories were adduced as evidence of God's purposive punishment, as a tyrannical scourge of God (Ribner, 1953 256). George Whetstone's *English Myrror* (1586), a probable source for the first of Marlowe's plays, accordingly stresses Tamburlaine's elevation from the condition of a 'poore labourer, or in the best degree a meane souldiour' (79), but also comments that 'it seemed by his cruelty, that God raysed him to chasten the kings & proud people of the earth' (82). The two traditions converged in the theory and practice of Elizabeth's wars.

Gates's *Defence of Militarie Profession* for example commends the 'worthie people of our nation' then engaged as volunteers in the 'defensory warres' in Holland (1578, 58); and concludes its list of the scourges by which God has punished 'a wicked nation for sinne' with *'Tamberlan a heardman with the rude Scythians* to chastise *Bajezet* the *Turkish* Emperour and all his dominions. And lastly the *Spanyard* to chastise *France, Italy, Germany* and lowe *Duchland'* (1578, 20-21).[20] On the other hand, Tamburlaine was widely seen as a paragon of soldiership. Though it was commonly accepted that the Romans were the 'Fathers of all Marshiall affaires' (Churchyard, 1593, 89), Whetstone's *English Myrror* claimed, with much subsequent authority, that 'none of their martiall acts, deserve to be proclaimed with more renown, then the conquest and militarie disciplines of *Tamburlaine*' (79). The same author's *Honourable Reputation of a Souldier* uses his precedent to illustrate the dissolution of feudal status in the modern army, insisting instead on the fellowship of all who 'glorieth in the name of a *Souldier'*(25) – even 'the mightie king TAMBERLAINE, was in the beginning, a poore sheephard' (28).

Whetstone's *Honourable Reputation* was published at Leiden in 1586, in the form of a parallel text in English and Dutch, a language manual intended to smooth liaisons between the allies since 'the arryving of his *Excell.* in this Low Countreyes' (10). Some of the same intimacy between the military precedent of 'the mightie king TAMBERLAINE' described there and the Dutch theatre of war can be discerned in the plays Marlowe made, via Whetstone's own *English Myrror*, of his life. Written within two years of Leicester's expeditionary force reaching the continent, by an author with known connections in military intelligence, their soldier-hero at once wages war by instructively commanding the modern technologies proselytized by Thomas Hood; and embraces certain of the theoretical contradictions and ambivalences towards war we have rehearsed in the previous chapter.

Critics have tended to overlook the specific profile Marlowe's Tamburlaine presented to his original wartime audiences. Thus Richard Levin's useful account of his 'contemporary perception' ('a triumphant figure who possessed and wielded tremendous power') skirts about the military nature of that power, upon which so many of the references he cites focus (1984, 56); and the helpful discussion J.S. Cunningham's edition provides of the homiletic commonplace of the Scourge of God fails to note that, in particular, that term was a *sine qua non* of Elizabethan war theory.[21]

*The Honourable Reputation of a Souldier*, according to Whetstone, rested on deeds rather than blood, for 'basenes of parentage might be no blemish to those that deserved well: nor noble blood, a previledge for those that did amisse'. So, he argues, though the Emperor 'VALENTIAN was a Shoomakers sonne' (27), and Tamburlaine a shepherd, yet each displayed the valour which can 'raise a man from the Carte, to be a Soveraigne Captaine' (26). When Alexander the Great lay dying, he writes, 'So great was the Justice of his minde', that he preferred 'a Straunger' when naming his heir (29). Himself a shoemaker's son (Bakeless, 1, 10), Marlowe converts Tamburlaine's humble origins into a theatrical tableau of Whetstone's moral. His hero invests himself in the 'compleat armor' of his soldiership (*One*, 1.2.42): 'I am a Lord, for so my deeds shall proove, | And yet a shepheard by my Parentage' (34-5). His triumphant progress presses home the lessons taught by the professionalized wars of the century, that 'Your byrthes shall be no blemish to your fame' (*One*, 4.4.127), and exacts the exemplary 'punishments and severities of offences' on which Tamburlaine's reputation rested in contemporary martial literature (Lloyd, 1602, 193): 'great *Tamberlan* punished so severely one of his souldiers', reads Barret's *Theorike and Practike of Modern Warres*, 'that the rigor thereof did ... correct and discipline his campe' (10). Tamburlaine's murder of his own son, in the sequel, displays the working of such 'martial justice' on the 'obloquie and skorne of my renowne' (*Two*, 4.1.92-6), even as it constitutes a defiant attack on the principles of primogeniture: for Calyphas too, 'noble blood' is no 'previledge for those that did amisse'.

'Mercilesse villaine', exclaims the Soldan of Egypt,

> Pesant ignorant,
> Of lawfull armes, or martiall discipline:
> Pillage and murder are his usuall trades.
> The slave usurps the glorious name of war.
> (*One*, 4.1.64)

'Villaine ... Pesant ... trades': the old guard of military hierarchy voices repeated affront at what Cosroe calls Tamburlaine's 'Giantly presumption', 'to cast up hils against the face of heaven' (2.6.2-3). That allusion secures the elemental force of Tamburlaine's belligerence in the mythic origins of war itself, in the Iron Age, when (as Ovid again summarizes) 'Giantes went about the Realme of heaven ... to place themselves to raigne as gods ... and hill on hill they heaped aloft' (1567, B3v). Cosroe's outrage in part stems from the military insubordination he has suffered. He appoints Tamburlaine the 'Generall Lieftenant of my Armies' (2.5.8-9) – where in Whetstone's source he is promoted to 'chiefe captaine' (1586, 79) – but his lieutenant's 'thirst of raigne' (*One*, 2.7.12), hinged about the celebrated repetition of 'And ride in triumph through *Persepolis*' (2.5.49-54), is slaked by the novelty and force of his rank. The Lieutenant, as Barret writes, 'in the absence of his Captaine, carieth his roome' (1598, 22): by the end of his first play, 'this man or rather god of war' (5.1.1) has risen through even Olympian ranks. 'The God of war resignes his roume to me', he boasts,

> Meaning to make me Generall of the world,
> Jove viewing me in armes, lookes pale and wan,
> Fearing my power should pull him from the throne.
> (5.1.450-53)

The passage recasts in military mould the mighty precedent Tamburlaine had earlier provided to his own career, Jove's usurpation of 'his doting father' Saturn, in a paean to those aspiring 'faculties' that 'can comprehend | The wondrous Architecture of the world' (2.7.12-22). The cartographic resonance of that phrase is borne out in a later sequence, the Siege of Damascus, which spells out the extent to which, in Digges's phrase, '*Geographie* [is] for a Souldior requisite' (1579, 148).

Tamburlaine's Olympian defiance once more gains force from the procedures of contemporary warfare:

> *Zenocrate*, were Egypt *Joves* owne land,
> Yet would I with my sword make *Jove* to stoope.
> I will confute those blind Geographers
> That make a triple region in the world,
> Excluding Regions which I meane to trace,
> And with this pen reduce them to a Map,
> Calling the Provinces, Citties and townes
> After my name and thine *Zenocrate*:
> Here at *Damascus* will I make the Point
> That shall begin the Perpendicular.
> (*One*, 4.4.73-82)

The lines conflate a number of the contexts outlined above. Most evidently they allude to the ascendance of modern maps over medieval representations of the world, the abstract T-in-O maps that divided it into a 'triple region' pivoted about Jerusalem.[22] Yet the immediate context is a military siege: Damascus's fall will provide co-ordinates by which Tamburlaine's own 'Map' may be drawn with his pen-as-sword. The same principles of geometric construction necessary to survey and map a town are those necessary to open up a breach in its defences. In the strictest contrast to 'those blind Geographers', Menaphon had earlier and vividly described Tamburlaine's eyes as 'piercing instruments of sight' (2.1.14). It has been argued that the phrase informs Lodge's description of Scilla in *The Wounds of Civil War* (1588), whose 'sparkling eyes' are likened to 'burning brands'; the mechanized flavour of Marlowe's phrase, however, conveys something more specific than 'awful power' (W. Armstrong, 382). The earth 'knows the share' at Damascus both in terms of Iron Age mythology, and of fully contemporary military science. Tamburlaine's instruments of sight insist upon the piercing inscription of the art of describing.

One such instrument of sight features in the Siege of Balsera, by Tamburlaine's lieutenants, in the second play. 'Pioners away', orders Theridamas, 'and where I stuck the stake, | Intrench with those dimensions I prescribed'. Techelles replies:

> Both we (*Theridamas*) wil intrench our men,

> And with the Jacobs staffe measure the height
> And distance of the castle from the trench,
> That we may know if our artillery
> Will carie full point blancke unto their wals.
> (*Two*, 3.3.41-53)

'The chieffest peece of arte in the description of countries', wrote Worsop in his treatise on surveyance, 'is the taking of heightes, lengthes, and distances' (1583, C2r), not least in order 'to knowe how farre any peece beareth point blank' (C1v). The essential tool for such calculation was the theodolite, the 'Geometricall Instrument of wood called Jacobs staffe', as the military architect John Symonds called it in his 1597 will.[23] Thomas Hood's lecture included a spurious appeal to the biblical antiquity of such methods, referring to Adam, Abraham 'and *Jacob* also, whose staffe we use' (F. Johnson, 102), and the quibble becomes a serious joke in George Peele's *David and Bathsabe* (printed 1599), a play apparently influenced by *Tamburlaine*.

Before Balsera, Marlowe has Techelles warn its castellan that his pioneers 'shall cut the leaden pipes, | That bring fresh water to thy men and thee' (3.3.20-22). Peele's 'mighty captaines' employ the same tactics at the Siege of Rabath, 'to scale this kingly Tower, | Where all their conduits and their fountaines are'.[24] 'Ye fight the holy battels of Jehovah', says Joab,

> King Davids God, and ours and Jacobs God
> That guides your weapons to their conquering strokes,
> Orders your footsteps, and directs your thoughts
> To stratagems that harbor victorie:
> He casts his sacred eiesight from on high
> And sees your foes run seeking for their deaths.
> (171-76)

It is 'Jacobs God' not 'Jacobs staffe' that 'guides your weapons to their conquering strokes'; and His are the 'piercing instruments of sight', now sanctified into a 'sacred eiesight' cast on sinners 'from on high'. Peele's figure deftly insinuates the technique of modern war into the Christian theory of its waging.

The implications of Peele's emendation for the peculiar force of his model are worth pondering. For the relish with which Tamburlaine champions the geographic 'rudiments of war' signals the extent to which they seem to exist independently of any overtly divine sanction. By way of illustration, it is notable that the soldier-heroes of both Marlowe's and Peele's plays, Tamburlaine and David, each find mention in Gates's *Defence of Militarie Profession*. A parallel is drawn there, as we have seen, between the divine punishments bestowed on Bajazet by '*Tamburlan* a heardman', and on '*France, Italy, Germany* and lowe *Duchland*' by the Spaniard, 'to plague a wicked nation for sinne' (20-21). 'Yet this is our comfort', as C.G. later explained, 'he is but Gods Servant, and therefore he can doe no more then God will permit & appoint him' (1596, D4r; see above, p. 35). Gates accordingly relates how the Duke of Alva, 'who came into *Belgia* so glorious and dreadful, is daunted & returned into Spaine with shame and discredite' (30). 'God was with ye poore, against the prowde and mightie' (30-31), and now remains with 'ye people of *England*', as the work's closing prayer (62) for Elizabeth and her European allies declares:

> for the sword of the Almightie is drawne, and will not be
> put up till hee hath confounded, and utterly consumed all
> the enemies of *Jacob* from the face of the earth for
> evermore.

Gates also commends King David as a 'worthy captain & prophet ... by whose mightie value & martial prowesse, ye Lord stretched forth the kingdom of *Jacob*, to the promised bounds' (39), 'for by Armes the Lorde God vanquished and destroied the enemies of *Jacob*, and therefore is called the Lorde God of hostes' (13).

Much of the tone of this divine militancy is caught by Peele's description of 'King Davids God, and ours and Jacobs God', 'Laughing [His enemies'] labours and their hopes to scorne' (177), directing military operations like the 'High generall of all warres' Gates described (1579, 16). Marlowe's Tamburlaine, however, stridently assumes that mantle himself: 'this man or rather God of war' promotes himself to 'Generall of the world' – and stays there. There is no Richmond to dispatch the 'wretched, bloudie and usurping bore' after he has served his chastening purpose (*Richard III*, 5.2.7); no Lieutenant Stump to declare, 'But goe no further' (*A Larum for London*, 770). The 'promised bounds' of Tamburlaine's dominions are etched by the map he himself inscribes. The terms with which Stephen Greenblatt usefully sketches the impact of the plays' structure have particular force in this context of Elizabethan war theory:

> [In Part One] Tamburlaine is proud, arrogant, and
> blasphemous; he lusts for power, betrays his allies,
> overthrows legitimate authority, and threatens the gods;
> he rises to the top of the wheel of fortune and then
> steadfastly refuses to budge ... The effect [in Part Two] is
> ... to challenge the habit of mind that looks to heaven for
> rewards and punishments, that imagines human evil as 'the
> scourge of God'.
> (1980, 202).

Machiavelli for one (as we have seen) challenged the very 'habit of mind' that particularly imagined *war* as the scourge of God (see above, pp. 21-3), and Tamburlaine's inexorable progress accordingly depends upon the technology of victory rather than the theology of its justice. The pattern of *de casibus* tragedy he flouts suggests the autonomy of that military power. While Marlowe deploys 'instruments of sight' like the Jacob's staff, Peele is careful to rein them back to the instrumental directive of Jacob's God.

As well as jamming the spokes of the wheel of fortune, Marlowe's version of Tamburlaine's story also curtails the sequence of war's perpetual cycle, 'the olde saying' (17) which forms the moral of its telling in Whetstone's *English Myrror: A Regard Wherein* (as its full title reads) *al estates may behold the Conquests of Envy*. Whetstone's relevant chapter is titled, 'The wonderfull conquest of Tamberlaine, reconquered and his large kingdom overthrowne by the envy and discord of his two sonnes' (78). Marlowe's plays end with a single-minded sense of an ending: 'Meet heaven & earth', says Amyras, '& here let al things end' (5.3.249). It has been claimed that Part Two is an uneasily contrived sequel, 'confessedly an afterthought';[25] yet the fuller potential for a Part Three, positively urged by the sources, is resolutely quashed. '*Tamburlaine*, the scourge of God must die' (248), but he does so with his inheritance secured in Amyras (justifying his filicide), and the 'exquisite *Mappes & Plattes*' (Digges, 1579, 148) of an impending campaign embodied on stage, 'That these my boies may finish all my wantes' (125).

The two military texts Whetstone saw published in 1586, *The English Myrror* in London, and *The Honourable Reputation* in Leiden, offer distinct treatments of their theme, best exampled by the account each provides of the origins of war. 'Many yeeres after the beginning', reads *The English Myrror*, proscribing Envy as 'the extreamest of all evils' (2),

> every King quietly enjoyed the countries in his own possession, until *Ninus* ... envying the soveranity of his neighbour kings put him self in armes unlawfully to inlarge his owne dominions, by deposing other from their kingdoms. Thus by envy from the bottom of hell came war, & by war confusion of devine and human blessings.
> (10)

A similar genealogy is contained in the (probably later) Anglo-Dutch work, but a collateral line is traced:

> At what time *Ambition*, the *Impe* of miscreate *Envy*, upon desire of Soveraigntie, begat *Warre*: *Necessitie*, Inventress of all Pollicies, Artes, and Mecanicall Craftes, devised many Engines for Warre: the use whereof, gave first reputation unto the *Souldier*, who ever since hath beene honourably esteemed.
> (25)

At once the confounding of 'devine and human blessings', war's advent 'from the bottom of hell' proves the source of honourable esteem in its practitioners – 'the worst and best' (as Riche later put it), 'that ever Fortune could promise her favourites' (1604, 4-5). Marlowe's Tamburlaine inherits and embodies the twin aspects of Whetstone's pedigree.

The play certainly begins by rooting the rise and rise of its hero in Cosroe's bid 'unlawfully to inlarge his owne dominions, by deposing' his brother Mycetes from his throne. Enlisting Tamburlaine to his cause, however, he soon discovers that once summoned (rather like Robin's later conjuration of Mephostophilis), this 'God or Feend, or spirit of the earth' (*One*, 2.6.15) cannot easily be laid down again. 'Sent from hell to tyrannise on earth' (*Two*, 5.1.111), Tamburlaine's elemental '*Ambition, the Impe* of miscreate *Envy*' is set in train, achieving iconic representation in the plays' most celebrated *coup*, the entrance of '*Tamburlaine drawen in his chariot by Trebizon and Soria with bites in their mouthes, reines in his left hand, in his right a whip, with which he scourgeth them*' (*Two*, 4.3.SD). The emblem ties together a range of contemporary symbolism, while demonstrating Marlowe's peculiar instinct for graphic cruelty. Perhaps *The English Myrror* had planted the seed in Marlowe's imagination by the time he composed the sequel, for Whetstone describes there the miseries of war, in which 'vice mounted in her chariot of triumph, arrogantly treadeth pore vertue under foot' (10). On the other hand, Tamburlaine's prop renders literal the whip Thomas Becon had described, 'with the whych the holy and righteous Lorde doth beate and scourge us for owre vicious lyvinge' (see above, p. 33), the divinely sanctioned chastisement of Elizabethan orthodoxy. Yet while, for example, Ripa's emblem of the *flagellum dei* has a bearded patriarch wield the flail (1610, 178), Tamburlaine's (presumably armoured) entrance 'in his chariot' more strongly calls to mind the horse-drawn Mars, flail in hand, of traditional iconography.[26] Furthermore, as Emrys Jones notes, this 'famous tableau' also owes a debt to 'the opening dumb-show of [Gascoigne's] *Jocasta* in which Sesostris King of Egypt, representing Ambition, is drawn in a chariot by four kings' (1977, 123). The impression made upon Marlowe's contemporaries by the scene is the more remarkable for the ambivalence of the moral it presents.[27] Whether illustrative of the perpetual cycle of C.G.'s 'pride of Princes', the pantheon of 'Ethnick wryters', 'the puddle or sincke of all mischiefe' or 'nothing else but a divine scourge for sinne' (C1v; C4v; C2r), Tamburlaine 'usurps the glorious name of war'.

The Soldan makes that complaint as Tamburlaine's 'Basiliskes ... roaring, shake *Damascus* turrets downe' (*One*, 4.1.2-3), 'Without respect of Sex, degree or age' (62). The later tableau includes the comparably telling detail of the Kings of '*Natolia, and Jerusalem led by with five or six common souldiers*'. Chivalric resentment at the indiscriminate effect of firearms still found residual expression in the period, as Smythe and Barwick's exactly contemporary military debate shows.[28] Whetstone describes the generation, out of Envy by Necessity, 'of all Pollicies, Artes, and Mecanicall Craftes' and 'Engines for Warre', as the source of a soldier's meritocratic *Honour-able Reputation* (25). The basis of Tamburlaine's autonomous power is accordingly the 'Engines, never exercisde' he wields (*Two*, 4.1.191), 'the thunder of his martial tooles' which, as Orcanes says, 'Makes Earthquakes in the hearts of men and heaven' (2.2.7-8). Freed from the restrictions of chivalric hierarchy, Tamburlaine is also freed from medieval ordinances commanding limitation in war, enacting the consequences of Macchiavelli's view that 'no considerations of justice or injustice, humanity or cruelty, nor of glory or shame, should be allowed to prevail' (I. Clark, 51).

The military historian Michael Howard has described the period to which the play belongs as one 'in which warfare seemed to escape from rational control; to cease indeed to be "war" in the sense of politically-motivated use of force by generally recognised authorities, and to degenerate instead into universal, anarchic, and self-perpetuating violence' (1976, 37). Greenblatt's description of Tamburlaine as a 'machine' notices a comparable dynamic: 'Once set in motion, this *thing* cannot slow down or change course; it moves at the same frenzied pace until it finally stops' (1980, 195). The uneasy truce with which the first play stops draws the following, honest response from Cunningham:

> We speak habitually of ambiguity, sometimes almost as a
> point of doctrine: it was a truly painful feature of the play
> for us to reflect on as we applauded Tamburlaine – not
> just the play, but, embarrassingly, the hero – as he left this
> obscene stage in triumph.
> (Cunningham and Warren, 160-61)

The 'problem of ambivalence in *Tamburlaine*' (Cole, 100-101) has long absorbed its commentators. One writes of Marlowe's 'divided' mind at the scenes of cruelty he presents there, 'whether in pleasure or repulsion' (Steane, 85); another of Marlowe's 'Paradoxical Hero and the Divided Response' (Homan); 'in place of the explicit moral lesson', comments a third, 'he aimed almost consistently at inducing a double response' (Leech, 1986, 68). Yet the paradoxical subject of *Tamburlaine* is war itself, and the divided response was almost a 'point of doctrine' among Elizabethan theorists, as we have seen, 'neyther hath arte ever sought out a subject more ambiguous' (Riche, 1604, 4).

The development of sophisticated firearms in the early Renaissance was attended, we read, by a mixture of 'physical horror and perverse pleasure' (Nef, 44). Contemporary reaction to Gianbelli's 'fierie keele at *Antwarpes* bridge' (as Marlowe himself called it) was 'one not of outraged sensibility but rather of grudging admiration' (Hale, 1983, 412). That phrase precisely describes Sir Thomas Coningsby's account of artillery fire at Rouen in 1591, 'where we mighte heare such ratling of houses, and see it fly through one house and grace upon the other, as were yt not for charytie it were pleasure to behold' (40). The 'Flanckers, Parapets, and Cazimates' of contemporary war, as Dekker comments in *The Artillery Garden*, are resources 'which man both loves and hates' (1616, D1v).

Dekker's baffling vocabulary is glossed in *Tamburlaine* by its hero's set-piece lecture on the 'rudiments of war' (*Two*, 3.2.53-92): 'Parapets to hide the Muscatters: | Casemates to place the great Artillery, | And store of ordinance that from every flanke ...' (77-9). That speech – a sequence that immediately precedes the lieutenants' deployment of the Jacob's staff at Balsera – has afforded its author's critics a number of problems.

As is well known, the passage derives (some would say laboriously) from a military treatise by Marlowe's Corpus Christi contemporary Paul Ive. *The Practise of Fortification* was published in 1589, and it is thought Marlowe may therefore have consulted the work in manuscript. Let us pause to contemplate that proposition: one of the most successful plays of the Elizabethan period incorporated a lengthily technical disquisition on military procedures so modern that the printers' ink wasn't even dry on its source. While the value of scholarly caution is clear, it is perhaps worth stiffening the resolve of Paul Kocher's analysis: 'there are no such serious errors in [Marlowe's] use of the terms, nor any such slavish copying of single passages as would suggest that he did not understand what he was saying' (1942, 216).

'Also it may be the perfecter', reads Ive's prosaic original, 'because the angles that do happen in it, may be made the flatter or sharper' (2). Marlowe's paraphrase retains that overt practicality of tone:

> Then next, the way to fortifie your men,
> In champion grounds, what figure serves you best,
> For which the *quinque*-angle fourme is meet:
> Because the corners there may fall more flat.
> (62-5)

Critics and directors have variously observed the mighty line itself to fall flat here, and sought to explain its descent by insisting on its juxtaposition with Zenocrate's death. 'The hyperbolical laments for the dead Zenocrate', asserts one, 'ironically give way to a flat and passionless account of the "rudiments of war" ... Our view even of the Marlovian superman is qualified by incongruity and ironic deflation' (Pearson, 55). 'I had thought of it as a diversion', writes another, following Peter Hall's 1976 production, 'awkwardly stitched in from Marlowe's recent reading of a (known) military textbook', yet his re-appraisal merely re-defines the qualities of the 'diversion' it offers: 'It was spoken rapidly, as if learnt by heart, up to a moment of breathlessness, as a diversion of Tamburlaine's own attention from the fact of Zenocrate's death' (Cunningham and Warren, 161). Otherwise quite disparate critics at least agree that the passage's 'plodding instruction in the art of fortification' (Leech, 1986, 65) makes for 'a tiresome speech' (Shepherd, 1986, 207).

But the speech was neither 'tiresome' nor 'flat and passionless' to its first audiences. On the contrary, it comprises the clearest evidence of the military hi-tech which Tamburlaine espouses. Although there is merit in the view that it lends the scene 'authentic human point',[29] the crux of the matter remains that these rudiments are indeed 'learnt by heart', and far from being a diversion, Tamburlaine is never more himself than in the scene. For we must take care not to mistake the verve of technical instruction for any lacklustre pedantry, let alone any 'incongruity' of effect. The plays' first prologue, after all, contrasts the 'jygging vaines of riming mother wits' with the 'stately tent of War' it promises: it is here that the mighty line most squares with the blank verse 'Perpendicular' of Tamburlaine's military expertise.

'Marlowe's Tamburlaine is not a fourteenth-century Tartar, but a late sixteenth-century Englishman', claims one historian of geography with refreshing certainty: 'He speaks and acts as the average Elizabethan [man] imagined he himself would if he could ... take the field at the head of English troops' (McCann, 198-9). This is no idle speculation. Hood continued to lecture on military maths from 1588, when *Tamburlaine* was new, until 1594 (F. Johnson, 98), when it first appeared in *Henslowe's Diary*. Garrard's *Arte of Warre* indeed recommended to its readership of officers (but not necessarily gentlemen) 'that both what is written before, and shalbe written after in this booke, specially touching the marshal lawes of the field, they may ever read as a lecture to their souldiers' (1591, 22). Tamburlaine's lecture anticipates such practical advice. At a time when London's citizen militia was braced against invasion, and its Trained Bands increasingly being sent to the European theatres (Boynton, 166-8), its rudiments may even have proved useful in the field to his original audiences.

But there is an enduring artistic consonance to Marlowe's scene which raises it beyond the bald topicalities it reflected. Clausewitz (in whose opinion Machiavelli possessed 'very sound judgement') once referred to Napoleon as the 'God of War' (Earle et al., 25; 99). His description of the Napoleonic Wars captures some of the force of Marlowe's scene: 'Da der Krieg selbst gewissermassen auf dem Katheder stand' (96). It was as if war itself had given a lecture. Reordering – usurping – the homiletic common-place of war as the Scourge of God, Tamburlaine, 'this man or rather God of war' (*One*, 5.1.1.) converts the didactic function of tragedy into a lecture on the rudiments of his autonomous power, inspiring 'in place of the explicit moral lesson' (Leech, 1986, 68), a 'grudging admiration' (Hale, 1983, 412). The young Napoleon, it seems, was 'commissioned in the artillery' because of an evident flair for 'mathematics and geography' (Cronin, 46); that Marlowe's Tamburlaine champions each of these disciplines illustrates the endurance of the Military Revolution he announces (see G. Parker, 1988, 43). The parallel between these two soldiers struck Coleridge too. In a lecture of his own, in 1818, he noted that 'to power in itself, without reference to any moral end, an inevitable admiration and complacency appertains, whether it be displayed in the conquests of a Buonaparte or Tamerlane, or in the foam and thunder of a cataract'.[30] Part of that 'inevitable admiration' cleaves to the lecture Marlowe has Tamburlaine deliver to his wartime audiences, not 'awkwardly stitched' but intricately woven into the texture of his plays.

Garrard's *Arte of Warre* devotes an entire chapter to the principles of fortification, 'this warlike *Architecture*' (1591, 283), explaining

> howe with due Measures to forme Bulwarkes, *Cavalieres*,
> Platformes, straight and crooked, Casemates, Covers,
> Canoneers, Merlones, Curtines, Scarpes, false Portes,
> secrete issues for footemen and horse men, Counter-
> ditches, Ditches, Sholders, and Counterscarpes.
> (287)

*The Second Part of The Bloody Conquests of Mighty Tamburlaine* covers much of the same ground:

> The ditches must be deepe, the Counterscarps
> Narrow and steepe, the wals made high and broad,
> The Bulwarks and the rampiers large and strong,
> With Cavalieros and thicke counterforts,
> And roome within to lodge sixe thousand men
> It must have privy ditches, countermines,
> And secret issuings to defend the ditch.
> It must have high Argins and covered waies,
> To keep the bulwark fronts from battery,
> And Parapets to hide the Muscatters:
> Casemates to place the great Artillery,
> And store of ordinance that from every flanke
> May scoure the outward curtaines of the Fort,
> Dismount the Cannon of the adverse part,
> Murther the Foe and save their walles from breach.
> (3.2.68-82)

Of course the lines bristle with the jargon glossed by modern editors. But what they fail to note is the novel, foreign extraction of their technical terms – the fact that they needed glossing at the time. That service was later provided by Robert Barret, who appended to his *Theorike and Practike of Moderne Warres* a lengthy glossary of terms, for 'such as have not frequented forraine warres, nor have anie great insight in forraine languages' (1598, 248).[31] 'You are to understand', explains Barret, 'that most of our termes now used in warres are derived from straungers; as the French, the Italian, the Spaniard and the Dutch; wherein every one almost have their severall pronuntiation' (248).

So Tamburlaine demands that 'the rampiers [be] large and strong': '*Rampier*, a French word, and is a fortification or wall of earth'. 'With Cavalieros and thicke counterforts': 'an Italian word ... Cavaliere is a mount or platforme of earth, built and raised high, either within or without the wall for to plant great Ordinance upon'. 'And Parapets to hide the Muscatters': '*Parapet*, an Italian word, is the upper part of the wall, which shadoweth the souldiers from the sight and annoyance of the enemy'. 'Casemates to place the great Artillery': '*Cassamatta*, a Spanish word, and doth signifie a slaughter-house, and is the place built low under the wall or bulwarke, not arriving at the height of the ditch, serving to scowre the ditch'. 'May scoure the outward curtaines of the Fort': '*Curtine*, a French word, is the long wall running levell from bulwarke to bulwarke' (Barret, 1598, 249-52).[32] Time has moreover familiarized a number of Tamburlaine's words that are now standard English. '*Flanque*', '*Artillaria*' and '*Trench*', for example, all appear in Barret's list. Indeed, most of our present military vocabulary derives from this very period. Words such as *ambush, alarm, squadron, infantry, cavalry* and *artillery* comprised a linguistic invasion altogether more successful than any of Philip of Spain's armadas.[33]

England had been isolated by the Channel that protected her from the technological developments her European neighbours were experiencing at first hand. Tamburlaine's lecture must have sounded as strange to his first audiences as the litany of geographic exotica his 'warlike progresse' comprehends (*Two*, 3.5.23). It also directly engaged with the current debate between what Jorgensen calls 'English military provincialism' and the 'cosmopolitan stream of military science', by which native mythologies of the few were tempered by a necessary instruction in 'alien military doctrine' (1956b, 43-9). We have seen how Tamburlaine's victories evoked cries of 'foul' in his aristocratic victims, 'ignorant', as they call him, 'of lawfull armes'. The basis of his strength, however, is the absolute modernity of his methods, and the resentment of the older order which Marlowe dramatizes was felt by many at the assimilation of foreign terms into the English tradition.

Robert Greene's sneering ridicule of Marlowe's drama in 1588, 'daring God out of heaven with that Atheist Tamburlan', is well known (McLure, 29); but Sir John Smythe's rebuke to military modernists in 1590 shared some of its sarcastic venom: 'Are they newlie fallen from heaven', he asks, 'with some divine instinct and gift, to teach us the Arte Militarie?' (* 2 v). Like the Soldan's dismissal of Tamburlaine as a 'Pesant ignorant', Smythe's objections are reinforced by the social rank he himself held: 'What then? are they Noblemen themselves by title, or descended of noble and excellent fathers'? Like some Elizabethan Colonel Blimp, Sir John Smythe dismisses such upstarts as 'children', and his resentment – crucially – comes to focus upon language:

These our such men of warre before mentioned, in a manner, utterlie ignorant of all our auncient discipline and proceedings in actions of Armes, have so affected the *Wallons*, *Flemings*, and base *Almanes* discipline, (as some of them terme it) that they have procured to innovate, or rather to subvert all our ancient proceedings in matters Militarie, and therefore have left nothing in a manner untouched, without seeking to alter and chaunge the same: as for example; They will not vouchsafe in their speaches or writings to use our ancient termes belonging to matters of warre, but doo call a campe by the Dutch name of *Legar*; nor will not affoord to say, that such a Towne, or such a Fort is besieged, but that it is *belegard* ... The bodie of the watch also or standing watch (as we were wont to terme it) they now call after the *French*, or *Wallons*, *Corps du gard* with manie other such Wallon and Dutch termes, as though our language were so barren, that it were not able of it selfe, or by derivation to affoord convenient words to utter our minds in matters of that qualitie.
(B2r - B2v)

Barret's 'Table, shewing the signification of sundry forraine words' (248) indeed annotates the '*Corps du guard*, a French word' (250); and Tamburlaine's 'Cavalieros and thicke counterforts' receive a passingly flat snub in Smythe: 'the *Cavaleeres* (by us called Mounts)' (\*\*\* 3 r). It has become as much of a critical commonplace to write, as Greenblatt does, of the 'strategy of subversion' built into Marlowe's drama (1980, 203), as it is to consider ambiguity a 'point of doctrine' (Cunningham and Warren, 161). Both terms however hold a precise force within the context of Elizabethan warfare that *Tamburlaine* so directly inhabits. While the conclusion drawn by Riche's *Fruites of Long Experience* is the 'ambiguous' nature of his theme, Smythe's *Discourses Military* obliquely reveal the subversive force of Tamburlaine's words – the 'Vaine innovation of our ancient termes of warre', 'procured to innovate, or rather to subvert all our ancient proceedings in matters Militarie' (B2v).

As Barret's glossary shows, 'forraine warres' introduced 'forraine languages' into the language of war (248). Englishmen learned from European *Practike* as well as from the classical *Theorike* of Caesar, Vegetius, or Frontinus. Sir Francis Vere had seen service in the Polish army (C. Markham, 26), Sir Roger Williams in the Spanish (*Works*, ed. Evans, 28), and William Bourne recommended close study of his *Arte of Shooting* (1587) because 'other nations and countries have tasted better therof, as the Italians, French and Spaniardes' (A2r). 'A Souldier when he comes forth', reads Edward Grimeston's *Historie of the Memorable Siege of Ostend*, 'speakes like a Maister of fortifications, of Ramperes, Bulworkes, Spurres, Counterscarfes, Ravelins, Traveries, Parapets, halfe Moones, Reduites or Block houses and such like' (1604, A3r). For Marlowe's generation, as his Tamburlaine's uncompromising 'rudiments of war' show, contemporary military service constituted a grounding in a sort of Esperanto of War.

Not only was this because (*pace* Smythe) English vocabulary lacked the finesse of distinction demanded by 'a Maister of fortifications'; it was also because the armies ranged against each other across Europe often themselves comprised multinational coalitions – 'Noah's Ark armies', in the vivid phrase cited by Hale (1985a, 70). Parma's ostensibly Spanish army was reportedly made up of 'Spanyardes, Launceknights, Wallons, Italians, and Neapolitanes, footemen: also his horsemen Wallons, Flemminges, Italians and Rutters' (1592, News-Pamphlet 13, 1): small wonder William Blandy called them 'the froth and scomme of many nations' (1581, G2r). Likewise, English troops fighting for the Protestant cause found themselves rubbing shoulders with the 'many contrary nations' of which a later news-letter from Ostend complained: '*French, Scots, Wallons, & Duch*, and thereby a hotch:pot of contrary & dissonant humors' (1602, News-Pamphlet 26, A3r). It was to defuse a potential 'disjoyntment of affections' among his coalition forces that Leicester issued his *Lawes and Ordinances* in 1586 – 'whereas sundrie nations are to serve with us in these warres, so as through diversitie of languages occasion of many controversies may arise' (B1r) – and that Whetstone published the parallel texts of his *Honourable Reputation* in the same year, for a readership 'which among all of nature be most solicitous to be skylled in all tongues' (10).

Such a background perhaps lends immediacy to the tense negotiations which open the second *Tamburlaine* play, and qualify T.S. Eliot's lament at Marlowe's 'facile use of resonant names' in the play (121). The league proposed there between Orcanes and Sigismund displays no less of a 'hotch: pot of ... dissonant humours'. As well as 'stout Hungarians', Sigismund heads an army of 'Sclavonians, Almans, Rutters, Muffes, and Danes' (*Two*, 1.1.21-2; repeated at 58); Orcanes commands an expedient alliance of

> revolted Grecians, Albanees,
> Cicilians, Jewes, Arabians, Turks, and Moors,
> Natolians, Sorians, blacke Egyptians,
> Illirians, Thracians, and Bythinians.
> (61-4)

Greater than both, Tamburlaine 'brings a world of people to the field' (67). Parma, whose occupying armies of the Low Countries are described in another news-letter as a composite of 'all kinds of Nations, and people mingled togither', was (according to another) 'exalted' in Paris 'as the great *Tamburlayn*'.[34] The fragile United Nations coalition that assembles in Marlowe's play merely writes large the Elizabethan soldier's bewilderment at the European Babel in which he fought.

In his *Work for Armourers* (1609), Thomas Dekker described a band of veterans from such campaigns as '*Dunkirkes*, a mingle mangle of countries, a confusion of languages, yet all understanding one another' (*Non-Dramatic Works*, 4, 103) 'Some not unproperly, call *Ostend* an *Academie*', commented Grimeston, 'and excellent Schoole for Governours, Captaines, Souldiers, Ingeneurs' (1604, A2v). That analogy also struck Sir Roger Williams, whose 1590 *Discourse of War* more precisely likened 'a Campe continuallie maintained in action' to 'an University continuallie in exercises':

> when famous Schollers dye, as good or better step in their
> places. Especially in Armies, where there be everie day
> newe inventions, stratagems of warres, change of
> weapons, munition, and all sorts of engins newlie
> invented, and corrected dailie.
> (*Works*, ed. Evans, 27)

The participants of Breton's 1597 'Disputation pithily passed' between 'The Scholler and the Souldiour' (in *The Wil of Wit*) display an immediate and mutual understanding by speaking a common language; or rather a 'confusion' of common languages: '*Ben trovate Signore*', says the scholar, '*bien trouve Mounsieur, buene baliado, es la Vuestra merced. Salve Domine. Countreyman well met*'. 'Well met good friende', replies the soldier, '*Che sete voi? Inglese? Dou venes vous? amigo. Dic mihi quaeso*' (G4v). The chiming outcome of their encounter – 'togither they are gon about something' (K1r) – illustrates the ideal alliance of pen and sword, a standard *topos* of Renaissance thought and close cousin to the 'time-battered axes' of military debate between force and guile (see above, p. 23). The subtitle of Loys le Roy's treatise on *La Vicissitude ou Varieté des Choses en l'Univers* (Paris, 1575) was translated by Robert Ashley in 1594 as 'the Concurrence of Armes and Learning'. It has been argued that Marlowe's *Tamburlaine* owes a debt to le Roy's original (H. Smith). It is certainly true that the 'mingle mangle' jargon of its hero, and his 'confusion of languages', substantiate that concurrence: 'During the raigne of TAMBERLAN', reads Ashley's translation, 'began the restitution of the tongues, and of all sciences' (108v). Just as Faustus, the Scholar of Wittenberg, speculates on 'stranger engines for the brunt of warre', so Tamburlaine, the Scythian Warrior, delivers a lecture from a military academy which testifies to the 'newe inventions' Willliams admires, 'and all sorts of engins newlie invented, and corrected dailie'.

The century or so between Caxton's translation of Lull's *Ordre of Chyvalry* and Marlowe's *Tamburlaine* may be defined as one in which two mutually exclusive areas of endeavour coalesced. 'Medieval poets had debated whether the knight or the scholar made the better lover; and medieval lawyers whether precedence in rank should be given to the one or the other' (Kelso, 42). To Roger Ascham, however, what is sauce for the goose is sauce for the gander. *Toxophilus*, his encomium of the long-bow, reserves ingenious praise for that creature: 'How fit', he writes, 'even as her fethers be onelye for shootynge, so be her quylles fytte onelye for wrytyng' (1545, Book 2, 16). The instruments of scholarship and knighthood, 'the Boke and the Bowe' (t.p.), are furnished by nature for the modern captain, whose 'sleightes and pollicies' must complement 'the strength and cerefull forwardnesse of the souldyers' (Book 1, 24). (Morysine's translation of Frontinus's *Stratagemes, Sleyghtes, and Policies of Warre* had appeared in 1539.) Ascham's insistence on the mutuality of arms and learning, as sides of the same coin, was a formula reiterated throughout the century.

Ascham's goose-feathers are 'mans comfort in war & in peace slepynge and wakynge' (Book 2, 16). Lyly's portrait of Alexander the Great in *Campaspe* (printed 1584) likewise asserts the mutually reinforcing ideals of arms and arts: 'it resteth now that we have as great care to governe in peace, as conquer in war: that whilest armes cease, artes may flourish' (1.1.80-1). Alexander's ideal of 'joyning letters with launces' (82) was most commonly ascribed in the period to his fellow-Worthy Julius Caesar, 'the best Captaine that ever lived'. Whetsone called him that in his *Honourable Reputation*, going on to claim that 'he was so addicted to study, as there was a question: *whether he were more inclined to the Launce, or to his booke*' (66). The basis of such praise was Caesar's authorship of the *Commentaries* on the campaigns he waged: 'both CAESARS pen and sword' (18) represented the mutual skills of scholarship and war.

Caesar's opus found renewed relevance on the newly strategic battlefield of the sixteenth century (Hale, 1985a, 165-6), and also provided the model for Sir Francis Vere's own *Commentaries*, posthumously (and lavishly) published in 1657, an imitation spelled out by the dedicatory verse on the verso of its title-page:

> And what his Sword *indited*, that his Pen
> With like success doth here *fight* o're agen:
> What *Mars* performed, *Mercurie* doth tell;
> None e're but *Cesar* fought and wrote so well.
> Why may not then his Book this title carry,
> *The second part of Cesar's Commentary*?

The topos of arms and letters was consistently invoked in the period by reference to these two deities.

While Bellona gradually superseded images of Mars as a chivalric knight in sixteenth-century iconographies of the harsh impact of war (see above, p. 27), Mercury increasingly featured as an emblem of military scholarship, instructing Riche's *English Souldier* that 'bookes maye bee greatlye beneficiall to the knowledge of martiall affaires' (1574, D1r). Such books (as John Dee insists in his preface) included Billingsley's Euclid (1570), whose frontispiece sports an emblem of Mercury, *caduceus* in hand. Abraham Fraunce's mythography stressed as well Mercury's 'especially mathematicall knowledge' as his 'eloquence, elegancy, learning' among the god's 'divers influences in mens minds' (1592, 38). The specifically Elizabethan alliance of Mercury and Mars, mathematical scholarship and military expertise, forms the symbolic climax to *The Cobbler's Prophecy*.

Like its source, Riche's 1574 *Dialogue*, Wilson's play links a warning at soldiers' neglect to the antipathy between 'mighty Mars and wary Mercurie', who, now reconciled, flank the soldier Sateros's entrance to its last scene, and to each of whom he 'gives thanks and vowes his duety' (1640-41). 'Mercurie ... With me shall passe unto my warlike house', says Mars (1636-7), and the relevance of the moral is drawn by the play's Duke, who presides over the 'blessed concord' (1407) between the Soldier and the Scholar. 'Embrace the Scholler', he tells Sateros:

> For Armes and Learning may not live at jarre,
> Counsell prevents, counsell prevailes in warre ...
> Then with due praise to heaven let us depart,
> Our State supported both by Armes and Art.
> (1686-96)

Breton's 'disputation' between *The Scholler and the Souldiour* reaches the same conclusion: 'There is such a love and union betwixt them, and the one is so necessarie unto the other, that some men thinke, the one and the other is as it were *Alter ipse*' (1597, I4v). Breton was step-son to the soldier-poet George Gascoigne, a fact apparently acknowledged in the motto with which he closes his work. Breton's '*Marti Mercurius*' (K1r) modifies, with the force of a new literary and military generation, Gascoigne's ubiquitous tag, '*Tam Marti quàm Mercurio*'; and emphasizes the newly mutual relationship between his two speakers, rather than their equal facility with pen and sword. Two works, from a still later generation, illustrate the period's union of knight and doctor. Francis Markham's *Epistles of Warre* (1622) advises against the specialism of either the 'meere Scholler' or 'meere Souldiour', instead commending 'the compounded man which consisteth of equall and excellent parts' (6). Two complementary emblems from *The Mirror of Majesty* (1618) render graphic that 'compounded' ideal. 'Virtus Unita Fortior' shows a composite figure, split down the middle, half gowned scholar, a book under one arm, half armoured soldier, a lance held in the other; 'Perfectus in Utraque' repeats the formula in a figure, half Mars in armour, half winged Mercury, lance and *caduceus* in either hand (reproduced in Frye, 1984, 173-4).

'Mars and Mercurie are both of a broode', as the Elizabethan *Myrrour for English Souldiers* asserted, which is why 'Poets descipher Pallas to have a helmet on her head, and a Booke in her hande' (1595, B2r).[35] The death of Sir Philip Sidney, that exemplary soldier-scholar, was mourned in verse in precisely the same terms. John Palmer's '*Martis et Mercurii Contentio*', published in the 1587 *Lachrymae*, relates an argument between the two gods as to whether Sidney's '*Artes*' or '*arma potentia*' were the more laudable, and each claims him as his own until Pallas intercedes. She argues that since Sidney is skilled in both ('*His utrumque tenet*'), he should rightfully belong to her. When her request is granted by Jove, Mars kills him in spite, and he is raised to heaven by Pallas (van Dorsten et al., 97-8). It should be noted that the contention Palmer imagines in terms of myth, had been directly addressed by Sidney himself in his *Apologie for Poetrie*.

Remnants of medieval distinctions lingered on in many military writers of the sixteenth century, evidenced by the brusque impatience many of them reveal for 'a worlde replete and glutted with letters', in which readers will only pay attention to that which 'senteth lyke a flower, and in shew, and hue be lyke a Lillye' (Blandy, 1581, B2r). Lyly's own *Campaspe* illustrates the sapping of Alexander's military prowess through love, now that 'youthes that were woont to carry devises of victory in their shieldes, engrave now posies of love in their ringes' (4.3.13-14). Sidney's *Apologie* takes care therefore to refute what it terms 'the principall, if not the onely abuse I can heare alledged', that poetry 'abuseth mens wit, trayning to wanton sinfulnes, and lustfull love' (H1v). This he does, as Edward Berry has demonstrated, by insisting on the fusion, not the mutual exclusivity, of war and letters. 'The most consistent metaphors for the poet's role are those of war' (1989, 27), as Sidney transforms a treatise on poetry into a call to arms, turning this 'abuse' on its head by casting England's low estimate of poetry into a symptom of her martial decline, 'not being an Art of lyes, but of true doctrine: not of effeminatenes, but of notable stirring of courage' (I2r).

A comparable conversion of the 'doctrine' of poetry is discernible in *Tamburlaine*, perhaps completed within a year of Sidney's death. 'And tis a pretty toy to be a Poet', muses the weak Mycetes in the first play (2.2.54), confessedly 'insufficient to expresse the same: | For it requires a great and thundring speech' (1.1.2-3). When Tamburlaine later hymns the beauty of divine Zenocrate, beyond the grasp of 'all the pens that ever poets held' (5.1.161), he rebukes himself that he should 'harbour thoughts effeminate and faint' (177). And when Zenocrate dies in the sequel, Tamburlaine again alludes to 'wanton Poets' for whom she would have 'bene the argument | Of every Epigram or Eligie' (2.4.94-5). Tamburlaine's own response is to 'wound the earth' (97), and 'Raise Cavalieros higher than the cloudes' (103). The 'Epitaph' he plans is to be 'Writ in as many severall languages, | As I have conquered kingdomes with my sword' (134-6). The lines suggest an identification in Tamburlaine between the 'thundring speech' Mycetes covets and the 'thunder of his martial tooles'. Certainly the 'severall languages' of his epitaph anticipate the lecture he delivers in his next scene – its 'war termes and words, as we do borrow from straungers' – which so many critics have found an incongruous 'diversion'; and echo too his earlier act of cartographic remembrance ('with this pen reduce them to a Map, |

Calling the Provinces ... After my name and thine *Zenocrate*'). It is as if Marlowe has restored to Sidney's defence of poetry, 'as an imaginative ground-plot of a profitable invention' (H1r), the origins of his figure, Thomas Hood's 'platforme laied for the better increace of the Mathematicall science'. 'But now my boies, leave off, and list to me ...': what follows is not 'an Art of lyes, but of true doctrine: not of effeminatenes, but of notable stirring of courage' (I2r).

The two surviving portraits of Marlowe's heroes from the period, those depicting Tamburlaine in the 1590 Octavo, and Faustus in the 1624 Quarto, show the complete armour of the Soldier, and the gown and book of the Scholar. The emblem of the Soldier-Scholar in the 1618 *Mirror of Majesty* could almost be a montage of their designs, but also renders graphic the mutually informing resemblance Marlowe presents between their respective status in the geographic crucible of war. 'The God of war resignes his roume to me', says Tamburlaine (*One*, 5.1.450), but it is what Fraunce calls Mercury's 'eloquence, elegancy, learning, and especially mathematicall knowledge' that has enabled his boast: 'Not *Hermes* Prolocutor to the Gods', says Theridamas, won with his words, 'Could use perswasions more patheticall' (1.2.210-11). In Tamburlaine, 'Mars and Mercurie are both of a broode'.

From being mutually exclusive in the Middle Ages, then, and mutually complementary in the earlier sixteenth century, the scholar's pen and the soldier's sword came to be identified as a single implement of knowledge during the Elizabethan war-years. In Lyly's prewar *Campaspe*, Alexander pledges to his tutor Aristotle that his 'court shalbe a schole, wherein I will have used as great doctrine in peace, as I did in warre discipline' (1.3.62-3). Peele's *Honour of the Garter* (1590) interpreted Edward III's victories in France by conflating Lyly's doctrine and discipline: 'rife was French those days with Englishmen', he comments,

> They went to schoole to put together Townes,
> And spell in Fraunce with Feskues made of Pikes.
> (B3r)

It is once more as if war is giving a lecture, using France as its blackboard, since a fescue was the stick or pin used for pointing out the letters to children learning to read.

Such a figure renders literal *Campaspe*'s 'joyning letters with launces', and spells out the implicit moral of Whetstone's *Honourable Reputation*, which has 'nombres joyned before every worde' to facilitate the construing of its Anglo-Dutch text (10): 'and no doubt, among the English Captaines, there are some, that can use both CAESARS pen and sword' (18). The knighting of the Black Prince in *Edward III* (c.1590) is overlaid by a comparably Elizabethan emphasis:

> Receive this lance into thy manly hand;
> Use it in fashion of a brasen pen,
> To drawe forth bloudie stratagems in France,
> And print thy valiant deeds in honors booke.
> (3.3.193-6) [36]

The image is singularly intelligent: the lance is likened to a burin, which at once secures the metaphor (it is sharp, like a lance) and implies the modern expertise of cartography with which war was so intimate, even as it is France whose copperplate will monumentalize the acts performed there. With his 'brasen pen', the Black Prince will 'drawe forth ... And print' his 'bloudie stratagems'. If he fails, as his speech of acceptance declares, he will 'remayne the map of infamy' (218); if he succeeds, he will have reduced France, in Tamburlaine's words, 'to a map'.

Like Bacon's traveller, Tamburlaine achieves 'some Entrance into the Language', and he later carries 'with him some Card or Booke describing the Country, where he travelleth': the map he calls for at the end of Part Two. 'Give me a Map, then let me see how much | Is left for me to conquer all the world' (5.3.123-4). With this command, his previously stated intention to render obsolete the *mappae mundi* of 'blind Geographers' is graphically fulfilled. As long ago as 1924, a direct correlation was established between *Tamburlaine* and Ortelius's *Theatrum Orbis Terrarum*. One plate in particular from that collection was singled out by Ethel Seaton as a direct source for the play: the combination of place-names and description contained in the 'Africae Tabula Nova', concerning Prester John and the Amazons, is so overwhelming that, as Seaton concludes, 'one can almost follow Marlowe's finger travelling down the page as he plans the campaign' (18). Such research counters Eliot's view of Marlowe's 'facile use of resonant names' (121), and has recently fuelled an absorbing correlation between Tamburlaine's map and the trade-routes of the Muscovy Company (R. Wilson, 54). The broader impact of the play's scene, however, deploys the 'aura of knowledge possessed by maps' in the period (Alpers, 133) in the immediate context of war. At a time when news of *The Besieging of Bergen op Zoom* (1589) reached Londoners in the form of a news-map, Tamburlaine traces his own campaigns by reference to the same narrative technology.

There are historical and literary precedents for the military map Tamburlaine calls for in his dying moments, and their symbolism measures both 'the extention, and limits' by which Hexham had recommended his atlas to his potential readership. Emperor Charles V had recognized the symbolism of conquest provided by a map. Du Bellay records that, so absorbed was he in 1536 by 'une carte des Alpes et du Païs Bas de Provence ... que désjà il presumoit d'avoir le païs en son bandon, ainsi comme il en avoit la carte' – he convinced himself he owned the country as absolutely as he owned its map. [37] Mercator – like Faustus and Barabas in his fictional wake – actively contributed to his emperor's military campaigns: Charles V was so pleased with the globe the cartographer made for him in 1541, that he commissioned a set of surveyors' instruments, which he took with him into the field (L. Brown, 159). By the same token, when Henry II of France triumphantly entered Rouen in 1550, his parade included a series of banners bearing cityscapes of the English and Scottish towns he had conquered (Strong, 1973, 34). How redolent of Tamburlaine's final survey that at his abdication in 1555/56, Charles V should have at that moment recalled his travels, through the Netherlands, Germany, Italy, Spain, France, England, and Africa, asserting the 'geographic extent of his universal monarchy', even as it ebbed (Strong, 1973, 83).

*Tamburlaine*'s final tableau has theatrical precedents too: 'a geographical lecture with practical demonstrations' had been delivered in the form of John Rastell's *New Interlude and a Mery, of the Nature of the Four Elements* (c.1518).[38] Using the 'fygure' (690), that scholarship has variously explained as a map or globe,[39] it is the role of Experience to 'expownyd connyngly | Dyvers poyntes of cosmogryfy' (1037-8) to Studious Desire, including the space where 'within this twenty yere, | Westwarde be founde new landes' (736-7). Rastell, in other words, 'hit on a method of popular (and probably royal) education through the medium of the stage' (E. Taylor, 1930, 8). The interlude's structure is also that of a morality play (Humanity goes to the pub when Experience instructs Studious Desire), and its blend of moral and technical teaching reflects the basis of an earlier geographic text, Caxton's *Mirrour of the World*.[40] While Caxton insists there that knowledge of the world is a branch of piety, 'ffor men coude not knowe ne fynde no resons of God but only by his werkis' (23), Marlowe's later heroes revealingly displace that spiritual cartography.

Thus, while Caxton explains that 'helle is in the myddle of therthe' (106), the answer to Faustus's characteristic question, 'where is the place that men call hell? ... but where about?', gains its force from hell's evasion from the power of a map: 'Hell hath no limits, nor is circumscrib'd | In one selfe place, for where we are is hell' (562-8). On the other hand, Caxton's assertion that 'Alle the erthe that is in the world enhabited is devided in to thre parties' (66) clearly marks him as one of 'those blind Geographers | That make a triple region in the world' that Tamburlaine confutes, instead usurping to himself the 'hye puissances & domynacions' (184) that Caxton attributed to God. Marlowe's geography replaces Caxton's or Rastell's moral didacticism with the autonomously militant power such knowledge confers on his Soldier-Scholars.

Ortelius claimed that geography comprised the 'eye of History'.[41] In 1589 Thomas Blundeville agreed, commending his *Briefe Description of Universal Mappes and Cardes*, as 'Necessarie for those that Delight in reading of histories' (t.p.). 'I Daylie see many that delight to looke on Mappes', he writes, for without geography 'the necessarie reading of Histories is halfe lame' (A2v). Among the many recent enthusiasts he observed may be counted the audiences of Marlowe's history of Timur the Lame. Like Rastell before him, Marlowe hit on a method of popular education through the medium of the stage, but as Thomas Hood's lectures were simultaneously proving, the syllabus of geography was now 'most convenient for militarie men'. Marlowe boldly transplanted into drama that instructive delight, fusing the military hi-tech of the map with its newly narrative function, Gascoigne's 'riming sport' with his 'Cartes ... Mappes, and ... Models made'. 'The reading of *Histories*', continues Ortelius, 'dothe both seeme to be more pleasant, and in deed so it is, when the Mappe being layed before our eyes, we may behold things done, or places where they were done, as if they were at this time present and in doing'. The map annexed to the end of *Tamburlaine* recapitulates the events of his own chronicle history: 'Here I began to martch towards *Persea*, | Along *Armenia* and the Caspian sea, | And thence unto *Bythinia*, where I tooke | The Turke and his great Empresse prisoners, | Then marcht I into *Egypt* ...' (126-30).

While the *Theatrum Orbis Terrarum* contained a 'certaine briefe and short declaration and Historicall discourse of every Mappe' (1606, Preface), *Tamburlaine*'s history concludes with an emblem of its own theatrical and 'warlike progresse' (*Two*, 3.5.23), which measures how much the soldier has conquered, and 'how much | Is left to conquer' (5.3.123-4), the 'extention, and limits' (Hexham) of his kingdoms, and his life. Like Everyman, Tamburlaine is at last summoned by 'the uglie monster death ... aiming at me with his murthering dart' (5.3.67-9), and the play sees, with Shakespeare, 'as in a mappe the ende of all' (*Richard III*, 2.4.53), 'lifes triumph in the map of death' (*Lucrece*, 402): 'Tamburlaine, the Scourge of God must die' (248). But Leigh's preface to his *Science of Surveying* also addressed every man '(inasmuche, as the thyng it self, appertaineth to every manne)' (A2r), and Marlowe's map emblematizes too the cosmopolitan *polypragmatism* of Hood's 'Mathematicall science' of 'Martiall affaires'.

'More than any other drama the source and original of the Elizabethan history play',[42] *Tamburlaine*'s subject unprecedentedly coalesces with its style. Its Prologue's 'high astounding tearms', the 'termes Italianate, | Big-sounding sentences and words of state' that Joseph Hall mocked,[43] declare themselves distinct from 'jygging vaines of riming mother wits'. Its hero's 'thundring speech' precisely emulates the 'thunder of his martial tooles' in a new military poetry, 'not being an Art of lyes', (in Sidney's words), 'but of true doctrine'. In what we may call its point blank verse,[44] *Tamburlaine* presents and teaches the shock of the new, with a relish for the 'termes now used in warres' (Barret, 248) that was thought by some to 'subvert all our ancient proceedings in matters Militarie' (Smythe, B2r). The contradictions of Marlowe's mythos, as atheist subversive and government agent, meet in the urgent context of his 'stately tent of War'.

'Certainly', writes a recent editor of *Shakespeare's Sonnets*, 'sonnets and soldiery do not mix'.[45] The evidence she cites from *Henry V*, of the Dauphin's inappropriate composition of a sonnet in praise of his horse

(3.7.39-67), squares with the militarist's disdain we have noted for 'a worlde replete and glutted with letters' (see above, p. 82). Yet, as the wars went on, the Elizabethan imagination seems increasingly to have played on the coincidences of literary and military production. With great wit, for example, the eponymous hero of *Edward III* disguises the sonnets he has commissioned to woo the Countess of Salisbury, as the jottings of military embattlement: 'thou knowst not how to drawe a battell; | These wings, these flankars, and these squadrons | Argue in thee defective discipline' (2.1. 184-7). We have noted the proliferation of military text-books in the period. Their 'plattes of fortifications' and 'formes of imbattailing', the 'Cartes ... Mappes, and ... Models' of the art of war, seem, finally, to have left their impression on contemporary literary industry. Shakespeare's self-demeaning comparison in Sonnet 32 between his own sonnets and 'ranckes of better equipage' urge a kinship beween the printed stanza and the so-called Bologna method of military diagrams (Hale, 1988) that is elsewhere made explicit.

Sharing Shakespeare's 'punning production of the written page in *equipage*' (Vendler, 174), for example, the 'stanzaes' of Marston's *Metamorphosis of Pigmalions Image* (1598), 'like Soldados of our warlike age, | March rich bedight in warlike equipage'.[46] Barret's typical account of 'these proportions of Diamant, Triangle, Sheeres, and Saw battels' (81), and the alphabets he fits into their geometric shapes, suggest a critically neglected influence over 'figured poetry', 'which' (as Elizabeth Cook's otherwise full discussion tells us) 'enjoyed a vogue in the late sixteenth and early seventeenth centuries' (21). 'Renaissance printers were certainly keen to demonstrate their skills in the display of uniform type in clearly contoured diagrammatic forms' (Cook, 28), skills honed in setting, for example, the 'figure' explained in Whitehorne's *Certaine Waies for the Ordering of Souldiours* (1588), of '25. men standing in fashion foure square ... and to cause it to be better understoode, I have thought good to make this figure with the 25. letters of the a.b.c.' (I3v-14r). Tourneur's *Funerall Poeme. Upon the Death of ... Sir Francis Vere* (1609) pressed the figure home. Woken to 'a hotte *Alarme*', its subject would

> His troupes *direct*; the service *execute*;
> As practis'd Printers, *Sett* and *Distribute*
> Their Letters: And more *perfectly* effected;
> For what he did, was not to be *corrected*.
> (C4r - C4v)

In 1628, Dekker claimed to be 'No Souldier, yet my Pen playes the *Captayne*, and Drils a *Company* of verses on *Foote*, in a *Field* of white *Paper*. The *Discipline* I teach them, is ... *Printed* in their *Memories*' (*Warres, Warres, Warres*, A4r). If soldiers variously mixed with sonnets 'in a *Field* of white *Paper*', the military doctrine of their 'warlike equipage' found broader literary expression elsewhere, in a theatre of war where soldiers and players indisputably mixed, and where Captains Vere and Tamburlaine were both played: it is to that stage that we shall now turn.

## Notes

1. W.S. Gilbert, *Ruddigore* (1887), *Savoy Operas* (1962), 458.
2. See E. Taylor (1947), 124.
3. See L. Brown, 160-64; Ortelius, *Theatrum*, ed. Skelton (1964), v-x.
4. Keuning, 42: L. Brown, 164; Braun and Hogenberg, *Civitates*, ed. Skelton (1965), 1, xix.
5. The work was reprinted in 1578, 1588, 1592 and 1596. Quotation is from the 1577 edition.
6. Coleridge, *Works*, ed. Coleridge (1912), 297; on the confluence of war and agriculture in the period see Low (1985), *passim*.
7. Including *TECTONICON* (1562) (whose subtitle provides this phrase); and *A Geometricall Practise, Named PANTOMETRIA* (1571).
8. So Garrard, for example, notes the 'Proportion of a battell out of M Digges Stratioticos' (1591, 195). See also Bourne (1587), A4v.
9. Compare for example the plates in Garrard's *Arte of Warre* (1591), 313, and in Phillippe Danfrie's 1597 *Déclaration de l'Usage du Graphomètre* reproduced in L. Brown, 231.
10. News-maps like these seem to have been regularly published in London throughout the war-years (eg News-Pamphlet 5), but are now rare, presumably due to the decorative functions Dee described.
11. Mercator and Hondius, *Atlas*, tr. Hexham, ed. Skelton, (1968), 1, xx.
12. Reference is to the lineation of the 1604 A-Text, from *Doctor Faustus: Parallel Texts*, ed. Greg (1950), unless otherwise stated.
13. See *OED* entries of 'peripheria' (= circumference), 'periphery' and the nineteenth-century terms 'periphractic' and 'periphraxy'.
14. *Friar Bacon and Friar Bungay*, MSR, lines 247-50.
15. *Doctor Faustus*, ed. Jump (1962), 123.
16. And later Vermeer's, whose *Art of Painting* (*c*.1666-67) 'irrevocably binds the map to his art' (Alpers, 122), and whose 'oldest known signature' (dated 23 April 1653) is to be found on a 'document about fortifications' that were constructed in Zeeland by his uncle, a 'military engineer' (Blankert, 8).
17. *Doctor Faustus*, ed. Jump (1962), xliii.
18. *Essayes*, ed. Kiernan (1985), 57.
19. F. Johnson (1942), 99. This article contains the full text of the lecture.
20. Whetstone's account of Tamburlaine in *The English Myrror* is swiftly succeeded by an account of the 'Tyrannie of the Spaniards in the lowe countries' (1586a, 96).
21. *Tamburlaine the Great*, ed. Cunningham (1981), 72-81.

22. Garber (1984) draws attention to the quibble on punctuation in Tamburlaine's 'Point', as well as the script of Faustus's 'Lines, circles, signs, and characters', but overlooks the military currency of each passage.

23. PCC 1597 (Public Record Office, PROB 11 / 90 fo. 61).

24. *David and Bathsabe*, MSR, lines 187-9.

25. Marlowe, *Works*, ed. Tucker Brooke (1910), 4.

26. See the illustrations in Pictorius (1558), 50; and Seznec (1980), 174.

27. On the contemporary fame of the scene see R. Levin (1984); Pendry (1974), 41-2; and below, p. 167.

28. See *Bow versus Gun*, ed. Heath (1973), v-xv; Smythe, *Discourses*, ed. Hale (1964), xli-lvi.

29. *Tamburlaine the Great*, ed. Cunningham (1968), 260.

30. *Lectures and Notes on Shakespeare*, ed. Ashe (1907), 334.

31. Much as a Glossary is appended to *Bravo Two Zero* (McNab, 407).

32. For useful modern diagrams illustrating these terms, see Hale (1977), 12, and G. Parker (1988), 11.

33. The process continues into our own century, as the incorporation into English of *jeeps, the Blitz, Molotov cocktails* or *Scuds* testify.

34. News-Pamphlet 12 (1592), A2v; News-Pamphlet 9 (n.d. [1591]), 5.

35. Sir Thomas Kellie's book of *Militarie Instructions for the Learned* was entitled *Pallas Armata* (1627).

36. Quotation is from *The Shakespeare Apocrypha*, ed. Brooke (1908).

37. *Mémoires*, ed. Bourilly and Vindry (1908-19), 3, 118-19.

38. *Rastell Plays*, ed. Axton (1979), 12.

39. *Rastell Plays*, ed. Axton, 6-7; E. Taylor (1930), 8-9; Parr (1948), 239.

40. The work was printed in 1480 from a far earlier work, and reprinted as late as 1527 (Caxton, *Mirrour*, ed. Prior, 1913, v-vi).

41. Ortelius, *Theatre of the Whole World* (1606), tr. W.B., Preface.

42. Tucker Brooke, quoted in Siemon (1985), 120, n.17.

43. *Virgidemiarum* (1597), quoted in R. Levin (1984), 53.

44. The 'blank' of both 'point blank' and 'blank verse', refers to the same idea, respectively a target's white centre, and the white of an empty page, and therefore 'empty' of rhyme. Both terms were current in the 1580s.

45. *Shakespeare's Sonnets*, ed. Duncan-Jones (1997), 45.

46. Marston, *Poems*, ed. Davenport (1961), 65.

# CHAPTER THREE

# Theatres of War

*'A battle must obey unities of time, place and action'* [1]

On New Year's Day 1569/70, Humphrey Gilbert was knighted for making 'short warres' of the Munster Rebellion (Churchyard, 1579, Q4r). Shortly afterwards, he submitted a proposal to the Queen for the foundation of an 'Achademy of Chivallric pollicy and philosophie', which included plans for the teaching of 'rules of proportion and necessarie perspective and mensuration': 'matters of accion meet for present practize' in the new arithmetical discipline of war.[2] Churchyard's account of his 'maner' in Ireland, however, makes us (as Cassio was to say of Iago) 'rellish him | More in the Souldier then in the Scholler' (*Othello*, 2.1.165). The following is from *The Generall Rehearsall of Warres* (1579):

> His maner was that the heddes of all those ... whiche were killed in the daie, should be cutte of from their bodies, and brought to the place where he incamped at night: and should there bee laied on the ground, by eche side of the waie leadyng into his owne Tente: so that none could come into his Tente for any cause, but commonly he must passe through a lane of heddes, whiche he used *ad terrorem*, the dedde feelyng nothyng the more paines thereby: and yet did it bryng great terrour to the people, when thei sawe the heddes of their dedde fathers, brothers, children, kinsfolke, and freendes, lye on the grounde before their faces, as thei came to speake with the saied Collonell.
> (Q3v)

Such brutalities, Churchyard continues, had been 'in effect ever tofore used toward the Englishe' (Q3v), but he could equally have cited the precedent that Frontinus provides of Sulla, who displayed to his besieged enemy 'the heedes of their capitaynes slayne in battayle, sette upon speares endes and so abated ... their obstinate frowardnes'.[3] 'There was muche blood saved through the terror', comments Churchyard (Q4r), and his rationale anticipates a later elegy on another knighted soldier. Tourneur's *Funerall Poeme* on Sir Francis Vere (1609) also takes care to justify his subject's disciplinarianism, 'which in the sense | Of *vulgar* apprehension, seem'd to bee | A disposition unto *crueltie*':

> *Tradition* and *experience* made him know,
> That men in *Armies* are more *apt* t'offend;
> And faults to *greater* danger doe extend
> *There*, then in *civill* governments...
> ... and that there's nothing can restraine
> Their *dissolute* affections, but the *Reine*
> Of *strict* and *exemplarie* punishment.
> (B3v-B4r)

In Gilbert's grotesque headquarters we may discern something distinct from either the '*exemplarie* punishment' with which Vere disciplined his own men, or the admonitory display of heads with which Sulla outfaced his enemy. For as well as the 'greate terrour' his lane publicly procured, the nightly ritual of its assembly was centred on Gilbert himself, and comprises an exemplary artifice of self-presentation. His position of authority is dramatized through the careful stage-management of his bivouac. Churchyard's assurances that 'the dedde felte no paines' stress the transformation into props their bodies undergo, and may further be seen in the context of the 'devises of warre' and military 'showes' that Churchyard himself had composed during the 1570s (Adnitt, 31; 66).

The dramatic sense of life commonly identified as integral to Elizabethan experience achieved its first solid manifestation in the decade between Gilbert's suppression in Ireland and Churchyard's *Rehearsall* of it, with the construction of the first public playhouses in London. To an extent, the inherent theatricality of Gilbert's macabre procedure in Munster was to be confirmed on these and subsequent stages. The temporary bivouacs used in the field were reproduced in the pavilions and tents erected on their boards to allow 'battle scenes [to] merge into camp scenes', or to represent 'two opposing camps' (Chambers, 1923, 3, 53-4). Gilbert's inventive desecration of the dead was to be echoed in the 'iiij Turckes hedes' itemized by Henslowe's *Diary* in a 1598 inventory of props (318). Tamburlaine's 'stately tent of War' is pitched upon a stage that promises to 'make a bridge of murthered Carcases, | Whose arches should be fram'd with bones of Turks' (*One*, Prol.3; *Two*, 1.3.93-4). Poetic licence aside, the historical model for Marlowe's plays, as we have seen, was cited approvingly by contemporary military theorists, Lloyd detailing the exemplary disembowelling of one of his soldiers (1602, 193), and Barret the efficacy of such methods (1598, 10). Gilbert and Vere evidently deployed equivalents to Lloyd's 'punishments and severities of offences' (193).

'Brave *Vere* was by his *Scarlet Cassock* known', as Tourneur's *Funerall Poeme* relates (D2r). Marlowe's Tamburlaine was known, so it seems from Henslowe's inventory, by his 'breches of crymson vellvet' and 'cotte with coper lace' (321). The two soldiers' respective theatres of war converged one afternoon in October 1599, as Rowland Whyte reported to Robert Sidney:

> Two Daies agoe the overthrow of *Turnholt*, was acted
> upon a Stage, and all your Names used that were at yt;
> especially Sir *Fra. Veres*, and he that plaid that Part, gott
> a Beard resembling his, and a Watchet Sattin Doublett,
> with Hose trimd with Silver Lace. You was also
> introduced, Killing, Slaying, and Overthrowing the
> *Spaniards*, and honorable Mention made of your Service,
> in seconding Sir *Francis Vere*, being engaged.[4]

Sidney's reaction to his impersonation is not recorded; but perhaps
something of its flavour is caught by Jonson's Captain Tucca in *Poetaster*
(1601): 'I heare, you'll bring me o' the stage there; you'll play me, they say:
I shall be presented by a sort of copper-lac't scoundrels of you: life of
PLUTO, and you stage me, stinkard; your mansions shall sweat for't'
(3.4.197-200).

One military commander employs exemplarily theatrical methods, supported by solid Classical precedent, to reduce rebellion to servitude in six
weeks; another general is himself 'plaid' on a stage to celebrate his
victorious campaign; a third '*Man of warre*' (122) – both fictional and
Roman – enquires whether he is to be played in the copper-laced doublet of
Tamburlaine, himself both a theatrical and military precedent. This chapter
runs its thumb upon the double-edged blade of the Elizabethan theatre of
war. Elaine Scarry has noted that such blends of the real and the fictional
are nowadays 'quietly registered in the language of theatres of battle,
international dialogues, scenarios, and stages' (62). The apparatus of fiction
has formed a series of uneasy coalitions with twentieth-century war (often
forcing inverted commas around the word 'real'), whether between the Gulf
War and virtual-reality video-games (Baudrillard, 1991); Vietnam and
television (Hallin, 1986, 104-13); World War Two and cinema (Virilio,
1989); or World War One and music hall (Fussell, 1975, 194-5). In the
sixteenth century, the technologies of war and the resources of fiction
overlapped even more explicitly, if only because the theatrical sense of life
was more pronounced.

### Playing at soldiers

'The Spaniards invade England' reads one of the more surprising glosses in
the margins of Camden's *Annals*. The event in question occurred in July
1595, when a small force landed on the Cornish coast, fired a church 'and
presently retired, not having slaine or taken one man'; and 'these were the
first and last *Spaniards* that ever made any hostile landing in *England*'
(1625, 4, 73). Though a footnote in military history, the episode is granted a
greater profile in Heywood's *Apology for Actors*, where the battle-honours
are awarded to a troupe of travelling players,

> who, playing late in the night at a place called *Perin* in
> *Cornwall*, certaine *Spaniards* were landed the same night,
> unsuspected, and undiscovered, with intent to take in the
> towne, spoyle and burne it, when suddenly, even upon
> their entrance, the players (ignorant as the townes-men of
> any such attempt) presenting a battle on the stage with
> their drum and trumpets strooke up a lowd alarme: which
> the enemy hearing, and fearing they were discovered,
> amazedly retired, made some few idle shot in a bravado,
> and so in a hurly-burly fled disorderly to their boats.
> (G2r)

This extraordinary tale of genuine hostilities seen off by their fictional
'presenting' prompts questions about the extent of their differentiation, and
ones enacted by Heywood's subtle prose. 'It is necessarie', reads Riche's
*Path-Way to Military Practise* (1587), 'that every company have two
drums' (G2r). In Heywood's narrative, it is the appropriation by a theatrical
'company' (G2r) of real military equipment, 'their drum and trumpets', that
reduces the invader to a state of theatrical vacuity: 'some few idle shot in a
bravado'. Rather cleverly, Heywood here restores the word 'bravado' to its
Spanish originators, but applies it to a flourish of real bullets. Conversely, it
is the players' 'lowd alarme' on stage that precipitates the retreat, and that
military word too is of continental extraction, only recently incorporated
into the English lexicon of war (see above, p. 35), as into the shorthand of
playwrights' stage-directions. A comparable mediation, or oscillation, between players and soldiers attaches to the fulcrum of 'their entrance' among
the subclauses of Heywood's long sentence: 'when suddenly, even upon
their entrance, the players ...'. The words float between referring back to the
Spanish soldiers entering the town, and forward to the English players
entering 'on the stage', an ambivalence enhanced by the rhymes that
elsewhere chime through the passage ('hearing, and fearing ... hurly-burly').
'At the report of this tumult', it continues,

> the townes-men were immediatly armed, and pursued
> them to the sea, praysing God for their happy deliverance
> from so great a danger, who by his providence made these
> strangers the instrument and secondary meanes of their
> escape from such imminent mischife, and the tyranny of so
> remorceless an enemy.
> (G2r)

The passage hangs the semantic overlap of player and soldier upon a point
of doctrine. We have seen how defence of the just war rested on the
instrumental function of its wagers, 'inferior instruments unto God to punish
the offences of the wicked' (Gosson, 1598, C1v). Heywood affords that

role to the company of players, the 'instrument and secondary meanes' of a divinely sanctioned resistance. Where *A Larum for London* intelligently deploys the expressive rank of Lieutenant to characterize the delegation of divine authority on earth, Heywood's 'hurly-burly' reversals of fact and fiction (the soldiers' bravado, the players' alarm) enhance the sense in which these players are doubly secondary. 'Presenting a battle on the stage', they also represent God's deliverance in the larger theatre of war, and taking His place. Actor and soldier merge because it is the role of both to be representative instruments.

Heywood's story forms a test-case for his *Apology* as a whole, an extreme example of the practical benefits to be derived from drama. Earlier in his treatise, he adduces a series of classical examples of the uses of imitation. Julius Caesar, he explains, emulated the example of Alexander; Alexander had learned from his tutor Aristotle, who ordered 'the destruction of Troy to be acted before his pupill', so that 'all his succeeding actions were meerly shaped' after the 'patterne' of Achilles; Achilles, in turn, had imitated Theseus, Theseus Hercules, and Hercules Jupiter (B3r-v). Heywood then insists that this mimetic pedigree of war stretches forward to 'our domesticke hystories':

> What English Prince should hee behold the true portrature
> of the famous King *Edward* the third ... would not bee
> suddenly Inflam'd with so royall a spectacle, being made
> apt and fit for the like atchievement. So of *Henry* the fift.
> (B4r)

The 'spectacle' of war effects the 'like atchievement' in the field, 'as if the Personater were the man Personated' (B4r). The inadvertent victory over the Spanish invader at Cornwall, 'some 12 yeares ago' (G2r), proves for Heywood the military value of eroding the distinction between Personater and Personated.

'Poetrie is the companion of Campes', Sidney had declared in his *Apologie for Poetrie* (1595, H3r), one of the earliest texts, as we have seen, devoted to the theme of the soldier and scholar's mutual benefit. Heywood's *Apology for Actors* makes the same claims for drama, 'not being an Art of lyes,' (as Sidney had written) 'but of true doctrine: not of effeminatenes, but of notable stirring of courage' (I2r). That too is the basis of Nashe's Elizabethan defence of plays in *Piers Penilesse*, celebrating 'our forefathers valiant acts ... than which, what can be a sharper reproofe to these degenerate effeminate dayes of ours?' (1, 212). For Nashe, as for Heywood, such plays invite imitation in their audience 'to encourage them forward', providing pragmatic examples of 'all stratagems of warre ... most lively anatomiz'd' (1, 213). Exclusively military writers were more cautious of such claims for the tactical value of theatrical emulation. Sir Roger Williams, for example, in his *Briefe Discourse of Warre* (1590), dryly notes that 'Divers play *Alexander* on the stages, but fewe or none in the field' (*Works*, ed. Evans, 6). C.G. elaborates the same point in *A Watch-worde for Warre* (1596):

> Alas, it is an easie matter to play *Hercules* in our houses, or *Alexander* uppon the stages: but it is somewhat to follow them in the field, where every bullet doth threaten death.
> (D1v)

Warnings like these confirm the currency during the war-years of Heywood's thesis, but also echo in a minor key residual resentments at the wantonness not only of poetry, but of drama, as voiced by a number of contemporary militarists. One of the dedicatory poems of Riche's *Allarme for England*, for example, bids the reader 'sort thy selfe from Comedies, and foolish plaies of love' (** ii v); Gyles Clayton's *Approoved Order of Martiall Discipline* (1591) darkly cites the example of the Greeks who, by laying aside their weapons and 'taking pleasure in Comaedies' were conquered by Philip of Macedon (A3v); the third of the *Foure Paradoxes* Dudley Digges published in 1604 passingly pronounces 'play bookes and base pamphlets unfit studies for dying men' (84). Most vituperative of such critics was Gabriel Harvey. In *Pierces Supererogation* (1593), his venom extends beyond wanton comedies to include 'Marlowes bravados' (*Works*, ed. Grosart, 2, 115) among 'the shreds of the theater' (99), and asks, 'Were some demaunded, whether Greenes, or Nashes Pamflets, were better penned: I beleeve they would aunsweare; Sir Roger Williams Discourse of War ... and M. Thomas Digges Stratioticos' (99). But in prosecuting his animus against Nashe, Harvey invokes a singularly inept metaphor: 'the winde is chaunged, & there is a busier pageant upon the stage' (96). Inept, that is, to Harvey's purpose, for as the most fervently antitheatrical of old soldiers testified in their treatises, the Art of War was very much an art of feigning.

It is not that soldiers were urged to 'play *Alexander* ... in the field'; rather that theatrical methods of disguise, pretence, and deceit comprised the essence of the *Stratagemes, Sleyghtes, and Policies of Warre* by which in 1539 Richard Morysine translated the title of Frontinus's influential work. 'Speake one thing to thine enemie, but doe another', advised the author of *A Myrrour for English Souldiers* (1595, C1v); 'Always faine to have good newes that your souldiers faint not' (D1r), and (most tellingly perhaps), 'He is most wise that in cases of warre can best dissemble' (D2v). Similar catalogues of pretence can be readily assembled: the 'common Stratageme' Sutcliffe describes, 'to cover our counsels and enterprises by contrary pretenses', or his assertion that 'Vaine shewes do often deceive the enemy' (1593, 192-4). But it is Mercury, in Riche's *Dialogue betwene Mercury and an English Souldier* (1574), whose martial advice most anticipates the alarums and excursions of the late Elizabethan stage. The god instructs the soldier there in the values of feigning, relating how King Alfred put 'himselfe in ye habite of a Mynstrel, & by these meanes ... came into [the enemy] Campe', and won it from within (E7r). Alexander, he says, 'sent forth certayne of his men in the Illiriens apparell' (F5v). Levinus struck panic in the enemy by wielding a bloody sword, pretending to have slain their king (E8r). Most elaborate is the stratagem he describes of Pelopidas. Simultaneously besieging two nearby towns, Mercury relates, the general 'commaunded that foure Knightes shuld come from the one siege to the other, with Garlands on their heades, as though they brought tydings of victory'. Furthermore, to assist 'this dissimulation', a nearby wood was set on fire, 'to make a show as though the Towne had burnt', and some soldiers were dressed 'in Townes mens apparell', pretending to be enemy prisoners. 'Thinking them selves halfe overcome', the enemy surrendered (F8r).

Sidney's *Apologie* had mocked those plays that have 'two Armies flye in, represented with foure swords and bucklers, & then what harde heart wil not receive it for a pitched field?' (K1r). But Riche's classical precept insists on the paradoxical efficiency with which 'foure Knightes' can incite belief in a 'pitched fielde' even in a pitched field, wresting victory through 'dissimulation', 'apparell', and the making of 'a show'. Riche speaks true when he comments that 'such sleyghtes as hath been used by the noblest Captaynes ... would not a little norish the imaginations of such as should peruse them' (G1r). Camden's appraisal of Vere's feigned parley at Ostend suggests such nourishment, 'excusing himselfe by that military Axiome, *To delude the enemie by cunning devises and stratagems, is not onely just, but pleasant also, and profitable*' (4, 198) – possessed (in other words) of that 'vertue-breeding delightfulnes' by which Sidney had defined the value of poetry (L2v). For all his disdain for 'taking pleasure in Comaedies', Clayton recommended the tactic of 'a shew as if men were slayne' (27).

'All warfare is based on deception', reads Sun Tzu's *Art of War*, written circa 500 BC. 'Therefore, when capable of attacking, feign incapacity; when active in moving troops, feign inactivity. When near the enemy, make it seem that you are far away; when far away, make it seem that you are near'.[5] Modern variations on the enduring theme of military seeming include the faked radio broadcasts, dummy parachutists, impersonated generals, fictional airfields, and phantom armies that comprise Young and Stamp's history of *Deception Operations in the Second World War*. The Allies' entirely fictional invention, ahead of D-Day, of a 'huge and spectral force' of 150,000 men (Howard, 1992, 121) confirmed Frontinus's maxim that 'It is better to vanquyshe thyn ennemy ... with terror, than with fyghtyng in playne battayle' (N6v).

Various sources testify that such theatrical theory was frequently put into successful military practice on the Elizabethan battlefield. At the siege of Leith in 1560, for example, as Sir John Hayward relates, an English soldier was 'trayned from his companie, by nine French men, apparelled like women, who stroke of his head' (*Annals*, ed. Bruce, 55-6). According to Holinshed, the Dutch commander Martin Schenk, when besieging the town of Waale, 'clad certeine of his men in the bours apparell, sent them into the towne to sell the vittels, and one of them broke his waggon in the gate ... and he suddenlie entred the towne without resistance' (2, 1429). Camden notes that a number of English troops, 'feigning themselves to be fugitives', lured many of the besieging enemy to their deaths at Bergen op Zoom in 1588 (3, 146). After the failure of the Cadiz expedition in 1596, Ralegh's ships reconnoitred at Corunna, 'manned by sailors dressed in Spanish clothing' in order to throw off suspicion (Cruickshank, 276).

On one celebrated occasion, such theatrical methods paid dividends. In May 1591 Sir Francis Vere

> caused sundry of his souldiours, secretly to be apparrelled in the habite of poore Market folks, as well of men as women, some dryving of Oxen, some of Kine, some of sheepe ... [and these] were pursued & chased by some Souldiours, as though they had beene their enemies, by meanes whereof the Cattle and poore people were received by the enemie, intending to succour them, while without any suspision those poore people being couragious souldiors, having got the gates opened, seazed uppon the keepers thereof, so that in the meane time the other issued, and immediatly sir *Frauncis Vere* folowed with a sufficient troupe of horsmen, and foote.

So was achieved *The Politique Takinge of Zutphen Skonce*, as the news-pamphlet calls it, 'as well by force as pollicie' (News-Pamphlet 10, 8-9). That slightly qualmish phrase quickly yields to the relish with which the author tells the story, in all its elaboration. Part of his enjoyment derives from the diversity of what Vere himself, in his *Commentaries*, called his 'sleight' (17). Riche had recommended a general 'sending Souldiers under the colour of market men dryving beastes' (1574, F8v). So had Frontinus, who further cited Epaminondas's disguising of his troops 'in womens apparaylle' (H8r). Vere manages to accomplish both sets of disguise ('as well of men as of women') and further enacts the 'shew' of their fleeing from their own army, who pretend to chase them, 'as though they had beene their enemies'. Sutcliffe's *Practice, Proceedings, and Lawes of Armes* (1593), includes such tricks of 'Men disguised like women, or like Countrey people, or *armed like the enemies* [who] *entring within their strength doe now and then abuse them, and give their felowes meanes of entrance*'. With a footnote to Virgil, he immediately resumes, 'In these late troubles of *France* divers negligent Governors have by these practises bene surprised' (195). Vere's ruse comprises something of a compendium of such sources, gathered from both classical prescription and contemporary example.

At once a direct imitation of classical methods, and one itself based in imitation, Vere's *Politique Takinge of Zutphen* might be said to add flesh to the metaphorical bones of the 'theatre of war', an image common to a variety of military literature of the time. Riche's *Souldiers Wishe* (1604) included in its catalogue of definition the observation that war 'is the Theater wheron Nobilitie was borne to shew himselfe' (4-5); 'Armes and Soulderie', agreed Francis Markham, 'are the Cronicles of Princes, the hazards of battayles their Theaters' (1622, 8). Their stress on 'Princes' or 'Nobilitie' suggests affinities with the medieval tradition of the tournament's chivalric displays. 'Real war and tournaments', writes Richard Barber, 'are never very far apart throughout the history of chivalry' (193); Vale agrees that the 'distinction between participants in "real" and "sham" warfare was not yet made quite as sharply as has been imagined' (99). Castiglione's recommendation to his courtier 'at skirmish, or assault, or battaile' equally pictures the field as a place of display:

> he ought to worke the matter wisely in separating him
> selfe from the multitude, and undertake notable and bolde
> feates which he hath to doe, with as litle company as he
> can, and in the sight of noble men that be of most
> estimation in the campe, and especially in the presence and
> (if it were possible) before the very eyes of his king or
> great personage he is in service withall.
> (quoted in Whigham, 1984, 46)

The inhabitants of the theatre of war have changed places: the nobility is now its audience, rather than being 'borne to shew himselfe' on its stage to the 'multitude'. 'The theater of war summons an audience of the highest rank', as Whigham comments (47). Castiglione's emphasis upon individual prowess, 'with as litle company as he can', represents a chivalric legacy to Renaissance thought, as Vale asserts (78-9), and one which placed 'rhetorical concerns above ... following orders ... or acting in accord with military strategic concerns' (Whigham, 1984, 47). Chivalry and policy were traditionally opposed military ideals, as we have seen, but they shared a common analogy with 'acting', and the theatre. The different emphases of this application might be illustrated by reference to the poems of two writers more celebrated for their work on the stage.

In *A Monumental Columne* (1613), Webster compared the dead Prince Henry with Edward the Black Prince:

> He that of working pulce sicke *France* bereft,
> Who knew that battailes, not the gaudy show
> Of ceremonies, do on Kings bestow
> Best Theaters, t'whom naught so tedious as Court sport.[6]

Perhaps understandably – his edition appeared in 1927, and he had served in the Great War – F.L. Lucas considered as Webster's 'most detestable lines' (3, 287) his paean to one who 'hath often made | Horror looke lovely, when i'th'fields there lay | Armes and legges' (85-7). But the neo-chivalric cult centred on Henry is given its most militant form in them, as the distinction between 'real' and 'sham' warfare is invoked to be conflated in the 'Best Theaters' bestowed on kings.[7] Henry's place in this 'specious Theater' (48) is directly comparable with Heywood's *Apology for Actors* (to which Webster contributed prefatory verses), and its pedigree of military emulation stretching from Hercules to Henry V. 'Him [the Black Prince] did He [Henry V] strive to imitate', continues Webster, 'and was sorry'

> Hee did not live before him, that his glory
> Might have bene his example.
> (96-8)

Heywood's prefatory poem in the *Apology* begins with the larger assertion that 'The world's a Theater, the earth a Stage'. 'Kings have their entrance in due equipage' (A4r), but so too do their 'Citizens': 'All men have parts, and each man acts his owne', and '*Jehove* doth as spectator sit, | And chiefe determiner to applaud the best' (A4v). The same convention introduces Dekker's poem, *Warres, Warres, Warres* (1628), which makes its own play, as we have seen, on the monumental columns of warlike equipage (see above, p. 87):

> Pitch'd *Fields* those Theaters are, at which the *Gods*
> Look downe from their high Galleries of *Heaven*,
> Where *Battailes, Tragedies* are, to which are given
> *Plaudits* from Cannons, *Buskind Actors* tread
> Knee deep in blood and trample on the Dead.
> (B1v)

These soldier-actors, 'knee deep in blood', recall the emulative examples of Heywood's *Apology*, 'to see a souldier shap'd like a souldier ... besmered in blood' (B3v). With Webster, they make 'Horror looke lovely'.

Dekker's poem proceeds to suggest a further reason why late sixteenth- and seventeenth-century warfare was described in terms of theatre, even for 'common fighting Men':

> *Death*, the grave *theame*, of which is writ the story,
> Keene *Swords* the *Pens*, texting (at large) the glory
> Of *Generals, Colonels, Captaines*, and *Commanders*,
> With common fighting Men ... Souldiers all,
> And Fellowes (in that name) to th' *Generall*.
> (B1v - B2r)

We recognize the components of the Renaissance ideal, the Soldier-Scholar, whose sword-as-pen anticipates Dekker's subsequent image of war as a 'S[c]hoole where honor takes degrees' (B2r). These degrees, however, punningly reflect back on the hierarchy of ranks - the meritocracy of the newly professionalized army (the army of Tamburlaine or Stump) not the chivalric hierarchy of blood.

Many military treatises of the time systematically prescribed these 'Officers in degree, with their severall duties' (Barret, 1598, t.p.). Blandy's *The Castle, or Picture of Pollicy* (1581) is an early example. Before sorting the army into 'braunches' (F2v), its formal dialogue between Blandy and Geoffrey Gates includes a telling exchange of metaphors. Gates asserts that

> The reasonable part in every well governed bodye, hath the dominion, and ruleth principally. The duetye and action of the other, may not unfitly be compared ... to a faythfull Corporall, who diligently attendeth the watchfull ... call of his *Sentenell*, or to a ready valiaunt souldiar, who executeth most speedely the will of his commaunder. (B1v)

The modern army's distribution of duties echoes the 'partes of a commonwealth' (t.p.) as well as its microcosmic model, the body. That conceit prompts the quiet pun in the word 'Corporall' here, and elsewhere extends to the etymology of 'Captain', which Morysine's Frontinus teases out in describing Sulla's display of the severed 'heedes of their capitaynes slayne in battayle' (G8v). Falstaff parodies the convention in his paean to sack in *2 Henry IV* (4.2.104-109), though there the 'vitall commoners ... muster me all to their captaine, the heart'. Blandy is next minded to conceive the 'well governed bodye' in terms of the theatre of the world: 'I perceave by your assertion, that every man in this lyfe (as on a Theater or stage) playes one parte or other, which meriteth shame ... or deserveth ... commendation' (B1v). Perhaps it is for this reason that the precepts of military theorists so often sound like Theophrastan character-sketches. Thomas Digges, for example, presents contrasting portraits of good and bad muster-masters (1604, 30-4); and Riche came to remodel from his *Martiall Conference* (1598, B3r-B3v) its description of soldierly inexperience, in the straightforwardly satirical portrait of Captain Swag in *Faultes, Faults, and Nothing Else but Faultes* (1606, D4r).

For a variety of reasons, then, the 'Pitch'd *Fields*' of Elizabethan warfare drew an almost instinctive comparison with the theatre. The chivalric display of the tournament furnished a precedent for the battlefield being a 'high stage' (Sutcliffe, 1593, B2r). Humanist example recommended the merits of using the models of Caesar or Alexander as the basis of imitation. The reorganization of the army into precisely segregated ranks (acknowledged in the rank of Lieutenant) highlighted the broader tradition of the *theatrum mundi* by dint of its chiming with the commonplace that 'all men have parts, and each man acts his owne'. The *topos* was further reanimated by the coincidence of the greater geographic precision spawned by the exigencies of war: Garrard's *Arte of Warre* (1591) reaches for such an image in detailing the usefulness of maps, and their 'true description' of terrain, by which 'Prince, Generall, Collonell, or Captaine'

> may with the eye of his mind, run over & peruse the
> whole ... briefly & plainly in a table, as ye view of a gallant
> Theater, from whence the veile of the shading curtaine is
> suddainlie drawne, and make apparent to the eyes of all
> the beholders, the sight of some sumpteous shew.
> (129)

Vere's stage-management of his soldiers at Zutphen provided them less with the 'set of inverted commas' of *sprezzatura* one critic describes (Saccone, quoted in Hanning and Rosand, 60), and more with a set of systematic stage-directions: but for both Vere and Castiglione, the battle-field is an arena of imitation, though for different audiences and to different purposes. The *Strategemes, Sleyghtes, and Policies of Warre* advocated by so many theorists confirmed the *theatrum belli*, since to this host of classical precedents was added the technique of theatrical illusion: the 'feigning', 'dissimulation', 'apparell', and 'show' of prudent policy. It is unsurprising that such pervasive traditions of theatricality should be reflected on London's newly constructed stages during these war-years; that these imitations of the classics, and their own strategies of imitation, should themselves have been imitated there.

Sir Thomas Coningsby's 1591 *Journal of the Siege of Rouen* repeatedly lays stress upon the spectacle or sport of combat-experience. In part this is due (as Garrard's 'gallant Theater' indicates) to the techniques of military surveyance. A day is spent, for example, 'viewing the places of the batterie' (18); another involves climbing a nearby hill 'only to vewe the towne ... where we mighte verie playnely discerne the scituation of it' (21-2). But the demands of siege warfare further guaranteed to military service a literally captive audience, as his entry for 7 November relates: 'there was an hott skyrmysh, both of horse and foote, nere to the castle of St. Katherin's, where the people of the towne stoode uppon the bullwarks of the towne and beheld it as though it had bene a tryumphe of sporte' (36). Battle and 'sporte' (leisure, games, play) often coalesce in Coningsby's account. He describes how, while on an expedition 'coursing the hare', his party encountered a company of armed 'curasers on horseback ... who toke us for ennemy, as we did them' (24); and later recounts a day spent 'playinge at tennys in the forenoone, and at playinge at ballon in th'afternoone with the lieutenant-gouvernor of Deape', adding (in a phrase lent force by its context), that 'the victorie fell on our syde' (30). On 6 December, Coningsby began his entry by noting that 'we all expected some sporte' (here the sport of battle) 'when th'ennemye should come unto his *cors de gard* of the half moone, which was within twenty pykes' (56).

It is important to bear in mind both the theory of martial literature and the practice of contemporary combat when considering the representation of war on the Elizabethan stage. *3 Henry VI* (*The True Tragedy of Richard Duke of York*) displays a contiguity between Coningsby's eye-witness journal and the treatment of war the play presents. Just as Coningsby's vocabulary of battle and sport blurs, Warwick enters one scene weary from combat, 'Sore spent with toile as runners with the race' (2.3.1). The metaphor is embellished, perhaps in revision, in the Folio, where the scene ends with George's promise to his troops 'such rewards | As Victors weare at the Olympian Games' (52-3). Coningsby's hare-coursing in the fields outside Rouen threatens to merge into conflict: 'some other Chace' occurs to Richard as he claims from Warwick the quarry of Clifford, 'For I my selfe will hunt this Wolfe to death' (F 2.4.12-13). Rouen's citizens spectated upon the skirmishes before them as though a 'tryumphe of sporte': Richard likens his father's bearing in battle to another spectator sport,

> as a Beare encompass'd round with Dogges:
> Who having pincht a few, and made them cry,
> The rest stand all aloofe, and barke at him.
> (F 2.1.15-17)

The plight of the baited bear was often to strike Shakespeare as a vivid image of suffering,[8] but the Bankside origins of playhouse in blood-sports found renewed point when allied to the represented spectacle of the theatre of war. Even in the brand new Globe, Agincourt is re-enacted in a 'Cock-Pit' (*Henry V*, 1.Ch.11). Warwick's rebuke to the sons of York extends to the audience of his play, but resonates with the spectatorship Coningsby had described from the front:

> Why stand we like soft-hearted women heere,
> Wayling our losses, whiles the Foe doth Rage,
> And looke upon, as if the Tragedie
> Were plaid in jest, by counterfetting Actors.
> (F 2.3.25-8)

The vertiginous sense of such lines was elaborated in *King John* (*c*.1595), in the Bastard's contemptuous exclamation before the besieged walls of Angers:

> By heaven, these scroyles of Angiers flout you kings,
> And stand securely on their battelments,
> As in a Theater, whence they gape and point

> At your industrious Scenes and acts of death.
> (2.1.373-6)

According to Lois Potter, the lines 'emphasise the contrast between the reality of war and the fictitious spectacle which [the Bastard] feels the non-combatant citizens are making of it' (Jones-Davies, 1990, 89), and the same might be said of Warwick's earlier rebuke. The 'contrast' must have reverberated to the play's real audience, minded of their own status as spectators watching 'counterfetting Actors' 'in a Theater'. As the rebuilt Globe intimately reveals, *King John*'s fictional audience on the walls of Angers completed the raised circle of its own spectators within the design of the Theater itself.

Jonathan Dollimore likens such meta-dramatic instances to Brechtian *Verfremdungs-Effekt* (64-6). Alan Dessen makes the discrepancy between war's reality and drama's spectacle the basis of his challenging argument for the 'symbolic logic' of Elizabethan stage-violence (45). Battle scenes, he maintains, can 'generate symbolic possibilities and initiate larger patterns significant for the plays as a whole, but only when we ... sidestep misleading assumptions about "realism"' (67). In a context of war, however, in what Sir Thomas Kellie described as a 'Theatre of Honour and Glorie' (1627, ¶ v), it begins to seem that the 'theatrical *italics*' by which Dessen describes his symbolic dramaturgy (50) was also felt by 'real' soldiers in 'real' battles.

The Siege of Angers in *King John* is at once formally symbolic and topically realistic. At the intersection between the two sit the Bastard's lines quoted above. 'By heaven', his outburst begins, an oath that echoes the insistent pieties of the contending kings in the scene as a whole. The symmetrical grouping of the staged scene (French and English armies on either side, the citizenry aloft on the walls in the middle) emphasizes the sense in which their battle comprises what a recent scholar of war calls 'corporate trial by battle' (J. Johnson, 62), and what its eponymous King declares a 'dreadfull triall' (2.1.286). The 'Scenes and acts of death' that are judged by the citizens 'as in a Theater', partake of the symbolic structure of *theatrum mundi*. The 'starre-galleries' Heywood later imagined in his macrocosmic theatre provides an auditorium 'in which *Jehove* doth as spectator sit' (A4r). But in *King John*, this stage, pitched between 'heaven or hell' (407), is presided over by no such 'chief determiner' (A4v): on the contrary, the Siege of Angers results in 'undetermin'd differences of kings' (355), which are amplified by the mutually contradictory speeches of victory delivered by the French and English heralds. It is at this point of impasse that the Bastard's analogy with 'a Theater' occurs. The 'hot triall' (342) results in a hung jury, and the extraordinary suggestion that Angers be laid flat and thereafter fought for.[9] The patterning of Dessen's 'symbolic logic' finds graphic confirmation in the play's substitution of the citizen's self-interest – 'Commoditie, the byas of the world' (575) – for the divine judgement of heaven.

On the other hand, Shakespeare portrays this twelfth-century siege as a firmly modern campaign. Its original participants had no recourse to the 'Artillerie' (403) that provides a constant stream of imagery throughout the scene. Holinshed's account mentions only the 'bands of his footmen, & all his light horssemen' (2, 170), *The Troublesome Raigne of King John* (printed 1591) his 'English bowes' and 'crossebow shot' (Bullough, 4, 90, lines 687-93). Shakespeare's was an 'age of siege warfare rather than of mobile warfare' (C. Wilson, 10), so perhaps it was the the topical resonance of John's siege (as opposed to the set-battle) which impelled Shakespeare to reflect so precisely on the contemporary art of war. Angers's walls are depicted with an eye on current practices of fortification, with their 'round[ure]' (259) and 'circumference' (262), their 'plots of best advantage' laid by the 'cheefest men of discipline' (39-40). Such an attention to realistic detail accompanies the Bastard's reproach to the citizens on their battlemented auditorium. Coningsby's report of the citizens of Rouen watching a skirmish from the 'bullwarks of the towne', as if 'a tryumphe of sport', rescues the episode in *King John* from any purely symbolic reading. In fact, the tone of its lines finds an exact precedent in a news-pamphlet describing another siege, the *Streight Siedge laide to the Cytty of Steenwich* (1592) (News-Pamphlet 12). Its author describes the bombardment Steenwyk received from its Protestant besiegers,

> after which storme they of the Citie came out with broomes to sweepe the walles in a mockage, least forsooth the dust of the shot should have fouled the walles, making so light of the matter, as if they had no harme by the cannon that had so furiouslye barked at them all that while.
> (B1v)

Such 'mockage' paradoxically confirms the sensations which Warwick describes ('as if the Tragedie | Were plaid in jest') and the Bastard condemns, as peculiarly realistic representations of war.

It has been noticed that Shakespeare's treatment of the Siege of Rouen in *1 Henry VI* glances at Essex's current (1591) campaign for that city, chronicled by Coningsby.[10] The first scene of the play to feature Rouen, however, has more in common with Vere's deeds that year further west:

> *Enter Pucell disguis'd, with foure*
> *Souldiors with Sacks upon their backs.*
> PUCELL   These are the Citie Gates, the Gates of Roan,
> Through which our Pollicy must make a breach.
> Take heed, be wary how you place your words,
> Talke like the vulgar sort of Market men,
> That come to gather Money for their Corne.

If we have entrance, as I hope we shall,
And that we finde the slouthfull Watch but weake,
Ile by a signe give notice to our friends,
That *Charles* the Dolphin may encounter them.
(3.2.1-9)

The source for this scene is often given as the 'imbusshement' Hall records, by which the castle of Cornill had been captured by the English, having 'apperreled six strong men, lyke rusticall people' (Z6v). Its adaptation (as Brockbank commented) significantly reversed an English victory into the treacherous 'Hellish Mischiefe' (3.2.39) of the French (78). That reversal gains depth when we recall Vere's *Politique Takinge* of Zutphen in May 1591. A recent cause for pride in English ingenuity is tempered into a test-case for the confrontation the play explores between chivalry and policy. 'What will you doe, good gray-beard?', taunts Joan from the captured city-walls, 'Breake a Launce'? (50). The supra-national sanctity of oaths, of the 'faith ... leage and solemne covenant' celebrated in *Edward III* (3.3.58-9), overtly flounders on the rocks of what Talbot castigates as 'Trecherie' (37). Chivalry, like Bedford, is 'brought in sicke in a Chayre' (40 SD), and that is the scene's 'symbolic logic'.

But as Vere's recent victory had demonstrated, Joan's 'happy Stratageme' (18) was also topically realistic. It is surely the theatrical premise of Vere's costuming his troops, 'most ... apparelled like the country women of those parts' (*Commentaries*, 17), that lends dimension to this staged representation. 'Foure Souldiors' enter with their captain 'disguis'd'. They are advised to 'talke like the vulgar sort of Market men', elaborating the sequence of deception Vere's ploy entailed by substituting for his variety of action ('some dryving of Oxen, some of Kine') the suiting of the word to the action. Players play soldiers playing market men. They *'Enter'* in order to seek 'entrance': 'even upon their entrance', as Heywood was to write, blurring the roles of player and soldier. Vere had disguised his men as civilians 'as well of men as women'; Shakespeare's scene is further complicated by the generic confusion engendered by Joan herself – 'A Woman clad in Armour' (1.5.3), played by a boy, who enters (before) Rouen triply 'disguis'd'; and who aids her impersonation by slipping into French for the first and only time in the play (3.2.13).

David Riggs has instructively written of the 'virtual parody' Joan constitutes of the prototypical Marlovian soldier-hero Tamburlaine (22). Her base parentage, status as warlike scourge, and command of modern tactics each informs her theatrical ancestry. But it is not precisely that she embodies 'fake', unnatural valour (Riggs, 128), that she is 'generically, an impostor' of English chivalry (107). Rather, that the network of imitation initiated by this scene emphasizes the theatricality of war as a necessary adjunct to the mathematical rudiments of war Tamburlaine had espoused. We have seen how Tamburlaine's lecture anticipated the advice offered in

Garrard's *Arte of Warre* that its contents be 'read as a lecture to their souldiers' (1591, 22). Whetstone noticed the theatrical overtones of such a lecture, explaining from Roman precedent that 'When any Captaine had any notable victorie, hee ... presently mounted upon a *Theatre*, and generally praised the whole Army' (1586b, 28-9). The terms in which Riggs describes Joan ('fake', 'parody', 'impostor') themselves make up the language of contemporary military discipline: 'He is most wise that in cases of warre can best dissemble' (Frontinus, D2v). It is *1 Henry VI*, after all, that probably forms the basis of Nashe's defence of drama in 1592, wherein 'all coosonages, all cunning drifts ... all stratagems of warre ... are most lively anatomiz'd'. The staging of Joan's capture of Rouen imitates a strategy of disguise, imitated from the classics in earnest at Zutphen, in a play which played its own part in wartime, as Nashe implies: 'what hopes of eternitie are to be proposed to adventrous mindes, to encourage them forward'.

'Layd owt for the company the 4 of septemb[er] 1602 to bye A flage of sylke the some of xxvj s 8 d': the document from which this purchase is cited also details payments that year to 'the armerer for targattes' (shields) and for the acquisition of 'iiij Lances'. But though the author was a churchwarden (and so involved with the maintenance of the armouries church-halls had become), and though 'the Campe-maister devides his regiment into companies' (Barret, 1598, 15), these purchases belong to the accounts of Henslowe's diary, and were made to furnish the stage of the Rose Theatre (215-17). The overlap of player and soldier is perhaps nowhere better glimpsed in miniature than in this document. Although the modern sense in which a 'troupe' of actors calls to mind the military terminology of Vere's 'troupe of horsmen' dates from the eighteenth century (*OED*, 'Troop', sb 1e), the same ambivalence attended the word 'company' in the sixteenth, as Barret indicates above. Indeed, it was in the 1590s that the precise sense of a 'company' of infantry (corresponding to a 'troop' of cavalry, or a 'battery' of artillery) came into being (*OED*, 'Company', 8b). That Henslowe's 'company' of players furnished more work for armourers consolidates their employer's dual expenditure on military props for them, and on military equipment for the real army. For immediately before his accounts of the takings for 'hary the v' and 'tambercame' in 1596 (47), there is entered 'A notte of what charges my Soger petter hath stode me in this yeare', which includes the provision of a 'head pesse', 'a sorde & a dager', 'A bealte & a gerdell', and 'viij li of powder' (46). If soldiers behaved like players in the field, players equally appropriated the matériel of war for the stage. There is evidence for such procedure in the German descendant of *Hamlet*, *Der Bestrafte Brudermord*, in which the prince welcomes the leading actor, and instructs him to

> prepare the stage in the great hall: whatever wood you
> may require, you can get from the master-builder; if you
> want anything from the armoury, or if you have not

dresses enough, make known your wants to the master of
the robes or the steward.
(Bullough, 7, 140)

It might seem anomalous that Henslowe's 1598 inventory includes no
reference to the firearms that feature so prominently through such plays as
*Tamburlaine* and *Henry VI*. The omission may perhaps best be explained by
Henslowe's access to the real thing: their absence from his scrupulous
accounting testifies to the unremarkable practice which rendered the local
armoury a convenient props-department.

Such a hypothesis gains credence from the account Philip Gawdy provides, in his letter of November 1587, of a recent incident at a London
playhouse. It seems probable from its date that the theatre in question was
the newly opened Rose; and it has been plausibly conjectured (Chambers,
1930, 684) that the relevant 'devyse' was the episode in *2 Tamburlaine*
whereby the Governor of Babylon is executed on its walls (5.1.151-8):

> My L[ord]. Admyrall his men and players having a devyse
> in ther playe to tye one of their fellowes to a poste and so
> to shoote him to deathe, having borrowed their Callivers
> one of the players handes swerved his peece being
> charged with bullett missed the fellowe he aymed at and
> killed a chyld, and a woman great with chyld forthwith,
> and hurt an other man very soore.
> (*Letters*, ed. Jeayes, 23)

We can take the parenthetical provenance of these weapons ('having
borrowed their Callivers') to indicate a common practice, and further
remark the plural: a number of these expensive weapons was apparently
available. Garrard, in his *Arte of Warre*, warns against using too much
gunpowder in battle, which 'I account more apt for the show of a triumph
and wanton skirmish before Ladyes and Gentlewomen then fit for the field'
(5). Gawdy's anecdote from four years before testifies that the stage itself
could on occasion (as C.G. wrote of the battlefield) 'threaten death'; that
Alleyn's Tamburlaine really could knock them dead in the aisles. 'How they
will answere it', continues Gawdy's letter, 'I do not study ... but in
chrystyanity I am very sorry for the chaunce but God his judgementes ar not
to be sear[ched] nor enquired of at mannes handes. And yet ... ther never
comes more hurte then commes of fooling' (23).

That last remark (a parting shot) would come to be echoed in I.G.'s 1615
*Refutation* of Heywood's *Apology for Actors*, which interprets the players'
deliverance of Perin from the Spanish invader quite otherwise. For I.G., the
actors themselves were the cause, not the saviours, of the town's invasion,
the villains and not the heroes, 'as sometimes [God] useth the Divels
themselves for his instruments ... to teach them to be wary' (43). If the

'devyse in ther playe' that misfired in 1587 was from *Tamburlaine*, the didactic, lecturing militarism of its hero could hardly have been more aptly supplemented than if God himself had, in I.G.'s phrase, 'turned their present enterlude to a good use' (43).

The Arte of Warre and Theater of Warre were as integral as their anagram suggests. If the Elizabethan field of battle deployed the resources of the theatre, so too did the London playhouses stand in close proximity to the needs of wartime. The audience into which the player's loaded weapon fired was an audience steeled for war. There is 'no lyklyhood', as Gawdy wrote some six months later, 'but that we are like to have warres as well with ffraunce as Spayne' (39). Only a month beforehand, he had reported 'a generall mustering and a preparation for powder throughout all England' (18). It is to the application of the theatre to this 'generall mustering' that we shall now turn.

## War games

Fifteen years or so after the accident at the Rose, Gawdy wrote another letter featuring the invasion of wartime reality into theatrical fiction. 'Ther hath bene', he wrote in May 1602, 'great pressing of late, and straunge, as ever was knowen'. He relates that a proclamation had recently been published to the effect that 'no gentleman, or serving man shold any more be impressed' – the result, as he explains, of an embarrassing government tactic. For the week before,

> their meaning was that they shold take out of all ordinaryes all cheting companions, as suche as had no abylyty to lyve in suche places, all suche as they cold fynd in bawdy howses, and bowling allyes ... All the playe howses wer besett in one daye and very many pressed from thence, so that in all ther ar pressed ffowre thowsand besydes fyve hundred voluntaryes, and all for flaunders.
> (121)

Unfortunately, 'they did not only presse ... sarvingmen, but Lawyers, Clarkes ... knyghtes, and as it was credibly reported one Earle' (120-1). Gawdy's list of 'suche places' calls to mind the 'foure extreames' Nashe described a decade earlier, claiming that of 'gameing, following of harlots, drinking, or seeing a Playe', the last is 'the least' (1, 212). War interrupted these Londoners at their play as urgently as it had dampened the merriment in the Boar's Head: 'We must all to the wars' (*1 Henry IV*, 2.5.547).

That imperative held an especial force for the play's original audiences. The perpetuity of the European wars was pressed home for them by the regularity with which men were not only pressed into service overseas, but mustered and trained at home. *2 Henry IV* opens with news of 'fearefull musters, and prepar'd defence' (Prol. 12), 'this mustering in everie parte of the realme' that Riche described at the outset of his *Martial Conference* (1598, A4r). Such alarms and excursions were a continual feature of London life, and the press-gang at the 'playe howses' in 1602 was merely an extreme example. A similarly heavy-handed tactic was deployed in 1596, for example, when the 'aldermen of London posted guards on church doors during the Easter communion ... until they had persuaded enough men in the congregation to make up a force of 1000' for service in France (Hale, 1985a, 78). But just as the playhouses mirrored the theatrical nature of contemporary warfare, so too did the auspices under which England's national defence was organized.

This doubly-sourced theatricality is acknowledged in Robert Wilson's *Pleasant and Stately Moral of the Three Lordes and Three Ladies of London* (printed 1590). Allegorizing recent events, the play (like *The Cobbler's Prophecy*) attempts to redeem policy from its alien taint. Policy, indeed, is one of the eponymous Lords (the others are Pleasure and Pomp), and the play begins with his chivalric challenge in defence of the Ladies. Later, as the 1588 Armada approaches, Policy declares to his audience that he 'might advise ye now, | To carrie as it were a carelesse regard':

> As showes and solemne feastes,
> Watches in armour, triumphes, Cresset-lightes,
> Bonefiers, belles, and peales of ordinance,
> And *pleasure*, see that plaies be published,
> Mai-games and maskes, with mirth and minstrelsse,
> Pageants and school-feastes, beares, and puppit plaies,
> My selfe will muster upon *Mile-end* greene,
> As though we saw, and fear'd not to be seene.
> (F2v)

Policy's policy depends upon a theatrical deceit, 'as though we saw, and fear'd not to be seene', upon a careful artifice of 'carelesse regard'. His alliance with Pleasure (by which 'Mai-games and maskes' accompany his 'muster upon *Mile-end* greene') subtly intimates the festive overtones of the military training demanded by the times.

Mustering and training, as Boynton's definitive history of the Elizabethan Militia explains, were distinct occasions, the first being a formal inspection of troops, and the second a gradually effective rise to the challenges of modern war undertaken throughout Elizabeth's reign. The 1558 Militia Act was the first review of feudal obligations to national defence since 1285, and Goring has described the state of military decline to which England had sunk in the twenty years before Elizabeth's accession. It was not until 1573, and the inauguration of the Trained Bands (by which each county system-atically assembled a professionally trained regiment of civilian soldiers), that the administrative infrastructure was set in place to undertake a 'unitary military organisation' (Boynton, 90-125; Goring, 197). As late as December 1578, Geoffrey Gates – Blandy's collocutor in *The Castle* – argued that it 'were a small matter for the citie of *London* to have five thousand citizens of special manry, trained in arms, booked, devided into bands, and ready at a moment, if need were' (1579, 54). It was not until the 1580s that such an organization proved at least rudimentarily effective.

Between 1558 and 1588, a general muster of troops was held every three years, and more frequently in times of national emergency (Boynton, 14). Although in the immediate wake of the 1588 Armada training was relaxed, the 1590s saw renewed fears of invasion. After 1588, the Trained Bands were no longer held in reserve at home, but were increasingly sent overseas along with the less desirable echelons of society who had previously borne the brunt of foreign service (Boynton, 166-8). The General Muster was usually held during the Easter, Whitsun, Michaelmas, or Christmas festivals, and constituted 'something of a holiday in the country' (18-19), a context which lends dimension to the London aldermen's press-gang at Easter 1596. Training, too, for the Trained Bands 'was to be on holidays, or convenient working days' (114). Guillaume du Bellay's treatise, translated by Paul Ive as *Instructions for the Warres*, recommended 'that the Souldiers should be accustomed therein, as often as they might possible, especially uppon Sundays and holidays' (1589, 35), a tip perhaps borrowed from Machiavelli's *Arte of Warre* (translated by Whitehorne in 1588), which proposed that citizens should train on holidays 'to exercise them',

> For that where vilie on the holy daies thei stande idell in
> tipplyng houses, thei will go for pleasure to those
> exercises, for that the handlyng of weapons, as it is a
> goodly spectacle, so unto yong men it is pleasaunt.
> (ed. Henley, 54)

As early as 1549, Sir Thomas Wyatt the Younger's *Treatise on the Militia* had specified 'the tyme apointed of gatheringe togeather sometyme on this holyday, sometyme on that'.[11] The associations of such suspensions of the normal working cycle seem to have attended the occasions of both muster and training. Soldiers often turned up 'decked out in ribbons', Boynton tells us, and one group of officers was instructed to 'forbeare their fyne coortlyke sutes during the tyme of musters' (27). These festive overtones were made explicit in the scheme proposed in 1567 by William Pelham, by which the training of a corps of harquebusiers could be financed by members of the public paying to watch, replacing such traditional entertainments as 'Robin Hood' or 'Midsummer lords and ladies' (59). The scheme, though never adopted, is readily understandable. 'The basis of folk plays', as Bradbrook noted, 'is most frequently a fight or a mock fight', as the only surviving Robin Hood May Game testifies (1962, 109). The mock fight also formed an important part of training.

Queen Elizabeth was the honoured audience of a series of such mock fights and shooting competitions throughout the 1570s, themselves held on holidays (Boynton, 115-16; Bradbrook, 1962, 150). Stow's *Survay of London* records 'divers warlike shewes' that once accompanied the 'severall mayinges' of London's citizenry, as well as the 'marching watch' that would parade through the streets, with 'divers Pageantes, Morris dancers, Constables' around midsummer (1598, 73-5). These parades had waned since the reign of Edward VI, he comments, but 'some attempts [to revive them] have beene made thereunto, as in the yere 1585' (76): 1585, of course, was the year in which Elizabeth effectively declared war on Spain by committing her troops to the Dutch campaign. Such specifically military pageantry formed an integral part of the folk-rituals of holiday. With the rise of 'unitary military organisation', Stow's 'sportes and pastimes' (67) were elided with the pragmatism of national defence, now 'transmuted into sterner stuff' (Boynton, 18). That such festive origins were barely concealed is evident from a controversy that arose in Oxford in May 1598, when the mayor allowed a company of citizens to 'try their pieces' and return to the city in battle array. On their return they were attacked by a group of scholars on the grounds that the townsmen

> with drum and shot and other weapons, and men attired in women's apparel, brought into the town a woman be-decked with garlands and flowers, named by them the Queen of May. They also had Morrishe dances and other disordered and unseemly sports.[12]

The transition of these Oxford soldiers from battle formation to 'Morrishe dances' had European roots. In medieval Italy 'the first of May was a festival of the army', and their 'encampments became also the centers for ... fairs and markets' (Cope, 1973, 204). Stow noted that the 'sportes' described by the twelfth-century chronicler Fitzstephen 'have beene continued till our time, namely in stage playes' (1598, 69).

'See that plaies be published', advises Wilson's Policy in a play itself published in response to the attempted invasion it dramatizes. The 'showes' he describes – its 'Watches in armour', 'Mai-games', 'Bonefiers', and 'Cresset-lightes' – embrace at once the civic pageantry detailed by Stow (67-77); the 'plaies' of the popular stage (themselves profoundly informed by the rituals of the festive calendar); and the 'muster' Policy marries to the 'mirth and minstrelsse' of Pleasure. The etymology of *muster* declares its kinship with these other theatrical displays.[13] And though the spectacle of beribboned soldiers and finely suited officers was discouraged, a similar sense of sartorial occasion evidently persisted. Camden describes as a 'peculiar vanity of the *English* when they goe to the warres' their habit of marching 'with their Feathers waving, and glittering in their gay clothes' (4,

102). Holinshed's chronicle too describes how in July 1585, 'certeine souldiers were pressed' in London, 'furnished for the warres, and clothed in red cotes' (2, 1413), and how in the previous May they had 'mustered ... and skirmished before the queenes majestie' (1402). The demands of wartime enlisted (as Wilson's Policy says) 'Mai-games' and 'maskes' to the national effort. It is significant that with the passing of both Elizabeth and her wars, the Jacobean court found the opportunity to deploy in its masques the 'first large-scale employment of technical skills, other than for military purposes' (Yates, 1969, 78). Agnew quotes that description in his account of *The Market and the Theater*, and notes how 'doubly apt' it is: 'for the masque offered nothing less than a dramatistic equivalent of war, a symbolic assertion of sovereignty in which the mercenaries had changed from soldiers to players' (146). Setting aside its questionable portrayal of the largely conscripted English army as 'mercenaries', the change he describes is more accurately a 'dramatistic' *return* from Boynton's 'sterner stuff' of wartime.

Elizabethan soldiers, then, were instructed in the ways of theatrical disguise to achieve politic victories in the field; but their manner of training at home also partook of theatrical models. In the days before systematic uniforms, they dressed up in 'gay clothes' or 'red cotes'. They assembled on holidays, but 'theatergoing was holiday' too (Bevington, 1984, 37). Thus mustered, they would either march in a 'goodly spectacle', or present mock battles to entertain invited audiences, performances repeated in the alarums and excursions of the stage, some of whose play-texts were published as a constituent part of the war-effort itself. But though Wilson's Policy married Muster to May-game, other military advisers urged caution against too great an identification between them and real combat.

C.G.'s contemplation in 1596 of the 'easie matter' of playing '*Alexander* uppon the stages', as compared to the bullet-threatening field, occurs in a section that condemns 'unskilfull persons' who

> rejoyce at war because they know not what it is ...
> because in ordinary traynings, they use to skirmish for
> theyr learning: or in theyr May-games for delight; They
> thinke warre to be a matter of merriment.
> (D1v)

Riche makes the same point in his *Martiall Conference*, a dialogue between the experienced Captain Skill, 'trained up in the ... Low Countrey Services', and the foolish Captain Pill, 'only practised in Finsburie Fields' (1598, t.p.). The professional soldier-authors of the 1590s seem to have regarded the Trained Bands and ritually mustered citizen militia with the same slighting disdain as today attaches to members, respectively, of the Territorial Army and the Sealed Knot. Thus, to Captain Skill's example of Alexander's battle-hardened soldiers, Captain Pill replies that men 'were not so capable in those days as they are now':

for now there be some, if they have but seene Souldiers
trayned up on *Mile-end-greene*, or have borne office in a
Midsummer fight, or have bin at the fetching home a
Maie-pole, they wil by and by put themselves into a
Captaines trayne, and ... looke as big as *Haniball*.
(B3r)

Riche has Pill condemn his stupidity from his own mouth, but he recognizes
the common identification of festive forms with the needs of domestic
training, even as he stresses the gravity of the art of war. 'God blesse me,
my countrey and friendes', exclaims Captain Skill in the later *Souldiers
Wishe*, 'from his direction that hath no better *Experience* then what hee hath
atteyned unto the fetching home of a Maye-pole, at a Midsomer fighte, or
from a trayning at *Milende-Greene*' (1604, 33). Such views perhaps
stemmed from Riche's own experience in training London's civil defence at
Mile End (Cranfill and Bruce, 92), a post that apparently earned him ridicule
from his peers (F. Wilson, 81); but the difference he points up between Skill
and Pill also found expression on the stage.

When Ralph at last meets Mars in *The Cobbler's Prophesy*, for example
(a play based on Riche's first military *Dialogue*), he is initially dubious: 'Are
you he I cry you mercie, I promise you I tooke you for a morris dauncer
you are so trim' (874-5). The joke operates out of the flabby state of
English martial readiness the play addresses, and which is galvanized by
Mercury's regime of joining 'Armes and Learning' (1686). The 'true
souldier', as the anonymous *Choice, Chance, and Change* recounts, 'Pre-
fers a March before a Moris daunce' (1606, K2v); the same gibe informs the
criticism levelled by his nobles at the King in Marlowe's *Edward II*. His
disastrous military defeats in France, Ireland and the North are squarely
ascribed to the 'idle triumphes, maskes, lascivious showes | And prodigall
gifts' by which Edward has sapped his kingdom's strength in bestowing on
Gaveston (2.2.157-8). Mortimer contemptuously takes up the theme:

When wert thou in the field with banner spred?
But once, and then thy souldiers marcht like players,
With garish robes, not armor, and thy selfe
Bedaubd with golde, rode laughing at the rest,
Nodding and shaking of thy spangled crest,
Where womens favors hung like labels downe.
(182-7)

'Ballads and rimes', we are told, have been composed about Edward's
effeminate military weakness (178), and a 'Jig' written by the 'fleering
Scots' (188-9). Edward and his troops stand accused in other words –
C.G.'s – of thinking 'warre to be a matter of merriment', and the basis of
the complaint closely resembles the scorn with which Gabriel Harvey

contrasted the 'most profitable, and valorous *Mathematicall Arts*' of war with 'Tarletons trickes, or Greenes crankes, or Marlowes bravados'.[14] Of course, Marlowe's Tamburlaine clearly espouses the 'Mercuriall and Martiall Discourses' Harvey recommended (2, 108); but his later English king acknowledges the theatricality by which the 'busier pageant of war' made itself felt to the citizens of Elizabethan England, in the 'Mai-games and maskes' which underlay their 'ordinary traynings'. 'With their Feathers waving, and glittering in their gay clothes', these men rehearsed their new military roles. Elizabeth's soldiers, like Edward's, 'marcht like players'.

And fought like morris-men. The objective of Tamburlaine's rudiments of war is to 'make whole cyties caper in the aire' (*Two*, 3.2.61). In *2 Henry VI*, York relates how he has seen Jack Cade 'capre upright, like a wilde Morisco, | Shaking the bloody Darts, as he his Bells' (F 3.1.365-6). When Dekker recalled the 1588 Armada in *The Whore of Babylon* (1607), he saw Spanish 'dancers | Revell in steele' (4.3.15-16), and 'bravely plum'd' English, 'flockt togither in gay multitudes', as if for 'May-games, and for summer merriments' (5.2.172-8). Examples like these bear witness to the frequency with which 'bloud be-sprinkled warre' was depicted in terms of festival on stage,

> Who whilst he shewes wilde Friscoes in the streetes,
> And with his Gamballes, overthrowes huge buildings ...
> Shall as an Anticke in thy sight appeare.
> (*A Larum for London*, 1025-30)

Many critics have traced the formula in Shakespeare's plays, whether accounting the Cade rebellion 'anarchy by clowning' (C. Barber, 13); observing its 'vivid connection between dancing and bloody warfare' (Brissenden, 18); perceiving that in *Henry V* 'War is play. War is festive. War is a spectator sport' (G. Taylor, 1985, 134); or citing evidence from anthropology to the effect that 'la similitude de la guerre avec la fête est ... absolue' (Jones-Davies, 1990, 34). It should be emphasized, I think, that such associations were cemented for Shakespeare's generation in something more than a fictive conceit: that, in short, this is what war felt like to its participants.

Dekker's nostalgic portrait of Elizabeth's 'royal Court' at Tilbury has her substituting 'for revellers | (Treading soft measures) marching souldiers' (5.6.6-7). The Queen herself, however, had reversed that paradigm by grumbling that the Rouen campaign of 1591 seemed 'rather a jest than a victory' (Wernham, 1932, 173). Although both remarks erect a contrast between a mock fight and the real thing, John Hale records how blurred was the distinction in the field. 'The conquerors' entry into a hard-fought-for city', he relates, was 'only too likely to develop into the military form of Carnival or All Fools' Day, a sudden, obscene release from arrears of pay, hardship and fear into the rituals of misrule' (1985a, 195). Even when besieged cities held out, comparable rituals were performed. The citizens of Ostend, 'attracting the wonderment of the world' for their unprecedentedly extended defiance, were aware of their own celebrity and created a sort of holiday of their own: 'As every anniversary of its opening came round they celebrated it with a *Feu de joie* in which every imaginable weapon joined, even the women being ordered to strike up a din on their pots and pans' (Burne, 246).

Documentation like this lends texture to the stream of festive imagery critics have noted throughout *Henry V*. The Chorus's apologies for presenting battle in the 'Cock-Pit' of the 'Woodden O' (11-12), or Henry's vow to match rackets to the Dauphin's tennis-balls and 'play a set, | Shall strike his fathers Crowne into the hazard' (1.2.261-3), mediate between war and sport in a manner familiar from Coningsby's journal. The bloodbath of misrule Hale describes serves as an implicit rebuke to the Dauphin's slighting of Henry's invasion, as 'if we heard that England | Were busied with a Whitson Morris-dance' (2.4.24-5). The staged representation of war as carnival seems to have been true to military experience: but it was true, too, to the experience of those who remained at home, anticipating battle. In particular, the specific context of the muster provided a crucible for the fusion of player and soldier. William Rankins's acerbic critique of the 'spotted enormities' caused by plays (t.p.) reflects in its *Mirrour of Monsters* (1587) the accoutrements common to both.

Perhaps exploiting in his title their verbal kinship,[15] Rankins presents a monstrous muster in which players are cast as a hostile, subversive army 'sent from their captaine Sathan (under whose banner they beare armes)' (B2v). In order to 'to immitate *Mars*', he relates, Pride 'thought it best in compleat Armor richlie wrought in martiall maner to march to the Chappell' (C1r), namely 'The Theater & Curtine', which 'may aptlie be termed for their abhomination, the chappell *Adulterinum*'(B4v). Players, he complains, 'take upon them the persons of Heathen men imagining themselves ... to be the men whose persons they present, wherein by calling on *Mahomet* ... doo most wickedly robbe God of his honour' (G1v). It seems at least possible that Rankins has Alleyn's Tamburlaine in mind. Certainly in his first play, Marlowe's soldier dresses himself in 'compleat armor' (*One*, 1.2.42), and boasts that the 'God of war resignes his roume to me' (5.1.450); in his second – and immediately after the 'devyse' Gawdy's letter may have described in November 1587 – he indeed calls on Mahomet (*Two*, 5.1.186). The satire is anyway effective by reason of Rankins's shrewd depiction of players as men who in a general sense 'immitate *Mars*': 'The Banners were displayed, the Drummes strooke uppe, and the Trumpets sounded', 'to cal menne to Plaies' (C1v).

As Chambers notes, 'drums and trumpets were used as advertisements in the city' (1923, 2, 547); and Henslowe enters the purchase of a 'drome when to go into the contry' in February 1600 (130). 'Banners' or flags were likewise raised atop the playhouses to signify their readiness for performance. But military organization in sixteenth-century England also deployed 'Banners', 'Drummes', and 'Trumpets' to secure regimental solidarity. Each company employed an exemplary soldier to carry the ensign, which 'wee corruptly call *Antient*' (Markham, 1622, 73), a banner about which it could rally. It was in the later fifteenth century that the English army began to emulate the Swiss practice of using the beat of a drum and the melody of wind instuments, by which to marry an effective communication-system to that sense of loyalty (Farmer, 1945, 49-53). 'Droumes and fyffers' accompanied the march of a London muster from Mile End to Westminster in 1539 (Farmer, 1950, 66). 'The medieval tabor was increased in size to become the deep military side-drum' (Vale, 152). And while flageolets, tabors, and pipes were the 'simple instruments of the poor' (Fletcher and Stevenson, 10), the tunes of these early regimental marches were evidently those of 'popular songs and dances ... perhaps most likely to evoke some response from the troops' (Vale, 153). The 'Drummer and Fife' coveted of the English in *The Famous Victories of Henry the Fift* (*c.*1588) were integral to regimental organization;[16] but the 'drumme | And the vile squeaking of the wry-neckt Fiffe' which Shylock warns Jessica against heeding in *The Merchant of Venice* belong to festive 'maskes' (Q1 2.5.28-30). The common props of masker and soldier are clearly illustrated in two prints of the period. Whitney's *Choice of Emblemes* includes one dedicated to Norris, 'Collonell Generall of the Englishe Infanterie, in the lowe countries', which illustrates the posthumousness of valour (1586, 194). Two drummers are shown playing the instruments slung from their shoulders, with pavilion tents and marching pikemen in the background. The lefthand figure, carrying a smaller drum, and also playing on a 'wry-neckt Fiffe', bears a strong resemblance (though the engraving is cruder) to the accompanist, beating a drum and blowing a pipe, depicted on the title-page of *Kempes Nine Daies Wonder* (1600). Indeed, the signal difference between them is the more extravagant, plumed headgear – worn by the soldier.

The following chapter will consider the pedigree of the Elizabethan Braggart in detail. For the moment, it should be noted that the doubly theatrical nature of such fictive soldiers is often signalled by reference to the banners, drums and trumpets that Rankins derides. Thus both Spenser's Braggadochio and Strumbo in *Locrine* are each attended by servants named Trompart. Shakespeare's Pistol holds the rank of Ancient, and his quotation of old plays makes him a walking advertisement of performance. The humiliation of Parolles in *All's Well That Ends Well* is likewise concentrated on the loss of a drum, while his slandering of Captaine Dumaine overtly signals the common worlds of festive drama and military reality:

> ha's led the drumme before the English Tragedians: to
> belye him I will not, and more of his souldiership I know
> not, except in that Country, he had the honour to be the

Officer at a place called *Mile-end*, to instruct for the
doubling of files.
(4.3.270-74)

That play's strange collisions and collusions between fairy-tale ritual and the
unflinching details of disease and war (contrasts enhanced from *Henry V*)
are true to the 'doubling of files' it describes, and form a sustained 'dialogue
betweene the Foole and the Soldiour' (100-101). 'Tragedians' (271) and
'militarist[s]' (145) overlapped in contemporary perception: but why should
the association have proved so durable?

The apparent contradiction is addressed in an observation cited by the
theorist and historian of war Quincy Wright: 'To people fraught with
uncertainties the huddling together in the mass rhythm of war-time brings a
momentary resolution of many doubts and the sense of fulfilment' (287).
William McNeill has described the 'primitive reservoir of sociality' that was
tapped by the gradual systemization of drill (131). But George Wyatt's
*Treatise on the Militia* (post-1588) challenges McNeill's patronizing claim
that the 'powerful psychological impact' of such regimented training,
'creating sentiments of solidarity and esprit de corps', was but 'dimly
comprehended' by its inaugurators (126). 'When Leaders and Souldgers',
writes Wyatt, 'are dulie chosin and fitlie banded and combined togather with
mutual regards of contrie acquaintance naighbehud aliance and kindred, ther
both al commands are carried with more love, care and authoritie, and
obedience given with more cheire reddines and respect' (*Papers*, ed.
Loades, 65). Bearing in mind the festive infrastructure built into these early
military organizations, it is unsurprising to note that many of the plays that
dramatize the muster's recruitment lay stress upon their erosion of
distinctions between actor and audience, fiction and reality, insisting thereby
on the single unit of the playhouses' community, 'fitlie banded ... togather'.

That is the effect, as Jackson Cope has seen it, of the conscientiously
festive structure of the May-Day muster-scene in Beaumont's *Knight of the
Burning Pestle* (1607): 'we have *participated* as celebrants against [Lon-
don's mercantile] society' (1973, 210). A similar notion of participation also
informs G.P. Jones's discussion of *Henry V*, the 'most metadramatic of
Shakespeare's plays' as Thomas Berger calls it (92). 'Such insistence on the
participatory role of the audience is not generally characteristic of the
Elizabethan public playhouse', writes Jones (98), arguing for the Chorus
being an addition for a court performance subsequent to the 1600
publication of the (Chorus-less) Quarto. That hypothesis is damaged, however, both by the specifics of Act Five's reference to events in 1599, and the
limited accuracy of his rejection of theatre-audiences' 'participatory role'.

Sharon Tyler's 1987 reply to Jones's claim acutely discerns the artistic
consonance of the choric intrusion (stressing the difficulty of representing
the Battle of Agincourt) on the matter being dramatized (the difficulty of
fighting the battle in the first place). 'Despite the apology', she writes of Act

Four, '– because of the apology – the impression of small numbers, poor condition, an impossible undertaking, becomes inescapable' (74). This observation illuminates the persistent force of the play in modern productions; but if we consider neither an abstract nor a modern audience, and instead imagine the particular one addressed in 1599, the critic's comments on the gradually co-operative role enjoined of it take on a richer meaning. When she writes, for example, of the way in which the 'we' of Act One (we the players, 1.Ch.26) has become by Act Five the 'we' of both players *and* audience (5.Ch.42) (74); or of the fact that in Act Four 'the audience, like the army, must sit quiet and watchful while Henry moves through the camp' (73); or again that 'the ultimate supporting cast is seated beyond the stage' (74); her observations are both aesthetically and contextually true. For the 'now' of the Chorus ('Now entertaine conjecture ... O now, who will behold ...', 4.Ch.1-28) was also the 'Now' Camden recorded: 'Now was the state of *Ireland* in a manner desperate' (4, 137). Indeed, between Camden's criticism of those 'subtill kinde of enemies' who deliberately built up expectations of Essex's mission to Ireland (138), and his flat report that he returned 'sooner than all men thought' (143) – between the parameters provided, in fact, by the Chorus's benediction on Essex (5.Ch.29-34) – we read that 'rumors grew rife' of another armada, and 'Leavies therefore of men were sharply made in all places' (142). Many thousands of men – Stow numbers the muster at 30,000 (1631, 789) – were trained at Mile End in August, and not stood down until September. We need only recall Gawdy's report, from May 1602, of 'the playe howses ... besett in one daye and very many pressed from thence', to discern with what force the following comments would have struck those audiences: 'Like Henry, the Chorus is a man whose job is to rouse his hearers to unusual effort' (Goldman, 59); '*Henry V* is a play concerned to force upon its audience a creative participation far more active than usual' (Barton, 1994, 217); *Henry V*'s 'non-combatant audience' is 'inducted into combat duty' (Altman, 19).

The 1599 invasion-scare was not, however, universally believed:

> insomuch as the vulgar sort abstained not from scoffing speeches, saying that in yeere 88, that invincible armado arrived from *Spaine*, and now this yeare arrived another armado invisible; and they muttered that if such May games had been played in the beginning of May, they might have beene thought more sutable.
> (Camden, 4, 147)

Once again the prompt associations are made – here held as contrasts – between emergency wartime mustering and 'May games'. To the same tense summer belong the first performances of Dekker's *The Shoemakers' Holiday* (entered in *Henslowe's Diary* in July 1599), a play which, in the opinion of one critic, maintains the same, contrastive association. 'Feasting and gaiety represent both the answer to human hostilities and the reward provided by brotherly love' (Burelbach, 105). The 'confraternité universelle' the play celebrates (106), however, constitutes the manner of its waging, as well as the rewards of victory, as the turn effected there in Lacy's account of London's musters demonstrates:

> The men of Hartfordshire lie at Mile end,
> Suffolke, and Essex, traine in Tuttle fields,
> The Londoners, and those of Middlesex,
> All gallantly prepar'd in Finsbury,
> With frolike spirits, long for their parting hower.
> (1.1.58-62)

These 'frolike spirits' underpin the variously common ground that has been observed between this play and the 'festival terms' (Rabkin, 286) of its rival at the Globe, *Henry V*. Both plays observe, adapt and partake in the 'busier pageant' on London's stage that summer, whose 'ultimate supporting cast' was indeed seated beyond it. For, from the 'May-Morne' of the King's youth (1.2.120), via the 'Whitson Morris-dance' of his invasion (2.4.25), to the 'fellowship' of the 'Feast of *Crispian*' (4.3.39-40), *Henry V* rests on the festive infrastructure of the training that supporting cast was being urged to perform – and not merely by Shakespeare's Chorus.

*Henry V* achieves an extraordinary artistic correlative to those sentiments of solidarity such training was embryonically creating. Henry's rhetoric of the few, by which so much is owed by so many to a 'band of brothers' (4.3.60), catches at the very vocabulary of Wyatt's judgement of the 'cheire reddines and respect' earned 'when Leaders and Soldgers are dulie chosin and fitlie banded togather with mutual regards'. Wyatt's words occur in a passage which places training within a sequence of military priority that holds true to the mustering spirit of *Henry V*. Firstly, honour is to be placed in God, 'next is placed and is sorting with the other that shild of a good cause under which men fight with greater confidence and alacritie'. Though such pieties of war theory – continually observed by Shakespeare's King – are not peculiar to the circumstances of the muster, it is interesting that Wyatt lays stress on their bonding effects among the soldiery: with such 'provitions', he continues, 'the wars are more strongly united intertained and carried'. When a citizen-army is mustered in this way, 'their coragise wax invincible that unarmd sumtimes we see equal the virtue of th'enimise'. Though the word had yet to be coined, this is a definition of morale, and forms a precedent to Henry's rebuke to Westmoreland ('The fewer men, the greater share of honour', 4.3.22), which culminates in his festive invocation of the 'fellowship' of St Crispin's Day. That unifying emphasis is Wyatt's too: 'Like wise by Neighbours Assotiates and frends the removinge of impediments and the gaininge of succours both bringe more authoritie and comoditie to Armes'. Scene after scene of *Henry V* urges a comparable 'removinge of impediments' from among the social and generic range of its cast.

The first we see of the play's 'Irregular Humorists', for example, concerns Bardolph's sustained mediation between Nym and Pistol: 'What, are ... you friends yet?' (2.1.3). After Bardolph's bribes ('I will bestow a breakfast to make you friendes', 11-12) and threats ('By this sword ... [an'] thou wilt be friends be frends', 98-9), it is Falstaff's death which at last fulfils Pistol's pledge that 'friendshippe shall combyne, and brotherhood' (109) – 'Yoke-fellowes in Armes, let us to France' (2.4.50-1). Bardolph's role is next assumed by Captain Gower, who steers a diplomatic path between Henry's Irish, Scots and Welsh captains: 'Gentlemen both, you will mistake each other' (3.3.77). The national speech-prefixes used in the Folio throughout the scene suggest affinities with contemporary European campaigns, where the 'sundrie nations' of coalition armies often led to 'disjoyntment of affections' between them (see above, p. 78). Immediately succeeding the Boy's joshing account of 'these three Swashers' (3.2.27), however, the scene inherits its comic tone, and bridges the span between the national and the parochial. Gower considers Macmorris 'a very valiant Gentleman', and to Fluellen '*Jamy* is a marvellous falorous Gentleman' (3.3.11-22): the frictions between them are contained in – or at least postponed by – what Wyatt had called the 'mutual regards of contrie acquaintance naighbehud aliance and kindred'. The pattern repeats on the night before Agincourt, when instead of 'three Swashers', 'three Souldiers' nervously anticipate the morning. Again, a comic framework holds 'a Quarrell betweene us', here between the king disguised and Michael Williams (4.1.204); and again the scene contains (or postpones) that quarrel: 'Be friends, you English fooles, be friends, wee have French Quarrels enow', as John Bates, after Bardolph and Gower, insists (220-21).

Of course, in each of these cases, Wyatt's 'removinge of impediments' between 'Neighbours Assotiates and frends' is compromised and darkened by the play's inescapable ambivalence. Anne Barton has definitively demonstrated the frustration of comic expectation in Williams's 'suppressed anger and resentment' (1994, 217); Paul Jorgensen has likewise restored the troubling force of Macmorris's complaint regarding his 'nation' (1956a, 77-81); and of the three 'sworne brothers in filching' (3.2.45-6), '*Bardolfe* and *Nym* ... are both hang'd' (4.4.69), bequeathing to Pistol the bruised solemnity of his braggart-veteran role. Wyatt's 'naighbehud aliance' becomes a 'Royall fellowship of death' (4.8.103). Yet all these frissons gain their purchase from the contrast they each effect with the structures of festive solidarity to which the play repeatedly appeals. The co-operative and co-opted participation made of its audiences emulates the ritual of London's 1599 musters, fusing military duty with a sense of theatre. That Elizabethan military service so often resembled theatrical participation, whether as spectator or player, provides a historical basis for the sense of collective intimacy between players and audience that was such a feature of the play's inaugural performance at the reconstructed Globe in 1997.[17]

*Henry V* claims its place in a series of Elizabethan dramatizations of this perennial preoccupation, from the 'mouster' paraded in *Horestes* (1567),[18] via the comic pressings of Strumbo in *Locrine* (1595) and Dericke in *The Famous Victories of Henry the Fift* (c.1588), to the darker humour of Falstaff's pricking in *2 Henry IV*. That so many parties to these scenes are braggart soldiers cements the kinship of player and soldier we have traced, a kinship elaborated in Marston's *Histrio-Mastix*, composed c.1598. Dramatizing the Elizabethan commonplace of war's natural cycle (see above, p. 21), its allegorical sequence of acts (Peace, Plenty, Pride, War ...) is ingeniously complemented by the fortunes of a company of players at the mercy of those circumstances. Marston's fictional troupe is formed in Peace; in time of Plenty they perform at a 'Morrice-daunce of neighbours' (C2v); they are then 'growne so proud' that they '*fall a sleepe on the Stage*' (E1v), and 'Fier-eied *Warre*' enters to correct and punish their complacence. For the first and only time in the play, the act next begins by immediately focusing attention on the players, once the choric abstractions have had their say – in this case an apocalyptic litany of 'grimme Warre' (F1v). The company's leader, Belsh, then enters '*setting uppe billes*', 'Text billes for Playes' (F2r). Belsh's name suggests kinship with Shakespeare's Sir Toby, and his actions certainly smack of the 'Cakes and Ale' disparaged in *Twelfth Night* (2.3.111). Chambers, for example, quotes a letter that reproves 'Histriones, common playours' who 'speciallye on holydayes, sett up bylles' (1923, 2, 547); and Rankins's *Mirrour of Monsters* bemoans how 'the streetes of *Terralbon* were stuck with their bylles, and almost every post was a witness to these pompous proceedings' (C2r). But if Shakespeare's Belch was cousin-german to Falstaff, for Marston's Belsh the boot was on the other foot.

For to him there enters a recruiting Captain who gives him 'presse money' to join his ranks. 'What Playes in time of Warres?' asks the Captain, in a disdain for Belsh's profession shared by such as Harvey and Rankins. Marston's Captain substitutes the voice of national emergency for Falstaff's unscrupulous profiteering. But just as Rankins had found grounds for his critique of players in their affinity with soldiers; and just as Harvey had deployed images of the theatre to express his contempt for Marlowe's distraction from the 'busier pageant upon the stage'; so the exchanges Marston presents between Captain and Players bristle with double-meanings that at once distinguish between their roles and confirm their close kinship.

'Hold sira', warns the Captain when Belsh explains his play-bills, 'Ther's a new plott': the pun knowingly elides the back-stage abstracts of fictional narration known as plots or plats with the '*Plattes, Mappes,* and *Models*' of the Art of War (Digges, 1579, 143). When the Captain offers Belsh his press-money, this fictionalized Henslowe misinterprets it as the entrance fee to his theatre: 'How many meane you shall come in for this?' 'Presse me', he then protests, 'I am no fit Actor for th'action'. But the Captain replies in kind, by quibbling on plays and glaives: 'Text billes must now be turn'd to Iron billes' (F2r). When Belsh is then joined on stage by his company, the player Gulsh inadvertently suggests his profession's comparison with soldiery by pleading that 'we are a full company'. 'If these soldiers light upon our playing parrell', comments Belsh (in another echo of Henslowe's Diary) 'they'le strout it in the field, and flaunt it out' (F2v). The player Gut's complaint at being pressed into service is one which brings this chapter full-circle. 'Alasse sir, we Players are priviledg'd', he implores,

> Tis our Audience must fight in the field for us,
> And we upon the stage for them.
> (F2v)

This back-stage exchange is typical of the metadramatic techniques by which the muster, and more largely war itself, found dramatic expression in the Elizabethan period. Soldiers were encouraged to behave like players on the battlefield, by dissembling intents or by dressing up. Meanwhile, players represented soldiers on their stages, mimicking in some cases their counterparts' player-like behaviour, as in Joan's policy in *1 Henry VI*. Yet Marston dissolves a further distinction here, that of the privilege on which Gut insists. *Histrio-Mastix*'s mordant wit lies in its supply of a third plane in-between: its players play players privileged to play the soldier on the stage, who are forced against their will, to play the soldier 'in the field'. The press-money offered by the Captain is indeed a sort of entrance-fee, as Belsh initially thinks, but to a theatre of war, not to a wartime theatre: 'A shrewd mornings worke for Players', as Clout comments. The last we see of Belsh's company in the act confirms his suspicions about the fate of his costumes. 'Enter a Captaine with Souldiers:', reads the stage-direction, 'the Souldiers having most of the Players apparrell; and bringing out the Players among'st them' (G1r). These considerable ironies are then compounded by what one of the soldiers then declaims – the last word in the play's 'dialogue betweene the Foole and the Soldiour':[19]

> Come on Players, now we are the Sharers
> And you the hired men: Nay you must take patience,
> Slid how do you march?
> Sirha is this [how] you would rend and teare the Cat
> Upon a Stage, and now march like a drown'd rat?
> Looke up and play the *Tamburlaine*: you rogue you.
> (G1r)

This is the army, Mr Jones: the sergeant-majorly tone is richly acerbic in voicing that last command. It is as if the debt incurred by Elizabethan drama to the Art of War, embodied in Marlowe's model of the modern major-general, were at last being called in; as if the Scourge of God were at last rounding on his own representation.

Marston's account of the fortunes of Belsh's company was both accurate and proleptic. The reversal of which his soldier speaks, 'now we are the Sharers | And you the hired men', gains nuance from the probability that soldiers themselves seem commonly to have invaded the stages of the time as 'hired men'. A 'probability' because decisive evidence on this point is sparse. The urgent circumstance of the Elizabethan muster lends support to Richard Southern's hypothesis of an 'undefined number of supernumeraries' assisting in the battle-scenes of Pickeryng's *Horestes*, 'possibly drawn from a group of local men-at-arms' (497), and should temper one critic's dismissal of it as 'wishful thinking' (MacIntyre, 33). Certainly the dumb show that precedes the fifth act of *Gorboduc* (1562) seems unambiguous:

> First the drommes and fluites began to sound, during which there came forth upon the stage a company of hargabusiers and of armed men all in order of battaile. These, after their peeces discharged, and that the armed men had three times marched about the stage, departed; and then the drommes and fluits did cease.[20]

True, the third act's dumb show includes a 'company of mourners' (240), and it would of course be inappropriate to imagine these supernumeraries genuinely stricken. On the other hand, 'a company of hargabusiers' sounds more professional than, say, the way in which the Lord Admiral's Men 'borrowed their Callivers': the army used 'drommes and fluites', as we have seen, to regulate marching, and *Gorboduc* directs its 'armed men' to march about the stage to their tune. Though the stage-business is explicitly symbolic, it is difficult to picture merely symbolic 'hargabusiers'.

If *Gorboduc*'s stylization, 'in order of battaile', resembles the muster's parade, the 'lively battel' demanded in *Horestes* savours more of the mock fight such training was beginning to involve: 'Go and make your lively battel', reads one of Pickeryng's stage-directions, 'and let it be long eare you can win the citie' (line 725). It was in 1567 (the year *Horestes* was published) that Pelham devised his scheme by which soldiers might be financed to train by the income generated by audiences of their training. Such manoeuvres formed part of the system eventually adopted by the government. If Southern's hypothesis holds, the need for extensive rehearsal would be effectively reduced if it were local men-at-arms which the stage-direction addressed, and might explain its markedly direct tone, 'make *your* lively battel', so to say 'now do *your* bit'.

Both *Gorboduc* and *Horestes* predate the construction of London's public theatres. But stage-directions such as those found in *Sir John Oldcastle*, describing the entrance of insurrectionists 'prepared in some filthy order of warre' (1194); or the 'scurvy march' bidden by Chettle in *The*

*Tragedy of Hoffman* (performed 1602)[21] imply a convention recognized by audience and company alike in the playhouses. Likewise, in *Clyomon and Clamydes* (printed 1599), Alexander the Great enters 'as valiantly set forth as may be, and as many souldiers as can':[22] as can be simulated, or as can be hired? Certainly, in the seventeenth century, members of the local militia would on occasion be paid to attend funerals, to lend status to the deceased (Gittings, 152). The gusto with which Marston's soldier gloats over the reversal of sharers and hired men would gain a dimension consonant with the scene's larger ironies if such were the case indeed. Players, after all, *had* accompanied Leicester's 1585 expedition to the Low Countries, though not as the soldiers Marston turns them into.[23] The London theatres for which his player Gulch touts, when he 'steppes on the Crosse, and cryes a Play' ('Come to the big Towne-house and see a Play') (B4v), were in truth the sites of the London musters – and not just on that single afternoon in 1602.

'Is this More fields to muster in?', asks the jovial porter in *Henry VIII* (1613) (5.3.32-3), equating the crammed audience at the Globe with the press of the King's press. The line serves as a further reminder that 'the Curtaine in Moorefeildes', as a document from 1601 calls it (Halliwell-Phillipps, 415), and the Theater by Finsbury Fields to the north stood within sight of the very scenes they so often dramatized. Finsbury Fields, as one historian puts it, 'bears a definite relation to the military history of England', since it constituted 'the drilling-ground of the trained bands', the site of 'periodical musters and inspections of the city troops' (Ordish, 36). Captain Pill, Riche tells us in his *Martiall Conference*, is 'only practised in Finsburie Fields' (1598, t.p.). When Ralph makes his comic entrance in *The Knight of the Burning Pestle*, 'with a forked arrow through his head' (5.276.SD), he burlesques that of the wounded Clifford in *3 Henry VI* (Q.2.6.SD), just as his speech guys the dead Andrea's opening words to *The Spanish Tragedy*. The wit of Beaumont's parody derives in part from the proximity it remembers between London's drilling-grounds and the playhouses in which those old military roles were first played. After being elected 'Lord of The May' (297), and 'chosen captain at Mile End' (300), Ralph 'took ... up my bow and shaft in hand, | And walked into Moorfields' (314-15), where he is struck by Death's arrow – presumably fired from the archery ranges in the neighbouring Finsbury Fields. A similar accident befell the soldier in *The Trial of Chivalry*, who, he tells us, received his limp 'as I was fighting in S. Georges fields, and blind Cupid ... tooke his shaft, and shot me right into the left heele, and ever since, Dick Bowyer hath been lame' (C1v). St George's Fields, to the south of Southwark, was the site of the 'first theatre south of the river... known to historians as Newington Butts' (Schoenbaum, 136); it was also, as one of John Chamberlain's letters details, the site of an emergency muster, in August 1599.[24]

Both plays find such perils ludicrous. On at least one wartime occasion, however, they were real enough. The military surgeon William Clowes recorded the incident, 'at a great mustering and training up of soldiers at

Mile end greene, neer London', in his *Profitable and Necessarie Booke of Observations* (1596): 'Amongst those bands of trained men, there was appointed a certaine number of Archers ... it chanced in their shooting at a marke, about six or seaven score off, by misfortune one of their arrowes did hit a gentlemans servant ... into the outside of his left leg' (65).[25] The accident took place', he writes, 'a few yeeres past' – at about the same time, perhaps, that Clifford first made his entrance, 'wounded, with an arrow in his neck', a few score yards from 'the archers of *Finsburie*' (1.1.49).

That last phrase belongs to a sequence of such familiar references by which Jonson's revising pen transformed the vaguely Italianate setting of *Every Man In His Humour* (1598, Q 1601) to the vivid London 'in which he had really first conceived it' (F 1616).[26] It is striking that many of those revisions concern the city's wartime training grounds. The scenes of the servant Musco's comic plotting, 'disguised like a soldier' (Q 2.1.SD), consolidate in revision the overlap of player and soldier they present: in F, now called Brainworm, he announces his plan to intercept his master as he walks 'over *More-fields*, to *London*' (F 2.2.9). At once the site of London's musters and of the theatre (the Curtain) in which the play was first performed, Moorfields was also the area where (as we shall shortly see) sometimes fraudulent war-veterans begged a meagre living. Jonson's revisions repeatedly feature such ironic equations. Musco's dubious war-service sounds, in Q, 'very strange, and not like those a man reads in the Romane histories' (4.1.68); 'or sees, at *Mile-end*,' continues F (4.6.73). It is only Brainworm whose relish at deceiving his master extends to crowing that 'Hee will hate the musters at Mile-end for it, to his dying day' (F 2.5.142-4). Again, the ironic praise levelled at Stephano's military career in Q – 'as I remember you serv'd on a great horse, last generall muster' (3.2.139-40) – is pitched in F towards a wry topicality: 'as I remember your name is entred in the artillerie garden?' (3.5.149-50). The topicality was temporal as well as geographic, for the revised version of Jonson's play was published in 1616 (at the outset of his *Works*), the same year that Dekker published his ode to the 'New-founded schoole of soldiery', *The Artillery Garden* (D2v). What was originally an Elizabethan joke (in the style of Riche's Pill and Spill) at the expense of those who 'thinke warre to be a matter of merriment', here becomes a Jacobean gibe at the institutionalizing of peacetime defence, now that – as Dekker put it – 'Boyes blush that Men should loyter out an Age, | Never to heare Drum beate, but on a stage' (C2v). But the Artillery Yard already stood beyond Bishopsgate in the 1590s: newly-cast cannon were tested there, and gunnery skills perfected (Holmes, 52-3), probably within earshot of the alarums and excursions which seem otherwise to have been staple fare at the Curtain, and from which Jonson took pains to distance himself in the Prologue he added to the play for the 1616 publication.

It is difficult not to be reminded of the Chorus to *Henry V* – perhaps itself first played at the Curtain – when reading Jonson's Prologue. The allusions (if that is what they are) usefully illustrate the distinct effects shaped by each play from the material of a common theme. Shakespeare's Chorus apologizes for the 'foure or five most vile and ragged foyles' (4.49) with which Agincourt is to be represented, eliding the play's theatrical resources with its King's military ones – and each is lent reinforcements by the audience. Jonson's Prologue punctures those exhortations, 'with three rustie swords, | And helpe of some few foot-and-halfe-foote words' (9-10). The Chorus invests in the matériel common to company and troupe – 'the nimble Gunner | With Lynstock now the divellish Cannon touches, | *Alarum and Chambers goe off* ...' (3.32-3). The Prologue sees mere stage-effect, a 'nimble squibbe ...to make afear'd | The gentlewomen', as clumsy a device as the 'roul'd bullet' (17-18) or cannon-ball used to simulate thunder (and which was itself perhaps borrowed from the Artillery Yard). Where Shakespeare enlists his audience to an effort of military participation, Jonson, spurred perhaps by his own experience of military service, perceives only the empty theatricality of such training. Yet both plays exploit and explore the common ground at Moorfields between playhouse and muster, Curtain and *Curtine*.

For the very name of the Curtain, the second custom-built London playhouse, erected in 1577, and shaped 'very like a castle keep' (Linnell, 37), brought with it military associations. It has been generally accepted that its name derived from the land, on the northern fringes of the city, upon which it was built, named 'the Curten' as early as 1538 (Halliwell-Phillipps, 416). But to this ascription should be added the fact that the earliest recorded usage of the word 'curtain' specifically to mean that 'part of the wall which connects two bastions, towers, gates' (*OED* sb. 4) dates from 1569, just eight years before 'the Curtaine in Moorefeildes' was built. The gloss of modern jargon it came to reflect is evidenced both by its inclusion in Barret's index of military terms in 1598 ('a French word, is the long wall running levell from bulwarke to bulwarke', 250), and by its appearance among John Davies's earlier satiric parroting of a pretended war veteran's 'warlike wordes' ('Of parapets, curteynes and Pallizadois ... he prates').[27] The Swiss tourist Thomas Platter visited the Curtain in 1599, and his account of 'diverse nations and an Englishman struggling together',[28] is cited by one theatre- historian as evidence that this playhouse 'flourished upon shows that ... consisted entirely of battles' (Linnell, 22) – the sort of shows to which Jonson's Prologue seems to have been retrospectively aimed. The Curtain also seems the most likely venue for the performance of 'the overthrow of *Turnholt*', that was 'acted upon a Stage' in October 1599. The 'seconding' of Francis Vere in that production would gain retrospective weight in Hexham's account of his bearing at the Siege of Ostend three years later, in the posthumous *Commentaries*. If Vere's 'Personate' trod the stage of the Curtain in 1599, the 'Personated' without doubt trod upon a similar construct in the field:

> Upon the curtain of the old town, between *Sand-Hil* and a
> redoubt called *Schottenburch*, a most dangerous place,
> which he feared most, being torn and beaten down with
> the sea, and the enemies Cannon, Sir *Francis Vere* stood
> himself with Captain *Zeglin*, with six weak companies to
> help to defend it.
> (167)

Vere fought 'Upon the curtain' of Ostend, 'with six weak companies';
Fynes Moryson's *Itinerary* counted 'foure or five Companyes of players' in
London, but the turn of his phrase suggests the military context of their
plays, 'to which and to many musterings and other frequent spectacles, the
people flocke in great nombers' (quoted in Gurr, 1980, 10).

Wartime invaded the stages of Elizabethan London, and that invasion was
itself incorporated into the plays presented there. Conversely, the resources
of the theatre were adopted (notably by Vere himself) in the waging of
those wars. Marston's 'Souldiers having most of the Players apparrell; and
bringing out the Players amongst them' is as succinct an expression of
Elizabethan theatres of war as one might hope to find. The Soldier's
dizzying rebuke there to the Players' privilege ('Looke up and play the
*Tamburlaine*') endorses C.G's warning of the 'easie matter to play ...
*Alexander* upon the stages: but it is somewhat to follow them in the field,
where every bullet doth threaten death'. But it also sharpens another of
Jonson's revisions to *Every Man In His Humour*. So good was Musco's
disguise as a soldier, we are told, 'thou wouldst have sworne he might have
beene the Tamberlaine, or the Agamemnon of the rout' (Q 3.2.20-22); it is
the 'Serjeant-*Major*, if not Lieutenant-*Coronell* to the regiment' we could
have sworn we had seen in Brainworm's performance (F 3.5.21-23). That
substitution enacts the 'hurly-burly' blur of fictive and actual war that forms
the basis of Heywood's *Apology for Actors*, either composed or published
at the same time as Jonson's revisions were probably made.[29]

Heywood's account of the theatres of Ancient Rome lend the authority of
classical precedent to the equation. He relates that Julius Caesar 'raised an
Amphitheater, *Campo Martio*, in the field of *Mars*', which 'farre excelled
*Pompeyes*, as *Pompeyes* did exceed that of *Caius Curios*' (D2v); 'Nero
erected a magnificent Theater in the field of *Mars*' (D4r). Sadler's 1572
translation of Vegetius explains that

> the aunchient Romaines, whiche by so manye warres and
> continuall perylles, came to be excellent in all warre
> matters, chose the field *Campus Martius*, harde by the
> ryver *Tyber*, that in the same when they had lefte
> exercising their weapons they mighte washe of cleane all
> the sweate and duste.
> ([5]r)

The playhouses of Elizabethan London stood in a similar relationship to its own fields of Mars, whether the Theater and Curtain, near the exercise of weapons in Moorfields; the Rose, Swan and Globe, 'harde by the ryver', 'on the other side of *Tyber*', as the player Histrio says to Captain Tucca in *Poetaster* (3.4.194); or the theatre at Newington Butts in (the martial-sounding) St George's Fields. While Morysine's Frontinus itemized the theatrical 'traynes and disceytes' of the front line (F1v), Sadler's Vegetius drew a parallel from the home front: 'The cunning stage plaiers do not leave of their exercises, loking onlye for prayse and commendation of the common people: a souldiour then ... ought not to ceasse, discontinewe or bee slacke in the exercise of chivalrie' ([24]v).

In a culture that perceived drill as rehearsal, combat as performance, and both the *Theorike and Practike of Moderne Warres* as representation, it is peculiarly appropriate that Shakespeare's Globe, its timbers so often the representative cockpit of the world at war it surveyed, should itself twice have fallen victim to collisions between the real and the fictional. For on 29 June 1613, a stage-direction in *Henry VIII* proved as suddenly actual as the loaded gun that may have interrupted *Tamburlaine* in 1587: '*Drum and Trumpet, Chambers dischargd* '. 'What warlike voyce, | And to what end is this?', asks Wolsey (1.4.49-52). And down went all before them. Like Ralph in Beaumont's *Knight of the Burning Pestle* (Q 1613), the burning down of the Globe was a belated casualty of wartime theatre, and of the shared apparatus of player and soldier.

'Come on Players, now we are the Sharers | And you the hired men': Marston's extraordinary meditation on the mutual duties of soldier and player proved proleptic of the fate in store for the Second Globe too. For in 1642 all the theatres were ordered to be closed in deference to another 'busier pageant' abroad, so long as

> the distracted Estate of England, threatned with a Cloud
> of Blood, by a Civill Warre, call for all possible meanes to
> appease and avert the Wrath of God appearing in these
> Judgements ... and whereas publike Sports doe not well
> agree with publike Calamities, nor publike Stage-playes
> with the Seasons of Humiliation.[30]

In 1643/44, a former sharer in a theatrical company voiced the complaint that 'our Hired-men are dispersed', and then resonantly added, 'some turned Soldiers and Trumpeters'.[31]

## Notes

1.  Keegan (1976), 16.
2.  *Queene Elizabethes Achademy*, ed. Furnivall (1869), 5-12.

3. Frontinus, tr. Morysine (1539), G8v.

4. Collins, (1746), 2 , 136.

5. *The Art of War*, ed. Hanzhang (1993), 101.

6. *Works*, ed. Lucas (1927), 3, 267-92 (lines 89-92).

7. Webster seems to have revisited the lines in his contribution to the 1615 Overburian Characters (ed. Paylor, 47-8): the 'Worthy Commander in the Warres ... knowes, the hazards of battels, not the pompe of Ceremonies are Souldiers best theaters'.

8. See *1 Henry IV*, 1.2.71-2; *King Lear*, 3.7.53; *Macbeth*, 5.7.1-2. See also *Edward III*, 5.1.143-5.

9. The scene bears a disturbing resemblance to a modern anthropological study of war, which observes that hostilities among other primates are 'often carried to such an extreme that they end in the complete destruction of the objects of common desire' (Bramson and Goethals, 85).

10. Bullough, 3, 24-5; *1 Henry VI*, ed. Dover Wilson, (1952), xvi-xxi.

11. *The Papers of George Wyatt*, ed. Loades, 169-70.

12. *Historical Manuscripts Commission Calendar of the Marquis of Salisbury* (1883-1940), 8, 201-3.

13. 'ME. *mostre, moustre* a. OF. *mostre, moustre* fem.(later in learned form *monstre*, fem., whence mod. F. *montre*) ... a com Rom, verbal noun f. *mostrare* to show :- L. *monstrare*', *OED*, 'Muster, *sb* 1'. See n.15.

14. Harvey, *Works*, ed. Grosart, 2, 74; 115.

15. 'OF. *monstre* (= Pg., It. *monstro*), ad L. *monstrum* monster, something marvellous ... f. root of *monere* to warn.', *OED*, 'Monster, *sb*. and *a*'. Riche's description of the duties of 'The Munster master' (1587, F3r) perhaps inadvertently invokes the Irish destination of so many mustered Englishmen.

16. Bullough, 4, 331, line 1100.

17. Mark Rylance felt that intimacy in terms of the current and charge of electricity: 'When I was playing Henry V ... I ran down to the front to deliver "Once more unto the breach, dear friends" and I could sense that the groundlings were ready to jump on stage and follow my charge ... you can sense that electric current between stage and yard' (*The Daily Telegraph*, 27 January 1998, 17).

18. *Three Tudor Classical Interludes*, ed. Axton (1982), line 454.

19. *All's Well That Ends Well*, 4.3.100-101.

20. *Specimens of ... Drama*, ed. Manly (1974), 2, 258.

21. *The Tragedy of Hoffman*, MSR, line 1127.

22. *Clyomon and Clamydes*, MSR, lines 358-9.

23. See Rosenberg (1955), 305; Mithal (1958); Bald (1959); Strong and van Dorsten (1964), 84-7.

24. *Letters*, ed. McLure (1939), 1, 83.

25. The next case Clowes details relates the cure of a man who 'received a notable wound in his head ... by a fall out of the gallery in the Beare

garden, at that time when all the gallery there did fall downe' (68).

26. *Every Man In His Humour*, ed. Seymour-Smith (1979), xxviii.

27. Davies, *Poems*, ed. Krueger (1975), 139. See also Digges (1579), 165.

28. *Thomas Platter's Travels*, tr. Williams (1937), 166.

29. 'The probabilities favor 1607-8 and 1612-13' (Gabriele Jackson, cited in Barton, 1984, 353). *An Apology for Actors* was printed in 1612, and its reference to 'some 12 yeares' since the invasion of Perin in 1595 dates its composition to circa 1607-08.

30. Bentley (1941-68), 2, 690.

31. Bentley, (1984), 65.

CHAPTER FOUR

# Rumours of War

*'In the mighty British Army*
*Rumour is the only issue*
*That arrives at units larger*
*Than it leaves the Base Supply Park'*[1]

The last decade of the sixteenth century opened amidst renewed fears in England of an imminent Spanish invasion. Convening on St George's Day 1590, the Privy Council dispatched a series of letters ordering the placing of 'all such forces both of the old garrisons and newe' in Ireland, and 'all the forces [in Devon and Cornwall] ... in a readines for the defence of the same against whatsoever may fall out'. The measures were taken in response to the reported sighting of a 'certeine fleete of shippes' off Cape Finisterre. Over a week later it transpired 'that the number of shippes so seene were hulkes laden with salte', blown off course and seeking to 'passe homewarde rounde about Ireland and Scotland'. Not only was this a false alarm, 'by reason of the mistie weather', but at the same time as it was being sounded in London, equally urgent and groundless fears for an English fleet were 'so great at Lisbon that the people sent their goods 30 leagues inland'.[2] These two chimerical fleets demonstrate, in Wernham's words, 'how thick was the fog of war that enveloped both sides' (1984, 240). The 'mistie weather' of rumour did not disperse until the new century.

To read accounts of England in the 1590s is to be struck by the regularity of such fears. While it is true that the brunt of war was suffered the more keenly abroad, England's insularity amplified its fears as effectively as it prevented their realization. The 'rumors of warres' which 'began now to increase every day' early in 1588 had proved justified (Camden, 3, 128); but what Walsingham called the 'half-doing' of the first Armada led the more cautious of Englishmen to 'interpret their temporary success as a reason to expect even greater troubles in the future' (Wiener, 52).

The 1590 alert was renewed in February 1592/3, when another Spanish attempt was 'credibly advertised' (*APC*, 24, 53). Fresh 'rumours' were heard in 1595, as Camden reports, 'not obscure, but with loud and unanimous voyce ... that the *Spaniards* were now ready to set sayle with a stronger Armado than before, for the Conquest of *England*'. 'All men', he writes, 'buckled themselves to warre' (4, 71). The fall of Calais in 1596 initiated a 'constant rumour [that] grew daily stronger and stronger' (4, 90) of yet a further attempt. In October 1597 'the most Part of the Gentlemen of every Cownty, [were] commanded to goe Home for the Defence of the [western] Sea Coast'.[3] In 1598 Robert Barret explained the relevance of his military treatise by referring to 'the rumour of this troublesome world towards, I meane ... the great preparations of the ambitious Spaniard, pretended as is thought against us' (1). And in 1599 'rumors grew rife, and ranne all over the kingdome' not only of an 'Armado ... prepared' (Camden, 4, 142) but 'newes (yet false) that the Spaniardes were landed in the yle of Wight', prompting panic in London streets.[4]

Calais fell in 1596, Camden tells us, 'with mutuall thundring of the Ordnance, (the report whereof we heard as farre as *Greenwich*)' (4, 89). The ambiguity of that phrase well illustrates the sense of encroachment which the European wars fostered in England throughout the decade. Fear of invasion seems to have been an almost constant discomfort, and though Sutcliffe's military treatise acknowledges 'this time of peace and securitie', he admonishes those who 'mislike nothing more, then to have their ears grated with the sound of drummes, and rumors of warres' (1593, A2r). It is to this period of 'assured rumors' (Camden, 4, 71) that belongs the composition of Shakespeare's histories.

War threatened more to Elizabethan playgoers than it ever delivered. It is equally true that invasion-scares, forced musters, printed news-reports and word-of-mouth rumours ensured that such anxieties were never allowed to be forgotten. It is the aim of this chapter to illustrate the creative precision with which certain of Shakespeare's plays reflect the experience of war as it was felt at home. In drafting a pedigree for the Elizabethan *miles gloriosus*, it seeks to demonstrate Shakespeare's sustained engagement with war-news, in plays as generically distinct as *Love's Labour's Lost* and *Henry V*. Although Armado, Pistol and Parolles stand down-stage of their plays' principals, they once reflected the solemnity and trauma of their first audiences' preoccupation. One day the rumours may have come true.

## True reports

It is important not to underestimate the force of rumour in this pre-technological era. Proclamations were regularly issued in the turbulent years before Elizabeth's accession to silence those who would 'stir up Rumours, raise up Tales, imagin News' (Aydelotte, 53).[5] A ballad was printed in 1570 (in the wake of the Northern Rebellion) which urged its audience 'to leave this murmoring spight'.[6] This 'rumerous devell' became even more troublesome in wartime. In 1586, the first year of direct English engagement in the Low Countries, instructions for musters were issued, which regretted

> that many lewdlye disposed are given to the spredyng of
> false rumours and reports, and idle and vayne newes of
> matters either abrodde or at home whereby many
> incideynes doe appeare bothe to the dishonour of the
> State and otherwise.[7]

But wartime rumour threatened more than 'dishonour' to the state: in fact, as many military pamphlets asserted, it constituted of itself a powerful weapon. 'A *General*', reads one, 'may sometimes invent and spreade *Rumors* of ayde and assistaunce from *Forraine Princes*, or such like, to Annimate his owne people, & terrify his adversarie' (Digges, 1579, 169).[8] Our own century confirms the force of both these accounts. The *Daily Mirror* of 4 September 1939 printed a list of advice, 'first, and most important of all things' being its appeal, *'Don't Listen to Rumours'* (24). 'In wartime', on the other hand, as Churchill observed, 'truth is so precious that she should always be attended by a bodyguard of lies' (Young and Stamp, 1). In Elizabeth's wars as in Churchill's, Rumour was both friend and foe, in the field and at home.

Biblical and classical sources strengthened the associations of war with rumour. On the one hand, the eschatological overtones encouraged by Protestant propagandist interpretations of the first Armada's defeat reanimated the force of Christ's prediction of the Day of Judgement at Matthew 24, 6: 'And ye shall hear of wars, and rumours of wars: see that ye be not troubled: for all these things must come to pass, but the end is not yet'. Thomas Becon had prefaced his 1543 *Policy of War* with reference to this passage (*Early Works*, ed. Ayre, 238), and it is echoed in C.G.'s account of the 'mutabilitie of reports' (A4r) in his *Watch-worde for Warre* (1596). Published 'by reason of the disperced rumors amongst us' (t.p.), C.G.'s work vividly sketches the 'constant rumour' Camden described,

> for one while there runneth nothing but rumors of warre,
> an otherwhile there passe manie speeches of peace; the
> same mouth that saith at one time, the Spanyard will
> come, another time affirmeth, we neede not expect his
> comming.
> (A4r)

On the other hand, this description also sounds echoes of the most extensive *locus classicus* of the theme, Ovid's description of the House of Fame in *Metamorphoses*, where it is Fama who makes known to the Trojans the imminent landing of the Greek fleet. Golding's 1567 translation reverberates with the same anxieties as were voiced in proclamations against 'seditious words and rumors' in the 1550s,[9] and subsequently felt in England's beleaguered isle:

> And millions both of trothes and lyes ronne gadding every where,
> And woordes confusely flye in heapes. Of which, sum fill the eare
> That heard not of them erst, and sum Colcaryers part doo play
> Too spread abrode the things they heard. And ever by the way
> The thing that was invented growes much greater than before,
> And every one that getts it by the end addes sumwhat more.

> Lyght credit dwelleth there.There dwells rash error: There dooth dwell
> Vayne joy; There dwelleth hartlesse feare, and Brute that loves to tell
> Uncertayne newes uppon report, whereof he dooth not knowe
> The author, and Sedition who fresh rumors loves too sowe.
> (V4v)

That Golding himself 'addes sumwhat more' to his source (the uniquely observed 'Colcaryers') emphasizes its sustained relevance to his times.

Where Ovid described her effects, Virgil supplied a more detailed description of Fama herself,

> pedibus celerem et pernicibus alis,
> monstrum horrendum, ingens, cui, quot sunt corpore plumae,
> tot vigiles oculi subter (mirabile dictu),
> tot linguae, totidem ora sonant, tot subrigit auris.
> (*Aeneid* 4, 180-3)

> right swift of pase,
> And swifter, far, of wing: a monster vast,
> And dreadfull. Looke, how many plumes are plac't
> On her huge corps, so many waking eyes
> Sticke underneath: and (which may stranger rise
> In the report) as many tongues shee beares,
> As many mouthes, as many listening eares.

This translation is from *Poetaster* (1601) (5.2.83-9), and Jonson's decision to have Virgil recite this particular passage perhaps illustrates its contemporary relevance; apt to the play's theme of slander, it also belongs in a sequence of treatments of the topos in the period.

There is much documentation of the extensive familiarity in Tudor times of what Boitani calls Virgil's 'iconographic nightmare' (12). Variously denoted, dressed in 'Ies tonges and eares', 'crimsin sattin full of toongs', or 'all in feathers',[10] the figure provides a variety of functions in pageant and drama ranged between 'glory and gossip' (Loewenstein, 1984, 16). 'Report' gathers 'the certain true report' of Bosworth in *The True Tragedy of Richard the Third* (line 2003); 'Rumor' enters 'running' in *Clyomon and Clamydes* to 'publish [off-stage events] ... at large' (lines 1196-1210); 'Vanitie' acts as chorus to *Liberality and Prodigality*, her multicoloured feathers denoting her 'mutabilitie' (line 10); 'Report', as Greene's Helenus in *Euphues His Censure* (1587) says, is 'a false Heralte of humaine Actions' (*Works*, ed. Grosart, 6, 204); and Linche's *Fountaine of Ancient Fiction* (1599) describes Fame as the herald of Mars's chariot, borrowng the 'swiftnesse' and 'infinite numbers of eares, and tongues' (V3v) from Virgil's description. The proleptic function Linche ascribed to *fama* recurs as a statement of flat fact in C.G.'s *Watch-worde for Warre*. 'Rumors are commonly fore-runners of warre', he writes (A4r), and the same applies to the unsettling chorus to Shakespeare's *2 Henry IV*, Rumour, who enters (as the 1600 Quarto specifies) 'painted full of Tongues'.

The strands of historical and literary precedents are overtly woven into the first lines of Rumour's commanding address:

> Open your eares; for which of you will stop
> The vent of hearing, when lowd Rumor speaks?

Clad in Virgil's tongues, Rumour's speech is animated by the blusterous wind-tunnel of Ovid's House of Fame. Rumour blows his words into his audience's 'vent of hearing', but is himself 'a pipe, | Blowne by surmizes, Jealousies conjectures', played upon by the 'wav'ring multitude' (15-20). Both agent and instrument, Rumour rides – or is blown by – the wind, '(Making the wind my poste-horse)' (4). Such shifts of focus trouble the mind's eye, even as the speaker's later self-rebuke – 'But what meane I | To speake so true at first' (27-8) – unsettles the conventions of the Prologue. Dr Johnson thought the speech 'wholly useless, since we are told nothing which the first scene does not clearly and naturally discover';[11] yet it is the disconcerting nature of rumours to thwart clear and natural confirmation. 'The same mouth that saith at one time, the Spanyard will come,' as C.G. wrote, 'another time affirmeth, we neede not expect his comming'. 'Rumors tongues' (39) manage to say both at the same time:

> And who but Rumor, who but onely I,
> Make fearefull musters, and prepar'd defence,
> Whiles the bigge yeare, swolne with some other griefe,
> Is thought with child by the sterne tyrant Warre?
> And no such matter.
> (11-15)

The *Henry IV* plays are usually dated 1596-7. Humphreys' edition suggests they were first performed 'in the winter season' of that year, before being revised to remove their original references to Oldcastle for performance in the following winter season 1597-8.[12] The topicality of Rumour's 'fearefull musters, and prepar'd defence' to the earlier date seems transparent: Calais had fallen; a 'constant rumour grew daily stronger'; and an almost unprecedented national muster was held in the winter of 1596 (Boynton, 19). Thomas Nun's *Comfort Against the Spaniard*, itself published in 1596, opens with the sobering enquiry, 'Is it true that the Spanyardes will com this spring?'. Shakespeare's lines marry windy inflation to the swelling growth of both brooding and bruising: 'the bigge yeare', nearing her term, is 'thought with child by ... Warre', but is 'swolne with some other griefe'.

It might be argued that Rumour's false alarm ('no such matter') benefits from the hindsight afforded by the Spaniards' failure to arrive in the spring of 1597. Whether or not the lines were revised at the same time as the Oldcastle/Falstaff changes a year later, however, the coalitions they forge between literary, biblical and topical precedents sustained their relevance into the new century. Camden notes that during the 1599 invasion-scare, 'the vulgar sort abstained not from scoffing speeches, saying that in yeere 88, that invincible armado arrived from *Spaine*, and now this yeere arrived another armado invisible' (4, 147). The phantom pregnancy Rumour describes acknowledges postponement not cancellation. Rumour's remained a 'wel knowne body' to his milling 'houshold' (21-2), the Theater or Curtain playhouses, in the fields where the 'wav'ring multitude' of his audience practised 'fearefull musters, and prepar'd defence' in the winter of 1596, and 'all men buckled themselves to warre'. At once housing a precise iconography and an anxious currency, this 'false Heralte' of the 'sterne tyrant Warre' strikes the keynote – with the insinuating blare of an air-raid siren – for our subsequent experience of his play.

There is a further chiming of the topical with the mythic in the speech, however, and one which demonstrates that Shakespeare, like Golding's 'Colcaryers', 'addes sumwhat more':

> Upon my tongues continuall slanders ride,
> The which in every language I pronounce,
> Stuffing the eares of men with false reports.
> (6-8)

Why does he speak 'in every language'? To answer this fully, it is necessary once more to turn to the variety of social consequences effected in London by the European wars.

We have seen how Jonson extracted the House of Fame for recital in *Poetaster*. *The Staple of News*, Jonson's return to the stage in 1626, builds an entire play around the lines. ''Tis the house of *fame*, Sir', explains the Register, 'Where all doe meet, | To tast the *Cornu copiae* of her rumors' (3.2.115-19). This play, and Jonson's earlier masque on the same theme, *News from the New World* (1620), were precisely rooted. The first English-language serial newspapers date from the early 1620s, their demand stimulated by the resumption of European hostilities in 1618 (Frank, 3; Cust, 69). The extraordinary '*Project*' attributed to Spinola in the play, 'to bring an army over in corke-shooes, | And land them, here, at *Harwich*' (3.2.87-9), though exaggerated, reiterates the fears exploited by Shakespeare's Rumour thirty years before. 'Be't true or false, so't be newes', says the Printer in the masque (18-19), with a timeless disregard for truth gloated over by the earlier Prologue (37-9):

> the postes come tyring on,
> And not a man of them brings other newes,
> Than they have learnt of me, from Rumors tongues.

There is some evidence that Elizabethans learned much of (what we might call) their current affairs from the theatres, which, though sketchy, is consistent. At the Rose, Marlowe's *Massacre at Paris* dramatized events from August 1589, and though Henslowe's Diary marks it as new in January 1592/3, we have already noted the extreme modernity of Marlowe's earlier lecture on the rudiments of war. The impresario later commissioned the first part of the 'syvell wares of france' from Drayton and Dekker in September 1598, just four months after the peace treaty of Vervins (98), and while its contents remain conjectural, the title of the play he bought for the Rose in 1600, 'Called straunge newes out of poland', resembles that of a news-pamphlet (134). The 'overthrow of *Turnholt*' re-enacted at the Curtain in October 1599 probably drew on the news-letter of (more or less) that name, which was printed in 1597 (News-Pamphlet 15). Like yesterday's newspapers, few of these plays survived their currency. The text of Richard Vennar's *England's Joy* is also lost, though in this case probably because it was never written. This was the hoax-play advertised for performance at the Swan in 1602, whose ticket-sales were misappropriated by the author with no play performed. Perhaps it was the promise of a news-play about the Irish wars which boosted those sales, for that is the subject of Vennar's poem of the same name, published the previous year: 'O England, never better newes can be: | Then thus to heare, how God doth fight for thee' (A2v). If the Swan, the Curtain and the Rose acted as news-rooms, why not the Theater and the Globe? Certainly, Fynes Moryson's *Itinerary* commented on London playgoers' eagerness 'to heare newes' (quoted in Gurr, 1980, 10); and in 1599 the Swiss traveller Thomas Platter saw the London playhouses in the same light: 'With these and many more amusements the English pass their time, learning at the play what is happening abroad'.[13]

Such a context would add resonance to the theatrical contrivance of Jonson's *Staple of News* – much as *Bartholomew Fair* (1614) exploits the 'closest parallels between the new theater and the new market' (Agnew, 119), and *The Alchemist* (1610), 'a play about transformation' (Barton, 1984, 137), transmutes experience 'within the walls of a stripped and deserted house – or a theatre' (152). But it would also lend even further acerbic force to Rumour's question, 'what need I thus | (My wel knowne body) to anothomize | Among my houshold?' (20-2). The king's reference in the first play to the 'fickle changlings ... Which gape and rub the elbow at the newes | Of hurly burly innovation' (5.1.76-8) would cast its rebuke further than the confines of its own play when spoken in a milling wartime playhouse.

The 1590s saw a boom in the publication of news comparable to the 1620s, and for comparable reasons (Webb, 1952, 241). 'War news is one of the first kinds to appear at the beginning of the sixteenth century' (Shaaber, 1929, 121); and it seems clear that Elizabethan war-correspondents aimed their dispatches at a readership anxious to counter the uncertainties of word-of-mouth rumour, 'to aunswere', as one such writer put it in 1591, 'the slanderous bruites raised of late' (News-Pamphlet 11, t.p.). Gascoigne's *Spoyle of Antwerpe* (1576) purports to correct 'manyfolde light tales' and 'doubtfull reportes' (A2r, A3v), while W.C.'s 1578 *True Reporte of the Skirmish* was published because 'manye tales goe, and men are desirous to kno the truth' (3). The formula of W.C.'s title was to be applied in the *True Relation*, *True Discourse*, *True Declaration* and *True Newes* continually issued as the wars went on.[14]

The nature of contemporary news-gathering ensured however that such pamphlets often ended in conjectures as improbable as Spinola's 'corke-shooes'. *A Discourse ... of the Late Overthrowe ... at Turnehaut* (1597), for example, is quick to speculate about 'those *Rodomons* soldats, *Neapolitans* of the regiment of the marques of *Trevicques* ... which are said to teare armed men with their teeth' (News-Pamphlet 15, A3v). The Scholar's distrust of Fame in Fenne's 1590 dialogue between them understandably despairs of the 'messengers of uncertaintie' that 'daylie so flout and mock me', and tellingly appeals to the 'true reports of your owne mouth' (B1r, P3v). Such 'doubtfull reportes' featured more than once in the plots of contemporary plays. Ralph's death, for example, is wrongly reported in *The Shoemakers' Holiday* (1599). 'Heres a letter sent', says Hammon to Jane,

> From France to me, from a deare friend of mine,
> A gentleman of place, here he doth write,
> Their names that have bin slaine in every fight.
> (4.1.83-6)

Printed news-letters indeed featured such casualty-lists, 'the names of such men of accompt as have beene either slaine, hurt, or taken prisoners' (1600, News-Pamphlet 17).[15] Jane's anguish – and Dekker's pathos – is pressed home by reading these roll-calls of Captains, Lieutenants and 'Ancients slaine', besides 'More of ours slaine and missing, 560' (B1v-B2r). Moreover, as Tourneur demonstrates in *The Atheist's Tragedy*, Fenne's 'true reports of your owne mouth' were as unreliable as the 'messengers of uncertaintie' Dekker had exposed. 'Souldier! what newes?', asks D'Amville of Borachio there, 'wee heard a rumour of a blow you gave the enemie'.[16] 'Tis very true', lies Borachio, before his false account of Charlemont's death at the Siege of Ostend. 'Twas rumord here in London thou wert dead', protests Hammon to the crippled Ralph in Dekker's play (5.2.44). It is in the uncertain news-pamphlets of his times that we may ground the 'false reports' of Shakespeare's Rumour, and provide an explanation of why they are pronounced 'in every language'.

Worcester had pictured 'Supposition ... stucke full of eyes' (*1 Henry IV*, 5.2.8), but it is Rumour's tongues to which the sequel's prologue draws attention, out of the feathers, tongues, ears and eyes available from tradition. Contemporary military news-letters were also variously known by a motley language, 'full of Tongues'. Many were (often rudimentary) translations of French or Dutch originals;[17] some were reprinted in London untranslated; others themselves comprised multilingual texts, such as the *Songe to be Printed in Duch. French or English of thoverthrowe of the Spanysh navie*, recorded in the Stationers' Register of 1589 (Shaaber, 1929, 129). The first European news-digest, *Mercurius Gallobelgicus*, was printed (in Latin) in 1594 (Shaaber, 1929, 310), and prompted John Donne to address its unreliabilty in an epigram: 'thou art like | *Mercury* in stealing, but lyest like a *Greeke*'.[18]

Such reports, whether true or false, circulated in Latin, Dutch, French and English. But then, such was to be expected from the coalition armies in which and against which Elizabeth's soldiers found themselves fighting – the 'hotch:pot' described in 1602 (News-Pamphlet 26, A3r). The language *of* war, 'as we do borrow from straungers' (Barret, 1598, 248), was accordingly incorporated into the reports of service circulating in London, because of the foreign originals on which they were often based; because the details of siege-warfare demanded its nuances; and because so many of the accounts were authored by soldiers. 'A Souldier when he comes forth', reads Grimeston's *True Historie of the Memorable Siege of Ostend*, 'speakes like a Maister in fortifications, of Ramperes, Bulworkes, Spurres, Counterscarfes, Ravelins ... and such like' (1604, A3r). Such vocabulary indeed peppers Borachio's report from Ostend in *The Atheist's Tragedy* (2.1.40-69), but also lends authority to an earlier news-letter, *A True Reporte of the Service in Britanie* (1591). Employing the relish of a connoisseur, its author describes 'a verie great *Ravelin*' (A3r), or 'pretie conceited *Turnepike* or *Barricado*' (A3v), before culminating *con brio*: 'I am enforced to leave my penne, and betake myselfe to the launce, for the trompet soundeth, *mont'a cavallo*' (B2r).

The panache with which he signs off is enhanced by the equal facility he professes with pen and lance. The phrase declares its author a model Soldier-Scholar of the sort we have examined, and echoes Whetstone's question of Caesar, 'whether he was more inclined to the Launce, or to his booke' (1586b, 66). That work's parallel English-Dutch text, exemplified the need it asserts 'to be skylled in all tongues' (10), a skill flourished in this news-pamphlet, but disturbed by Shakespeare's Rumour:

> Upon my tongues continuall slanders ride,
> The which in every language I pronounce,
> Stuffing the eares of men with false reports.
> (6-8)

Further, the ideal alliance of arms and learning found pithy homage in a series of mottos (Gascoigne's *Tam Marti quàm Mercurio*, Breton's *Marti Mercurius*) which elided Mars the god of war with Mercury the god of learning, of language – and of fame. Thus, in Breton's 'Disputation', the soldier at first rebukes the scholar for reading 'the famous acts of gallant Souldiours, such as *Caesar, Alexander, Hanniball, Hector, Achilles*' while staying safely at home; but the scholar replies by asking how 'the *Fame* of your gallant Souldiours remaine in Memorie, had there not bene Schollers willing ... to set them out' (1597, H2v).

The tradition of the Nine Worthies is the most enduring literary seat of such memory, and it is Fame who conventionally presents them. Carroll has traced the progress of the Worthies as chivalric paradigms, portentous illustrations of the *ubi sunt* theme and of the military ideal of 'arts and arms commixt' they came to embody (229-35). Hawes's *Passetyme of Pleasure* (1509, reprinted 1554) includes Dame Fame, clad 'with fyry flame | Of brennynge tongues', who sounds her trumpet 'After the dethe of many a champyon', and whose tongues record 'theyr grete actes'.[19] Later in the poem, she introduces the Worthies (5495-5606) and pronounces a 'swete reporte' on each of them. The figure is often cited by editors as an ancestor of Shakespeare's Rumour, who 'still unfold[s] | The acts commenced on this ball of earth' (4-5). That function was also shared by many news-letters from the wars in Europe, as much to commemorate as to inform. Lingham's *True Relation of all Suche Englishe Captaines and Lieutenants, as have beene slaine in the lowe Countries*, for example, praises Norris, 'whose deedes is by fame sounded through the whole Worlde' (1584, A3r), and prefaces his roll of honour with a direct allusion to archetypally 'gallant Souldiours':

> But if ever Greece had cause to spred the praise of
> *Achilles* and the residue of their renowned captaines, or
> haplesse *Troy* to sound forth the due deserts of unfortunat
> *Hector*, Then hath Englande triple cause to declare the
> exceeding courage of her faithfull Countrimen.
> (A2r-A2v)

W.C.'s *True Reporte* had also linked present conflicts to an explicit emulation of earlier Worthies, praising the 'valiant wightes of Britaine blood, whome strangers rightlye terme, a second *Hercules*, a second *Hector*' (7). Ripa's emblem of *Fama Chiara* depicts Mercury, the leash of Pegasus in one hand, the *caduceus* in the other (1611, 155): '*Mercury* denotes *Fame*, for he was the Messenger of *Jupiter*, as also the Efficacy of Speech, and a good Voice, that spreads and is diffus'd' (1709, 30). It is for this reason that the word 'Mercurius' was a more or less constant feature of serial newspapers since *Gallobelgicus* in 1594 (Cranfield, 6-16).

One of these news-letters, *Mercurius Rusticus*, depicts the god on its title-page.[20] Wearing the winged *petasus* on his head, but otherwise dressed in the jerkin and boots of a contemporary Civil War infantryman, *Rusticus*'s running figure bears a banner before him 'Recounting the Sad Events of this

Unparraleld WARR'; and, in a direct iconographic allusion to Mars, wields a flail – the Scourge of God. The figure bears direct comparison with the composite Soldier-Scholar (dressed in gown and armour, holding book and lance) and Mars-Mercury (wearing a half-helmet, half-*petasus*) in the 1618 *The Mirror of Majesty* (see above, p. 81), at the same time as casting Mercury as a soldier bearing news. As such, *Mercurius Rusticus* constitutes a belated emblem of the Soldier-Scholar war-correspondents whose dispatches from the front in the 1590s were issued in a hotch-potch of what Jonson calls 'some *Gallo-belgick* phrase' (*Poetaster*, 5.3.553). As Donne's epigram on *Gallobelgicus* indicates, however, Mercury's status as a messenger of fame was compromised by his equal reputation for thievery, imposture and double-dealing (Comes, 1627, 431). Fame awaited the gallant actions of England's war-dead; but the actions they achieved were also shrouded in Rumour. Mercury's name attached to the news-pamphlets which awarded them their 'due deserts' and answered 'slanderous bruites'; but that name was also a by-word for the malicious dissemination of false reports.

It is this reputation to which William Rankins refers in one of his *Seaven Satyres Applyed to the Weeke* (1598). 'Behold a Bruite', begins Wednesday's 'Contra Mercurialistam' (as in *mercredi*), 'that scarce can hold his pen, | Yet thinkes he hath *Caduceus* in his hand' (7). Golding's Ovid personifies 'Brute' as one 'that loves to tell | Uncertayne newes uppon report', but Rankins brings such instabilities of report firmly up to date, ridiculing the 'patched Pamphlet' and 'ballet-fraughted ship' with which this 'fellowship of seemers' practises its 'counterfaites' (8-10). Shakespeare's later ballad-monger Autolycus was 'lytter'd under Mercurie' (4.3.25), and recent criticism has seized upon him as an embodiment of the 'deferral of reference' and 'problematization of language' that characterize *The Winter's Tale* (Parker and Hartman, 15-16). Rankins's rancour demonstrates the currency of such distrust in Shakespeare's wartime England, to which Riche's contemporary account of fifth-columnists lends a solemn urgency:

> You shall have them inquiring of newes, spreading of rumours, lying, forging, counterfeiting and dissembling ... What good newes hath there come over which they have not paraphrased, what enterprise so justly attempted, which they have not eclipsed, or what exployt so bravely accomplished, which they have not methamorphised.
> (1587, C3v)

Sutcliffe's later text-book confirms the theory of such warnings as well as *The Practice, Proceedings and Lawes of Armes*, by recommending their offensive deployment: 'Rumours of succours comming encourage our souldiers, discourage the enemie'; 'Wordes making for us comming to the enemies eares doe often strike a terror in them'; 'Suborned messengers are dangerous, if credit be given unto them' (1593, 194-5). Such passages sketch the anxious context against which Shakespeare suborned his own messenger at the outset of *2 Henry IV*, whose 'false reports ... speak of peace, while covert enmity, | Under the smile of safety, woundes the world' (8-10). Rumour's counterfeiting and dissembling tongues flick at a lexicon of military topicality: the Esperanto of war demanded by the theory and practice of modern conflict; the tactic of dis-information deployed in the field; the dubious authority of dispatches from the front; and the 'brennynge tongues' of Dame Fame pronouncing elegy over the fallen.

While it is true that Richard Davies's 1610 pageant *Chester's Triumph* distinguishes between Fame ('a Trumpet in her hand') (A3v), Mercury ('Tongues-man of the *Universe*') (B2r), and Rumour (who delivers an oration on St George) (A4r), it is clear that the three figures contested iconological ground in the Elizabethan war-years. Although there is nothing in the text to identify the gender of Shakespeare's Rumour,[21] it seems likely that the play bears in mind Davies's distinction between a female Fame (as Virgil's *fama*) and a male – more precisely a mailed – Rumour of the sort depicted as an 'Huomo armato' by Ripa, reproduced on the jacket of the present volume.

Like his later 'Prologue, arm'd' (*Troilus and Cressida*, Prol. 23), Shakespeare's Rumour announces his affinity with the captains and soldiers that, as Nashe reported, frequented the 'houshold' of the London theatres. We have considered the extent to which the plight of neglected veterans was aired on the stages of the time. Casualties of war were a common sight in London but the virtuous duty celebrated in Stump or Bowyer should be balanced against the 'lame beggar' of another of Donne's epigrams: 'if he say true, hee *lies*'. Returning from the wars, Ralph enters *The Shoemakers' Holiday* 'being lame', after his death is 'rumour'd here in London': that entrance bears out Senator Johnson's maxim from 1917 that 'the first casualty when war comes is truth'.[22]

### Old soldiers

'A fig for fame', declared the septuagenarian old soldier Thomas Churchyard in 1596, bemoaning the contrast between the rewards once bestowed on veterans, and their present neglect (B4v). 'Warres in our times being ended', agreed Sutcliffe, 'are the beginning of beggarie and calamitie to many poore souldiers' (1593, 298-9). Uprooted from civilian life, subject to sickness, hunger, and the extortion of their captains as well as 'the event | Of the none-sparing warre',[23] such men were discharged on debarkation in England, often owed their pay, and expected to find their own way home. Their 'colde reward' (Riche, 1578, E2v), at a time when welfare structures were rudimentary, was as pitiful to them as troublesome to the government, since their discontent often erupted into civil unrest (Judges, xvii-xviii;

Walter, 127). The problem of their enforced vagrancy was incremental in the 1590s. 'Of wandryng souldiers ther are more abroade then ever weare', complained one JP to Burghley in 1596, and the Act 'for Punyshment of Rogues, Vagabondes and Sturdy Beggars' was issued in 1597, reiterating that veterans should carry the 'lawfull pasportes' of their service so scorned by Lieutenant Stump (see above, pp. 38-9).[24]

It is perhaps paradoxical then that a further consequence of this explosion in the numbers of discharged, masterless men, was a widespread impersonation of them. Burghley's correspondent in 1596 elaborated on the problem, enclosing in his letter 'this Counterfect passe'. The reasoning behind such deceits is best summarized by the Proclamation issued on 28 February 1591/92:

> Concerning such persons as wander abroad in the habite of Souldiers, there are divers persons pretending to have served in the late warres and service as Souldiers ... whereof some are maymed, others have received hurtes and woundes ... And some amongst these have neither bene maymed nor hurt, nor yet served at all in the warres, but take that cloak and colour, to bee the more pitied, and doe live about the Citie by begging.[25]

It is a piquant irony that while Sir Francis Vere successfully captured Zutphen by causing 'sundry of his souldiours, secretly to be apparrelled in the habite of poore Market folks', London was simultaneously the site of an equivalent 'cloake and colour', this time by vagabonds of discharged soldiers. A soldier, it seems, was never what he seemed.

The false sympathy evoked by such men, together with the genuine grievances voiced by the real veterans who threatened riot at Bartholomew Fair in 1589, constituted a potent force for disorder. The threat posed by the combined might of disgruntled veterans and the deceit of their impersonators was perceived as still more dangerous. Another proclamation was issued in 1598 regarding 'assemblies of rogues and vagabonds, coloring their wandering by the name of soldiers lately come from the wars', armed 'with shot and other forbidden weapons'.[26] Riche's *Faultes Faults, and Nothing Else but Faultes* appeals for ampler rewards for soldiers with 'good Testimonie of ... honest service', lamenting that 'beeing returned home, hurt, maimed, lamed, dismembred', they are forced to beg 'for a peece of bread' (1606, M4r); yet it also stresses the importance of a 'Testimonie' for clear military reasons:

> othersome againe, under the pretence of begging, have searched out the secrets of Citties ... have layed them open to an ennemy, have poysoned waters, and have sometimes fired Citties ... and it is strange that here ... we

> have long escaped these practises, when such multitudes
> of sturdy rogues have bin suffered ... to passe... under the
> pretence of begging Souldiors, that never crossed the
> Seas.
> (M3v-M4r)

We have seen how Riche's warnings against fifth-columnists in 1587 centred on their subversive attempts to 'paraphrase' and 'methamorphise' whatever 'good newes' should have been reported. It is notable that in this later satire, published two years after peace-talks, his warning about men 'that never crossed the Seas' is tempered by a more artful indulgence.

He lampoons, for example, in precisely the same terms those stay-at-home 'State-Apes' (C3r) who sing for their supper by relaying news 'from *Fraunce, Flaunders, Spaine,* and *Italy*': 'These men have a speciall gift, eyther to Metamorphise, or to Paraphrase, what newes soever' (C3r-C3v). 'Report', he later warns, 'is a lier' (N2v), and the same applies to 'Newes-mongers' (C4r), 'Travailers' (C4v), and to the 'counterfeit Souldiour' Captain Swag (D4r): 'he that will be *Thraso,*' he summarizes, 'shall never want a *Gnato*' (C2r). Just as the anxieties of the House of Fame gained particular resonance from the false reports of wartime, so the archetypally absurd teller-of-tall-tales, Terence's *miles gloriosus,* was solemnified in the same context. Both literary topoi share a vocabulary of counterfeiting and dissembling.

Thomas Digges's essay, 'That no prince ... doth gaine ... by giving too small entertainment unto Souldiers', well demonstrates the link between literary braggart, counterfeit soldier, and subversive rumour (1604, 1). He rebukes 'impudent Runawaies' who 'shal by Rumors, letters, or printed *Pamphlets* perhaps sometimes disgrace those valiant men that resolutely died in the place' rather than admit their own cowardice, 'extolling one another with *Heroicall* names ... to purchase friends, by such *Thrasonicall Stratagems*' (18). His critique extends to their counterfeiting the news-pamphlets of veterans, composed to their own glory rather than the due desert Fame owes to true heroes (just like the 'patched Pamphlets' of Rankins's Bruite). Riche proved the exactitude of that parallel by describing carpet-knights as men 'furnished with three or foure *Frenche, Italian,* or *Spanishe* wordes, thinking that the whole glorie consisted in beeing newfangled in their apparell, [and] straunge in their conceiptes'(1578, G1r). Mercury's various iconology, his presidency both of language and deception, elided in such counterfeit soldiers' enlistment of the Martial-Mercurial vocabulary of war, to lend credence to their imposture.

John Taylor's droll 'doggrell', *A Dogg of Warre,* illustrates the transition from jargon to braggery most succinctly: 'Yet all their talke is | Bastinado, | Strong Armado, | Hot Scalado, | Smoaking | Trinidado.| Of Canvasado, | Pallizado, | Of the secret | Ambuscado, | Boasting with | Bravado' (B8v-C1r). The basis of Taylor's Jacobean bathos is a common theme in earlier war-years. Puttenham, for example, describes as 'braggery' the practice of 'using some Italian word, or French, or Spanish, or Dutch ... ignorantly and affectedly', and suggests 'mingle mangle' as an equivalent to the Greek term '*Soraismus*'.[27] Dekker picked up the same term when he described veteran '*Dunkirkes*' as 'a mingle mangle of countries, a confusion of languages' in *Work for Armourers* (1609) (*Non-Dramatic Works*, ed. Grosart, 4, 103).

Donne's *Satyre IV* takes to task a spokesman of just such linguistic confusion, an 'Interpreter | To Babells bricklayers', whose voluble gossip collars the narrator,

> as if he'd undertooke
> To say Gallo-Belgicus without booke
> Speakes of all States, and deeds, that have been since
> The Spaniards came, to the losse of Amyens.[28]

'From the last comming of the D. of Parma into Fraunce, untill the eighteenth of May 1592', as the title of one news-pamphlet, 'Truely Sette Down', puts it (News-Pamphlet 13). Donne's 'thing' may serve to bind together the current stream of unverifiable war news, the 'slanders ... in every language' of Shakespeare's contemporary Rumour, and the '*Soraismus*' of Pedant and Braggart's 'motley tongue':

> This thing hath travail'd, and saith, speakes all tongues
> And knoweth what to all States belongs.
> Made of th'Accents, and best phrase of all these,
> He speakes no language; If strange meats displease,
> Art can deceive, or hunger force my tast,
> But Pedants motley tongue, souldiers bumbast,
> Mountebankes drugtongue, nor the termes of law
> Are strong enough preparatives, to draw
> Me to beare this.
> (35-43)

In each of these cases, *in extremis* with Donne's 'Makeron' (117), words run before their matter. The result can be disturbing, like Rumour's echoes of present anxieties; or richly comic, by dint of the dislocation of word from deed. The Braggart's threats and boasts of violence are revealed to be hollow; the Pedant's insistence on the theoretical language of learning is revealed as mere parade. Language itself lies at the heart of why these archetypal figures are funny – as it does not, for example, with the Cuckold or Miser.

Certain manuscripts of Donne's *Satyre* report that this weird traveller 'speakes *one* language' (38, my emphasis). It is to this 'one language' which is 'no language' that I shall now turn. For just as the Renaissance witnessed the blending of two hitherto distinct vocations, Knight and Doctor, into a single epitome of military learning, the Soldier-Scholar, so the stages that reflected Elizabethan theatres of war reanimated the archetypal comedy of the old soldier by reference to a burlesqued form of that Martial-Mercurial ideal: the Braggart-Pedant, whose consummate example may be found in the troubling timeliness of Shakespeare's Pistol.

Boughner's study of the Renaissance Braggart claims that 'the stupid *miles gloriosus* of the Roman poets became in the Renaissance a vehicle for the satire of any ridiculous lumber of the mind' (1954, 98), but stops short of equating such lumber with the stock-in-trade of Italian comedy's Dottore and his 'expert book knowledge' (Nicoll, 56). According to Boughner, the typical *commedia* Capitano 'asserts his equal talent with sword or pen, a theme amplified in other Cinquecento comedies' (48); and yet he refers to a 'persistent confusion of two popular figures ordinarily kept distinct by the dramatists' (307, n.8), the Braggart and the Pedant. It seems plain, however, that since the nature of warfare changed so dramatically – and did so in Italy – so the satirical portraits of boastful soldiers would accordingly be revised, as topically as those *commedia* Capitanos who reflected contemporary detestation of Spanish mercenaries (23). Far from the resemblance between Braggart and Pedant being 'superficial' (307), English *milites gloriosi* directly parodied the ideals embodied in the Soldier-Scholar, taking their cue from Italian precedents. The 'two popular figures' begin to merge in the plot of one such play, Pasqualigo's *Il Fidele* (1576), that was translated in 1584, probably by Anthony Munday, as *Fedele and Fortunio: The Two Italian Gentlemen* – the 'one sure example' of the influence felt in England of the *commedia dell'arte* (Salingar, 1974, 189).

## 'Vaine Basiliscos and Captain Crackstones'

*Fedele and Fortunio* includes both a sententious 'Schoolmaister', [29] Pedante, and the first English Capitano, Crackstone. The figures merge simply by dint of plot: Crackstone disguises himself as Pedante to gain an audience with one of Pedante's pupils, whom he loves, and stresses that his disguise is as linguistic as it is sartorial. 'Nay looke no more for Lattin now my gowne is gone', he declares afterwards, 'My learning with my reparrell goes off and on' (814-15). The lines echo his first (muddled) confession, that he 'bought this apparell of a Captain that was slain',

> And wearing the same abroad as you see:
> The Soldiers all the towne over, make a Captain of mee.
> One calles mee Captain Cheese, an other Captain Crust:
> An other brave *Crack-stone*, take which name ye lust.
> (61-5)

The sentiments are sharp about the 'beggarie' suffered by veterans 'for a peece of bread', but also reflect the gullibility for counterfeits Riche had admonished, 'thinking their whole glorie consisted in beeing newfangled ... and straunge'. Certainly, Crackstone's language is both. For one thing, he conveys the 'malapropism, confusion, and slapstick' of his role (Wiggins, 37) with the genius of ignorance:

> As when I give a charger to my foes in the open feelde,
> Or put Citties into sackes, and make thousands to yeelde.
> (1342-3)

Military tactics are superbly reduced to presenting horses to the enemy and dropping cities into sacks. For another, those 'three or foure *Frenche, Italian,* or *Spanishe* wordes' Riche had attributed to the carpet-knight appear, more or less, on Crackstone's lips, peppering his boasts with the Esperanto of war, as he warns that 'I would give you such a frezado, or canvazado' (1399). Barret's 1598 glossary explains that '*Canvasada* ... doth signifie the investing a shirt over the soldiers apparell or armour' for a night-raid (248). What Crackstone's threat precisely intends is obscure, though it sems appropriate to a man whose 'learning with my reparrell goes off and on'. John Eliot's language manual *Ortho-Epia Gallica* (1593) would later ridicule what 'many of our English doe commonly, who will begin one language to day, and another to morrow', men who after learning 'a *Beso las manos*: in Spanish ... thinke themselves brave men' (3) – men, in fact, like Captain Crackstone who announces to Fortunio, '*Basilus* Codpeece for an olde *Manus*' (50).[30] Riche includes the same expression among the 'few foolish phrases' he ridicules (1606, C4r), though Crackstone evidently thinks it a Latin or Greek one. Its suggestion of the Greek βασιλευς (king) provides a multilingual instance of Crackstone's most prominent verbal tic, his habit of coining latinate neologisms, portmanteau words of a Joycean dimension.

He boasts, for example, of his 'bravalitie' (55) and 'Magnaniminstrelsie' (129); he is a 'terrebinthinall' individual (846) and yet the 'perplexionablest man that lives' (1453). It is this trick of speech that Nashe would single out from Munday's play in his swipe at Gabriel Harvey's 'energeticall lines ... in ambidexteritie and omnidexteritie' (3, 44): 'he is such a vaine *Basilisco* and *Captaine Crack-stone* in all his actions & conversation, & swarmeth in vile Canniball words' (3, 102). It is notable that Nashe lampoons this 'precious apothegmaticall Pedant' (3, 77) by alluding to an English Capitano – evidence in itself of the more than superficial resemblance between Braggart and Pedant, recognized by the play's original audiences. Nashe parodies Harvey's 'encomiasticall Orations, and mercuriall and martiall discourses of the terribilitie of war' (3, 45), directly invoking the soldier-scholarly ideal Harvey had appropriated in the motto ('*Vel Arte, vel Marte*') he inscribed in a number of his books (Stern, 138). 'I am all *Mars* and *Ars*', says another braggart soldier, Lyly's Sir Tophas in *Endimion* (1585), a character that at least one scholar has considered a pastiche of Harvey himself (1.3.91).[31]

Even Boughner concedes that in Tophas the two types, Braggart and Pedant, occurred 'in combination' (307).

Crackstone had literally clad himself in the borrowed robes of soldier and scholar. Tophas both brags like the Capitano, threatening hyperbolic destruction to the animal kingdom (in a broadening of Chaucer's ironic portrait of Sir Thopas), and cites the *sententiae* of the *commedia* Dottore:

> TOPHAS   Freendes? *Nego argumentum.*
> SAMIAS   And why not freends?
> TOPHAS   Because *Amicitia* (as in old Annuals we find) is *inter pares.*
> (1.3.29-31)

Tophas's muddle between 'Annuals' (almanacks) and Annals (histories), which prompted scholarly correction from Blount, is surely one Lyly intends. It brings a hint of those 'Canniball words' Nashe described, by which Tophas the pseudo-scholar reveals his reading matter to be rather less high-brow than intended, a linguistic mistake like Crackstone's confusion of charge with charger. Certainly that character's conflation of magnanimity and minstrelsy into a single quality of 'Magnaniminstrelsie' is comparable to Tophas's proud parsing of his sword to Samias: 'it is my Simiter; which I by construction often studying to bee compendious, call my Smyter' (1.3. 88-9). His sword demands a new word, a scimitar that smites, and the equation of sword with word catches at the twinned expertise with pen and sword Tophas parodies: 'Commonly my words wound' (1.3.58).

'All Masse and Asse', as Samias comments (1.3.92), Sir Tophas inherits the hyperbole of the Braggart, and the bookish self-esteem of the Pedant. Like his own 'compendious' words (confessing his unrequited love by likening himself to 'a Nowne Adjective ... because I cannot stand without another', 3.3.17-19), he represents an alloyed updating of the *miles gloriosus* in a conscientious pastiche of the Soldier-Scholar. Tophas even cites Cicero's oft-quoted maxim, 'Take my gunne and give me a gowne: *Caedant arma togae*' (3.3.28-9), which Breton's Scholar cites to the Soldier to prove their mutual assistance (1597, H2v). One critic's appraisal of the 'inane schoolboy humour of his part' is no more accurate than Crackstone's Latin (Hunter, 1962, 237).

Neither Crackstone's nor Tophas's plays have anything but the most distant contact with war. Their military roles are subsumed to their secondary parts in the love-plots, in line with their descent from Latin and Italian comedy. The next generation in the pedigree of the Elizabethan Braggart took note of the new circumstance of open war, declared soon after *Endimion* was composed. Its advent may be illustrated by reference to the 'vaine *Basilisco*' with whom Nashe bracketed Crackstone. That is the name of a number of *commedia* Braggarts, but (closer to home) it is also that of the character that Kyd introduced to his main source for *Soliman and Perseda* (c.1590) (A. Freeman, 154). Its significance lies in its allusion to the basilisk, or cockatrice, 'the kinge of all Serpentes, of whome they are most afrayde, & flee from', 'for with his breth & sight hee sleath all thinges' (Legh, 1568, 61v), so named from the diminutive of βασιλευς suggested by the coxcomb on its head. Its long-distance hostility perfectly describes the Braggart's inflated word and diminished deed; its link with words is confirmed in the coinage by which Trompart, the Braggart Strumbo's page in *Locrine*, yokes 'cockatrices' to 'bablatrices' (911). Still more cogent to the context of war, however, is the fact that a basilisk was also a 'large cannon, generally made of brass, and of about 200 pounds weight' (*OED*, 3) – the 'Basiliskes, | That roaring, shake *Damascus* turrets downe' in *1 Tamburlaine* (4.1.2-3). The contemporaneity of Marlowe's play is emulated and parodied in Kyd's.

Despite his name, Kyd's Basilisco is not the Spaniard of Italian comedy like Don Armado, Spenser's 'Don *Braggadocchio*' (5.3.15) or Chapman's 'Martiall Spaniardo' Don Bragadino in Scene Two of *The Blind Beggar of Alexandria* (1596). Instead, he is 'a Rutter borne in Germanie' (1.3.66),[32] a German mercenary cavalryman of the sort Edward VI had employed, and who still fought in Europe's cosmopolitan armies (Goring, 195; News-Pamphlet 13, A2r). So dubious was their reputation that the word *rutter* had passed into thieves' cant, to mean, as Greene records, 'he that makes the fray' in a party of swindlers.[33] The chivalric context of the play's first act is immediately questioned by his mercenary origins, much as Tamburlaine the 'base-bred Thiefe' had offended his aristocratic enemies (*One*, 4.3.12).

At once a counterfeit swindler and a contemporary soldier, Basilisco's alien status is matched by the character of his language, which also signals his theatrical model: 'I fight not with my tongue, this is my Oratrix', he declares, 'Laying his hand upon his sword' (1.3.69). The sentiment echoes that of Marlowe's Techelles – 'Our swordes shall play the Orators for us' (1.2.132) – and the allusion to the Soldier-Scholar's word/sword is couched in the macaronic idiom of the Pedant ('Oratrix'), while also recalling the 'clinical language' critics have noticed in Marlowe's plays (Greenblatt, 1980, 210): 'orifex', 'Pericranion' (*2 Tamburlaine*, 1.3.101, 3.4.9). Basilisco later reveals a comparable fastidiousness when he itemizes the bones he has injured in the tournament ('My backe bone, my channell bone, and my thigh bone, | Besides two dossen of small inferior bones', 1.4.55-6). The irked dignity and learned self-importance of those lines recur in one of Kyd's most overt parodies of *Tamburlaine*, in a passage which converts Marlowe's chilling account of the 'uglie monster death' (*Two*, 5.3.67) into a comic assertion of love. Tamburlaine's Death 'Stands aiming at me with his murthering dart | Who flies away at every glance I give' (69-70). When Basilisco's page, Piston, jabs him on the bottom with a pin, he thinks it is Cupid who,

> Not daring looke me in the marshall face,
> Came like a coward stealing after me,

> And with his pointed dart prickt my posteriors.
> (4.3.44-6)[34]

'Posteriors': the latinate, circumlocutionary hyperbole is typical, and splendidly at odds with his declared taciturnity.

Mention of his 'Oratrix' leads to his providing an 'instance' for the 'feminine Epitheton' he bestows on it (1.3.71-77), and a further forty lines boasting of his military deeds. He considers himself a citizen of the world – 'the earth is my countrey' (1.3.79) – from which we might expect a version of the 'fantastic peregrination' that characterizes the vaunts both of Italian Capitanos (Boughner, 1940, 204) and Latin *milites gloriosi*.[35] What Kyd gives us however is importantly different. We have seen how Tamburlaine's exotic geography was rooted in the latest cartography; Basilisco's geography is also both relevant and genuine:

> As I remember, there happened a sore dr[o]ught
> In some part of Belgia, that the jucie grasse,
> Was seared with the Sunne Gods Element ...
> Upon a Time in Ireland I fought,
> On horsebacke with an hundred Kernes...
> Insomuch that my Steed began to faint;
> I, conjecturing the cause to be want of water, dismounted:
> In which place there was no such Element.
> (1.3.84-99)

His mythologizing of space ('Belgia ... the Sunne Gods Element') cannot disguise those trouble-spots of the 1580s and 1590s, Ireland and the Low Countries. But the desert-like terrain he describes belongs more to the Middle East of Tamburlaine's campaigns than the notoriously damaging damp climates of these current theatres of war (see Cruickshank, 182). Kyd's ear is ironic and sly in hearing the prosaic hyperbole to which Marlowe's soldier sometimes descends. 'And here in Affrick *where it seldom raines*', says Tamburlaine, 'Have swelling cloudes drawen from wide gasping woundes | Bene oft resolv'd in bloody purple showers' (*One*, 5.2.393-6, my emphasis). Basilisco effects a comparable miracle of nature by quenching the thirst of his 'Palfray' by the sweat he generates in 'three or foure houres combat' (102-5). But the comedy of his ignorance is tempered by the 'pollicie' he relates from Belgia:

> I held it pollicie to put the men children
> Of that climate to the sword,
> That the mothers teares might releeve the parched earth.
> The men died, the women wept, and the grasse grew,
> Else had my Frize-land horse perished.
> (1.3.87-91)

Though of course manifestly fabulous, the massacre he describes is closer to home than, say, the Capitano's alleged banqueting on 'Jews, infidels, and Lutherans' (Boughner, 1940, 208); and a deal less innocuous than Tophas's assaults on the 'wilde Mallard' and 'terrible Trowte' (1.3.72-78). The Elizabethan opposition of policy to chivalry confirms Basilisco's currency. William Blandy had praised the 'worthye actions done by our nation in *Friseland*' against the Catholic armies that were 'gathered together of the froth and scomme of many nations' (1581, G1v-G2r). The self-confessedly cosmopolitan Basilisco perpetrates 'mercilesse massacres' of the sort attributed at the time to that same enemy (*An Oration Militarie*, 1588, A4r), but does so merely to feed his 'Frize-land horse'. The smile at the conventionally risible hyperbole here freezes in the face of wartime.

Like Tophas, Crackstone, and their forebears, Basilisco is subject to love: 'an humor of Venus beleagereth me' (1.3.127). But as his usage of that military word denotes – the same modish Dutch that John Smythe had deprecated in 'our chiefe men of ... warre' (1590, B1r-B2v) – Basilisco brings a new vocabulary of war to bear on his condition. When Piston mis-delivers another well-known Ciceronian tag, '*O extempore, O flores!*' (1.3.140), his master rebukes this 'un-edicate illiterate pesant' for 'abus[ing] the phrase of the Latine' (141-2). It is to Piston, then, that Kyd attributes the dog-Latin of the native vice-braggart, exemplified in *Thersytes* (performed 1537).[36] For Basilisco, however, Latin has a robuster foundation, like the (extemporized) *commedia* Dottore's. His inflated style ('saunce dread of our indignation') prompts Piston to comment, 'what languidge is that? I thinke thou art a word maker by thine occupation' (144-6). Basilisco takes the Pedant's part against his page, while bragging of his military exploits in discernibly modern theatres of war. He emulates the Soldier-Scholar Tamburlaine's vocabulary, and carries the refined absurdities of Sir Tophas's Braggart-Pedant into the field. Both Lyly's and Kyd's warriors study 'to bee compendious'; and each is a 'word maker by ... occupation'. *O tempora, o mores* indeed.

Pyrgopolinices, Plautus's original *Miles Gloriosus*, employs his servant to record his deeds in a notebook. Basilisco relies on his own oral testimony rather than the 'table' of written record:

> I repute myself no coward:
> For humilitie shall mount.
> I keep no table to character my fore-passed conflicts.
> As I remember ...
> (1.3.82-4)

His lines anticipate the comic topicality of Donne's 'Makeron', 'as if he'd undertooke | To say Gallo-Belgicus without booke'; and of Jonson's Shift in *Every Man Out of his Humour* (1599), who 'waylayes the reports of services, and connes them without booke, damming himselfe he came from them, when all the while he was taking the dyet in a bawdy house' (Ind. 16). Like Donne's subject too, Basilisco 'hath travail'd, and saith, speakes all tongues', combining 'Pedants motley tongue' and 'souldiers bumbast':

> I have no word, because no countrey,
> Each place is my habitation,
> Therefore each countries word mine to pronounce.
> (1.3.111-13)

In each of these particulars, Basilisco's news from Belgia bears a more forceful resemblance to Rumour's tongues than the 'bokes' of Hawes's Dame Fame (5519). Like Shakespeare's Rumour, he purveys 'continuall slanders ... in every language', and both characters embody aspects of the 'counterfeiting and dissembling' voices of Elizabethan war. Kyd's portrait of this 'counterfet foole' (1.3.223) brilliantly incorporates into theatrical tradition the social pressures of London's home front. At a time when wild rumours were circulating about the course and outcome of the wars, when so many were counterfeiting 'the name of Souldiers' that proclamations were being issued, Basilisco's version of Tamburlaine's supreme modernity was exactly attuned. It is difficult not to remember the 'one chamber' their authors once shared (A. Freeman, 181).

Riche was to give an enduring sketch of the veterans who will settle international affairs 'but in one dinners discourse' (1598, E2r). Basilisco has similar tendencies, but, with a sharply comic spin, he flinches from the least contact with weaponry, even as he accepts the charity his counterfeit fellows exploited. 'Last night', reports Piston, 'he was bidden to a Gentle-womans to supper, | And, because he would not be put to carve, | He wore his hand in a scarfe, and said he was wounded' (1.3.216-18). As the lines perhaps intimate, Basilisco's comedic profile shadows darker themes. His mixture of 'mirth' and 'melancholy' (3.3.25) well describes his role in this 'tragicomicall' play (5.2.143). For Death, as well as Cupid, steals upon him as he finds himself embroiled in the main catastrophe. Called upon, like Crackstone before him, to act as assassin, Basilisco's reluctance is more sombre than that captain's comic incompetence. Amidst the climactic slaughters, he '*feeles upon the point*' of a dagger, and then delivers an uncharacteristically monosyllabic meditation:

> BASILISCO   The point will marre her skin.
> PERSEDA     What, darest thou not, give me the dagger then,
>             Theres a reward for all thy treasons past.
>             *Then* Perseda *kils* Lucina.
> (5.3.51-4)

Nestling among the glib atrocities, Basilisco achieves an extraordinary dramatic poise here, the more affecting for the suspicion that Perseda misreads his reluctance. In the following scene, Kyd is scrupulous not to afford his Braggart the indomitability of previous examples: Basilisco is abruptly bumped off on stage (5.4.72). Before he dies, however, he is granted a remarkable speech on mortality. His soliloquy begins by bearing the hallmarks of his macaronic diction ('I will ruminate: Death ... Hath deprived *Erastus* trunke from breathing vitalitie', 5.3.63-5), but gradually turns to a more sober litany, listing eight valiant warriors, Hercules, Alexander, Pompey and so on. Where are they? Dead (67-76). Describing himself as 'worthy' (89), Basilisco's speech clearly evokes the Nine Worthies tradition. Its particular tone may be illuminated by reference to two further literary Braggarts.

Udall's Roister Doister boasts that he has been mistaken for Lancelot, Hector and the like, by the 'enamoured' women he meets.[37] His self-comparison mocks the amorous delusions he inherits from his Roman and *commedia* counterparts, and deviates from the *ubi sunt* theme that characterizes Gower's or Lydgate's treatments of the Worthies (Carroll, 230). Nearer in time to Kyd is the speech of 'the Bragger' in Eliot's *Ortho-Epia Gallica*, who literally asks that question of the Nine, but does so to erect his own bravery over their absence:

> Where is Alexander, the great drunkard of Greece? I will
> make him drinke a carouse ...
> Where is this quaking-quivering coward Julius Caesar?
> that I might horse him on the end of my Pike and Lance.
> (1593, S2r)

By contrast, Basilisco's rumination restores to the genre of the Worthies' parade the solemnity of their medieval representations:

> Where is the leader of of the Mirmidons,
> That well knit *Accill* ? dead ...
> Where is tipsie *Alexander*, that great cup conquerour,
> Or *Pompey* that brave warriour? dead:
> I am my selfe strong, but I confesse death to be stronger.
> (5.3.71-7)

This archetype of counterfeit Fame paradoxically reaffirms the *memento mori gravitas* with which Hawes's Dame Fame is superseded by Time and Eternity. The sentiment is at once contextually and symbolically eloquent:

> I am wise, but quiddits will not answer death:
> To conclude in a word, to be captious, vertuous, ingenious,
> [Are] to be nothing when it pleaseth Death to be envious.
> (81-3)

'In a word ... captious, vertuous, ingenious': such 'quiddits' are typical of the vociferous motley tongue of the Braggart-Pedant. Ovid's House of Fame mixes 'trothes and lyes': so the truths of contemporary 'pollicie' may be discerned behind Basilisco's vaunts; and so the comic conventions of the *miles gloriosus* mingle-mangle with the topicalities of counterfeit veterans, unverifiable news-reports from the front, and the martial paradigm of the Soldier-Scholar – all this mediated by his shadowing of Marlowe's dramatic version of that paradigm.

One of Basilisco's braggart brothers, Strumbo in *Locrine*, lurks in his conqueror-play much as Basilisco does in his. He recommends the seductive power of 'new coined words' (410), threatens his muster-captain with 'a canvasado with a bastinano' (632-3), and compendiously rails on the enemy 'Shitens, the Scithians' (729). His (vulgarized) characteristics testify to a contemporary expectation of the traits we have assembled of the Braggart-Pedant. It is surely further significant that its author spells out Strumbo's identification with Mercury. Strumbo's 'mansion cottage', we are told, now destroyed by the war, used to stand 'hard by the temple of *Mercury*' (726-8), and he himself is taken for '*Mercury* | In clownish shape' by the conquered Humber (1655-6). Kyd's Basilisco is an altogether more sophisticated Mercury in clownish shape. A pretender to scholarship, and to fame, a 'word maker' of tongues and languages, but like Mercury in stealing, and in fraudulence, Basilisco also mediates between the living and the dead. 'I will play least in sight' (5.3.95), he announces as the play's bodies pile up, but his self-consciousness as a player emphasizes that we die in earnest, and that's no jest. That is the central truth that skulks within Kyd's mixture of fictive tradition and current warfare, underpinning the technologies of the Martial-Mercurial Soldier-Scholar, as much as the stratagems of the Braggart-Pedant: 'quiddits will not answer death'.

## '*The Pedant, the Bragart ...*'

'Among contemporary dramatists only Shakespeare seems to have been much taken by the play', writes Freeman in his defence of *Soliman and Perseda* (158). The most prominent evidence for this is the Bastard's allusion to Basilisco in *King John* (1.1.244), and it is significant that it is he who later likens the battlements of Angers to an auditorium for war's 'industrious Scenes and acts of death' (see above, pp. 102-3). Basilisco mounts an on-stage ladder to be a spectator of the off-stage tournament (1.3.181 SD) immediately after the passage Shakespeare recalled, and his next entrance is made, extraordinarily enough, '*riding of a Mule*' (1.4.46 SD). 'Is that horse *real*?': Anne Barton amusingly records that response by a modern playgoer to an equivalent (though directorial) coup, as part of a discussion of 'Realism in Shakespeare's Last Plays' which includes the later exit, '*pursued by a Beare*'. (1994, 199). The figure of the Braggart is a supreme example of such metatheatrical tactics, as of the mutual informing of theatre and war, since his performance on the battlefield extends into the pretence of valour he maintains after the war. This redoubling of performance may explain why Braggarts are, again in Barton's phrase, so 'theatrically attractive' (1984, 86). Shakespeare's first *miles gloriosus* is, accordingly, to be found in a play which, as a recent editor writes, 'explores the theatricality of culture'.[38]

*Love's Labour's Lost* was probably written within a year of *King John*, around 1595. Like all Shakespeare's plays with an original plot, it reflects on its own status as drama, not least in the stereotypy of its comic characters, which are itemized by Berowne as 'The Pedant, the Bragart, the Hedge-Priest, the Foole, and the Boy' (5.2.538), and which are inter-mittently deployed in both Folio and Quarto speech-prefixes. The comic vice held in common by Pedant and Braggart is their promotion of words over deeds, and the play as a whole, as one critic puts it, 'is about *words*' (R. Berry, 1969, 69). It is for his words, as the King says, that Armado is retained at court, providing relief from study by relating 'In high borne wordes the worth of many a Knight: | From tawnie Spaine lost in the worldes debate' (1.1.170-71). Like those of the 'word maker' Basilisco, or of the 'compendious' Tophas, Armado's 'high borne wordes' are possessed of linguistic novelty, as the King and Berowne both agree. Armado is 'A man in all the worldes new fashion planted | That hath a mint of phrases in his braine'; 'A man of fier new wordes, Fashions owne knight' (162-76). And while Tophas wittily declares himself a 'Nowne Adjective', Armado's name (like Basilisco's) was itself a fire-new word.

*Armado* was a common variant spelling of *Armada*, and was included as late as 1598 in Barret's glossary of 'forraine words', which explains it can also mean 'one great ship of warre' (249), an object of weight and firepower – like the piece of artillery called the basilisk. The word's slow incorporation into English is perhaps attested by Dull's struggle to pronounce it: 'Signeour *Arme Arme* commendes you' (1.1.185). Named for an odd word, Armado also has a word, a Mote, for a page, as Kerrigan's edition notes (160-61). Such textual self-consciousness (as well as his primacy in its oddly alphabetical *dramatis personae*) highlights the play's emphasis upon the written word, its letters, scripts and sonnets, that have as much difficulty reaching their audience as its clowns' verbal fumbling.

Armado first entertains us with his words, rather than in person, in his letter to the 'Great Deputie the welki[n]s Vizgerent, and sole dominatur of *Navar*' (1.1.216-17). Carroll's description of the character's idiom as 'the dead end, within a decade, of Tamburlaine's "high-astounding terms"' (17) perhaps finds confirmation in the hollow echoes Armado sounds of that Soldier-Scholar's geographic sway: 'It standeth North North-east & by East from the West corner' (1.1.240-41). (Mad north by north-west?) Although the critic's appraisal of Armado's rhetorical *cul de sac* applies the more appropriately to his written than his verbal word, it suggests kinship with the latinate, high-falutin, and periphrastic styles employed by Crackstone,

Tophas, and Basilisco. With a rich and knowing comedy, Armado's subsequent letter to Jaquenetta approvingly quotes that model soldier Julius Caesar's pithiest axiom:

> *Veni, vidi, vici*: Which to annothanize in the vulgar, O
> base and obscure vulgar; *videliset*, He came, See, and
> overcame: he came, one; see, two; [   ]overcame, three.
> Who came? ...
> (4.1.67-70)

Just as Sir Tophas commandeers a Ciceronian tag to describe his amorous conversion (see above, p. 148), so Armado appropriates Caesar's military commonplace in prosecuting his suit. But the very point of the saying, the 'certaine short grace' North's Plutarch commended,[39] is laboriously missed. Caesar's brevity of words designate massive deeds. Contrariwise, Armado's insistent parsing of the phrase, amidst his customary 'magnanimous ... pernicious and indubitate' verbosity (4.1.64-6), disguises the vacuity of whatever deeds can be discerned it. Armado bungles the soldier-scholarly merits of this paradigm; and his letter goes undelivered.

Boughner insists that Shakespeare 'differentiates sharply' between the Pedant and the Braggart in this play (1954, 307). This is true inasmuch as the two characters are differentiated into type only to have their similarity revealed. What's in a name? Holofernes suggests to Kerrigan the 'familiar "tyrant" of medieval Miracle plays' (188). As such, the Pedant's name is one the domineering Braggart might covet, especially since Holofernes's Biblical tyranny had been cited by contemporary English propagandists to describe Philip II's war-aims. W.C.'s *True Reporte* (1578), for example, closes with a prayer 'to strengthen our *Judeth*, that shee ... maye strieke downe that proud *Holifernus*, whose intent is to overthrowe thy house' (11-12). Like Armado, then, Holofernes brings with him associations of Spanish belligerence.

It seems of further note that the strict distinctions various critics have discerned between the two characters' tyranny over language themselves savour of the pedantic finesse in which each revels. C.L. Barber, for example, attributes to Armado 'Euphuistic tautology and periphrasis', and to Holofernes 'inkhorn terms, rhetorical and grammatical terminology, even declensions and alternate spellings' (96) – yet surely such niceties paper over the theatrical similarity of both types. In his first scene, Armado explains his calling Mote a 'tender juvenal', 'as a congruent apethaton apperteining to thy young dayes' (1.2.12-14). It has been suggested that 'apethaton' (F 'apathaton') represents a confusion from a manuscript 'appellat[i]on',[40] though editors follow the later Folios by correcting the typesetter's – or Armado's own – attempt at 'Epitheton'. Basilisco had lengthily explained why his sword-cum-'Oratrix' may 'very well beare a feminine Epitheton' (1.3.77): both soldiers seem keen to deploy the 'grammatical terminology' which Barber ascribes exclusively to the Pedant. Furthermore, Armado's epithet, he says, is a 'congruent' one, a word Shakespeare uses just twice – here, and in the mouth of Holofernes, when he has him approve Armado's deployment of the word *'posteriors'* (5.1.84): 'The *posterior* of the day, most generous sir, is liable, congruent, and measurable for the after noone: the word is well culd, chose, sweete, & apt' (86-9). 'Apt' indeed if we remember Basilisco's conscription of the same word into use when he jocularly borrows from *Tamburlaine*. Echoes abound between the hollow vessels of Armado and Holofernes. Each delivers lists of near-synonymous words, and though the Pedant (arguably) teases out more rigorously accurate nuances, their techniques are directly comparable (4.2.66-8 and 5.1.105-7, for example). It is sometimes forgotten that Armado's lines in the pageant, so redolent of his 'incessant role-playing' (R. Berry, 1969, 74) are actually written by Holofernes.

Plot and tradition lead one to expect this pair to come into conflict, as they do in *Fedele and Fortunio*. Holofernes delivers a tirade about Armado's 'vaine, rediculous, & thrasonicall' behaviour, criticizing his 'discourse' and 'tongue' much as Pedante had Crackstone's (5.1.9-12; lines 1442-3). Armado immediately enters, whereupon ... the two men get on famously. The 'peale' Mote announces (5.1.43) is less the 'clanging' Kerrigan hears (210), more a chiming of minds. Mote is in no doubt as to their common linguistic stock: that 'great feast of Languages', whose 'scraps' they have stolen (36-7). From the theatrical casserole of these 'strange meats' (so Donne described the Pedant-Braggart's 'motley tongue') arises the notion of the Nine Worthies parade, exemplary of the 'Fame' that strikes the first note of the play (1.1.1), and of the 'arts and arms commixt' (and parodied) in Armado's meeting with Holofernes.

The presence of 'arms' in *Love's Labour's Lost*, that most Lylyan of Shakespeare's plays (Hunter, 1962, 330), is a distant one. Armado's contact with war is more hypothetical than the German mercenary Basilisco's. 'Where the play uses history, it uses it as something to escape from', reads Kerrigan's edition (11). This is true so long as we recognize our history to be Shakespeare's audiences' current affairs. For in addition to the Spanish tyrannies evoked by the names of Armado and Holofernes, those of Dumaine, Berowne, and Navarre are recognizable variants of the participants of the French civil wars. They probably featured in the cast of the lost four-part play Henslowe commissioned in 1598, when *Love's Labour's Lost* was published; they were certainly familiar from news-pamphlets when it was first performed. These allusions have been noticed before: I mention them not to support the complex political allegories some have suggested, rather to highlight the self-conscious distance from war the play presents, from its metaphorical presence in Berowne's early analogy of study with siege (1.1.144) to the Five Worthies parade with which the play ends. Just as this 'ostentation' (5.1.106) is also a parade of Wordies, so the King describes war as 'the worldes debate' (1.1.171).

Armado both partakes of and departs from the role of the traditional Braggart. His exaggerated echo of the main love-plot, and his status as 'a Souldier, a man of travayle, that hath seene the worlde' (5.1.102) declare his generic origin. But his 'Minstrelsie' (1.1.174) sees war as a matter of words, and to this extent he exemplifies the new breed of comic warrior, the Braggart-Pedant, evidenced by his companionship with and mutual regard for Holofernes. If a basilisk on paper, however, his performance in person is a deal less incorrigibly voluble than the Capitano, typically leaving it to Mote to explain the traditional conceit of gunpowder-terms: 'My words wound', Tophas had declared (1.3.58); 'is not Lead a mettal heavie, dull, and slow?' asks Armado, himself dull and slow in the business of war (3.1.57). Most importantly, Armado never actually boasts of his military expertise, unlike all the *milites* we have considered. He is retained to narrate the worth of 'many a Knight', and not his own; his words brag of learning, not war. Less bellicose than Eliot's Bragger, O.J. Campbell's description of him as 'a fop in manners' holds true (1925, 23); his weapon is the 'Spaniards Rapier' (1.2.169), not Basilisco's mercenary firearm. In his first Braggart, Shakespeare draws a surprisingly genial portrait of a man named after the worst fears of an enemy invasion. But though a crowing ridicule of the Spanish, and the failure of their 1588 Armada, may in part explain that tone, there is an incremental solemnity to Armado's role which is astonishingly broad of view. By way of comparison and contrast stands the figure of Spenser's Braggadocchio in *The Faerie Queene*.

'What plume of fethers is he', exclaims the Princess when she reads Armado's love-letter to Jaquenetta, 'What vaine? what weathercock?' (4.1.93-4). The lines invest in the imagery Spenser lavishes on Braggadocchio, and the 'vaine of glory vaine' he mines there (2.3.4). The aviary of 'fearefull fowle' (2.3.36) to which Spenser likens Braggadocchio, his 'painted' and 'borrowed plumes' (2.3.6, 2.3.36, 5.3.20), and the windy bluster of his 'smoke of vanitie' (2.3.5) are pleasingly compressed into Shakespeare's sequence of imagery (from plume to vain vane to weathercock), forming a shorthand of contemporary resonance. In *A Mirrour to all that love to follow the Warres*, for example, R.B. reflects that 'the *Dukes* great bragges [the 1588 Armada] to smoke and wind did turne' (1589, B1r), while the second of Rankins's *Seaven Satyres* mocks the bragging soldier who 'can wear a feather all a flaunt ... And sweares he will make the haughty foe to yeeld' (5-6). Riche's Captain Swag is known 'by his Plume' (1606, D4r); and even *STRATIOTICOS* warns against counterfeit soldier-scholars: 'If every *Birde* should pul hir owne feather, like *Esops Daw* [they] might daunce naked' (1579, 70). In the course of their narratives, both Armado and Braggadocchio come to stand plucked and naked, but the rituals of come-uppance they suffer present parallel but distinct treatments.

The comedy of the tilt Braggadocchio evades in Book Three ('Once having turnd, no more returnd his face', 3.8.18) is only allowed indulgence in Book Five, after Talus strips the Spanish Braggart of the appurtenances of knighthood, and thrashes his page Trompart. 'Now when these counterfeits were thus uncased', comments Spenser, 'And in the sight of all men cleane disgraced, | All gan to jest and gibe full merilie' (5.3.39). The close of *Love's Labour's Lost* also features aristocratic mirth at a 'glorious shew ... made in all their sights'. Before it dramatizes Armado's 'uncasing' however (5.2.695), before he reveals the 'naked trueth' of his 'Woolward' penance (5.2.704-5), Shakespeare's Braggart chides the nobles' flippant mockery of his portrayal of Hector in the pageant:

> The sweete War-man is dead and rotten,
> Sweete chucks beat not the bones of the buried:
> When he breathed he was a man.
> (654-6)

Divesting himself of his part, Armado claims fifth-act centre-stage, at the same dramatic juncture as Kyd's Basilisco had taken pause to rehearse the theme of the Nine Worthies, so assiduously shorn of the vainglorious vaunts of his kind. Armado's *memento mori* also serves as a reminder of the pious origins of the 'device' (657) he presents. 'Where is the eldest sonne of *Pryam*', Basilisco asks, 'That abraham-coloured Trojon? dead' (5.3.68-9). *Soliman and Perseda* is framed by a wrangling chorus, Fortune, Love, and Death, who contest their influence over the play's events. Basilisco's rumination prefigures the final entrance of Death, all triumphant, who nine times applies the *ubi sunt* theme to the play's entire cast. 'Wheres *Basilisco* but in my triumph?' (5.5.22). In *Love's Labour's Lost*, and with a similar dynamic, the note Armado strikes is swiftly succeeded and reinforced by the solemn news Marcade then brings, 'heavie in my tongue' (714). Marcade's 'tale' (714), like the ones Armado tells, concerns one 'lost in the worldes debate' (1.1.171) – the Princess's father.

It has been noticed that the name of this 'Messenger Mounsier Marcade' (5.2.709 SD) bears more than a passing similarity to Ralph's attempts at 'Mercury' in *The Cobbler's Prophecy* (Nosworthy, 105-14). As we have seen, that play, following Riche, celebrates the soldier-scholarly ideal, and rebukes the effeminizing influence of Venus over Mars. Marcade, like *Mercurius Gallobelgicus*, bears 'newes' (710), news which makes him, like Tourneur's later witness from Ostend, 'the cursed messenger of death' (2.1.110). Editors agree that Marcade's name, while suggestive of marring Arcady, is 'basically the French surname Marcadé', and that 'Marcadé or Mercadé' may be 'an historical person'.[41] Ralph's confusion of Mercury and 'Markedie' was certainly shared by contemporary news-pamphleteers, who noted in 1591 that 'Duke Mercurie' or 'Mercoeur' was 'Governour of Britanie for those rebellious Leaguers', who had 'joyned with 4000. Spaniards' (News-Pamphlets 7, A2v, and 11, A2r). While the names of Armado and Holofernes betoken current preoccupations with war, then, so too does Mercury-Marcade's: there is a real sense in which Shakespeare's

Marcade joins with his Spanish Armado.

'Mercury comes and all vanish', reads the 'platt' of *The Second Parte of the Seven Deadlie Sinnes* (*c*.1588).[42] Certainly Marcade's entrance dispels the pageant's theatrical illusion. 'Worthies away', cries Berowne, 'the Scaene begins to cloude' (715), as if Armado's reproach ('The sweete War-man is dead and rotten') had not clouded it already. The archetypally theatrical role of Armado's presence is intricate with the play's immanent solemnity. His 'fier new wordes' and 'mint of phrases' bespeak his mercurial role as a guardian of words, his kinship with Holofernes the martial-mercurial ideal he apes (the Worthy Caesar's, for example). Like 'feathered Mercury' (*1 Henry IV*, 4.1.107), his 'plume of fethers' (4.1.93) at once alerts us to the borrowed plumes of his learning and restores to the symbolism of vainglory the feathers (*plumae*) of Virgil's *Fama*. 'Vanitie' enters *Liberality and Prodigality* 'all in feathers'; that 'fearefull fowle', Spenser's Braggadocchio, 'has feathers foule' (2.3.36); and the plumed Captain Swag would have us think 'the *Nine Worthies* were but fooles in comparison' (D4v). In contrast to all these emblems of vainglory, the comedy of Armado's *miles gloriosus* comes to yield profounder warnings: the vain glory of Hector.

Marcade's entrance follows the announcement of Armado's 'pennance' (5.2.705), and prompts the new Queen's bidding the suitors to 'some forlorne and naked Hermytage' (788) for a period 'too long for a Play' (865). Marcade/Mercury, 'Hermytage'/Hermes: 'The wordes of Mercurie, are harsh after the songes of Apollo' (914-15). The bold type of that enigmatic phrase in the 1598 Quarto serves, perhaps, to present a Shakespearean coda to that series of mottoes, *Tam Marti quàm Mercurio*, *Vel Arte, vel Marte, Marti Mercurius*, that summarize the military text-books of the time; an *apologia* for his 'Pleasant Conceited Comedie' at a time when (as Harvey complained) there was 'a busier pageant upon the stage'. In the Folio text the phrase is assigned to the one character whose command of words, familiarity with the dead, aspiration to military scholarship and stereotypical vanity uniquely qualify him for the role he afterwards dispels. Armado ('Braggart' in Q's bald speech-prefix), for the second time in his play, steps out of his role to speak it. And all vanish: 'You that way; we this way' (F 5.2.915).

## 'A Stronger Armado Than Before'

'This is no world | To play with mammets, and to tilt with lips', exclaims Hotspur to Kate in a play probably written within a year of *Love's Labour's Lost* (which had closed with a similar message) (2.4.88-9). In 1595, 'All men buckled themselves to warre', Camden notes, and 'a stronger Armado than before' was expected. War was evidently too important to be left to men like Armado, hence the vehement impatience with which Hotspur deals with the 'neat and trimly drest' lord he meets at Holmedon, 'perfumed like a

Milliner' (1.3.32-5). That scented 'Popingay' (49), with his 'many holiday and lady terms' (45), perhaps remembers the word-maker Basilisco, who, as Kyd tells us, 'weres Civet' (1.3.221). Hotspur's fictional disdain, however, was shared in earnest by Thomas Digges, who condemned alike the captain who is 'brave and gallant ... in his apparrell', 'perfumed perhaps with Muske and Syvet' (1604, 11), and the muster-master who claims 'the *Daw* ... an *Eagle*, & the *Cucko* a *Nightingale*' (33). Hotspur's antipathy stems in part from that man's shrinking dislike of 'vile guns' (62). Far from being 'unlearned in the new Renaissance military science' (Siegel, 137), Hotspur champions the rudiments of modern warfare. Even in his sleep, as Kate chides,

> thou hast talkt
> Of sallies, and retyres of trenches tents,
> Of pallizadoes, frontiers, parapets,
> Of basilisks, of canon, culverin,
> Of prisoners ransome, and of soldiors slaine,
> And all the currents of a heddy fight.
> (2.4.50-5)

'We must have bloudy noses, and crackt crownes, | And passe them currant too', he later remarks (90-91), and indeed his lexicon of war is 'fier new' and 'currant', fresh from news-pamphlet and military treatise. The style of Kate's mockery perhaps suggests the influence of John Davies's epigram 'In Gallum' (*c.*1592-1595) whose subject 'hath bin this Sommer in Friesland':

> He talkes of counterscarfes, and casomates,
> Of parapets, curteynes and Pallizadois,
> Of flankers, Ravelings, gabions he prates,
> And of false brayes, and sallies and scaladose.[43]

Both parroted passages, in any case, guy the jargon of the new Esperanto of war, whose most influential literary exponent was Marlowe's Tamburlaine. Hotspur's emulation of Marlowe's high-astounding terms has been noted,[44] and it is consequently difficult not to be amused by his exclamation, at the beginning of Act Three: 'a plague upon it, I have forgot the map' (3.1.5).

The appraisal Hotspur's widow delivers in Part Two reiterates as eulogy his military expertise: 'In militarie Rules, Humors of Blood, | He was the Marke, and Glasse, Coppy and Booke' (F 2.3.30-31). Hotspur seems to have been much missed: his name appears on the title-page of all his play's early quartos (1598-1622), and shares with Dukes Humphrey (*2 Henry VI*), York (*3 Henry VI*) and Richmond (*Richard III*), the exclusive distinction of a non-eponymous appearance in the Folio's titles. It also seems likely that Kate's lines of remembrance were added in revision (Kerrigan, 1990, 29). The death of so popular a character left a gap in the *dramatis personae* of the sequel, an absence filled on the 1600 Quarto title-page (as an added incentive to purchase) by 'swaggering Pistoll'.

It is Pistol who appears in the scene that immediately follows Lady Percy's reminiscences, and his re-inscription of Hotspur's 'Coppy and Booke' has not gone unremarked. In general terms, Rabkin is right to say that 'Ancient Pistol, who adds fresh attraction to the tavern world, performs one of the functions of the missing Hotspur by giving us a mocking perspective on the rhetoric and pretensions of the warrior' (282). But such would be the case if Pistol were merely the 'filthy, dirty rogue' one historian thinks him (Schwoerer, 10), if it were his 'gross humor' alone that 'paid off superbly in box-office appeal' (Jorgensen, 1956a, 82). Boughner's comment that 'living, not literary models sat for this portrait' is only partially accurate (1936, 226). For in Pistol, Shakespeare leaves us his most thoughtful and ambiguous modern warrior, and one whose precise force has often been overshadowed by the sheer girth of his Captain Falstaff. Pistol's 'fresh attraction' lies in his status as heir to Armado, a comic Soldier-Scholar – a Braggart-Pedant – who belongs not in the rarefied park of a surprisingly un-war-torn France, but on the battlefields of the 1590s.

Omitting the curious fact that the names 'Pistail' and 'Bardoulf' appear on a muster-roll of artillerymen at the siege of St Laurens des Mortiers in 1435,[45] where does Pistol get the name which he so proudly flaunts? One answer seems provided by his first exchange with Falstaff: 'I will discharge upon her sir John, with two bullets' (2.4.111-12). A pistol, then as now, was a firearm, 'an unruly, blustering weapon', as Jorgensen notes (1950, 73), and as such perfect to the 'swaggering rascal' Doll thinks him (2.4.68). Riche later pictured Captain Swag 'discharging some two or three volies of oaths' (1606, D4v), and perhaps the native mistrust for these unpredictable weapons of fire (as likely to explode in the hand as propel a missile) lies behind the common tradition of associating their noisy inefficacy with the Braggart's bluster. Sir Petronel Flash in *Eastward Hoe* (1605) makes the same point in a (slightly) higher social circle. A pistol was a modern weapon, in sharp contrast to the clinquant world Hotspur's name implied. Kyd's Basilisco, Munday's Crackstone and his model, Pasqualigo's Frangipietra, are each collateral ancestors to Pistol's lesser calibre; Armado's freighted firepower is reduced into a handheld weapon.

'With two bullets': Pistol's 'filthy, dirty' aspects have also endured.[46] Hale's essay on gunpowder in the Renaissance tells us that 'from the middle of the sixteenth century ... guns began to take their place in the symbolism of love', replacing the phallic sword 'at about the same time that [gunpowder] became a symbol of war itself' (1983, 409). The bawdy is stressed in the Hostess's version of contemporary pronunciation, 'Captain Peesel' (2.4.158): 'pistol' as in 'castle', or 'pestle' (Kökeritz, 135). Such phallic connotations help determine Pistol's descent from the amorously inclined Plautine or *commedia* Braggarts we have noted. His family resemblance to Basilisco is further signalled by what the Page says of him in *Henry V*: 'for

*Pistoll*, hee hath a killing Tongue, and a quiet Sword; by the meanes whereof, a breakes Words, and keepes whole Weapons' (3.2.34-7). With the cockatrices Basilisco and Spenser's Braggadocchio (3.10.24), Pistol wields a 'killing Tongue'; like Crackstone and Tophas he 'breakes Words' to make his 'Sword', an anagrammatic quibble that shares his forebears' soldier-scholarly aspirations. 'Sword is an oath', he later insists (2.1.101).[47]

There is a third resonance still to Pistol's name, one which adds a gloss to his word-breaking, and to which Falstaff alludes as he beats him downstairs: 'Quaite him downe Bardolfe like a shove-groat shilling, nay, and a doe nothing but speake nothing, a shall be nothing here' (2.4.189-91). His gibe is in keeping with the play's wider preoccupation with money. Both at court and in the tavern, money, or its lack, are seldom far from the characters' minds, whether its theft, loan or debt. The King's coffers 'sound | With hollow povertie' (1.3.74-5); the price is enquired of a pair of bullocks at a Gloucestershire market (3.2.37); Falstaff's debts are called in, 'both in purse and in person' (2.1.118). In addition, however, and as a personification of the theme, Pistol's name plays on the coin of that name: the Pistole, 'a Spanish gold coin minted first in 1537, a double *escudo*, worth 16s.11d.' (Fischer, 105). 'The merchant community', writes one economic historian of the period, 'was well used to handling French, Spanish, German and Low Country coins, and many of these were virtually legal tender' (Outhwaite, 32). Nashe provides contemporary confirmation of this, and helps explain why Falstaff's insult leads into a criticism of Pistol's language ('a doe nothing but speake nothing'). The singular fitness of the following passage, from *Christ's Tears Over Jerusalem* (1594) deserves full quotation:

> For the compounding of my wordes, therein I imitate rich men who, having gathered store of white single money together, convert a number of those small little scutes into great peeces of gold, such as double Pistols and Portugues. Our English tongue of all languages most swarmeth with the single money of monasillables, which are the onely scandall of it. Bookes written in them and no other seeme like Shop-keepers boxes, that containe nothing else save half-pence, three-farthings, and two-pences. Therefore what did me I, but having a huge heape of those worthlesse shreds of small English in my *Pia maters* purse, to make the royaller shew with them to mens eyes, had them to the compounders immediately and exchanged foure into one,and others into more, according to the Greek, French, Spanish, and Italian?
> (*Works*, ed. McKerrow, 2, 184)

This metaphor of language as currency was a relatively new one at the time, and one to which Nashe returned in 1596 when he described an Italian with 'halfe a dosen several languages in his purse' (2, 255). His mints of 'Greek, French, Spanish, and Italian' recall the *soraismus* or 'mingle mangle' which Puttenham described, the linguistic cosmopolitanism which was such a feature of military jargon. Cross-reference to Barret's glossary shows that Hotspur's 'currant' terms include French, Italian and Spanish words. Falstaff's description of Pistol speaking 'nothing' chimes too with Donne's exactly contemporary 'Makeron', who despite being 'made of th'Accents and best phrase' of all languages, likewise 'speakes no language'.

All the Elizabethan Braggarts we have considered share Basilisco's 'occupation' as a 'word maker'. Crackstone pronounces words ('Magnani-minstrelsie') that indeed seem to have been taken to the compounders and 'exchanged foure into one'; Tophas studies 'to bee compendious', deeming Latin a more valuable currency than 'a world of silver' (1.3.102-3); Strumbo relishes his 'new coined words' (410); and Armado, with his 'mint' of 'fier new wordes', presents to Costard a 'Remuneration', which the swain misunderstands as 'the latine word for three-farthings' (3.1.132-3). Pistol's indignation is superb when Fluellen tries, in *Henry V*, to remunerate him for force-feeding him a leek: 'Me a shilling'! (Q 5.1.57). But the riposte has a literal significance, too, since Pistol is neither a shilling, nor the 'groat' by which the Folio devalues him, but rather the compendious Pistole – the coin that may have given its name to the weapon (Clephan, 147). That this was a Spanish coin further ingeniously signals the *commedia* origins of Pistol's braggardism (a stronger Armado than before), and casts his cosmopolitan compounding of words in the mould of the Soldier-Scholar.

What appears to be Pistol's motto, 'si fortune me tormente sperato me contento' (2.4.178, repeated with variation, at 5.5.95), is a perfect example of his compendious study, a garble of Latin, Spanish and Italian. Comments the Arden editor, 'which language he thinks he is speaking is uncertain',[48] and this is very much to the point. For there is a sense in which this 'arrant counterfeit Rascall' (*Henry V*, 3.6.62) is worth rather less than his face-value, aspiring to the scholarship he parades, but which like his soldiership is based on a lie. His language is sprinkled with Latin throughout his plays, though its meaning has long vexed editors: 'are & caeteraes, no things?' (*2 Henry IV*, 2.4.181), 'Tis *semper idem*, for *obsque hoc nihil est*' (5.5.28), 'Solus' (*Henry V*, 2.1.44-6), '*Quondam*' (76), '*Pauca*' (77), '*Caveto*' (2.3.49), 'Gallia' (5.1.85). More often, like his forebears', it is phrased in a latinate diction which recalls the macaronic speech favoured by the Pedant. So he tells us that Falstaff's heart is 'fracted and corroborate' (*Henry V*, 2.1.119), and that Nym is 'egregious' (44); he commands Le Fer to 'perpend' his words (4.4.8). 'Shall we have incision?', he likewise asks in Part Two (2.4.193), impugns Shallow as 'most recreant' (5.3.93) and describes the 'base durance' of Doll's 'contagious prison' (5.5.34).

Pistol's use of French is similarly fracted. He seems *au fait* with standard imports like 'puissant' (*Henry V*, 4.1.41), but more taxed when confronted by a real Frenchman at Agincourt, when he relies upon a parroting echo of

his adversary's tongue ('Owy, cuppele gorge permafoy pesant', 4.4.36).
The perils of editorial intercession are particularly apparent in Pistol's
textual history. Editors since Rowe have tried to excuse his French. When
he meets the King before Agincourt in *Henry V*, for instance, he gives his
version of 'Who goes there?'. 'Ke ve la?' reads the Quarto; 'Che vous la?'
the Folio (4.1.36). Rowe substituted 'Qui va la?' in 1709 and ever since a
joke has been missed.[49] The Folio renders Le Fer's and Katherine's French
perfectly fluently; while the Quarto's more eccentric spelling of their lines
achieves a certain phonetic accuracy. But Pistol's challenge is inaccurate
French in the Folio, inaccurate phonetics in the Quarto. Surely Pistol's
confusion is intended, reflecting as it does the standard routine of the
sentinel, as explained in Garrard's *Arte of Warre* (1591): he must demand
'*Qui vala?* Who goes there? to which when answere is made, Friende' (12).
'A friend,' replies Henry to the challenge (4.1.37). Marston's exactly
contemporary swaggerer in *The Scourge of Villanie* has at least mastered
this most basic of soldierly duties, 'thinking still | He had beene Sentinell of
warlike Brill. | Cryes out *Que va la?* zownds *Que?*' (*Poems*, ed. Davenport,
143). Pistol botches even this rudiment, apparently conflating the Italian
'Che' (F) or Spanish 'Ke' (Q) and rendering 'va' as either 'vous' or 've'
into the Esperanto compound of his motto. This is a minor point, to be sure,
but is I think substantial to an understanding of his role in a play where, in
the Princess's words, 'les langues des hommes sont plein de tromperies'
(5.2.116-17) – as full of mistakes as the 'deceits' her maid translates (119).

Trooper that he is, Pistol knows how to swear in the languages he
elsewhere botches, and cannot resist translating his own expletives: 'Dye,
and be damn'd,' he says to Fluellen, 'and *Figo* for thy friendship ... The
Figge of Spaine' (3.6.55-7). He also deploys military terms *as* expletives,
rounding on Justice Shallow in Part Two: 'Under which King, Besonian?
speake, or die' (5.3.114, F '*Bezonian*'). Churchyard regretted the scorn
with which soldiers were treated as common hirelings, '*bezoingnies* or
necessarye instruments for the time' (1593, 85), and Barret's glossary
explains that '*Bisognio or Bisonnio*, a Spanish or Italian word ... is, as we
terme it, a raw souldier, unexpert in his weapon, and other Military points'
(1598, 249). The meaning is glossed by modern editors: but Pistol's words
*are* his weapons, and his inexpert handling of this one (apparently
understanding it to mean an inhabitant of Besonia) reveals the way in which
his 'fier new wordes' tend to flash back in his face.

There is one modern term however which Pistol understands perfectly,
one which derives from the most prominent campaign of the 1590s, the
Low Countries War. In *Henry V*, Pistol declares his connection with the
camp: 'for I shal Sutler be unto the Campe, and profits will accrue'
(2.1.106-7). Sutlers, or victuallers, were the men responsible for supplying
provisions to the army. Pistol's role recalls that of Captain Crackstone's,
who has 'nicked [the soldiers] of their measure' while 'vittail[ing] the
Camp' (57-8). But like the use of the 'Dutch name of *Legar*' for the English

word 'camp' which so irritated Sir John Smythe (see above, p. 77). 'Sutler' was also a recent military import into the language. One of its earliest recorded occurences is in the *Ordonances and Instructions for the Musters* issued in 1590, which threatens punishment to unscrupulous 'victuallers (called in dutch *Sutlers,*)'. The joke of Pistol's full understanding of the word subtly depends on the profiteering notoriety of the Elizabethan spiv.

S.S. Hussey comments that in Pistol's language Shakespeare 'goes far beyond the register of rogues and vagabonds and creates a genuine dramatic idiolect' (135), yet stops short of specifying the military cosmopolitanism in which it consists. Best described as the 'Gally-mawfry' he himself mentions in *The Merry Wives of Windsor* (F 2.1.110), Pistol's linguistic quilt is stitched from the 'hotch:pot of contrary & dissonant humors' which characterized the allied armies at Ostend (News-Pamphlet 26, A3r). His Dutch 'Sutler', his Spanish or Italian 'Besonian', his French 'rendevous' (*Henry V*, 5.1.79), even the ghost of the Irish song Malone detected in his tirade against Le Fer (4.4.4),[50] bespeak his presence in the current theatres of war. 'From the Orient to the drooping West', Pistol has seen service – or so it would appear; a man of tongues like the Prologue who speaks those words (3). Like Rumour, and like the Prince who succeeds to the throne in his first play, Pistol accumulates idioms, 'studies his companions, | Like a strange tongue wherein to gaine the language' (4.4.68-9). This troubling three-way relationship between Rumour, King and Braggart, alerts us to the fact that this Pistole is an 'arrant counterfeit', a 'double Pistol' in a quite separate sense to Nashe's compound.

'Pistoll speakes nought but truth', he declares in his first play (5.5.38), in a proposition that recalls the riddle of the Cretan liar as much as the third-person Caesarean voice. Pistol's ostentatious expertise in 'Military points' represents a sustained devaluation of the currency of Hotspur's terms, exchanging 'Besonian' for 'pallizadoes', 'Sutler' for 'parapets'. That metaphor was current too, for the circulation of the Spanish Pistole during the period was thought evidence at the time of the steady inflation induced by its wars. The 1581 edition of W.S.'s *Discourse of the Common Weal* has its Doctor cite the 'infinite sums of gold & silver, whych are gathered from the Indies & other countries' to explain the phenomenon.[51] Modern historians confirm the 'likely' accuracy of this diagnosis (Outhwaite, 48), and support W.S.'s primary reason, the 'basenesse of our Coyne in the time of king Henry the eight' (186): Henry's debasement of coinage in the 1520s and 1540s arose from the need to provide money to wage war. The status of money as the sinew of war was a commonplace of the period, 'in the warres of this our age, where treasure is indeed becom *Nervus Belli*' (Digges, 1604, 1). The following assessment of inflation brings resonant implications to a proper contemplation of Pistol's role: 'The eventual development of coins whose politically authorized inscriptions were inadequate to the weights and purities of the ingots into which the inscriptions were stamped precipitated awareness of quandaries about the relationship between face value ... and substantial value' (Shell, 1).

To Costard, 'Remuneration' is 'a fayrer name then French-Crowne' (3.1. 137-8). Pistol's character is stamped with a fairer name than his groatsworth of 'substantial value', an inflation embedded in his language. Like the gold Timon addresses, he speaks 'with everie Tongue, | To everie purpose' (4.3. 391-2), and this capacity was thought by some a military stratagem in itself. Barret cites a series of historical precedents for 'the Captaine Generall ... to corrupt with money ... as principally doth King *Phillip* of *Spain* corrupt with his golden Pistolets the most parts of Europe' (172). The increasingly disembodied nature of abstract money, which has been identified as a defining preoccupation of the period (71), is nowhere more eloquently stamped than in the unanchored verbiage of this apparent military imposter. Nashe's 'double Pistolls' came to be known as doubloons; the sobriquet was often attached to the coin for which Pistol was in part named.[52]

The series of aspects Shakespeare's Pistol presents are each two-faced. His doubleness, for example, is featured in his floating rank. First flagged as 'Antient pistol' (2.4.66), the modern Ensign 'wee corruptly call *Antient*' (Markham, 1622, 73), his entrance swiftly confounds contemporary prescription that the holder of this office was 'the verie foundation of the Companie' (Barret, 1598, 19), an example of the 'gross misapplications of esteemed offices' Falstaff's band comprises (Jorgensen, 1956a, 65). Hotspur's chivalric name and modern expertise are mirrored in the gunpowder terms and 'ancient' rank of Pistol's title. Perhaps because she cannot cope with the modern army's technical hierarchy, perhaps simply in order to placate him, the Hostess repeatedly confers on him the rank of Captain (2.4.133; 157). Yet though Doll Tearsheet eight times exclaims at the error (135-44), Falstaff too confers promotion on Pistol later in the play. 'Come lieftenant Pistol', he says, after the new King Henry's mortal snub, 'I shall be sent for soone at night' (5.5. 87-8). The detail has been explained as 'Shakespeare's inattention'.[53] In fact it displays an attentive subtlety consonant with the complex patterning of the plays' sequence.

I have previously stressed that the Elizabethan rank of Lieutenant bore the traces of its etymology (see above, pp. 34-5, 93-4). Pistol seems to hold the ranks of both Ancient and Lieutenant in *Henry V* (2.1.25; 2.1.37; 3.6.12). Contemporary prescription defined the Lieutenant's role, as we have seen, as the wielding of 'authoritie in the absence of the captaine', 'as if the Captaine were in presence'. Critics have ingeniously deduced from the broken promise of Part Two's Epilogue (24-6), the phantom presence of Falstaff behind the lines now given to Pistol in *Henry V*.[54] Promoted in his Captain's last full speech, Lieutenant Pistol certainly comes to duplicate his authority in the sequel: the fat knight's capture of Coleville (4.2.1-21) is perfectly shadowed by his deputy's capture of Le Fer (4.4.1-63). Pistol's lieutenancy extends beyond the strictly military, and is signalled as early as the Battle of Shrewsbury in *1 Henry IV*.

'Sir John, I am thy Pistol and thy frend', he tells Falstaff in Part Two

(5.3.94), but Falstaff had already offered his 'pistol' to Prince Hal in Part One. One of the stock props of the braggart warrior, as E.E. Stoll's study of the theme relates, is the 'weapon ... that is no weapon but a fraud' (428). Falstaff's is his 'pistol', which he has Prince Hal draw from his holster on Shrewsbury field:

> *Fal.* Nay before God, Hal, if Percy be alive thou gets not
> my sword; but take my pistoll if thou wilt ...
> *The Prince drawes it out, and finds it to be a bottle of Sacke.*
> *Prin.* What, is it a time to jest and dally now?
> (5.3.50-55)

Hal's question is appropriate to Shakespeare's first battle-scene since *King John*'s 'Scenes and acts of death'. For Shrewsbury is fought in a strategic theatre of deception as current as Hotspur's jargon. Sir Francis Vere had captured Zutphen with a mixture of costume, acting, and stage-management, proving Sutcliffe's maxim that 'Vaine shewes do often deceive the enemy' (1593, 194). Riche's catalogue of military ruse – one king's disguised infiltration of the enemy camp, another's assassination by a disguised soldier (1574, D6v, D8r) – prompts in him the thought that a knowledge of such dissimulative precept 'would not a little norish the imaginations of such as should peruse them' (G1v). Shakespeare's battlefield in *1 Henry IV* imaginatively feeds on the detail Holinshed provides of three knights, 'apparelled in the kings sute and clothing' (Bullough, 4, 191), who are slain by the Earl of Douglas. Sir Walter Blunt, 'Semblably furnish't like the king himself' (5.3.21), is the first casualty at Shrewsbury (though his true identity goes unrecognized by audience and Douglas alike until Hotspur's entrance): 'some tell me that thou art a king', says the Earl; 'They tell thee true', lies Blunt (5-6). When Douglas encounters the true king, he suspects 'another counterfet' (34).

Falstaff's fifth-act meditation over Blunt's 'grinning honour' (5.3.59) resembles those of Armado or Basilisco, and like the latter, Falstaff's instinct is to 'play least in sight'. Accordingly, he 'fals downe as if he were dead' (5.4.75 SD): 't'was time to counterfet' (112). That it is Douglas, scourge of the 'borrowed title' (5.3.23), who prompts Falstaff's ruse, however, disturbs the broad comedy modern audiences discern there. For the 'colours' and 'shadows' (5.4.26-9) of theatrical illusion informed contemporary military precept, and Falstaff's tactic ironically complies with Clayton's *Approoved Order of Martiall Discipline* (1591), which recommends a 'shew', whereby 'certaine of the Companie shall fall, heere some, and there some, as if they were slaine' (27). The amateur theatricals of Falstaff's earlier impersonation of the King (2.4) extend into the battlefield, where he shares the military techniques of the King's professional company. The strict distinctions between heroism and cowardice, valour and discretion,[55] dissolve in the tactics of dissimulation deployed by King and Braggart alike. Shrewsbury is a battlefield of counterfeits: kings, princes, heroes, deaths and pistols. The theatre of war enlivens another stock feature of the *miles gloriosus* tradition: his aspiration to kingship.

Basilisco's name apparently incorporates the Greek βασιλευς; that of Jonson's turn-of-the-century braggart Bobadilla seems more exotically indebted to a 'corruption of Abu'Abd Allah ... the last king of the Moors in Spain'.[56] It is one of Falstaff's favourite quibbles to play upon crowns and coins, and the numismatic Pistol inherits his captain's role of the Player King, 'to make the royaller shew' (like Nashe's 'double Pistols'), 'meeting the true king in disguise' at Agincourt (Righter [Barton], 1962, 143).[57] Named in part for an inflationary currency, promoted to a rank that shadows the duties of his superior, and afforded the role of a substitute in the plays themselves, Lieutenant Pistol is best remembered for the relish with which he echoes Marlowe's 'generall lieftenant' Tamburlaine (*One*, 2.5.7). 'Holla, ye pampered jades of Asia', declaims that kingly Soldier-Scholar, the very emblem of Mars, as his chariot is drawn on stage by captive kings (*Two*, 4.3.1). 'Shal pack-horses, and hollow pamperd jades of Asia', echoes Pistol, 'compare with Caesars and with Canibals, and troiant Greekes?' (2.4.160-64). Hotson's description of Pistol astride a 'stuffed Pegasus' (Hotson, 56) nicely catches the inertia of the character's inadvertently 'hollow' jades. Elsewhere, Eliot's Bragger in *Ortho-Epia Gallica* has been cited as evidence that Pistol precisely means 'Canibals' and not Hannibal, despite the many critics who 'attributed to Pistol a certain confusion' on the point (Lever, 85). Confusion, however, seems a relatively mild description of Pistol's state of mind. 'The man has virtually become lost in the part', comments Barton, and as she intimates, his 'royaller shew' is so inflexibly maintained, his quotation so incessant, as to be distinctly unnerving (Righter [Barton], 1962, 140). 'Les pièces', writes one theatrical historian, 'où s'établit une comparaison entre le théâtre et la vie tirent toujours leurs effets d'un tel dédoublement des plans' (Jaquot, 345). Such is the case with Pistol's 'lovingly studied and contrived' role (Righter [Barton], 1962, 139). Muriel Bradbrook's vivid description of him as a 'tatterdemalion scarecrow of a player's nightmare' (1978, 128) acutely refuses to laugh, for Pistol's contrived fustian, more than any Shakespearean snipe at the old-fashioned tastes of the Rose (Rhodes, 63), represents that playwright's further enquiry into the implications of military dissimulation, more searching still than the troubling counterfeits of Shrewsbury.

Joseph Hall's 1608 Character *Of the Vain-glorious* concludes that 'hee is ever on the stage': 'Hee is a Spanish souldier on an Italian Theater; a bladder full of winde, a skin full of words' (139). This archetypal description of the *commedia* Capitano gains force if read against the Elizabethan proximity between wartime theatres and theatres of war. Ancient Pistol's rank is again to the purpose. The ancient or ensign was a term shared by the company's colours – the 'old fazd ancient' Falstaff describes (*1 Henry IV*,

4.2.31) – and the man who bore them, 'resolute rather to loose his life, then to loose hys Cullours' (Riche, 1587, G1v). In the field, an Ancient rallied soldiers round the flag; at home, similar colours mustered audiences to the play, advertising a theatre's readiness for performance (Chambers, 1923, 2, 547). The comparison comes easily to Dekker, whose *Work for Armourers* (1609) pictures the army of Poverty, in time of plague, 'spreading their tottered cullours which hung full of honour, because it was so full of holes, and was indeede no bigger, nay scarce so big, as the flagge of a Play-house' (*Non-Dramatic Works*, ed. Grosart, 4, 117-18). Ancient Pistol's snippets of old plays perhaps serve as an ironic poster for such performances, but his single-minded obsession with drama may be illuminated by Dekker's unflinching account of an earlier outbreak of plague, *The Wonderfull Yeare, 1603*. The passage deploys a metaphor drawn from combat-experience:

> We will therefore play the Souldiers, who at the end of any notable battaile, with a kind of sad delight rehearse the memorable acts of their friends that lye mangled before them: some shewing how bravely they gave the onset: some, how politickly they retirde: others, how manfully they gave and received wounds: a fourth steps forth, and glories how valiantly hee lost an arme: all of them making (by this meanes) the remembrance even of tragicall and mischievous events very delectable.
> (1604, 52)

This compelling account reveals a deep resemblance between the veteran's impulse to re-enact the 'tragicall and mischievous events' of his fallen comrades (now 'mangled before them') and the '*Thrasonicall Stratagems*' Digges had impugned, those 'impudent Runawaies' who appropriate others' valour to their profit (1604, 18). Dekker's psychological reasoning is keen and sophisticated, blurring the borders between counterfeited Vainglory and simple instinct – a truth that carries through the years, and stands comparison with more recent analyses.

In 1916, the *British Medical Journal* published an early account of what became known as shell-shock. The author describes the sense of relief felt by men ordered over the top, and continues:

> Men hit under such circumstances are stopped instantly, while all their faculties are at the highest tension; this sudden arrest gives rise to a psycho-physical state which manifests itself in a tendency to speak of the assault in which they took part as soon as they can and to take no interest in anything that does not relate to it. Together with this there is a desire to carry on the fight in order to settle accounts with the enemy.[58]

Pistol (so far as we know) has not been so wounded: but bullets are not unique in wounding, nor Stump and Bowyer war's only casualties. No particular assault can be discerned in Pistol's manic tirades, but his vocabulary derives from the active theatres of war of his time. And those outbursts are almost exclusively composed of the sorts of 'mischievous events' Dekker describes. A sober list of his preoccupations makes grim reading. In *2 Henry IV* he rants about bullets and hell-fire, and quotes violent war-plays; he pictures men dying like dogs, and blood being shed; surgical procedures, broadsides and 'grievous gastly gaping wounds'.[59] In *Henry V* he continues his fixation with 'doting death', gaping graves and gallows, cut throats, and blood-sucking horse-leeches.[60] Such a litany of horror sorts oddly with Hotson's claim that 'the spectacle of Pistol's verse-and-glory fixation ... would release the best of all laughs – at the comedy of ones own human folly' (65). In *2 Henry IV*, after all, his first appearance features his assault of Falstaff, and his last is prefaced by the news that he has beaten someone to death (5.4.16-18). 'This is chilling', notes a recent critic: 'These characters we have been prepared to laugh at have really meant what they have been saying all along. They really do kill people' (Cohen, 67). It might be added that the scholarship that has identified the dribs and drabs of the old plays Pistol quotes has tended to obscure the more or less deranged voice that speaks them.

One recent study of shell-shock is subtitled *A History of the Changing Attitudes to War Neurosis*. Despite the shifting terminology of its subject, its symptoms remain starkly consistent. A 'deep despair' was noted among soldiers suffering from 'nostalgia' during the Thirty Years War (Babington, 7), and veterans of the American Civil War were described as 'callous to moral sensibility' (16). In 1910 patients with 'neurasthenia' displayed 'insufferable restlessness ... abnormal irritability, defective control of temper' (44-5). During the Great War, the 'Shell-Shock Sick' (96), men 'quite incapable of self-control' (93), suffered 'acute confusional insanity' characterized by 'persistent hallucinations, ideas of persecution, and other symptoms' (109); Siegfried Sassoon, himself a sufferer, described an 'underworld of dreams haunted by submerged memories of warfare' (112). In 1943 the U.S. Army 'adopted the diagnostic terms of "battle-fatigue" and "combat exhaustion" to describe the disorder', manifest in patients' 'extremely bizarre' behaviour, with 'senseless gestures and alternating periods of excessive activity' (151-2). Post-traumatic stress disorder (PTSD) came to define the 'nightmares, insomnia, "flashbacks" to the scenes of battle, a tendency to be easily startled, depression, anxiety and ... emotional numbness' (168) presented by veterans of Vietnam. Diagnosis from history, let alone from fiction, is of course perilous, but it is striking how so many of these terms call to mind Pistol's bizarrely erratic, 'chilling' behaviour that critics have noted. Babington assigns the first systematic studies of the malady to the seventeenth century; we might at least mark Pistol's case 'NYDN' – the acronym devised by a sceptical officer-class in

1917: 'Not Yet Diagnosed, Nervous' (96).

The symptomatic dreams, nightmares and hallucinations of the condition in any case resonate with the theatrical self-consciousness Pistol shares with his braggart kind. That condition does not seem restricted to cases of shell-shock, as Paul Fussell has shown. His observation, in *The Great War and Modern Memory*, that among its combatants 'the temptation to melodramatic self-casting was everywhere' (195) further erodes the (perhaps complacent) distinction between a Braggart's vaunts and the disturbances of PTSD. Pistol's single-minded (but third-person) accounts of himself encourage the possibility of perceiving within his character a comparable severity of context, a harsher doubleness still to his lieutenancy. The testimonies Fussell assembles in his section on 'Being Beside Oneself' (191-6) provide a sobering gloss to Pistol's quotation from Marlowe, Kyd, Peele and *Locrine*. One soldier, for example, writes on the eve of battle of 'a queer new feeling ... A sort of feeling of unreality, as if I were acting on a stage'; another, overhearing himself talk tactics, suddenly realized that 'one half of me was convinced that all this was real; the other knew it was illusion'; a third 'felt an intense desire to see plays again, more intense than ever before or since'. E.E. Stoll absorbingly commented that 'the braggart captain ... is incompatible with himself' (431), and Ancient Pistol certainly conforms to Hall's Theophrastan stereotype. 'Hee is ever on the stage', but such self-performative display is neither necessarily comic nor self-advancing. If Hotspur bones up on Tamburlaine's command of technological war, his successor Pistol seems to confuse war with theatre, conflating the play with the blood and fear of the front line. 'Hee is a Spanish souldier on an Italian Theater' (as Hall continues) but Shake-speare's inflationary double-Pistol is also a cosmopolitan coin in a European theatre of war. If, as Thomas Digges wrote, 'treasure is ... becom *Nervus Belli*', Pistol is its nervous wreck.

The sombre portrait of Pistol thus developed is lent contrast by Jonson's contemporary Braggart, Bobadilla, in *Every Man In His Humour* (1598, Q 1601, F 1616). Whatever the exact extent or direction of influence,[61] Pistol's various traits are distributed three ways among the humourists of Jonson's play. Pistol's stage-struck relish for the bombast of old-fashioned plays is principally attributed to the plagiarist Matheo, though his praise for Kyd elicits full agreement from Bobadilla (1.3.126-42). Bobadilla himself shares the apparatus of his military imposture with Musco, who disguises himself on stage 'like a soldier' (2.1.SD). The distinction between these two figures is exampled by the swords they wield: Bobadilla claims his own surpasses the mythic '*Morglay, Excalibur, Durindana*', but dismisses Musco's as a cheap army-surplus 'Fleming' (2.3.138-147). Broadly stated, Bobadilla inherits the characteristics of the *miles gloriosus* and *commedia* Capitano, while the disguised Musco inhabits a more discernibly Elizabethan environment.[62]

Hall calls his vainglorious 'Spanish souldier on an Italian Theater' 'a bladder full of winde'. Jonson's knowledge of the same tradition is shown both in his description of Bobadilla and Matheo as 'two *Zanies*' in Q (2.3.53), and by its revision to 'wind-instruments' in F (3.1.62). Bobadilla's eulogy on his sword, and the taciturnity he both professes and belies ('I love few words', 2.3.75) echo by turns Tophas's 'Smyter' and Basilisco's 'Oratrix'. And though he does not mint them himself, Bobadilla shares his predecessors' predilection for 'high borne wordes', and their high-falutin, macaronic style. 'Fie veney', he exclaims, correcting Matheo's terms (with a surety that evades Captain Crackstone), 'most grosse denomination, as ever I heard: oh the *stockado* while you live Signior, note that' (1.3.218-19). When he explains the 'publique benefit of the state' he can provide by killing 40,000 of the enemy by duelling, at twenty a day (4.2.61-86), the distance between brag and battlefield is all too plain.

Bobadilla descends from literary precedents,then, but Musco's disguise as a veteran soldier itself impersonates the 'divers persons' denounced by Proclamation, 'pretending to have served in the late warres and service as Souldiers ... [who] take that cloak and colour, to bee the more pitied'. Jonson's revision of his play's setting from a vague Florence to an exactly Elizabethan London,[63] highlights the original topicality of Musco's disguise, impersonating the real counterfeit veterans who solicited alms at Moorfields and Mile End (F 2.4.9, 2.5.144). Q Musco's transition into F Brainworm is accompanied by an emphasis upon the soldier-scholarly apparatus of late Elizabethan war and its braggart-pedantic counterfeit. Thus, if he can intercept his master, he tells us in Q, '*Rex Regum*, I am made for ever' (2.1.17); exchanging the Braggart's kingly pretensions for the *locus classicus* of the Soldier-Scholar, his exclamation becomes in F, '*Veni, vidi, vici*, I may say with Captayne CAESAR' (2.4.18-19). His *alias* likewise changes from the vaguely portentous Portensio in Q (2.2.90), to the smoothly fitting Fitz-Sword (bastard son of word, or sword?) in F (2.5. 122). And where Musco's disguise suggests 'the Tamberlaine, or the Agamemnon of the rout' (Q 3.2.20-22), Brainworms's deception covers the 'Serjeant-*Major*, if not Lieutenant-*Coronell* to the regiment' (F 3.5.8-23), in a revision that acknowledges the contextual symmetries of the Elizabethan theatre of war (see above, pp. 125-6).

Musco and Bobadilla present discrete facets of military imposture. Bobadilla's oath, 'as I am a gentleman and a soldier' (Q 1.3.85-6), gains comic purchase from its gradually evident untruth. The disguised Musco also begs alms of his master by claiming to be 'a poor gentleman, a soldier', and his role as Zanni was emphasized by the coda Jonson added to his initial soliloquy: 'as I am true counterfeit man of warre, and no souldier!' (F 2.2.22-3). The pattern of deceit is sophisticated, (the actor playing) Bobadilla pretending to martial prowess, (the actor playing) Musco impersonating real counterfeit veterans. By comparison, however, Pistol attaches strings and mirrors to Jonson's comedy of humours. So while the plays of Marlowe and Kyd find reference in Jonson's and Shakespeare's,

Pistol's quotation-marks are harder to discern than Matheo's. Unlike Musco, there is no simple acknowledgement of the imposture Pistol adopts; and unlike Bobadilla, the parameters of Pistol's role are not defined by literary precedent.

Barton well describes Matheo and Bobadilla as 'two amusing boobies' (1984, 52); 'amusing', however, scarcely gauges Pistol's depth. It is true that cowardice has always appeared to be funny, and Bobadilla's shrinking scrabble for excuses when faced by Giuliano's challenge (4.2.120-24) certainly invites ridicule. Bobadilla (like Crackstone, Basilisco, and Bragga-docchio before him) is coweringly comic, and so (in the opinion of many commentators) is Pistol. Walter's 1954 edition praises the 'humour' to be derived from Pistol's 'abject terror' at Harfleur (xxxvii), and, to a more recent critic, he is the very 'image of cowardice' (Pugliatti, 244). Yet the distinction between cowardice and trauma is often moot (Babington, 55); and Pistol's service-record in *Henry V* is shrouded by the fog of war.

Driven to the breach at Harfleur by Fluellen, the Boy then impugns Pistol's killing tongue and quiet sword. The next we hear of him is Fluellen's own report of the battle. 'There is an aunchient Lieutenant there at the Pridge', he tells Gower, 'I thinke in my very conscience hee is as valiant a man as *Marke Anthony*, and hee is a man of no estimation in the World, but I did see him doe as gallant service' (3.6.12-16). 'The surprise of the identification', comments Taylor, 'is surely intended as comic',[64] but the joke is less emphatic than, say, Le Fer's praise of his captor at Agincourt (in both French and English) as 'the most brave, valorous and thrice-worthy signeur of England' (4.4.63-5). Gower flatly dismisses the report – 'Why, this is an arrant counterfeit Rascall' (60) – but Fluellen remains adamant: 'I'll assure you a utt'red as prave words at the Pridge, as you shall see' (62-5). Gower's reply, his description of the 'slanders of the age', persuades Fluellen that Pistol 'is not the man that hee would gladly make shew to the World hee is', but the 'gallant service' Fluellen saw at the bridge remains a quiet mystery which once again unsettles the expectations Pistol provokes. The behaviour Gower laments, furthermore, bears a curious resemblance to the terms in which the King himself later urges on his 'band of brothers'.

For while Gower condemns men like Pistol who 'now and then goes to the Warres, to grace himselfe at his returne into London, under the forme of a Souldier', Henry too predicts the soldier's safe return, for 'He that out-lives this day, and comes safe home, | Will stand a tip-toe when this day is named' (4.3.41-2). 'And such fellowes are perfit in the Great Commanders Names', continues Gower, bemoaning the effect a military beard and battledress will have 'among foming Bottles, and Ale-washt Wits' (3.6.70-80). King Henry actively coaches his audiences in the recital of such names, and under the same circumstances:

> Old men forget; yet all shall be forgot:
> But hee'le remember, with advantages,

> What feats he did that day. Then shall our Names,
> Familiar in his mouth as household words,
> *Harry* the King, *Bedford* and *Exeter*,
> *Warwick* and *Talbot*, *Salisbury* and *Gloucester*,
> Be in their flowing Cups freshly remembred.
> (4.3.49-55)

It is the time-honoured role of soldiers to 'remember, with advantages' their feats; yet one veteran's 'pardonable exaggerations' are another braggart's slander of the age.[65] Gower's description of theatrical rehearsal ('they will learn you by rote where services were done ... who came off bravely, who was shot, who disgraced') anticipates the performance Dekker was to observe among veterans ('some shewing how bravely they gave the onset: some, how politickly they retirde: others, how manfully they gave and received wounds'). Pistol too plays the soldier, and echoes, at his last appearance, his King's 'indulgently humorous' prediction of nostalgia,[66] 'Then shall he strip his sleeves, and shew his skars, | And say, these wounds I had on Crispines day' (Q 4.3.46-7):

> To England will I steale, and there Ile steale:
> And patches will I get unto these cudgeld scarres,
> And swore I got them in the Gallia warres.
> (5.1.91-3)

'The Gallia warres': Pistol's 'phrase of warre' (3.6.74) echoes the Tudor title of Caesar's *Commentaries, His Martiall Exploytes in the Realme of Gallia* (1565), in a final flourish of the soldier-scholarly expertise to which this comic, cowardly counterfeit pretends. Except that such a description is tempered by the brute fact that all his fellow 'Irregular Humorists' are now dead; that Fluellen could have sworn he 'did see him doe ... gallant service'; and that the wounds he will swear he received in the wars were indeed – albeit after the battle – 'had on Crispines day'. Pistol speaks nought but truth.

This Braggart-Pedant's troubling presence brings us back to the counterfeit soldiers that hung around London streets in the 1590s, 'some ... neither ... maymed nor hurt', who assumed the mantle of genuine veterans 'to bee the more pitied'; back to the paraphrasers and metamorphosers, who 'by Rumors, letters, or printed *Pamphlets*' pretended to heroic deeds; back to the multilingual unreliability of war-news, whether printed in news-letters or enacted on stage; back, in short, to Rumour.

'Rumour doth double like the voice, and eccho | The numbers of the feared' (*2 Henry IV*, 3.1.92-3). Warwick's lines themselves echo Ovid's House of Fame, where 'the thing that was invented growes much greater than before'. But if Rumour doubles, who doubles Rumour? The answer to this is surely Pistol. Like Rumour's continual slanders, Pistol (a slander of the age) pronounces his lies and truths in every language, reflecting both cosmopolitan militarism and the news-pamphlets of the times. His 'false reports' also find an echo in Pistol's very name. Falstaff's recruits, who 'feare the report of a Caliver' (*1 Henry IV*, 4.2.19-20), demonstrate the common ground between Pistol's and Rumour's noises off. After Rumour's prologue, the air is thick with the blended truths and lies of a whole sequence of posts, letters, messages and messengers. When Hotspur's death is confirmed, Morton turns to other rumours. He 'speake[s] the truth' of the York rebellion (1.1.187), and Northumberland confesses that, 'to speake truth, | This present grief had wip'd it from my mind' (209-10). The parallel scene in Act Five features Pistol who likewise 'speake[s] the truth' (5.3.118) of the old King's death. 'What wind blew you hither?', asks Falstaff, a question that emphasizes this newsmonger's kinship with Rumour, making the wind his posthorse: 'Not the ill winde which blowes no man to good' is Pistol's ironic reply, 'helter skelter, have I rode to thee, and tidings do I bring' (86-96). Stephen Booth has speculated that 'a heightening of a relationship already embodied in the text would result from doubling Rumour ... with Pistol' (141), and certainly, if played by the same actor, Pistol's 'tidings' would all the more suggest Rumour's 'smooth comforts false, worse then true wrongs' (40). For of course Pistol both speaks the truth and lies: Henry IV *is* dead, but the 'luckie joyes, and golden times' (5.3.96-7) he promises are far from the reality Falstaff encounters. 'Light credit dwelleth there', as Golding's Ovid reads, 'There dwells rash error: There dooth dwell | Vayne joy'.

Pistol is a 'stronger Armado than before' of the sort feared in the mid-1590s, and it seems that he deliberately alludes to his more genteel forebear when he delivers his news: 'I speake the truth: when Pistol lies, do this, and fig me like the bragging spaniard' (5.3.118-20). His final speech in *Henry V* brings 'News ... that my Doll is dead i' th' spital | Of malady of France' (5.1.82-3), and forms the jarring preface to another princess's elevation to the throne. But his fifth-act entrance in *2 Henry IV*, breaking into Shallow's celebrations, also recalls Marcade's, and like him brings news of the death of a king. Falstaff's earlier exclamation adds force to that recollection: 'a rascall bragging slave', he complains to Doll, 'the rogue fled from me like quicksilver' (2.4.229-30). The phrase is well calculated, for the metal's capacity 'to seem to dissolve other metals by forming alloys' is startlingly appropriate to Pistol's compendious coinages (Porter, 1988, 37). The author of that definition has traced the mercurian pedigree of *Shakespeare's Mercutio* in a study that confirms the prominence of that god in Elizabethan thought. Porter stops short, however, of expounding what I have shown to be his crucial role as the guardian of modern warfare. Certainly Mercutio invites comparison with Mercury; but the range of the god's attributes he assembles more readily applies to Pistol. So while conceding that Mercutio has nothing 'directly to say about theft, nor much about money' (124), Porter claims that Mercutio 'is easily ... Shakespeare's most phallic character' (155), notes that 'mere language has a particular prominence with him' (100) and (suggestively identifying Marlowe with Mercury) asserts that 'Hotspur's death at Hal's hand seems to complete the process of incorporation and exorcism' of Marlowe's influence (143). Yet it is Pistol who inherits and develops these resonances, as the authors of *Eastward Hoe* (1605) recognized in naming its apprentice, a character who repeatedly quotes Pistol's own scraps of quotation (1.1.105-8; 2.1.87-107): Quicksilver.

When Shakespeare fashioned Hotspur, *pace* Porter, he did not discard the mould. Pistol, the mercurial character that seeps into the space left by that 'Coppy and Booke', forms an alloy in the crucible of modern warfare, *Tam Marti quàm Mercurio* (or Mercutio). Pistol provides an NCO's-eye-view of the technological innovations that had changed the face of war; he calls attention to the economic crisis war precipitated at home; to the whispering gallery of fearful surmise England's water-walled bulwark had become; to the European theatres of war to which Englishmen were constantly being dispatched; to the social crisis they inflamed at home; to the theatrical essence of war itself. His final doubleness, his most perturbing ambivalence, lies in his inhabiting the queasy interface between laughably fictional comic archetypes and perturbingly modern casualties of war.

Carlyle's dictum that history is 'a distillation of rumour' is of special applicability to *Henry IV* and *Henry V*.[67] Pistol, himself an amalgam of 'trothes and lyes', is an illuminating spokesman for the symphony of contending voices they comprise. Dramatic lies like Shallow or Falstaff/ Oldcastle ('this is not the man', Ep. 32), blend with the 'truths' of Tudor chronicle, as the matter of history intrudes on Gloucestershire farms and London taverns. This is the force of Pistol's dramatic self-consciousness, just as his linguistic unscrupulousness echoes the political realities of power. It has well been said that the second Henriad 'dilates into retrospection' (Kerrigan, 1990, 29), an observation the more cogent in its applicability to war, simultaneously the catalyst of fire-new technology, and the most inherently nostalgic of institutions. Such a retrospective modernism informs Ancient Pistol's name, rank, and serial impostures; it also forms the basis of the military strategy employed at Gaultree.

At the end of *1 Henry IV*, the rebellion is scotched at Shrewsbury, and we see Hotspur slain in single combat by Hal. Towards the end of *2 Henry IV*, Prince John promises the safe conduct of the rebel forces after their surrender, but then arraigns their leaders with treason and sends them to execution. The victory does not sort comfortably with Hotspur's chivalric precedents. But as Jorgensen has definitively argued, Prince John's actions reflect the erosion of such ideals in the praxis of the 1590s campaigns, the victory of policy over chivalry (1961, 488-92). He cites Thomas Proctor's definition, in *Of the Knowledge and Conducte of Warres* (1578), of the ideal captain who

> ought to flye the faulte of infidelitie and untrothe, as from
> a rocke. For there is no regarde to bee hadde of the man
> that is not just & honest, and firme of his woorde, but
> fycle and variable of promise, which ought alwaies to bee
> perfourmed towardes souldiours, frende, & enemie.
> (E1r)

To this Jorgensen tellingly contrasts the increased desperation with which
the Irish wars came to be waged, evidenced in the Queen's 1595 declaration
that 'neither is a Prince bound by his contract, when for just cause the
contract turneth to the public detriment' (491). The corollary with Gaultree
is clear. 'Is this proceeding just and honourable?', asks the dismayed
Mowbray; 'Is your assembly so?', counters Prince John (4.2.110-11). The
watchword of the war Prince John wages is the one he breaks. If the first
casualty of war is truth, as Senator Johnson has it, the episode may also call
to mind the apophthegm of his namesake, Doctor Johnson: that patriotism is
the last refuge of a scoundrel.

   'Captain', Doll had exclaimed at Quickly's unintentional promotion of
Pistol, 'thou abhominable damnd cheter, art thou not ashamed to be called
Captaine ... you a captaine?' (2.4.135-9). Pistol, of course, is as 'firme of his
woorde' as Rumour, and it is no accident that the flicker of Rumour's
tongues attends the description of the rebel army at Gaultree:

>       our army is disperst already,
> Like youthfull steeres unyoakt they take their courses,
> East, weast, north, south ...
> (4.2.327-9)

No accident either that Prince John's policy is immediately succeeded by
Falstaff's capture of another Sir John, Coleville, who yields to his words
rather than to his sword. 'I have a whole schoole of tongs in this belly of
mine, and not a tongue of them all speakes any other word but my name',
he comments (4.2.18-20). It is here that Falstaff is granted his most
extended interview with the world of the court, delivering his prisoner to
Prince John himself: 'With the hook-nosde fellow of Rome', he says, 'I
came, saw, and overcame' (40-41). Prince John then chides Falstaff's
victory in terms that deflect on to his own: 'It was more of his curtesie then
your deserving' (42). His subsequent instruction sets a chill upon the
comedic convention of Coleville's surrender: 'Send Colleville with his
confederates | To Yorke, to present execution' (70-71). But the man he
instructs, though mute, speaks volumes for the passage of time since
Shrewsbury: 'Blunt leade him hence, and see you guard him sure' (73).
'Blunt's part could not be less onerous', comments one editor, 'he says
nothing, and this is the only time he does anything'.[68] But the name, a last,
blunt double, remembers the first play's counterfeit king Sir Walter Blunt,

whose presence in its very first scene, 'new lighted from his horse, | Staind with the variation of eache soile' from Northumberland to London to bring 'smothe and welcom newes' (1.1. 63-6) adumbrates the 'smooth comforts false' delivered by Rumour in the sequel, a 'blunt monster' (18), 'painted full of Tongues'.

### 'Passa Parola, *Advance the Word* ...'

Shakespeare seems to have been absorbed by the figure of the Braggart. 'Basilisco-like',[69] Armado, Falstaff, and Pistol each ripples the comic surface of their roles by pressing home the military stage on which they act. As Elizabeth's wars passed into history, the dramatist seems to have been reluctant to cede with them the resonant proportion of 'mirth to melancholy', theatre to war, such figures bestowed. Two of his earliest Jacobean plays develop the relations between Braggart and Rumour argued for in this chapter, both with significant thematic reversals.

*Othello*'s 'pervasive' debt to comedy, and in particular the Moor's odd resemblance to the *commedia* Capitano, has often been noted.[70] It is Iago's poisonous lies, however, that instigate the play's tragic catastrophe, and Everett's suggestion that Iago is 'dramaturgically perhaps descended from Shakespeare's Rumour' is richly pertinent (1989, 47). The incremental solemnity of Othello's braggart forebears finds apotheosis in a play which wrings the comedy from Sir Tophas's claim that, 'Commonly my words wound' (1.3.58). The Braggart's promotion of words over deeds underpins Shakespeare's last word on the subject, Parolles, the character he added to his source in composing *All's Well That Ends Well*.

'Hee's a good drumme my Lord', says Lafew of Parolles, 'but a naughtie Orator' (5.3.256), prompting Hunter to comment that the 'connection between *drum* and *orator* remains mysterious'.[71] In fact the line clearly signals the character's allegiance to Pistol's regiment, and further reveals the subtlety with which Shakespeare treated of military affairs. Of course Parolles is named for the words he flaunts (5.2.39-40), but contemporary military prescription lends depth to his imposture. His ironic description as a 'gallant militarist ... that had the whole theoricke of warre in the knot of his scarfe, and the practise in the chape of his dagger' (4.3.145-8), is certainly suggestive of such contexts – though attempts by earlier scholarship to identify Parolles as a portrait of Robert Barret himself (the author of *The Theorike and Practike of Modern Warres*) are best resisted.[72] It seems significant that this 'man of words (as his name indicates)' (*Works*, ed. Wells and Taylor, 965) also wields the name of the military command ('advance the word') detailed in Garrard's *Arte of Warre*, which forms the title of this section (1591, 172). The drum with which Parolles is constantly associated in his plot, furthermore, far from being 'mysterious', is absolutely appropriate to his name and role.

In the wars to which Parolles urges Bertram's escape, the regimental drum is lost to the enemy (3.6). Rising to the bait offered by the French captains (in their efforts to persuade Bertram of his fraudulence), Parolles undertakes to retrieve it. As he rehearses his means of counterfeiting valour, he is ambushed by the French captains, believing himself taken by the enemy (4.1). Unlike Pistol, Parolles's military rank is not specified; but his guardianship of the drum suggests a strong parallel between the Ancient (or Ensign), and the Drum (or Drummer). Like the Ancient, the Drum was regarded as a post suitable only to the most 'discreet and sober' of men (Riche, 1587, G2v), since what Bertram calls their 'instrument of honour' (3.6.66) rivalled only the ensign itself as the focus of a company's allegiance. As with Pistol, contemporary military text-books provide a running commentary on a running joke. The Drum, summarized Markham, should be 'indued with all these especiall vertues which should adorne a perfect Souldier, as *Obedience, Silence, Secrecie, Sobrietie, Valour*, and *Loyaltie*'; 'hee stands in the middest when Swords flie on all sides' (1622, 59-60). Markham's typical text, however, provides further salt to the jest, for 'the *Drumme* being the very tongue and voyce of the Commander', must 'bee also a good Linguist, and well seene in forraine Languages: for by the carrying of Messages, he must commerce and have to doe with people of sundry Nations' (58-9).

The rank Parolles travesties at last renders explicit the intimate relations between his military Esperanto 'smacke of all neighbouring Languages' (4.1.16) and 'Rumour painted full of Tongues', 'the sound of drummes, and rumors of warres' (Sutcliffe, 1593, A2r). This 'manifold Linguist, and ... army-potent souldier' (4.3.242) stages a postwar encore to the braggart-pedantic traits we have assembled in his ancestors. Armado acts as pilot to this 'vessell of too great a burthen' (2.3.206), and bequeaths his plumes to the woodcock Parolles (92), as he does to Pistol's turkey-cock (*Henry V*, 5.1.14). Parolles stamps his character in the base metal of Pistol's mould, revealing 'to what mettle this counterfeyt lump of [ore] will be melted' (3.6.38-9);[73] his kingly pretensions (1.1.106) and blatantly sexual bravado (110-24) are both mocked by Helena in their first scene. Like Pistol too, Parolles wears the scraps of Markham's 'forraine Languages' on his sleeve. 'The soule of this man is his cloathes' (2.5.43-4), and the words he both wears and embodies duplicate the range of Pistol's diction, from macaronic latinism ('facinerious', 'debile', 'egregious', 'plausive') to Riche's foolish phrases of cosmopolitan exclamation ('*Mor du vinager*', 'Caprichio', 'Coragio').[74] 'Those Drumers', according to Clayton, 'ought to have sundry languages', and to this extent Parolles's pretence aspires to his *Approved Order of Martiall Discipline* (1591, 17). Greatly revealingly, however, Clayton continues: 'If such Drums ... fortune to fall into the handes of the enemie, no gyfte, no faire speeches, neither force nor terror, shall cause them to bewray any secrets knowne to them'. Shakespeare's wit is substantial in the words Parolles immediately issues when he is captured, as he thinks, by the enemy:

If there be heere German or Dane, Low Dutch,
Italian, or French, let him speake to me,
Ile discover that, which shal undo the Florentine.
(4.1.72-4)

This unprompted flouting of military prescription – 'And all the secrets of our campe Ile shew' (86) – is prompted by the 'fine comic nemesis' of his undoing (Hapgood, 277).

We have heard Armado's language described as 'the dead end, within a decade, of Tamburlaine's "high-astounding terms"' (see above, p. 155). That ultimate cul-de-sac, however, is surely the 'terrible Language', the 'linsie wolsy ... Choughs language' (4.1.3-20), by which Parolles is gulled. More than mere 'fantastic gibberish' (R. Parker, 104), their lines return an echo of the exotic force of that soldier's 'rudiments of war': 'Bulwarks ... Cavalieros ... Argins ... Parapets ...'; *'Throca movousus, cargo, cargo, cargo ... Manka revania dulche ... oscorbidulchos volivorco ... Acordo linta ... Bosko Chimurcho ... Boblibindo chicurmurco'* (4.1.64 - 4.3.129).

Such apparently 'forraine Languages' and 'sundry Nations' seem to feature in the plural name of Parolles; they were also the particular concerns of the rank with which his play associates him. Like Rumour's, his portrait is 'painted full of Tongues', and *All's Well That Ends Well* relies upon their range to effect the promise of its title. As news of its wars are 'reported' as 'most credible' (1.2.4-5), Parolles, 'a notorious Liar' (1.1.99), brags of the 'reports' made of his service by the apparently spurious Captain Spurio (2.1.41-4). Bertram's passage to self-knowledge depends upon his abandoning one lie and accepting another. As his belief in Parolles, 'of verie valiant approofe ... And by other warranted testimonie' (2.5.2-4), wanes, another takes its place. Helena trusts that the 'pittifull rumour' (3.2.129) of her flight will recall Bertram from the wars, and 'the particular confirmations' of her death are later made to him, 'point from point, to the full arming of the veritie' (4.3.64-5). This false news is reported by the two French Captains immediately before their exposure of Parolles, 'this counterfet module' (as Bertram now calls him), who has 'deceiv'd mee, like a double-meaning Prophesier' (4.3.102-3).

Parolles's humiliation has been called 'almost more painful than amusing' (Righter [Barton], 1962, 174). That description gains force when one considers its equal application to his disguised tormentors. For with great irony, the information which this 'infinite and endlesse Lyar' (3.6.11) relates there, comprises a series of uncomfortable truths. 'A truth's a truth', as Parolles repeatedly insists (4.3.161, and see 132, 154, 165), and amidst the bluster of outrage his words provoke, the first Captain's quiet remark should not go unnoticed: 'He's very neere the truth in this' (4.3.155). Certainly his description of the 'muster file', who 'dare not shake the snow from off their Cassockes, least they shake themselves to peeces' (171-4) rings with the conviction of contemporary Elizabethan reports,[75] the bleaker for its contrast with 'the scarffes and the bannerets' of its speaker (2.3.204). And certainly, the 'dialogue betweene the Foole and the Soldiour' Bertram is so eager to witness uneasily reveals a different truth in the warning letter Parolles has written to Dian: 'And say a souldier (Dian) told you this ... the Counts a Foole' (4.3.233-5). Bertram's petulant reaction, 'He shall be whipt through the Armie' (239), anticipates the paradox of a later Fool: 'they'l have me whipt for speaking true, thou wilt have mee whipt for lying' (Q King Lear, 1.4.164-5). Even Captain Spurio turns out to be real (4.3.166). Henceforth, like Pistol before him, Parolles speaks nought but truth.

It is in this scene too, that the Braggart's natural inhabitat, the 'double-meaning' theatre of war, again comes into focus. If Pistol's Ancient rank suggests the playhouse flag of permanent performance, the drum Parolles describes in his account of Captain Dumaine bears the same symbolic weight: 'Faith sir, ha's led the drumme before the English Tragedians ... he had the honour to be the Officer at a place there called Mile-end, to instruct for the doubling of files' (4.3.270-74). In 1600, as we have seen, Henslowe bought just such a military instrument to drum up audiences on a provincial tour (see above, p. 115), while the efficacy of the Mile End musters was a common laughing-stock among military men. The double files of war and theatre merge in the plot that concerns Parolles and his drum.

In 1 Henry VI, Shakespeare's fictional soldier Pucelle had imitated the real Sir Francis Vere, in gaining entrance to Rouen by disguising her troops, and bidding them 'Talke like the vulgar sort of Market men' (3.2.4). The theatrical debt of her 'happy Stratageme' (3.3.1) is repaid with interest in All's Well That Ends Well. The Folio stage-directs the French soldiers' entrance with a military term, 'in ambush' (4.1.SD). Counterfeiting an 'Alarum within' (65 SD), they disguise themselves, like their forebears at Rouen, in language. 1 Henry VI had presented (players playing) soldiers acting as players; this scene in All's Well That Ends Well gives us (players playing) soldiers playing soldiers. Such attempts at frame analysis are pushed into almost infinite regression, however, by the object of their counterfeiture: the exposure of a braggart soldier, captured by soldiers (disguised as soldiers) while he ponders whether to counterfeit the military 'stratagem' of disguise (49-50).

Before the ambush, Parolles rebukes his own heart for 'not daring the reports of my tongue' (30-31). Thus 'incompatible with himself' like the Braggart Stoll describes, his words prompt the comment, 'This was the first truth that ere thine own tongue was guiltie of' (32-3): the first but assuredly not the last, as we have seen. Yet, within a scene that trains its camera on its own monitor, the line resonates with a distillation of Shakespeare's theatre of war and Ovid's House of Fame. In both households, 'millions both of trothes and lyes ronne gadding every where, | And woordes confusely flye in heapes'. Such a heap of words is Parolles.

Shakespeare's first Braggart at last presides over a wordy, theatrical pageant which clouds a scene of courtship with a cautionary truth that is subsequently confirmed by a messenger of death. His last Braggart begins his play by jarring an atmosphere of mourning, but after the theatrical exposure of his imposture, he ends by assisting at a resurrection: 'one that's dead is quicke' (5.3.305). The 'mingled yarne' of his clothes and soul recruit him to the truth of Churchill's wartime observation, which might stand as a motto to his play: 'truth is so precious that she should always be attended by a bodyguard of lies'.

*All's Well That Ends Well* ends so well for the subtle reversal it effects on the poignancy of wartime rumour, and its impression on the wartime stage. In *The Shoemakers' Holiday*, Ralph's death is 'rumord here in London' to his wife (5.2.44), but he returns limping to the fellowship of Dekker's comedy. 'The Army breaking' in Shakespeare's play, Bertram returns home from the wars, but it is his wife who is, again falsely, 'supposed dead' (4.4.10). 'Is there no exorcist | Beguiles the truer Office of mine eyes?': Helena's entrance, as 'the shadow of a wife' (5.3. 307-9), brings us to the subject of our next chapter. The Elizabethan veteran variously beguiled his audiences with news from the wars; more perturbing still was that other military revenant, the ghost.

## Notes

1. Owen Rutter, *The Song of Tiadatha* (1919), in Stephen (1988), 52.
2. *APC*, 19, 78-91; *CSP (Dom) 1581-90*, 665 (11 May 1590).
3. Collins (1746), 2, 72.
4. Chamberlain, *Letters*, ed. McLure (1939), 1, 81.
5. Aydelotte lists ten proclamations against rumours made in 1548-9 (63); see also *Whole Volume of Statutes* (1587), 239-41; 337.
6. *Collection of ... Ballads*, ed. Wright and Halliwell (1867), 240-42.
7. Chadwick (1960), 229; see also *Tudor ... Proclamations*, ed. Hughes and Larkin (1964-69), 2, 534-5.
8. See also Sutcliffe (1593), 194; and Riche (1574), E8r.
9. *Whole Volume of Statutes* (1587), 239.
10. *New Variorum 2 Henry IV* ed. Shaaber (1940), 12; *2 Henry IV*, ed. Humphreys (1966), 4; *Liberality and Prodigality*, MSR, line 2.
11. *Johnson on Shakespeare*, ed. Sherbo (1968), 1, 490.
12. *Henry IV*, ed. Humphreys (1966), xvii.
13. *Thomas Platter's Travels*, tr. Williams (1937), 170.
14. News-Pamphlets 2, 4, 6, 7, 12, 18, 23, 25 and 29.
15. See also News-Pamphlets 2, 4, and 24. Hammon's 'gentleman of place' both echoes and anticipates the description of such pamphlets' anonymous authors, 'Written by an English Gentleman of verie good account from Ostend, to a worshipfull Gentleman his friend heere in England' (1602, News-Pamphlet 26): see also News-Pamphlet 6 (1591, A3r).
16. *The Atheists Tragedie* (1611), D2r; *The Atheist's Tragedy*, eds. Morris

and Gill (1976), 2.1.35-7.

17. News-Pamphlets 1, 6, 9, 12-15, 18, 20-21, 23, 25 and 27.

18. 'Mercurius Gallo-Belgicus', *Poems*, ed. Grierson (1929), 69.

19. *The Pastime of Pleasure*, ed. Mead (1928), lines 176-7, 193-5.

20. Reproduced in Brooks-Davies (1983), 110.

21. H. Berger asserts that Rumour's gender is 'conspicuously obscure', and then that 'her [*sic*] spirit festers on' (1984, 64).

22. *Oxford Dictionary of Quotations* (1979), 273.

23. *All's Well That Ends Well*, 3.2.103-4.

24. Tawney and Power (1924), 2, 343-54; *England Proclamations*, 5 November 1597.

25. Hughes and Larkin (1964-9), 3, 105.

26. Hughes and Larkin, (1964-9), 3, 196-7.

27. *The Arte of English Poesie*, ed. Willcock and Walker (1936), 252-3.

28. *Poems*, ed. Grierson (1929), 140-49 (lines 64-5; 111-14).

29. *Fedele and Fortunio*, MSR, line 78.

30. The phrase crops up again in the mouth of the newly enlisted Dericke in *The Famous Victories of Henry the Fift*: 'How now ho, *Basillus Manus*, for an old codpeece' (Bullough, 4, 325).

31. Lyly, *Works*, ed. Bond (1902), 3, 100.

32. Lineation is from Kyd's *Works*, ed. Boas (1901), text from the 1599 Q.

33. *A Notable Discovery of Coosnage* (1591), *Works*, ed. Grosart, 10, 38.

34. *The Trial of Chivalry*'s Dick Bowyer tells us it was Cupid who shot him 'right into the left heele' (C1v)

35. Pyrgopolinices, Plautus's *Miles Gloriosus*, claims to have fought in Scytholatronia (*Works*, tr. Nixon, 1916-38, 3, 128, line 44).

36. *Three Tudor Classical Interludes*, ed. Axton (1982), 11.

37. *Roister Doister*, ed. Schuerweghs (1939), lines 208-28.

38. *Love's Labour's Lost*, ed. Kerrigan (1982), 12.

39. *Plutarch's Lives*, ed. Henley (1895-6), 5, 52.

40. See *Love's Labour's Lost*, ed. Kerrigan (1982), 161-2.

41. *Love's Labour's Lost*, ed. Kerrigan (1982), 232; ed. David (1956), 175.

42. Dulwich College MS 19.

43. *Poems*, ed. Krueger (1975), 139. The *Epigrams* were published with Marlowe's translation of Ovid's *Amores* in an undated Quarto. Krueger dates the poems 1594-5, but see Nicholl (1996) for a convincing argument for the earlier date.

44. *1 Henry IV*, ed. Humphreys (1960), 31 (1.3.199-205 n.); Porter (1989), 135-43.

45. *2 Henry IV ... New Variorum*, ed. Shaaber (1940), 5.

46. If, as has been claimed, The Sex Pistols were named after Shakespeare's character, the unlikeliest of people seem to know their Onions.

47. See Kaplan (1971), 400.

48. *2 Henry IV*, ed. Humphreys (1966), 75 (2.4.177 n.).

49. *The Works of Mr. William Shakespear*, ed. Rowe (1709-10), 3, 1340.
50. *Henry V*, ed. Craik (1995), 297 (4.4.4 n.).
51. W.S., *A Discourse*, ed. Lamond (1897), 187.
52. The 'double pistolets', for example, in *Captain Thomas Stukeley*, MSR, line 383.
53. *2 Henry IV*, ed. Humphreys (1966), 184 (5.5.88-9 n.).
54. *Henry V*, Walter, (1954), xxxviii.
55. On 'Shakespeare's Most Difficult Proverb', see Jorgensen (1976).
56. *Every Man In His Humour*, ed. Seymour-Smith (1966), 5.
57. On parallels between Hal and Pistol, see Rabkin, and E. Berry (1979); on the ramifications of royal doubleness see Kantorowicz, and Axton.
58. 'The Psychology of the Wounded Soldier', *British Medical Journal*, 15 April 1916 (564).
59. *2 Henry IV*, 2.4.112-13; 153-4; 160-66; 170; 192; 177; 194.
60. *Henry V*, 2.1.64-5; 3.6.41; 2.1.72; 2.3.53-4.
61. 'Bobadilla anticipates and indeed may have influenced ... Pistol' (Barton, 1984, 50-51), but if so, such an influence would have to be limited to *Henry V*.
62. There is also common ground between the two: each claims heroic service in exotic campaigns (2.1.55-64, 2.3.102-35), and spices his speech with the Esperanto of war (see 2.1.15, and 2.3.102).
63. Since Bobadill offers his plan 'to her Majestie' only there (F 4.7.65).
64. *Henry V*, ed. Taylor (1984), 186.
65. *Henry V*, ed. Walter (1954), 113.
66. *Henry V*, ed. Craik (1995), 290.
67. *The Oxford Dictionary of Quotations* (1979), 131.
68. *2 Henry IV*, ed. Humphreys (1966), 136.
69. *King John*, 1.1.244.
70. *Othello*, ed. Honigmann (1997), 77; de Mendonca (1968), 31-8.
71. *All's Well That Ends Well*, ed. Hunter (1959), 141.
72. Asserted by Chalmers, according to the *DNB*, where Barret is also pleasingly credited with composing the longest epic poem (68,000 lines) in the language.
73. F reads 'this ... lump of ours'. The suggestion in Hunter's Arden edition, that gold (the heraldic *or*) is being hinted at (89) would well duplicate Pistol's counterfeiture.
74. 2.3.30, 2.3.35, 2.3.217, 4.1.26; 2.3.45, 2.3.290, 2.5.91.
75. See below, pp. 205-6.

CHAPTER FIVE

# Ghosts of War

*'Old soljers never die they never die ...'* [1]

In 1600 the ghost of Christopher Marlowe was 'to be seene walke the *Churchyard* in ... three or foure sheets'. The author of this sighting, the publisher Thomas Thorpe, hastily explains, lest his readers 'should presently looke wilde now, and grow humorously frantique', that this 'ghoast or *Genius*' was Marlowe's translation of *Lucans First Booke*, only now 'rais'd' by him into print.[2] Thorpe's joke is darkly apt: the author of *Doctor Faustus* is to be conjured 'in all rites of perfect friendship'. But it is also appropriate to the translation itself, since the first book of *Pharsalia* was a frequently cited authority in sixteenth-century ghost-lore.[3] Its 'Wars worse then civill on *Thessalian* playnes' (1) are presaged by a series of 'dismall Prophesies' (562), including the spectres of Crassus (11), Marius (568) and Sulla (579), whose 'Ghoasts incounter men' (568). And in their English translation they were heralded into print by the 'spirit' of Marlowe.

Thorpe's 'bumptious humour' (Rostenburg, 18) tries to laugh off these ancestral voices prophesying war, but, as Gill notes, much of Lucan's matter had a 'grim topicality' (1, 89) when Marlowe composed his translation in the mid- to late 1580s, which (we should add) had not receded by the time of its publication. Lucan's analysis of 'this warrs seed' (159) chimes with a host of Elizabethan admonitions against the weaknesses bred of peace, anticipating, for example, Smythe's attack on Elizabethan 'effeminacies and superfluities' (1590, *4r) by describing Romans who 'tooke delight in jewels ... and ware robes | Too light for women' (164-6). Lucan's account of their rummaging for long-neglected weapons (241-5) must have held a peculiar force for Englishmen periodically armed against imminent invasion with the 'olde swords' (244) of parish church armouries. So too must his reworking of Virgil's 'Vaine fame', which 'increast true feare, and did invade | The peoples minds ... and swiftly bringing newes | Of present war, made many lies and tales' (465-8). Such 'newes' persisted in England into the new century, augmented by incremental fears of civil war as Elizabeth's reign waned and the succession remained apparently unresolved. Philip II died in 1598, but his son promised greater commitment to the wars, landing military supplies in Ireland in April 1600 (Falls, 1950, 263-4). And though the French wars ended in 1598, the peace talks held at Boulogne in July 1600 proved abortive: 'all was in vaine', as Camden records (4, 158). The beleaguered Rome presented in Marlowe's Lucan, culminating in the weird prophecy delivered by a Roman matron in 'th'amazed streetes' (675) provided an alarum for late Elizabethan London – itself the site of 'feare and consternation' in August 1599 'with such a crie of women, chaining of streets and shutting of the gates as though the ennemie had ben at Blackewall'.[4]

In 1600, then, Marlowe's ghost, wrapped in 'three or foure sheets', was as timely as his *Tamburlaine*'s 'stately tent of War' had been a decade earlier. As timely was another ghost whose 'warlike forme' (1.1.45) first walked 'in compleat steele' (1.4.33) around 1600 – Old Hamlet's. Shakespeare had begun the 1590s by apprenticing himself to a depiction of the 'wars worse then civill' of England's Plantagenet past. Concluding that sequence in 1599's *Henry V*, he turned his attention to the 'Domesticke Fury, and fierce Civill strife' adumbrated in Lucan's First Book (*Julius Caesar*, 3.1.266). The strong sense of continuity between *Henry V*, *Julius Caesar* and *Hamlet* has often been remarked and the plays themselves invite notice of their sequence. *Henry V*'s last Chorus likens the Londoners welcoming home their victorious king to the 'Plebeians' of 'th'antique Rome' who 'fetch their Conqu'ring *Caesar* in' (5.Ch.26-8). *Julius Caesar* opens amid exactly comparable celebrations, a 'Holyday to see *Caesar*, and to rejoyce in his Triumph' (1.1.30-31). That triumph soon sours, and Caesar's murdered ghost later appears on the field of Philippi – his apparition another commonly cited precedent of Elizabethan ghost-lore.[5] It is the 'high and palmy state of Rome' which occurs to Horatio as apposite to the 'portentous figure' of the murdered king in *Hamlet* (Q2 1.1.112-16).[6]

This chapter seeks to demonstrate that parallels such as these may be furthered by reference to the specifically military topicalities of the plays. In particular it shows that the overt presentation of the supernatural, which invites comparison between *Julius Caesar* and *Hamlet*, profoundly informs and disturbs the festive mustering by which *Henry V* gathers its inclusive strength: contemporary ghost-lore afforded wartime connotations and applications which the play systematically exploits. The following section restores to the seminal figure of Kyd's Ghost of Andrea in *The Spanish Tragedy* the emphasis of his military bearing, and the scrutiny of the boundary between war and revenge such emphasis prompts. That scrutiny is made the basis of my second section's reading of *Henry V* and the folklore of military afterlife it deploys and depicts. *Hamlet* is the subject at large of my sixth and final chapter.

## Soldiering on

Marlowe's was not the only thespian ghost seen walking in 1600. Jonson's Induction to *Cynthia's Revels*, performed that year, makes a calculated snipe at, among others, *The Spanish Tragedy*:

> They say, the *umbrae*, or ghosts, of some three or foure
> playes, departed a dozen yeeres since, have bin seen

> walking on your stage heere: take heed, boy if your house
> bee haunted with such *hobgoblins*, 'twill fright away all
> your spectators quickly.[7]

Jonson's preface shares with Thorpe's both its bumptious humour, and the fitness of its reference, for both Marlowe's and Kyd's now posthumous works were themselves concerned with the apparatus of military adumbration. 'While slaughtred *Crassus* ghost walks unreveng'd' at the outset of Lucan's *Pharsalia* (11), *The Spanish Tragedy* begins with 'the Ghoast of *Andrea*, and with him *Revenge*'.[8]

The dates Jonson provides for Kyd's play, 'departed a dozen yeeres since', approximate most modern appraisals. Freeman, following Boas, offers the parameters of 1585-87 (79), Pitcher's edition those of 'say, 1587 and 1592' (1998, xii). Though critical debate has hinged about the play's relationship to 'the Armada',[9] the anterior dates should alert us to the more substantial fact of its composition in the wake of open war with Spain. That context, I take it, profoundly informs the play, and should perhaps temper the brusque dismissal Edwards offers of Kyd's construction: 'He must start his chain of causation somewhere, of course, and he chooses to bury his start in those long-winded early scenes about the war on the borders of Spain and Portugal' (27). The words demonstrate a characteristic intimacy between the origins and afterlives of the play's themes and its textual history, transmission and criticism. Pitcher's 'uncanny sense of retrospection in and around the play' (xiii) is consolidated by the fact that this seminal war-play, written at the outbreak of war, itself begins in military aftermath; that its prologue features the most extreme type of veteran imaginable: a ghost.

Kyd indeed 'chooses to bury his start' in the 'late conflict with *Portingale*' (1.1.15), but he begins by encouraging the assumption that his originating ghost is restless for want of burial. Killed in the wars, Andrea is first delayed by 'churlish *Charon*', who 'Said that my rites of buriall not performde, | I might not sit amongst his passengers' (20-22). 'Let the souldiers be buried', beseeches Zabina in *1 Tamburlaine*, after desperately picturing 'the blasted banks of *Erebus*: | Where shaking ghosts with ever howling grones' hover for 'passage to *Elisian*' (*One*, 5.1.316; 244-47). 'Why sufferst thou thy sonnes unburied yet', asks Titus Andronicus, 'To hover on the dreadfull shore of Stix?': 'slaine in your Countries warres', they too are laid to rest in burial at the opening of the play (1.1.87-91). Each play rehearses the specifically military superstition later summarized in the 1665 edition of Scot's *Discoverie of Witchcraft*. The sight of 'millions of Apparitions in fields where battails had been fought, seeming to fight', it reads, is explained 'from the want of Burying. And from this arose the Poetical Romance of the *wandring of Ghosts besides the River Styx for an hundred yeares*'.[10] Andrea too has 'died in warre' (47). Perhaps he may be counted among the many examples to which the anonymous author then alludes, 'of such as has appeared to their surviving kindred and acquaintance, after they had been slaughtered in the Warrs, beseeching them to perform unto their bodies the Sacred Funeral Rites that their Ghost might return into Rest' (507). In fact we swiftly learn that his 'funerals and obsequies' (26) have been observed by his 'kindred and acquaintance', 'By *Don Horatio* our knight Marshals sonne' (25). The moment sets the tone of what follows. One form of military afterlife, the first in a series, is suggested, then discarded, in a pattern of frustrated definition repeated through the induction and the play.

Edwards finds the pattern of its early scenes 'long-winded' precisely because their sense of protracted aftermath exposes the difficulty with which the wars, like the buried Andrea, are laid to rest. His implicit distinction between war and revenge (the first to be dispensed with as quickly as possible for the second, the real business of the play, to begin) overlooks the play's characteristic occupation of 'the borders' between them, and Andrea's posthumous progress is once again to the point.

Passing across to 'the slimie strond' (28), Andrea is first assigned by Aeacus to the 'fields of love' (42), and then once again stayed:

> No, no, said *Rhadamant*, it were not well,
> With loving soules to place a Martialist,
> He died in warre, and must to martiall fields:
> Where wounded *Hector* lives in lasting paine,
> And *Achilles* mermedons do scoure the plaine.
> (45-9)

Long seen as an adaptation of the Senecan prologue, Andrea's posthumous topography is also closely modelled on Aeneas's descent to the underworld in Book Six of Virgil's *Aeneid*, and critics have variously accounted for this mixture of influence. Howard Baker, one of the earliest 'to emphasize the Virgilian rather than the Senecan element' of the play (1935, 29), claimed a kinship between Kyd's Induction and the apparatus of medieval metrical tragedy, and of the genre's abiding Elizabethan form, *The Mirror for Magistrates*. Replacing T.S. Eliot's assertion that Andrea and Revenge 'replace the Tantalus and the Fury of the *Thyestes*' (27), Baker offers a different model in which 'a ghost appears with a guide and begins telling a narrative of his life and death' (35). Kyd's Revenge, he claims, resembles the various personifications (Remembrance, Morpheus, Sorrow) who liaise between the tragic poet and his ghostly narrators. In particular, Sackville's contribution to the 1563 *Mirror* included an Induction derived (like Kyd's) from the sixth *Aeneid*, which is followed by the ghost of Buckingham's complaint and call for revenge. Baker's argument would apply the more thoroughly, however, if Andrea's progress had ended in the 'lasting paine' of 'Martiall fieldes'. For, with his soldiership further underlined, and his collocutor still unidentified, Andrea indeed resembles the spectral casualties of war who intermittently voice their homiletic admonitions through *The Mirror for Magistrates.*

In the first 1559 edition, for example, Glendower is described 'cumming out of the wilde mountaynes like the Image of death in all poyntes ... so sore hath famine and hunger consumed hym'.[11] Lord Clifford is shown 'all armed save his head, with his brest plate all gore bloud running from his throte, wherin an hedles arrow sticketh' (191). We are urged in the 1563 edition to 'ymagyne that [we] see [Hastings] newly crept out of his grave' (267), and in 1571, Glendower's 'Image of death' was enhanced by his added likeness to a 'ghost forpined' (120). These 'mangled' ghosts 'with blew wounds' (111) appeal not for the rest of burial, but to 'lament [the] great misfortune' of their fall (120), from a perpetual afterlife squarely identified by Sackville's induction with the *Aeneid*'s underworld terrain. 'An headles arrow strake me through the throte', says Clifford, 'Wherthrough my soule forsooke his filthy coate' (195); Andrea too is slain in battle, freeing 'this eternall substance of my soul ... imprisond in my wanton flesh' (1.1.1-2).

The testament of Sir Nicholas Burdet, added to the 1587 edition of *The Mirror for Magistrates*, is uttered by another bloody ghost: 'You must thinke then ... that you see him all wounded as he was slaine at *Pontoise*' (463). Despite this resemblance to his gory predecessors, however, the lesson Burdet teaches is quite distinct. The moral of Clifford's 1559 tragedy had been to 'warne the bluddy sort, | To leave their wrath, their rigour to refrayne', and his fatal arrow makes up an emblem of 'gods just award' for his 'straunge and abhominable cruelty' in revenging his father's death (192-195). The 'guerdon juste' of which Burdet speaks is awarded him not for his vice but for his virtue. In keeping with the wars declared since the work's previous edition, his complaint, far from being a plea for restraint, becomes a call to arms:

> Yf erst at Princes affayres wee counted were of truste,
> To fight in waeged warres, as Captayne gainst the foes,
> And might therefore alive receive the guerdon juste,
> Which ay his majesty employde on those:
> Why should wee so keepe silence now, and not disclose
> Our noble acts to those remayne alive,
> T'encourage them the like exployts t'achive?
> (463)

First released 'on stage' (464) in 1587, Sir Nicholas Burdet is a close contemporary to Don Andrea. Like Hector and Achilles they stand 'wounded ... in lasting paine', on opposing battle-lines, Trojan and Greek, English and Spanish. Kyd's audiences may well have expected a dramatized narration of (as Burdet says) 'what our warres were then, | The great exployts wee did, and where our armies laye' (464) – a play, in fact, not unlike the '*long alarum*' detailed in the later prequel, *The First Part of*

*Jeronimo* (3.2.SD). Andrea's progress, however, does not end in these martial fields. Provided, like all Elizabethan veterans, with a passport (54), he steers a path between 'the foresaid fields' and 'deepest hell', and is at last 'brought ... to the faire Elizian greene' (1.1.60-74).

Eugene Hill's important article on the play's 'Senecan and Vergilian Perspectives' begins by challenging Baker's. Kyd knew his Virgil *from* Virgil, he insists, needing none of Sackville's mediation (1985, 143-4). Instead, while Kyd's 'Induction introduces Seneca's notion of tragedy as the passage of passion on its obstructed path to infernal vengeance, it also presents Vergilian material that places the Senecan elements in an ironic light' which 'systematically define[s] Andrea's voyage as the inverse of Aeneas's' (164). So where Virgil has *pius* Aeneas descend alive to the underworld in anticipation of the founding of Rome, Kyd has proud Andrea posthumously ascend to set in train the self-destruction of a royal household (146-50). In the Spanish fall is tacitly asserted the corresponding rise of English empire.[12] 'Dilemmas of transition', notes Hill, 'dominate the play' (164), and his model of Kyd's 'inverted mirroring' of sources (147) is persuasive. It may be advanced, however, by lending attention to what I take to be the most dominant of the play's 'vain partitions' (156), namely that between war and revenge. It is on Kyd's 'Elizian greene', imported directly from Virgil, that this transition is most boldly announced.

Andrea's 'wandring Ghost' (35) indeed haunts the footsteps of Aeneas. Charon refuses passage to the unburied Andrea, while Palinurus appeals to Aeneas for burial: Virgil's is the 'Poetical Romance' cited by *The Discoverie of Witchcraft* as a fictive counterpart to the haunted battlefields it explains (see *Aeneid* 6, 327-71).[13] Placating Cerberus (1.1.30; 6, 417-25), Andrea and Aeneas are both shown 'our fields of love' (1.1.42; 6, 440-44) and 'martiall fieldes'. Neither Hector nor Achilles feature in Virgil's 'farthest fields, where the renowned in war dwell apart' (6, 477-8), but their 'lasting paine' finds a precedent in their ranks of soldiers 'still in arms' (485-6), and in the gory shade of Hector's brother Deiphobus, 'his whole frame mangled, his face cruelly torn ... lopped by a shameful wound' (494-9). It is not the rites of burial Deiphobus seeks from Aeneas (509-12), but the audience of his lament. In the course of Kyd's induction, then, Andrea's ghostly status shifts its focus in line with Aeneas's progress, and both journeys culminate in the 'Blissful Groves' (639) of 'the faire Elizian greene'.

Virgil's is a markedly military Elysium, where phantom arms and chariots wander the plain: 'Here is the band of those who suffered wounds, fighting for fatherland' (651-60). Aeneas receives there from his father the prophecy of Rome, 'and when Anchises had led his son over every scene, and fired his soul with love of fame that was to be, he tells him then of the wars he must thereafter wage' (888-90). Before turning to Kyd's treatment of the passage, it is worth noting its contemporary adaptation in the earliest of Riche's military treatises. As we have seen, the circumstance of open war prompted a shift in emphasis (from admonition to exhortation) in the 1587 *Mirror*. Soon after the first English volunteer force landed at Flushing in 1572, Riche published his *Dialogue betwene Mercury and an English Souldier*.

The work begins with Mercury transporting his soldier-narrator to the Court of Mars to deliver his message about soldiers' neglect. They alight on 'a very fayre greene' where 'great rowts of people' are engaged in the 'many exercises' of war: some 'running at the tilte, others at the turny others were pushing with the pike, som were throwing of the dartes, some were exercising the Caliver in manner of skirmishe, and many were on horsebacke, the one having the other in chace' (A5v). Riche takes care to distinguish between Virgil's 'farthest fields, where the renowned in war dwell apart', and the military Elysium further along Aeneas's way. 'No *Cerberus* is Porter in this place' (A6r), Riche's Mercury assures his English soldier:

> Loe, here quod he the Court of *Mars*, where thou mayst beholde those blessed wightes, who spent theyr passed dayes in defence of theyr Countery and right, onely to attaine prayse and noble fame, and not for filthye lucours sake, or hope of any Golde gaine: Where nowe their just desertes is quitte with like delight, what though their bodies intombed bee in clay thou seest their spirite doe here remaine in everlasting blisse, for here no yeres may make them olde, no barehead skul, no wrinkled browe may here be found.
> (A5v-A6r)

'They shall not grow old, as we who are left grow old':[14] like the 'guerdon juste' Burdet's ghost promises to his wartime audience 'the like exployts t'achive', Riche presents 'everlasting blisse' as the 'just desertes' of patriotic service. These 'blessed wightes' have fought 'in defence of theyr Countery and right', and Burdet 'for Prince and publique weale' (463). But while Burdet's wounds, like Deiphobus's, 'freshly bleede' at the memory of 'crafte and treason' (475), Riche insists on the rewards of Elysium.

A similar prospect was later made the basis of the Minister's duty, prescribed by Styward's *Pathwaie to Martiall Discipline*, to put soldiers 'in sure hope through faith in Christ to enter into the campe of everlasting life, where they shall ride amongst the souldiers on white horses, clothed in white and pure silke' (1581, 42). Riche's parable, however, clothes the uncompromisingly pagan apparatus of his model in a firmly Elizabethan guise. Supplementing the chariots Aeneas sees in Elysium with the modern weaponry of caliver and pike, his English soldier relishes his glimpse of fortifications far above 'anye human skyll' (A8r). And while Aeneas meets the shades of 'the fallen in war, the Dardan chiefs' (481-2), Riche counts among his roll-call of war-dead the spectres of real English soldiers, Captains Darcy, Sanders, Randel and Audley, and others 'I lykewise had knowne at Newhaven' (A7r-B1r). Anchises instructs Aeneas in 'the wars he must thereafter wage'; Riche's Virgilian induction prefaces the text-book of modern war his book becomes.

The details of Riche's Temple of Mars (its 'greate rowts' of troops and monuments of battle) suggest affinities with the 'horrors of war' represented by its ancient, medieval and Elizabethan counterparts (Fowler, 153). Sackville's 1563 induction bases its terrain and its monuments to 'hugie hostes' (313) on Virgil's hellish antechamber (268-81). Spenser's Ate presides over the same 'darksome delve farre under ground', 'Hard by the gates of hell', adorned by 'ragged monuments' of 'Nations captived and huge armies slaine' (4.1.19). The 'fayre greene' Riche describes, however, and the 'pure goulde' of its military monuments (A8v) strenuously distinguish between the reward due his 'blessed wightes' and the punishment owed the 'damned sprights' of Spenser's account (4.1.19).

The machinery of Kyd's induction to *The Spanish Tragedy* finds a variety of precedent, then. Possible models for Don Andrea and the so far silent Revenge may include: the Ghost and Fury of the Senecan prologue; Virgil's *pius* Aeneas and his Sybil-guide; the posthumous narrators and scribes of medieval complaint tragedy; their Elizabethan equivalents in the (no less than) six editions of *The Mirror for Magistrates* between 1559 and 1587; and the soldier-narrator and military pedagogue of Riche's *Dialogue*. Andrea appears by turns to belong among 'damned sprights', among the 'shaking ghosts' of unburied soldiers hovering for passage; among the bleeding ghosts whose exemplary falls admonish 'abhominable cruelty' or encourage military valour; and, lastly, among the 'blessed wightes' of a pagan or Christian Valhalla.

Such a range of military afterlife tempers one recent assertion that Andrea, and the ghosts that follow him on to the Elizabethan stage, are all 'recognizably evil' since their 'connection with Hell was constant' (McGee, 22). Categorical assertions like this typify many accounts of *The Spanish Tragedy*. Like the infernal judges who wrangle over Andrea's proper destination, with 'either sort containd within his bounds' (1.1.62), Baker's discussion of the play's Virgilian elements challenges the Senecan emphasis of Cunliffe, Boas and Lucas (27); and Hill's sophisticated account of the 'inverted mirroring' of Senecan and Virgilian sources, by which 'we see the same story running in opposite directions' (147), dismisses Baker's citation of *The Mirror for Magistrates*. The culmination of Andrea's journey in Elysium in fact importantly supplements the series of contrasts Hill notes between him and Aeneas, while testifying to the sustainedly elusive qualities of his military ghost.

Aeneas, the 'perfite souldier' of Elizabethan military prescription,[15] ends his underworld progress by receiving patriotic instruction from his father's shade in 'the wars he must thereafter wage', and passing through the gates of ivory (890-98). Andrea, a dead Spanish soldier, concludes his journey in the 'campe of everlasting life' reserved by contemporary propagandists for patriotic service in the newly declared wars. And at last he identifies his silent companion, and is shown Virgil's alternative gateway (E. Hill, 150): 'Forthwith (*Revenge*) she rounded thee in th'eare, | And bad thee lead me through the gates of Hor[n]' (1.1.81-2).[16] An expectation of military emulation is reversed and replaced by the promise of revenge. The last of the Induction's 'dilemmas of transition' occupies the space between the 'late conflict' and its future consequence, between war and revenge. Neither sort is contained within its bounds.

In the play's last scene, after its sequence of events has dominoed, Andrea's ghost promises to 'lead my freend *Horatio* through those feeldes, | Where never dying warres are still inurde' (4.5.17-18), back to the 'martiall fieldes' in which Hector's 'lasting paine' is endlessly re-enacted (1.1.47-8). 'Never dying warres' frame the sequence of violence that the play presents, and provide a depth of focus to 'the late conflict with Portingale' that initiates its particular action. The *late* conflict: these wars are both recent and (like the late Don Andrea) recently deceased. But like Andrea's ghost they are uneasily buried, for each of the Act's subsequent scenes provides retrospective, and (it is claimed) successively definitive accounts of the battle. Andrea's cursory account of his passage from 'life to death' is followed by the Spanish King's reception of the bare facts of his victory, and the 'Tribute and wonted homage' he has won (1.2.7-9). He then demands a fuller 'breefe discourse' (16) from his General. Perhaps the sixty-odd lines that follow sound 'long-winded' to modern audiences, but their self-conscious amplitude was tempered for contemporary ones by the currency of their 'news' (18): the General's 'breefe discourse' adopts both its content (as Freeman notes),[17] and the style of its title,[18] from contemporary news-pamphlets. The speech also echoes the rhetoric of the messenger's set-piece in the fifth act of Garnier's *Cornélie*, published in Kyd's own translation in 1594. Such a transplant of the classical conventions of closure on to *The Spanish Tragedy*'s opening scene enhances the sense in which its aftermath of war distends.

Beginning at the end (and starting thence away) the play's 'never dying warres' even find expression in the scene's precise stage-business: 'The Armie enters', they 'pass by', but then 'Enter again', at the King's request to 'march once more about these walles' (1.2.109-26). The double-entry, comments Mulryne, 'complements the high verbal flourish of the General's speech', 'extends the air of martial grandeur and confidence', and 'permits the theatrical display so dear to Elizabethans'.[19] It also provides a dramatic embodiment for the narrative recapitulation sustained throughout the act. Although the war seems to be concluded in the 'paper' (92 SD) (the Portuguese treaty of tribute) which the General delivers to the King, the following scene immediately doubles back over the same 'late' ground, this time at the Portuguese court, with another account (this time false) of the same battle.

Villuppo's narrative there initiates the ramifications of war into peace as he uses the occasion of public war to exact a private retribution, but the scene also sketches the origins of the 'late conflict':

> My late ambition hath distaind my faith,
> My breach of faith occasiond bloudie warres,
> These bloudie warres hath spent my treasure,
> And with my treasure, my peoples blood.
> (33-6)

His 'breach of faith' was the withholding of tribute, as we have learned (1.2.135), but such tribute cannot but imply a previous conquest. That retrospection deepens in the fifth scene, with the 'maske' Hieronimo presents at the Spanish victory banquet (1.5.23). Historically, Portugal had been conquered in 1580,[20] but the masque sets this campaign at the head of a sequence of earlier conquests, of Spain by England, in the reigns of King Stephen (27) and Richard II (38), and by John of Gaunt (49). Under the broader auspices of the first production of Kyd's play, it sounds the note of present conflict with Spain. Hieronimo's drum and his three knights, twice 'Dooing as before' (47 SD), symbolically revive the campaigns of the past, like the 'never dying warres' of the underworld that stretch still further back to Troy.

Revenge closes the first act with a promise to turn 'their peace to warre' (1.6.8), but that peace has only ever been as fragile as the 'paper' the King has received – the first of a great many such documents flourished during the play. These props demonstrate an ingeniously various relationship with the violence they typically struggle (and fail) to contain. There is the graphic 'Red incke', for example, specified for Bel-Imperia's 'bloudie writ' (3.2.25-6);[21] the petitions Hieronimo receives as a magistrate, and which, in despair at Justice, he destroys, 'Shivering their limmes in peeces with my teeth' (3.13.123); Pedringano's non-existent pardon in its 'bare empty box' (3.5.6);[22] and the 'severall abstracts drawne' (4.1.140) of the scripts Hieronimo distributes for the final play-within-the-play. 'Teare the Papers', reads one stage-direction (3.13.123). By the end of the play, the peace-treaty lies in pieces.

At the Portuguese court, the Vice-Roy makes 'endles moane' at his son's death in battle (1.3.9). Alexandro reassures him that 'still the Prince survives', that Balthazar is in Spain, 'a prisoner by mischance of warre', but his father assumes the worst:

> — Then they have slaine him for his fathers fault.
> — That were a breach to common law of armes.
> — They recke no lawes that meditate revenge.
> (43-8)

His father's 'fault' caused the war, a fault merged here with a suspected revenge for it. The exchange points up the blurred interface between the 'law of armes' and 'foule revenge' (49): between murder and death-in-battle. Villuppo's narrative, 'When both the armies were in battell joynd' (60), echoes the Spanish general's, but tells of a murder. Balthazar is first pictured 'amidst the thickest troupes', then 'in single fight', and then shot in the back by Alexandro, 'Under the colour of a duteous freend', 'As though he would have slaine their Generall' (61-8). The account is the 'wicked forgerie' Alexandro calls it; but it is interesting that the story is itself one involving an ambiguous moments of violence, a pistol-shot apparently aimed at the enemy which kills an ally – a counterpart of the use to which it is put by the dissembling narrator.

Horatio's account of the same battle (the fourth so far) to Bel-Imperia, makes much of Balthazar's 'ruthles rage' (1.4.23) against Andrea, 'Taking advantage of the foes distresse' (24) and killing him once his halberdiers surround him. The death renders Horatio 'incenst with just remorce' (27) and he captures Balthazar. One critic takes Rhadamanth's cue, and comments that Andrea 'dies quite legitimately in battle' (K. Briggs, 121), and, to an extent, taking advantage of a foe's distress is the very stuff of war. That sense is compounded by the fact that Andrea's death (outnumbered by foot-soldiers commanded by his rival) recalls that of Hector by Achilles and his Myrmidons, a moment enacted 'in lasting paine' in the 'Martiall fields' Andrea himself reports. To Bel-Imperia, however, Balthazar's actions comprise a 'murderous deed' (72):

> For what wast els but murderous cowardise,
> So many to oppresse one valiant knight,
> Without respect of honour in the fight?
> (73-5)

What else except perhaps the common law of arms? That question is pertinent to the visitation of Andrea's ghost, and to the play it frames. Its 'never dying warres' stretch back to Troy and the 'endles Tragedie' with which this tragedy ends (4.5.48). Where do the wars in which Andrea falls originate? With the withholding of tribute from Spain by Portugal? With Spain's conquest of Portugal? With the earlier conquests of Spain by England? With the Trojan War? Hector's death occurred at the end of that war, raising questions as to the origins even of that far-distant conflict, renewed *in perpetuum* in hell. As with the 'Martialist' Andrea, we are confounded as to an origin; and in both Hector's and Andrea's deaths, we are denied an absolute distinction between war and 'murderous cowardise'.

Where does the 'late conflict' take place? 'On the borders of Spain and Portugal', replies Edwards. The Spanish General, however, provides a more nuanced answer:

> Where Spaine and Portingale do joyntly knit
> Their frontiers, leaning on each others bound,
> There met our armies in their proud aray.
> (1.2.22-4)

Andrea falls, that is, in a war literally waged *between* Spain and Portugal, on their one common 'bound', the space where they do 'joyntly knit | Their frontiers' into a single border, neatly caught in Kyd's enjambment. The war is waged upon the ground that defines and distinguishes them, but its outcome is the dissolution of their 'frontiers': 'Spain is Portugal, | And Portugal is Spain' (1.5.17-18). We have noted Riggs's account of how the civil wars traced in *3 Henry VI* 'probe the uncertain boundaries that divide acts of war from crimes of blood' (see above, p. 49). His metaphor applies the more exactly to Kyd's seminal play, and its preoccupation with such geographic precision. These 'uncertain boundaries' have characterized the study of war from the sixteenth to the twentieth century. 'The most serious thing of all', argued Erasmus, 'is that this deadly pestilence cannot be contained within its own limits, but once it has begun in one corner it floods like a contagious disease into the surrounding regions'.[23] 'An investigation into the nature of war', comments Ian Clark, 'becomes a concrete task of drawing meaningful boundaries within the general realm of violence and consequent boundaries to demarcate the means by which this activity should be pursued' (18). The co-ordinates to just such a moral cartography, traced through *The Spanish Tragedy*, are announced by its Induction. Refused entry to the fields of war and love, with 'either sort contained within his bounds', the Ghost of Andrea (absent and present, dead and alive) instead proceeds to Elysian fields where military reward turns to private retribution. Like the contestants of the battle in which he dies, war and revenge occupy a liminal space, 'leaning on each others bound'. War is revenge, we may be prompted to deduce, and revenge is war.

A recent study of *The Elizabethan Hamlet* admits no such ambiguity. 'The condemnation of revenge', it reads, after assembling a range of homiletic evidence, 'is categorical': 'It is also obvious that revenge meant revenge and not justice. There is no ambiguity in the basic religious instruction of the Elizabethans. God was Justice and only he could revenge. Thus in human terms there was no such thing as "just revenge"'; such dramatic characters as use such zeugmatic pretexts, it continues, are ones whose 'motives were demonstrably evil', the ghosts that impel them 'recognizably evil' (McGee, 3-4, 22). But there was one Elizabethan context in which the formula of 'just revenge' not only existed but was urgently current: the context of war. We have seen how Stump's 'right | Of just revenge' (*A Larum for London*, 1085-6) dramatizes orthodox just war theory, summarized, for example, by C.G. in 1596: 'Just Warre is ... taken in hande at the commaundement of the magistrate, for the demaunding of thinges againe, or to repulse injuries, or to revenge them' (F3v).

Hieronimo is himself a magistrate, and yet, as we have seen, revenge is sanctioned as just only within the 'publike' and 'generall' auspices of war, as Robert Ward later specified (1642, 1). 'An implacable desire of revenge' is condemned by state and God alike, and 'justly taxed' in war (7). De Loque's *Discourses of Warre and Single Combat*, translated in 1591, makes the same distinction, defending the methods of 'christian Warre' (31-4), but condemning the uses of 'Single Combat' (43). Such private grievance, he claims, is transgressive of the same moral geography as Kyd's play explores, 'beyond the bornes of justice' (46).

*The Spanish Tragedy* may well have played its part in the propagandist imperatives of the wartime stage. The destruction it visits on 'the whole succeeding hope, | That Spain expected' (4.4.202-03) indeed suggests that English victory forms the substance of the notional Actus Quintus omitted from this four-act play since its first Quarto. This patriotic subtext probably accounts for Henslowe's payment to Jonson for 'adicions in geronymo' in 1601, the same year in which he commissioned the frankly titled 'Boocke called conqueste of spayne' (*Henslowe's Diary*, 124; 167). Kyd's, as Hill well puts it, is 'a *Spanish* tragedy that implies an English comedy' (151). But the terms by which the dramatist exhibits the process of its violence outlasts the topicalities it reflects. By levelling such unnerving scrutiny on the resemblance between contemporary models of martial exhortation and admonitions against revenge, Kyd reveals the enduring human difficulty 'of drawing meaningful boundaries within the general realm of violence'.

*The Castle*, Blandy's military treatise from 1581, records a battlefield oration by Sir Roger Williams, an Elizabethan 'model of martial skill and integrity'.[24] 'Let this lively sight of dead bodyes', he declared over the English dead, 'let fresh bloud newly spilt, stirr and pricke you forwardes, let desire of revenge and victory, lift up your mindes' (G4r). The exhortation is all but indistinguishable from the anguished appeals made by Horatio's parents over his murdered corpse: 'Seest thou those wounds that yet are bleeding fresh', cries Hieronimo, 'Ile not intombe them till I have reveng'd' (2.5.54-5). 'See where his Ghoast solicites with his wounds, | Revenge', echoes the suicidal Isabella, 'on her that should revenge his death' (4.2.24-5). Baker quotes these last lines, and Isabella's subsequent summons by 'sorrow and dispaire' (27), as evidence that Kyd 'reproduces ... the outline' of Sackville's 1563 Induction: 'in *The mirror*, the ghosts always appear as they do above – soliciting with their wounds, asking for notice of their deaths' (33). As we have seen, however, it is not simply notice of his death for which Burdet's ghost solicits in the first wartime edition of that work. His wounds 'freshly bleede' (473), but the lively sight of his dead body urge, with Roger Williams, 'revenge and victory' (G4r), for 'Prince and publique weale' (463).

Burdet's wounds solicit the prosecution of just revenge and victory; Clifford's (in the 1559 *Mirror*) 'warne the bluddy sort ... theyr rigour to refrayne': these two old soldiers straddle the 'bornes of justice' interrogated by *The Spanish Tragedy* at large, and by its military ghost in particular. It is notable that Beaumont begins his 'omnibus parody of earlier ghost scenes', in *The Knight of the Burning Pestle*,[25] by lampooning the stage-directed entrance of the wounded Clifford in *3 Henry VI*, and then the opening lines of Kyd's Induction (see above, p. 124). The passage we have traced there from military ghost to agent of revenge is revisited in miniature in the troubling doubling between Clifford and Richard in *The First Part of the Contention* (see above, pp. 46-9). Like both the soldier Roger Williams, and the magistrate Hieronimo, Clifford is impelled by the 'lively sight of dead bodyes' to swear revenge over 'fresh bloud newly spilt':

> O! dismall sight, see where he breathlesse lies,
> All smeard and weltred in his luke-warme blood ...
> Sweete father, to thy murthred ghoast I sweare,
> Immortall hate unto the house of Yorke,
> Nor never shall I sleepe secure one night,
> Till I have furiously revengde thy death.
> (H3r)

'Thy *murthred* ghost'? Clifford *père* is killed on stage in single combat with York, far more 'legitimately', in fact, than Andrea. Yet his son's revised address to war in the Folio text spells out its own dilemma of transition by counterpointing (with Kyd's Andrea) Senecan and Virgilian models:

> Meet I an infant of the house of Yorke,
> Into as many gobbits will I cut it
> As wilde *Medea* yong *Absirtus* did ...
> Come thou new ruine of olde Cliffords house:
> As did *Aeneas* old *Anchyses* beare,
> So beare I thee upon my manly shoulders.
> (F 5.3.57-63)

Andrea follows in the footsteps of Aeneas to the Elysian fields, but instead of receiving instruction from the ghost of Anchises 'in the wars he must thereafter wage' (6, 890), his companion is identified as Revenge. Clifford too emulates that 'perfite souldier', but his assumption of the burden of his father's body perfects the strange meeting he mirrors with the vengeful chameleon Richard, and by his father's ghost he swears 'Immortall hate'. In the passage between war and revenge begins another 'endles Tragedie' (4.5.48).

Of the '*umbrae*, or ghosts, of three or foure playes, departed a dozen yeeres since' that Jonson invoked in 1600, '*the old Hieronimo*, (as it was first acted)' (209-10) is the only one identified by name. Kyd's '*Spanish tragedy ... implies an English comedy*', as Hill comments; implies (that is) a play that would enact the hints he discerns there of 'the real Rome-like future of England' (151); and that might substitute for the ghost of Don Andrea's Spanish 'Martialist' the *English Souldier* of Riche's Dialogue; implies a play, perhaps, like the one that first appeared 'in (at the least) three or foure sheets' in 1600, and which reanimated both the *Famous Victories* and the '*umbrae*, or ghosts' of that other old play, 'departed a dozen yeeres since': *Henry V*.

## Airborne troops

'To The Commandos and Airborne Troops of Great Britain the spirit of whose ancestors it has been humbly attempted to recapture in some ensuing scenes This Film is Dedicated'. Laurence Olivier's stentorian inscription at the outset of his *Henry V* (1945) catches at the very tone of Shakespeare's own preface to *Henry V* (1599).[26] The same oddly-sorted blend of rhetorical inversion and self-deprecation attends the pardon begged of us by its Chorus for the 'flat unraysed Spirits, that hath dar'd, | On this unworthy Scaffold, to bring forth | So great an Object' (1.Ch.9-11). Olivier's 'great ... Object' is as much Shakespeare's play as the events it shows. But his bid to 'recapture' the 'spirit' of heroic 'ancestors' itself recaptures for the present the appeals to the past made to the king by his spiritual advisers in the play. 'Looke back', says Canterbury,

> into your mightie Ancestors:
> Goe my dread Lord, to your great Grandsires Tombe,
> From whom you clayme; invoke his Warlike Spirit.
> (1.2.102-4)

'Awake remembrance', agrees Ely, 'of these valiant dead, | And with your puissant Arme renew their Feats' (115-16). Part of the brilliance of the film is the gusto with which it accepts the play's own invitation to regard the present in terms of the past; to renew in film the play's feats, even as Agincourt was to be renewed in the Normandy landings of D-Day. But the military circumstances of 1944 echo not only those of 1415, but of 1599 as well: Olivier's dedication to what he later called his 'truly Shakespearian film' is true to the play,[27] but true too to the times that saw its first production. For in staying true to the apparently endless wars on the continent, Shakespeare's contemporaries were themselves continually urged to 'Looke back' to their ancestors, and to 'renew their Feats'.

Despite praising the 'worthie people of our nation' then voluntarily fighting for the Dutch cause, Gates's *Defence of Militarie Profession* more generally deprecated the fact that most of his countrymen now 'despise the profession of Armes' (1579, 58; 43). Such scant regard is particularly ironic since, as he writes, 'we are the sonnes of those our Fathers, whose strength and courage in martiall activitie, neither *Scots*, *French*, nor *Spanyards*, were able to resist' (57):

> this present generation of the *English* people, being
> trained and exercised under the like conduct, nourishment,
> & government as our kindred were under the moste
> famous kings, *Richard* the first, *Edward* ye first, *Edward*
> the third, *Edward* the blacke Prince, *Henry* the fifth, the
> Duke of Bedford, &c. wold shew it self to be the right-
> fully begotten children of the olde *English* Fathers, most
> valiant and famous in Militarie feates and knowledge.

The same notion of 'olde *English* Fathers' concludes the anonymous
manuscript on 'whether it be better for England to give an Invador present
Battaile, or to temporize' (*c*.1595), now held at Dulwich College:

> O what true English heart would live to heare his children
> wayle and cry upon the sepulchers of their Grandfathers
> and say, Behold the dead bodyes of those that in their
> lives defended the freedome and home of England; and
> now behold our owne ffathers living bodyes, that have
> utterly lost the same but rendred as captives to perpetuall
> slavery and bondage.[28]

It is particularly apt that Edward Alleyn should have owned this pamphlet.
He may have acted in the 'harey the vj' Henslowe recorded performed in
1592, and to which Nashe alludes in the same year's *Piers Peniless* in terms
strikingly reminiscent of the manuscript:

> How it would have joyed brave *Talbot* ... to think that
> after he had lyne two hundred yeares in his Tombe, hee
> should triumphe againe on the Stage, and have his bones
> newe embalmed with the teares of ten thousand spectators
> ... who, in the Tragedian that represents his person,
> imagine they behold him fresh bleeding.
> (*Works*, ed. McKerrow, 1, 212)

Dekker later agreed that histories are the 'soveraigne balmes to the bodyes
of the dead, that preserve them more fresh then if they were alive' (*Non-
Dramatic Works*, ed. Grosart, 4, 101). Their resurrection on stage in the
chronicle plays of the 1580s and 1590s shared a vocabulary with the
patriotic exhortations expressed both at home and (apparently) in the field;
in the wounds of the 1587 *Mirror*'s Sir Nicholas Burdet, whose wounds
'freshly bleede' in recounting his 'mangled tale', 't'encourage them the like
exployts t'achive';[29] and in the 'lively sight of dead bodyes', and of 'fresh
bloud newly spilt', that formed the spur to Sir Roger Williams's oration.

Certainly Heywood's *Apologie for Actors* takes for example Gates's 'moste famous kings' Edward III and Henry V, whose personaters make their spectators 'apt and fit for the like atchievement' (B4r). This sense of the reanimated relevance of English military tradition, by which Elizabethan soldiers were prompted to believe themselves 'not so far degenerate from the high courage and manlines of their ancestors & forefathers', was repeatedly urged in the military literature of the time.[30] Barret's *Theorike and Practike of Modern Warres* elides within a single sentence the victories of Edward III, the Black Prince, Henry V, and 'this present king of *Fraunce* ... in *Anno.* 1590' (1598, 171). When Shakespeare's Archbishops urge their King – and their audience – to 'awake remembrance of these valiant dead', to 'looke back' to 'mightie Ancestors', and 'renew their Feats', their words form commentaries upon the wartime status of their own play.

*Henry V* shadows the sentiment expressed in Alleyn's manuscript in another way, too. Its warning to every 'true English heart' is made effective not only by filtering the past through the present, but by further contemplating the future. Children are imagined looking back at their grandfathers' past, and at their 'ffathers living bodyes' in a direct speech that envisages a 'now' of 'perpetuall slavery'. Likewise Henry darkly warns the French ambassador that 'some are yet ungotten and unborne, | That shal have cause to curse the *Dolphins* scorne' (1.2.287-8). When that vow is about to be fulfilled at Agincourt, he once more predicts remembrance of 'this day':

> This story shall the good man teach his sonne:
> And *Crispine Crispian* shall ne're goe by,
> From this day to the ending of the World,
> But we in it shall be remembred.
> (4.3.56-9)

Such moments resemble the celebrated prediction in *Julius Caesar*, when Brutus and Cassius contemplate their 'lofty Scene' being 'acted over, | In State[s] unborne, and Accents yet unknowne' (3.1.113-14). Marjorie Garber comments of that scene that 'the "now" of Shakespeare's play already points to a ghostly "then"' (1987, 56), and the same is true of *Henry V*, a play composed within months of *Julius Caesar*.

'Now all the Youth of England are on fire ... the Scene is now transported ... There is the Play-house now' (2.Ch.1-36): the 'Now' of the Chorus indeed refers to 1599 rather than 1415, and hence insists that the models of emulation it presents, like Burdet, Talbot, or the 'blessed wightes' of Riche's Valhalla ('though their bodies intombed bee in clay') are now all long dead. Of course there needs no ghost come from the grave to tell us this, but the consistency with which *Henry V*, the last of Shakespeare's Elizabethan histories, is suffused with that truism might account for the sense of unease it has prompted in so many critics. The play's composition, somewhere between the perturbing prodigies of *Julius Caesar* and *Hamlet*, alerts us to a comparable sensitivity towards the uncanny at work within it; and one mediated (as I shall now argue) by the supernatural mythologies of military ghost-lore. The ghost of Caesar set loose by his assassins' 'lofty Scene' might serve as precedent for the entire cast of *Henry V*.

There comes a moment in the play when the French Earl of Grandpré sounds remarkably like that self-deprecating master of ceremonies, the Chorus. Describing the English camp on the eve of battle, he asserts that

> Description cannot sute it selfe in words,
> To demonstrate the Life of such a Battaile,
> In life so livelesse, as it shewes it selfe.
> (4.2.53-5)

With a flicker of the ambiguity that attends the word 'Battaile' (hostile encounter or arrayed army), this lifeless description echoes and supplements the earlier choric command:

> And so our Scene must to the Battaile flye:
> Where, O for pitty, we shall much disgrace,
> With foure or five most vile and ragged foyles,
> (Right ill dispos'd, in brawle ridiculous)
> The Name of Agincourt.
> (4.Ch.48-52)

We have seen how the apparent paucity of dramatic representation enhances the mimetic circumstance of the battle itself, conducted against all odds by playwright and character alike (see above, pp. 117-18). Grandpré's speech similarly plays by eliding the lifelessness of its own description with the lifelessness of what it describes. For there is a pronounced posthumousness which clings to the play, and which is first announced in the Chorus's apology for the 'flat unraysed Spirits' that the company can muster. Prospero, that later self-conscious spokesman for his author's 'rough Magicke' (*The Tempest*, 5.1.50), another master whose 'Spirits obey' the ceremonies he administers (2), reflects that

> Graves at my command
> Have wak'd their sleepers, op'd, and let 'em forth
> By my so potent Art.
> (48-50)

The role of dramatist-as-conjuror is of course particularly forceful within the context of a martial literature that encouraged belief in the inspiriting example of past military heroes, as well as their enduring spiritual reward.

The metatheatrical muster *Henry V* parades raises too the monstrous spirits of the uncanny. The presence of these dead is felt particularly at Agincourt, but their burden is assumed in earlier scenes.

In the first scene, for example (which takes its time to distinguish between matters temporal and spiritual), Henry's reformation is cast as a resurrection: his 'wildnesse' was 'mortify'd' and 'Seem'd to dye too', leaving his body a vessel for 'Celestiall Spirits' (1.1.26-31). The clergymen urge the King to wake 'our sleeping Sword of Warre' (1.2.22) by reference to the 'Warlike Spirit' of his ancestors (Edward III and the Black Prince) and its invocation at their tomb (102-5). Remembrance is woken here from the purposively prosaic pages of Holinshed's chronicle, and graves awake their sleepers. The 'hearts have left their bodyes here in England', we are told of Henry's nobility (128), transported overseas like the later Chorus's audience to Act Two (2.Ch.35-7). 'O let their bodyes follow', urges Canterbury (1.2. 130). The same imagery is deployed in Henry's considered response, casually referring to his own bones and grave, tongueless but for history:

> Or lay these bones in an unworthy Urne,
> Tomblesse, with no remembrance over them:
> Either our History shall with full mouth
> Speake freely of our Acts, or else our grave
> Like Turkish mute, shall have a tongueless mouth.
> (228-32)

Once again the Chorus's claims for this 'unworthy Scaffold' make themselves felt in the 'unworthy Urne' Henry pictures, just as his refutal of the mockeries shown him by the Dauphin anticipate the 'true things' minded 'by what their Mock'ries bee' of the later Chorus (4.Ch.53). Act Two closes with a quickening of the 'worme-holes of long-vanisht dayes' of Edward III (2.4.86), Henry's 'most fam'd, of famous Ancestors' (92), and the subject of the (partly Shakespearean) play reprinted in 1599. Canterbury recalls to Henry how the Black Prince 'on the French ground play'd a Tragedie ... Whiles his most mightie Father on a Hill | Stood smiling, to behold' him (1.2.106-9). The same events are rehearsed by the French King (2.4.53-62) – and form a memorable set-piece of the earlier play (*Edward III*, 3.5). The similarity in sequencing between *Edward III* and *Henry V* – arguably the first and the last of Shakespeare's Elizabethan histories – further enhances the sense of reanimation with which the later play is so concerned.

When Mountjoy rebukes the English with the warning that 'Though we seem'd dead, we did but sleepe' (3.6.118-19), the systematic accretion of such imagery stretches to the French camp too. But while appropriate to drama's 'rough Magicke', and to the propagandist rhetoric the play emulates, is there not a sense in which a certain discomfort at such magic is also awakened? In which the stage of *Henry V*, pitched between sleep and waking, life and death, anticipates that other royal play of *Macbeth*, where its 'imaginarie Puissance' (1.Ch.25) is matched by the 'fatall Vision' and 'false Creation' of hallucination?[31] Nowhere is this kinship more pronounced than on the eve of Agincourt.

Like Henry's meditation on 'Ceremonie' (4.1.263-82), Macbeth's disturbing vision of a dagger-of-the-mind moves into a meditation of night:

> Now o're the one halfe World
> Nature seemes dead, and wicked Dreames abuse
> The Curtain'd sleepe: Witchcraft celebrates
> Pale *Heccats* Offrings: and wither'd Murther,
> Alarum'd by his Centinell, the Wolfe,
> Whose howle's his Watch, thus with stealthy pace,
> With *Tarquins* ravishing s[tr]ides, towards his designe
> Moves like a Ghost.
> (2.1.49-56)

Perhaps the first thing to notice here is the markedly military nature of Macbeth's rumination: murder is 'Alarum'd by his Centinell', 'Whose howle's his Watch[-word]' – the wolf alerts his master like a sentry alerting his superior officer with the password. The same technical vocabulary forms the titles of two considered responses to Elizabethan wartime, *A Larum for London* and *A Watch-worde for Warre*. The same eerie stealth as Macbeth envisages, attends the 'creeping Murmure and the poring Darke' with which *Henry V*'s Chorus invites our conjecture of the 'foule Womb of Night' before Agincourt:

> The Humme of eyther Army stilly sounds;
> That the fixt Centinels almost receive
> The secret Whispers of each others Watch.
> (4.Ch.2-7)

Macbeth's speech is interrupted by the stage-direction 'A Bell rings' (2.1.61 SD), and that knell is echoed by 'the Clocks [that] doe towle' in the Chorus's description (4.Ch.15). And though similarly distanced by metaphor, the supernatural apparatus of Macbeth's 'Witchcraft' pertains there in the 'creeple-tardy-gated Night, | Who like a foule and ougly Witch doth limpe | So tediouslie away' (20-22).[32] And the lines that follow follow also the 'stealthy pace' of the 'Ghost' of murder:

> The poore condemned English,
> Like Sacrifices, by their watchfull Fires
> Sit patiently, and inly ruminate
> The Mornings danger: and there gesture sad
> Investing lanke-leane Cheekes, and Warre-worn Coats,

> Presented them unto the gazing Moone
> So many horride Ghosts.
> (22-8)

What *Henry V*'s Chorus describes was dramatized in *Richard III* on the eve of Bosworth, where in two opposing camps, the buckling on of armour and the sound of cocks and crows accompany a parade of horrid ghosts (5.5.72-165). The eve of Agincourt, like the eve of Bosworth, resembles a sort of military halloween.

The Chorus's account of the 'horride Ghosts' of the English army had its counterparts in many contemporary descriptions of the ravages of war. Spenser's *Vewe of the Present State of Irelande* (1596) described the ghastly efficiency of the English campaign in Ireland, remarking how 'Out of everie Corner of the woods and glinnes' the victims of the 'late warrs of mounster' 'came Crepinge forthe uppon theire handes for theire Leggs Coulde not beare them, they loked like Anotomies of deathe, they spake like ghostes Crynge out of theire graves'.[33] Such extremities were the fate of English soldiers too. John Smythe had written in 1589 of the 'sicke and starved Souldiors' who had been disembarked on to the coasts of southern England, 'of which foresaid great numbers of miserable & pitiful ghosts, or rather shadowes of men, the *Essex* and *Kentish* carts and carters (that carried them) can testifie' (1590, **** 4r). The same image occurred to Sir John Dowdall, who towards the end of 1599 reported that the 'most part of the army [in Ireland] ... seem fitter for their graves than to fight a prince's battle'.[34] Charles's scorn in *1 Henry VI* for 'the famisht English [who], like pale Ghosts, | Faintly besiege us' (1.2.7-8) seems to have a basis in contemporary observation. The Chorus's metaphor is followed by his reverberative 'now' ('... So many horride Ghosts. O now, who will behold ...') and the self-consciousness of the history again asserts itself. If they were *like* so many ghosts then, they are surely so 'now', in 1599, 1945 or 1999. Such an insistence might be thought conjectural, but it is notable that Shakespeare emphasises the 'ruin'd' nature of his army, in sharp contrast to the 'brave apparel' that the French repeatedly covet from their enemy in *The Famous Victories* (lines 1088-98, 1140). Though figurative, the Chorus's description of 'horride Ghosts' is reiterated throughout Act Four.

Henry stresses the rhetorical nature of his own simile in 4.1 ('Upon example') but his figure is apt:

> And when the Mind is quickned, out of doubt
> The Organs, though defunct and dead before,
> Breake up their drowsie Grave, and newly move
> With casted slough, and fresh legeritie.
> (4.1.20-23)

The rousing of Henry's drowsy army is here cast less as an awakening and more as a resurrection, 'defunct and dead before'. And later, the Constable of France boasts of the 'shales and huskes of men' to which mere sight of his army will reduce the English. Grandpré goes further, scorning 'Yond Iland Carrions, desperate of their bones' (4.2.18; 39); the soldiers, he says, are 'livelesse' (55), their mounts 'still and motionlesse' with 'pale-dead eyes' (48- 50). Still later, Mountjoy urges on the English a retreat from the fields where their 'bodies | Must lye and fester' (4.3.87-8), their only 'executors' the 'knavish Crowes' (4.2.51), as Grandpré has said. The soldiers 'stay for death' (4.2.56): but the repose of such a death, or the 'fresh legeritie' of resurrection Henry promises, are both reanimated in the horrid afterlife that one of their number, Michael Williams, contemplates, 'when all those Legges, and Armes, and Heads, chopt off in a Battaile, shall joyne together at the latter day, and cry all, Wee dyed at such a place, some swearing, some crying for a Surgean ...' (4.1.134-7). The King has an alternative afterlife in mind, however, for those of 'our bodyes' as 'Find Native Graves':

> Dying like men, though buryed in your Dunghills,
> They shall be fam'd: for there the Sun shall greet them,
> And draw their honors reeking up to Heaven,
> Leaving their earthly parts to choake your Clyme,
> The smell whereof shall breed a Plague in France.
> Marke then abounding valour in our English:
> That being dead, like to the bullets crasing,
> Breake out into a second course of mischiefe,
> Killing in relapse of Mortalitie.
> (4.3.97-108)

At the equivalent point in *The Famous Victories*, the King defies the French Herald's requests for ransom: 'Rather shall my bodie lie dead in the field, to feed crowes', he says, 'Then ever England shall pay one penny ransome | For my bodie' (1200-2). Shakespeare seems to have re-allocated the figure to Grandpré's 'knavish Crowes' (4.2.51), and dwelled instead upon the variable service of human flesh, in a graphic image of posthumous militarism. The inspiring shades of the glorious dead are queasily imagined as the weaponry of a sort of primitive germ warfare. A similarly 'bizarre mixture of putrefaction and ammunition' has been noted by one Great War historian, of the landscapes of the western front, as 'the perfect envirionment for the spread of tales of the supernatural' (Winter, 1995, 67-8). Henry's vaporous but deadly spirits might stand for the 'vile and ragged' English army Shakespeare depicts as a whole.

Editors suggest that the germ of the Constable's 'shales and huskes of men' is the speech that Hall records, promising victory over the English, 'for their force is clerly abated and their strength utterly decaied, so yt or the battailes shall joyne they shalbe for very feblenes vanquished &

overcom, & in stede of men ye shal fight with shadowes' (1550, H3v). The army we actually see on stage (as the Chorus continually insists) is a mere handful of actors: the remainder are absent to our eyes, but present through the 'imaginarie Puissance' of our mind's eye. Just as the play's festive descriptions of war invite its location in the context of the communal solidarity of the London musters, its army reinforced by the imaginary participation of its audience; so the play animates the 'Warlike Spirit[s]' of its 'mightie Ancestors'. In a real sense, Shakespeare's Battle of Agincourt is one which its audience 'shal fight with shadowes'. The 'flat unraysed Spirits' of its muster-roll and cast-list are the ghostly 'shadowes' for which Puck apologizes at the end of that other supernatural play, *A Midsummer Night's Dream*.

Victory is signalled by Mountjoy's re-entrance to beg leave of Henry to 'booke our dead, and then to bury them' (4.7.71). These shadowy hosts are raised from chronicle, and to chronicle they are returned. A series of dead warriors, though, has already been recorded on the battlefield, and their absences are felt as keenly as the 'horride Ghosts' who disembodiedly embody Henry's ruined band. The King, for example, has 'interred new' the body of Richard II (4.2.292); Bardolph and Nym, as the Boy puts it, 'had tenne times more valour' than Pistol ('this roaring divell i'th'olde play') but they are themselves both consigned to an old play (Shakespeare's own), 'both hang'd' (4.4.66-9). Dead too is the 'fat Knight with the great belly doublet' remembered here by Fluellen (4.7.46). The same bookish theoretician recalls too the campaigns of Edward III and the Black Prince, 'as I have read in the Chronicles' (4.7.90-93), and as audiences had seen on stage. Lyly prefaced his *Campaspe* (1584) with a contemplation of his 'calling *Alexander* from his grave';[35] his military precedent, and that of Pompey, are 'quickned' into 'fresh legeritie' in Shakespeare's play too, in a pedigree of war that stretches back to 'old Assyrian slings' (4.1.69-72; 4.7.19-37; 4.7.60).[36]

From first to last the dead are 'numbred' (4.8.73), and 'Prowd of their Numbers' (4.Ch.17). It is 'the Booke of *Numbers*' that Canterbury had adduced to prompt the campaign in the first place (1.2.98). The disembodied names of its casualties – 'the Earle of Suffolke, | Sir *Richard Ketly, Davy Gam* Esquire' (4.8.103-4) – clutter the unworthy scaffold, 'raised from the Grave of Oblivion' (as Nashe had written), 'borrowed out of our English Chronicles, wherein our forefathers valiant acts (that have lain long buried in rustie brasse and worme-eaten bookes)' are 'revived' (1, 212). And just as the English can posthumously kill 'in relapse of Mortalitie', so the French are doubly slain by their wounded steeds that 'Yerke out their armed heeles at their dead masters, | Killing them twice' (4.7.78-9).

'Worme-eaten bookes' have indeed been exhumed 'fresh bleeding' here on to the stage, 'freshly remembred' in the spirits that walk the wooden O. But the smell of the grave clings to their forms, and like Michelangelo's

Prisoners they struggle from the monumental stone from which they emerge. Henry V closes proceedings at Agincourt with a roll-call of names as disembodied as the Pepins and Childerics of Canterbury's chronicle, before himself being translated into the Latin lifted verbatim from Holinshed, '*Praeclarissimus Filius noster Henricus Rex Angliae & Heres Franciae*' (5.2.336-7), and before the play's blank verse yields to the Chorus's monumental sonnet, 'In little roome confining mighty men' (Ep.3).

Shakespeare's battlefield of Agincourt is a haunted site. Its band of brothers makes up 'a Royall fellowship of death' (4.8.101). As such, the play's representation of battle, and its single-minded attention to the posthumousness of its events, should be seen in the context of the widespread folklore of military spectres. Citing Pausanius, Noël Taillepied's 1588 *Psichologie, or Treatise upon Apparitions and Spirits* alludes to the *locus classicus* of haunted battlefields: 'At this spot' at Marathon, he writes, 'every night you may hear horses neighing and men fighting'.[37] According to one modern authority, phantom armies have 'been reported throughout history' (Haining, 185): 'the battlefields of medieval Europe', confirms another, 'were haunted places as greater and older battlefields had been before them' (Maple, 46). Lewes Lavater's *Of Ghostes and Spirites walking by nyght*, translated by R.H. in 1572, takes a more detailed note of such phenomena. 'There are heard and seene in the aire', he writes,

> or uppon the earth whole armies of men encountring togither, and when one part is forced to flye, there is heard horrible cries, and great clattering of armour. Gunnes, launces and halberdes, with other kindes of weapons and artillerie, do often times move of their owne accord as they lie in the armories.
> (81)

Lavater quotes from Appianus equivalent prodigies 'before the civill warres at *Rome*' (82), the same 'Clashing of armes' that *Lucans First Booke* records, 'heard, in untrod woods', and the attendant eerie noise with which 'An armed battaile joines' (567-78). He then updates the phenomenon by reference to the omens that preceded battle at Basel in 1444, and confesses to having omitted 'many suche lyke examples ... bothe of aunchient and also of newe writers' (85). Modern students of the occult demonstrate the same sense of continuity on which Lavater's 'Gunnes ... and artillerie' insisted.

A party of holiday-makers at Dieppe in 1952, for example, were troubled by the echoes of explosions detonated in the disastrous raid ten years before (Bardens, 211-14), a detachment of American marines in Vietnam in 1971 by the 'footsteps of a ghostly platoon' (Haining, 185). The most famous of such incidents took place in 1914, when beleagured English troops in the front line reported the apparition of a spectral host who reassured them of their divine support. The legend of the Angels of Mons has been traced to an avowedly fictional patriotic story by Arthur Machen, in which the ghosts of the bowmen of Agincourt rose from the mud and joined in the fight (Fussell, 1975, 115-16). Machen's story 'took on a life of its own' since its fabrication out of Kipling was 'fiercely contested' by the sworn testimony of many witnesses (Winter, 1995, 67-9): it is worth noting, however, the uncannily precise echo the legend sounds to Shakespeare's recreation of Agincourt, and the life of its own his battle gains from its posthumous participants. Belief in such phenomena was certainly current in the Renaissance.

We have seen how de Loier's 1586 *Treatise of Specters* attributed to Ate the turmoils of civil war (see above, p. 28). George Sandys's seventeenth-century translation of Ovid's *Metamorphoses* glosses its lines on the 'Armes, clashing in the aire with clouds o'r-cast' that augured disaster for Caesar, by referring to the currency of such 'Ostents' 'even this last yeare':

> Of the Latter we not onely read, but have heard of in our times. And even this last yeare, 1629. reported it was by some of good credit, how they saw two opposite Battalions, launcing out their speares, and discharging, as it were, their muskets in the aire, victory now reeling, and in the end one giving chase to the other.[38]

Some months after the Battle of Edgehill in 1642, Charles I sent three officers to investigate the 'Prodigious Noyses of War and Battels' that 'hath since, and doth appeare' in the skies above, 'strange and portentuous Apparitions of two jarring and contrary Armies ... where the corporeall Armies had shed so much blood'. The news-pamphlet that detailed these 'visions of horrour' weirdly revisits Riche's recognition, on an Elysian green, of the ghosts of his erstwhile comrades (see above, pp. 192-3): the 'Gentlemen of credit' Charles commissioned, it relates, 'distinctly [knew] divers of the apparitions or incorporeall substances by their faces, as that of Sir Edmund Varney and others that were there slaine'. Its author prefaces his account of this 'Great Wonder' by likening it to 'the things which our too superstitious ancestors called Elves, and Goblins, Furies and the like, such as were those who appeared to Macbeth ... and foretold him of his fortunes both in life and death'.[39] Catalogued by Robert Burton and Noël Taillepied, parodied by François Rabelais, and pooh-poohed in the 1665 edition of Scot's *Discoverie of Witchcraft*, the spectral phenomenon of Edgehill's airborne troops endured, and like Macbeth's air-drawn dagger, Renaissance soldiery saw them still.[40]

Drayton's second *Poly-Olbion* (1622) notes another such haunting. He relates how, on the eve of battle between Henry III and his Barons,

> In that blacke night before his sad and dismall day,
> Were apparaitions strange, as drad Heaven would bewray

The horrors to ensue, O most amazing sight!
Two Armies in the Ayre, discerned were to fight,
Which came so neere to earth, that in the morne they found
The prints of horses feet remaining in the ground.
(34)

'Thinke when we talke of Horses', commands Shakespeare's Chorus, 'that you see them | Printing their prowd Hoofes i'th' receiving Earth' (1.Ch. 26-7). In the absence of any Elizabethan play devoted to the life of Henry III, there is no way of establishing Shakespeare's familiarity with this particular chapter of history. Similar prodigies, however, are certainly incorporated into the play he composed immediately after *Henry V*. In *Julius Caesar* Shakespeare augmented North's Plutarch in Calphurnia's description of the 'spirits running up and down in the night' before Caesar's assassination:[41]

Fierce fiery Warriours fight upon the Clouds
In Rankes and Squadrons, and right forme of Warre
Which drizel'd blood upon the Capitoll:
The noise of Battell hurtled in the Ayre.
(2.2.19-22)

The Arden editor cites a lost Henslowe play, *Jerusalem* (1592), to account for the addition (51-2), but Josephus's account of the prodigies that preceded its fall was but one of many such models available in the period. Lodowick Lloyd's military text-book *The Stratagems of Jersualem* (1602) quotes Josephus's 'seven signes' (including 'Iron Charriots, and an host of armed men hovering about the citie in the cloudes') but also details examples of 'Many strange apparaitions ... seene in the ayre in many places of *Greece*', and 'At the destruction of *Constantinople* by the Turks' (221-5). Barnabe Barnes's play *The Devil's Charter* (1607) certainly anchors its Braggart's comedy in his audience's awareness of such 'strange Almanacks'. A worthy successor to Basilisco, Frescobaldi's set-piece vaunt describes how he blew up the entire Turkish army at the Siege of Malta:

Which when the wise Astronomers of *Greece*,
Prodigiously discovered from a farre,
They thought those *Turcaes* fiery meteors,
Which with their Pikes were pushing in the clowds,
The learned Booke-men writte strange Almanacks,
Of signes, and apparitions in the ayre.
(E3v)[42]

Shakespeare's phantom 'Rankes and Squadrons' formed the stuff of military superstition, their 'right forme of Warre' all the more aptly deployed in a play about 'the best Captaine that ever lived' (Whetstone, 1586b, 66).

Ghosts, walking the streets or battling in the sky, were popularly believed to prophesy war; and wars were waged in emulation of the shades of illustrious English martialists, as a series of patriotic texts testifies. But the aftermath of war was attended by fears for the shades of the slain, that, unburied they would haunt the site of their deaths. Furthermore, such battles might themselves come to be refought over the fields of conflict, from Marathon to St Albans to Edgehill. 'Many, indeed most, battlefields are haunted in a similar manner',[43] even as their veterans were described as 'pitiful ghosts, or rather shadowes of men'. Elizabethan ghosts haunted the fringes of warfare: and the body of this martial supernature is marshalled in the eerie posthumousness which attends Shakespeare's Agincourt. It is emblematized in the first scene we are offered of St Crispian's Day, in the strange meeting between Henry V with Ancient Pistol.

'Superstition, of one sort or another', commented Coleridge in his 1818 lecture on *Macbeth*, 'is natural to victorious generals; the instances are too notorious to need mentioning. There is so much of chance in warfare ... that the proper temperament for generating or receiving superstitious impressions is naturally produced'.[44] Michael Herr noticed the soldier's 'proper temperament' of superstition in other ranks too. Writing of the modern airborne troops of Vietnam, he commented that

> Men on the [helicopter] crews would say that once you'd carried a dead person he would always be there, riding with you. Like all combat people they were incredibly superstitious and invariably self-dramatic, but it was (I knew) unbearably true and close exposure to the dead sensitized you to the force of their presence and made for long reverberations; long.[45]

'It is true', wrote Taillepied four centuries before, 'that some classes of persons may be considered to be more aptly in the way of seeing ghosts; travellers, for example, [or] ... sentinels' (94). Perusal of modern compendia of ghosts and hauntings confirms the reverberations of his observation. In 1864, for example, a sentry was found unconscious at his post after seeing 'a ghostly figure' approaching him, and vainly lunging at it with fixed bayonet; more dramatically, a guard at the Tower of London reportedly died of shock in 1816 after being stalked by (that most Shakespearean of figures) 'a shadowy bear' (Bardens, 44-5). It will be remembered that Macbeth's breathless response to the air-drawn dagger envisaged an abstract Murder 'Alarum'd by his Centinell'. The isolated responsibility of that office, memorably described in the 'secret Whispers' of *Henry V* 's Chorus (4.Ch.7), certainly involves the tense suspicions of night-time. Robert Barret took note of the tricks the mind can play on soldiers engaged in such duties: 'For many times, unto one man alone, feare or imagination doth cause few people to seeme many, and many things to seeme to be, which are not indeede: and at no time, is the Alarme to be striken in the campe without good and urgent cause' (1598, 106). Shakespeare seems to have been absorbed by the dramatic potential of such 'imaginarie Puissance'.

In *Antony and Cleopatra* it is a *'Company of Souldiours'* on a 'carefull Watch' who hear the 'strange' *'Musicke of the Hoboyes ... under the Stage'* that signals Hercules's desertion of Antony (4.3.1-20). Though Shakespeare substituted Hercules for Plutarch's Bacchus,[46] 'songs ... heard in the ayre in the praise of *Bacchus*, and armed men ... seene in the aire' appear among the ominous phenomena listed by Lloyd (1602, 221-2). The supernatural pageantry that closes *The Merry Wives of Windsor* also finds a parallel in such military folklore, as a modern *Casebook of Military Mystery* reveals: Windsor Castle 'is the haunt of ... the ghost of Herne the Hunter, once a warden of Windsor Great Park ... Sentries at Windsor were quick to give the alarm whenever Herne appeared' (R. Brown, 113). The Ghost of Old Hamlet also appears to sentries on their nocturnal patrol (see below, pp. 224-6). And in *Henry V*, after borrowing a cloak from the old soldier Sir Thomas Erpingham, Shakespeare has the King encounter *his* sentinel, Ancient Pistol. 'Here', writes Anne Barton, 'at the end of his Elizabethan cycle, he effectively laid the ghost of Tamburlaine as a hero'; Pistol's 'histrionics', she asserts, are contrasted with the King's 'workaday prose', and the 'distance between one kind of theatrical fantasy and fact' is asserted (1994, 215). One of the most prominent kinds of theatrical fantasy explored by the play, however, is its insistent likening of the spirits of actors (causing 'few people to seeme many') to the posthumous walking of ghosts.

'Stories of ghosts seen on various battlefields', writes a compiler of *Mysteries of the Great War*, 'or in woods at dawn or misty twilight are not rare'. 'Was this', he asks after illustrating his comment, 'an example of the transference of thought producing a phantasm of the dead in the mind of the living whose state bordered closely on the hypnotic, or the dream-state of consciousness?' (Wilkins, 242-3). Christopher Sly asks a similar question in Shakespeare's Induction to *The Taming of the Shrew*: 'Or do I dreame? Or have I dream'd till now?' (F Ind.2.68). In Pistol's misty encounter with his King, according to Barton, Shakespeare 'laid the ghost of Tamburlaine'; another critic describes as a process of 'incorporation and exorcism' Shakespeare's literary negotiation of Marlowe's posthumous influence (Porter, 1988, 143). Such supernatural metaphors are indeed apt to the strange meeting Shakespeare contrives on the eve of battle, and bears comparison with the climactic encounter between Clifford and Richard from the beginning of his Elizabethan cycle.

We have seen how the spirits of Edward III, Henry V et al were deployed by martial writers to further the self-identity of Elizabethan Englishmen required to fight in Europe. The 1595 edition of Daniel's *Civile Wars* renders that spiritual visitation explicit. Meditating on Henry V's 'wracke of

*Fraunce*', he asks whether or not he sins 'to salute your ghostes | Great worthies, so renown'd in forraine coasts'.[47] His question raises the ghost of Henry himself:

> Who do I see out of the darke appeare,
> Covered almost with clowdes as with the night,
> That here presents him with a martiall cheere
> Seeming of dreadfull, and yet of lovely sight?

'Out of the clowdy darkenes of the night' – so that second line was revised in 1599 – appears the dead King to berate the poet for neglecting the 'wondrous Actions' of the past in merely tracing the calamities of England's *Civile Wars*. His lament, as Bullough comments, reflects an 'unusual awareness of England's shortcomings in heroic poetry' (4, 350), and one renewed in Shakespeare's apologetic Chorus. But the fact that it is a raised ghost that voices that sentiment, together with the 'imaginarie ground | Of hungry shadowes' Daniel describes (2, 175), should equally alert us to the ghostly apparatus of Shakespeare's 'unraysed Spirits'. 'Tell great ELIZA', commands Daniel's ghostly king, 'That she repaire what darkenesse hath defac't, | And get our ruyn'd deedes, reedifi'd' (2, 176) – an appeal to 'Awake remembrance' of a piece with both current military exhortation and *Henry V* itself. In his first encounter before battle, Shakespeare's King too appears 'out of the clowdy darkenes of the night' to a sentry, 'considered to be more aptly in the way of seeing ghosts', as the superstition had it.

'I am not *Barbason*, you cannot conjure mee', says Nym to Pistol (2.1.52), in a sequence identified by one editor as 'a parody of that part of the service of exorcism known as the "conjuratio"'.[48] Pistol's botched challenge at Agincourt, 'Che vous la?', seems a more successful conjuration (4.1.36; see above, p 165). When Shakespeare revisited the theme of the disguised ruler in *Measure for Measure*, that veiled authority is twice described as a 'ghostly Father' (4.3.46, 5.1.126). Certainly Henry's portrayal in his play is in the spirit of the 'olde *English* Fathers' that contemporary propaganda pressed home. One source for *Measure for Measure*, Riche's *Adventures of Brusanus* (1592), includes an encounter between the Prince of Hungaria, disguised, and one 'Signior Gloriosus' who wears 'a loose *Mandilyon*, like a counterfait souldiour', 'his haire hanging downe to both his shoulders, as they use to figure a hagge of hell, his beard cut *peecke a devaunt*, turnde uppe a little, like a vice of a play' (Bullough, 2, 526). Disguise meets fakery at Agincourt too, and the ironies of Henry's spirit of emulation encountering Pistol's ragtail incarnation of counterfeiture are apparent. But the peculiar force of this encounter rests also on the symmetry that had empowered that between Clifford and Richard in *The First Part of the Contention* – a mutual likeness that deploys not only the duplicitous implications of Pistol's parodies, but also the recognition that the word 'double' carried the sense of 'ghost' or 'apparition' in the period.

The issue informing Clifford and Richard's meeting is the distinction between the just cause of public war and the private grievance of revenge; or rather, their perturbing similarity. The measure of Henry's filial obligation to his father is taken at Agincourt. But how might Pistol be described as a spirit of revenge? In the previous chapter we laid stress upon Pistol's obligation to his only dramatic begetter, Marlowe's *Tamburlaine*. His mighty line, however, is overshadowed by the persistent obsession he displays with the Senecan apparatus of the underworld, most influentially adapted by Thomas Kyd. As editors tirelessly point up, Pistol's familiarity with Pluto's lake, Erebus, Cerberus and so on is perfectly suited to his manner – the 'fake "Senecan" verbosity' one critic describes (Thomson, 36). The Braggart's traditional argumentativeness finds expression in his sustained (and possibly deranged) demands for revenge. Within minutes of his first entrance in *2 Henry IV*, Pistol has vowed revenge on Doll Tearsheet (2.4.148), and the Kydian invocations of 'Ebon den, with fell Alectoes snake' (5.5.37) accompany his later rousing of revenge to her side when she is imprisoned (compare *The Spanish Tragedy*, 3.15.1-7). In *Henry V* Pistol centres his malice on Fluellen, using the symbol of his humiliation by which to swear: 'By this Leeke, I will most horribly revenge' (5.1.45) – though he accepts the groat offered him 'in earnest of revenge' (60). Of course these are comic moments, but just as Pistol's braggartism sounds darker echoes to its wartime context, so here does his quest for vengeance. To Gower, the leek is a 'memorable Trophee of predeceased valor' (5.1.68-9), and Pistol's appropriation of it to his own private vendetta recalls *The Spanish Tragedy*'s 'complementary emblems of remembrance' (Kerrigan, 1996, 174), Andrea's scarf and Horatio's 'handkercher besmerd with blood' (2.5.52). Named in part for the Spanish doubloon, Pistol's origins in *2 Henry IV* insist on his equally forceful resemblance to the dead Spaniard Don Andrea, as to the Spanish *memento mori* Don Armado.

'Sir', says the Drawer, 'Antient pistol's belowe, and would speake with you' (2.4.66-7). Having entered from 'belowe', the detail might easily have been allowed to lapse; in the event they are pressed home. 'Pray thee goe downe good Ancient', urges the stolid Bardolph, keen to the brewing quarrel (145). Pistol's vengeful exclamation prompts a further attempted placation from the otherwise quiet Page: 'Pray thee go downe' (149). 'For Gods sake', amplifies Doll after Pistol's tirades, 'thrust him down staires', a phrase immediately echoed by Pistol himself (185-7). 'Quaite him downe', Falstaff then orders Bardolph, who again insists, 'get you downe staires' (189-92), and then Falstaff too repeats it as the brawl erupts (201). Down, down, down: my prosaic assembly of these utterances does scant justice to the scene's dynamic, but Pistol himself provides a precedent for its laboriousness: 'Downe: downe Dogges, down Fates' (F 155). Pistol's first appearance, in short, is cast very much like that favourite of Elizabethan folklore, the spirit that once conjured from 'th'infernal deepe' (152) cannot easily be laid down: 'How now, *Mephostophilus*?' is his first line in *The*

*Merry Wives of Windsor* (F 1.1.121).

On the eve of Agincourt, the ghostly form of King Henry meets the lone sentinel. Equally, however, to the King appears this shadowy mock-king, 'like a hagge of hell', this attenuated spirit of Marlovian belligerence and Kydian revenge. A sense of the uncanny, 'of the hypnotic, or the dream-state' Wilkins described, attends both figures, and that ambience is consolidated by the symmetry their meeting constructs. We have noted how the newly promoted Lieutenant Pistol shadows the action of *Henry V* (see above, p. 167). 'All princes be | [God's] Lieutenauntes', according to the 1559 *Mirror for Magistrates*: bearing in mind the kingly voice and echo that Henry and Pistol's two bodies depict in the scene, it is worth noting the supernatural associations of the doubling they strangely enact. Robert Kirk's *Secret Commonwealth* (1691) notes the endurance of the superstition of second sight:

> Some Men of that exalted Sight ... have told me that they have seen at their Meittings [funerals] a Double-man, or the Shape of some Man in two Places; that is, a superterranean and a subterranean Inhabitant, perfectly resembling one another in all Points, who he notwith-standing could easily distinguish one from another ... They call this Reflex-man a Co-Walker, every way like the Man, as a Twin-brother and Companion, haunting him as his Shadow, as is oft seen and known among Men (resembling the Originall,) both before and after the Originall is dead.[49]

'This Copy, Echo, or living Picture', concludes Kirk, 'goes att last to his own Herd' (4). 'I am not a double man', Falstaff had claimed at Shrewsbury, that battlefield of counterfeits (*1 Henry IV*, 5.4.136), after his own comic (and probably phallic) '*ris*[ing] *up*' (Jorgensen, 1976, 154-6). But now that Falstaff has gone to his own herd, to '*Arthurs* Bosome' (*Henry V*, 2.3.10), the range of Kirk's catalogue of duplicates applies the more freely to his Lieutenant Pistol, a 'double man' indeed, who 'in his Captaines absence hath authority to directe all' (Riche, 1587, G1v), 'both before and after the Originall is dead'.

There is a profound point to Henry's and Pistol's spectral symmetry. Lieutenancy (the instrumental representation of God's will) forms the basis of Elizabethan war-theory, as we have seen, and one to which Henry alludes in his first scene:

> But this lyes all within the wil of God,
> To whom I do appeale, and in whose name
> Tel you the *Dolphin*, I am comming on,
> To venge me as I may, and to put forth

My rightfull hand in a wel-hallow'd cause.
(1.2.289-93)

The public ruler wages war by representing God's will, and by conducting it in His name. War is the 'sonne of hell', as Clifford had said, 'Whom angry heavens do make their minister' (2 Henry VI, 5.3.33-4); 'Warre is his Beadle, Warre is his Vengeance', as Henry reiterates to Michael Williams (4.1.167-8). Previous chapters of this book have dwelled on the dramatic implications of such military delegation, whether in Stump's emblematic handicap, Tamburlaine's didactic lecture, Pucelle's metatheatrical tactic, or Rumour's sombre braggartism. Between them, Henry and Pistol variously shadow all these roles, and here before Agincourt, we indeed see Kirk's 'Shape of some Man in two Places', as the King (Kirk's 'superterranean' authority, perhaps) meets Pistol, his 'Copy, Echo, or living Picture' (Kirk's 'subterranean' daemon). The ghost of ancestral military emulation, of the old English fathers, Henry V, meets the ricochet of Pistol's fake spirit of Senecan revenge. Their encounter comprises in itself a copy or echo of the earlier meeting between Clifford and Richard, breaking down the distance between war and revenge.

The private grievance Pistol expounds to Henry foreshadows Henry's own unsuccessful attempts to justify his wars to the soldiers he next meets. 'Tell [Fluellen] Ile knock his Leeke about his Pate', says Pistol: 'Doe not weare your Dagger in your Cappe ... least he knock that about yours', replies the King (4.1.55-8). But within minutes, that warning has waned to an 'embrace' of another quarrel, this time with Williams: 'Give me any Gage of thine, and I will weare it in my Bonnet' (205-7). These two private grudges, and the process of their resolution, are cemented by the common participation of Fluellen, substituted to answer Williams's challenge, as he later meets Pistol's. But both the quarrel over Henry's glove and Fluellen's glove end amidst grudges. Williams's 'suppressed anger and resentment' (Barton, 1994, 217) at the 'twelve-pence' offered him by Fluellen – 'I will none of your Money' (4.8.64-8) – is matched by the better part of valour Pistol displays in accepting an identical sum from Fluellen. 'I take thy shilling in earnest of reconing', says Pistol in the 1600 Quarto (5.1.60), a line revised in the Folio to diminish his value to a 'groat', and substitute 'revenge' for the more monetary 'reconing'. It is worth recalling that such private animosities were the subject of strict censure not only by theorists like Sutcliffe and de Loque, but in the Lawes and Orders of Warre published by the Earl of Essex in 1599: 'No man shall commit any murther, or kill any person or draw blood of any, or draw any sword in private quarrell, with intent to offer violence within the Campe of Garrison, upon paine of death' (4). The Earl of Leicester had printed comparable instructions at the outset of the Dutch campaign, that specify the 'sundrie nations' by which 'controversies may arise':

> It is ordeined, that if any person of English nation shall
> finde him selfe agrieved with any wrong profered him by
> any foreiner, that then without profering further revenge
> hee shall signifie the same unto his Captaine ... so, as no
> further quarrell growe thereof.
> (1586, B1r)

'Further revenge', however, between Williams and Henry, or between Fluellen (his 'Majesties Countreyman')[50] and Pistol, is precisely how their deferral of grievance may be defined. Lieutenant Pistol and God's Lieutenant meet at dawn, each with a 'private quarrell' to fulfill after the battle itself. But handy dandy, which is the justice, and which the thief? 'One of these men is *genius* to the other', wonders the Duke in *The Comedy of Errors*, faced with a set of comparable complexities, 'And so of these, which is the naturall man, | And which the spirit?' (5.1.334-5). Questions like this are prompted by this brief encounter in *Henry V*, between two ghosts, the emulation of public Augustinian war and the theatrical echo of private Senecan revenge, each leaning on the other's bound.

Olivier's film of *Henry V* features a Williams who '*laughs in close-up*' before his challenge, 'Let it be a quarrel between us', is edited away via the '*sound of a fanfare*' and another close-up on Bates's successful appeal for amity: 'Be ... friends, you English fools ... *He grabs* WILLIAMS *by the arm and they walk away*' (Olivier, 1984, 60). The film likewise erodes the original force of Pistol and Henry's symmetrical meeting, since the camera concentrates on Pistol, with Henry '*(off)*', throughout the exchange. The play's uncanny effect thus diminished may be illuminated by Freud's meditation on the subject – the product, like play and film, of war years.

'The Uncanny' (1919) skirts about the eeriness of the 'supernatural apparitions in ... *Hamlet, Macbeth* or *Julius Caesar*' by claiming they 'remain within their setting of poetic reality'.[51] But the play Freud omits deploys perhaps with greater force than those he lists the criteria he assembles. As Freud acknowledges, the First World War witnessed an explosion of spiritualism, and hundreds of tales were told of revenant dead soldiers.[52] Shakespeare's *Henry V* testifies to the same notion of the military supernatural, and also to the transgressions of 'poetic reality' of which Freud speaks. That queasy uncertainty of which Pistol and Henry's meeting partakes pervades the play, and resonantly anticipates the terms of Freud's *Unheimlich*: 'doubts whether an apparently animate being is really alive; or ... whether a lifeless object might not be in fact animate'; 'characters who are considered identical because they look alike'; 'a doubling, dividing and interchanging of the self'; 'the constant recurrence of the same thing ... of the same crimes, or even the same names through several generations'; 'an uncanny effect is often and easily produced when a distinction between imagination and reality is effaced' (17, 226-44). The relationship between 'imagination and reality' is the constant theme of the play's Chorus, and the effacement of their distinction lies at the heart of the play's mustering energy, its darkly inverse posthumousness, and of Olivier's marshalling of its forces to the exigencies of 1945. How rich, then, sounds the misquotation he includes after the misty uncanniness of that dawn meeting:

> *A man is scrabbling in the undergrowth. It is* FLUELLEN,
> *who stands up and jumps down to a trench.*
> GOWER: (*off*)  Captain Fluellen!
> *Pan to show* GOWER *approaching.*
> GOWER:  Captain Fluellen!
> FLUELLEN *jumps up beside him.*
> FLUELLEN:  Sh! Sh! In the name of Beelzebub, speak lower.
> (Olivier, 1984, 56-7)

'In the name of Beelzebub'? Fluellen swears 'In the name of Jesu' in the 1600 Quarto, of 'Jesu Christ' in the Folio (4.1.66). But who is it that swears so?

> Knock, Knock, Knock. Who's there i'th' name of
> *Belzebub?* ... Never at quiet. What are you? but this place
> is too cold for Hell. Ile Devil-Porter it no further.
> (*Macbeth*, 2.3.3-16)

'Remember the Porter' (2.3.20): Olivier indeed seems to have remembered his play here, a play consummately replete with uncanny doublings and 'wicked Dreames'. His (Freudian) slip speaks volumes for the darkly eerie force of Shakespeare's original *Henry V*, and the 'Airborne Troops' conjured on to its stage.

Taillepied's *Treatise of Ghosts* includes a story of a peculiarly effective military strategy, deployed by a general who 'on the eve of battle with the King of Britain' (48),

> set the dead bodies of certain of his warriors who had
> been slain on horseback like living men, and mustered
> corpses to fight. And as the sunbeams struck the great
> mass of dead and senseless shapes it seemed a mighty
> active host so that the Britons, terrified at the spectacle,
> fled conquered by the dead.

The policy is reminiscent of the 'contrary pretenses' catalogued in Elizabethan military text-books that lent such theatrical colours to the art of war. It reverses Clayton's 'shew as if men were slayne' (1591, 27) by mustering corpses to fight. Taillepied calls the story 'dark and mysterious' because he interpolates into his source the detail that 'it would appear that the Spirits of these corpses returned to them a while at least' (48), while his original author confesses to being doubtful 'whether to think more of the cunning or of the good fortune of this victory'. That interpolation recalls Shakespeare's presentation in *Henry V* of a 'mass of dead ... shapes', the 'flat unraysed Spirits' that fight at Agincourt, temporarily mustered from their graves. *Henry V* treats contemporary military exhortations as a series of perturbing exorcisms. Within a year of writing that play, Shakespeare turned from Agincourt to Elsinore, a reorientation we shall now follow. Our passage is assisted by Taillepied since the general whose macabre policy he elaborates is Amleth, and his source is Saxo Grammaticus.[53]

## Notes

1.  David Jones, *In Parenthesis* (1963), 84.
2.  Marlowe, *Works*, ed. Gill (1987-91), 1, 93. Reference is to the lineation of this edition.
3.  See for example Lavater (1572), 62; Taillepied (1933), 50.
4.  Chamberlain, *Letters*, ed. McLure (1939), 1, 81.
5.  See for example Laveter (1572), 56; Taillepied (1933), 45-6.
6.  See below, p. 242. On quotation from *Hamlet*, see above, p. vi.
7.  Induction, 194-8. '*Hieronimo*' is alluded to at 209-11. On the lines' possibly subsequent insertion, however, see Barton (1984), 14-15.
8.  Lineation of *The Spanish Tragedy* is from Kyd, *Works*, ed. Boas (1901) and the text from 1592 Quarto.
9.  *The Spanish Tragedy*, ed. Edwards (1959), xxiii. See also *The Spanish Tragedy*, ed. Mulryne (1989), xiv.
10. Scot, *Discoverie*, ed. Nicholson (1886, repr. 1973), 507.
11. *The Mirror for Magistrates*, ed. Campbell (1938), 120.
12. See also Mulryne (1991), 67-89.
13. Reference to the *Aeneid* is from the Loeb edition, tr. Fairclough (1935).
14. Laurence Binyon, 'For the Fallen', in Stallworthy (1988), 209.
15. *A Myrrour for English Souldiers* (1595), A2r.
16. Q 1599 reads 'gates of Horror' in an illuminatingly graphic error.
17. A. Freeman (1967), 53-4.
18. Compare too the titles of News-Pamphlets 3, 9, 11, 15, 16, 24 and 25.
19. *The Spanish Tragedy*, ed. Mulryne (1989), 14.
20. See S.F. Johnson (1963), 34-6.
21. See Kerrigan (1997), 174-81.
22. See Baines (1980), 41-51.
23. *The 'Adages' of Erasmus*, tr. Phillips (1964), 314.
24. *The Works of Sir Roger Williams*, ed. Evans (1972), xviii.
25. *The Knight of the Burning Pestle*, ed. Zitner (1984), 159 (5.290.n).
26. Quotation from the play *Henry V* is from the Folio text. Quotation from Olivier's film is from Sinclair's transcript, *Henry V, 1945* (1984), though its dedication does not appear there.

27. *Henry V, 1945*, ed. Sinclair (1984), v.

28. Dulwich College, MS 29, 36r.

29. *The Mirror for Magistrates*, ed. Campbell (1938), 473; 482; 463.

30. Gates (1579), 58. See also Churchyard's commendatory verse in Riche (1578), ** i v: 'loes not your old renown, O baebs of brittayn bloed'.

31. *Macbeth*, 2.1.36-8.

32. On the likeness between the Chorus's 'Witch' and Ate, see above, p.40.

33. Spenser, *Prose Works*, ed. Gottfried (1949), 158.

34. Quoted in Altman (1991), 10.

35. See G. Roberts (1996), 148-9 (where the figure is related to *Doctor Faustus*, Nashe's *Unfortunate Traveller*, and *Love's Labour's Lost*).

36. Ornstein notices this pedigree, commenting that 'since time immemorial the battlefield has provided the supreme test of nobility', but stops short of equating that pedigree with the ghost-players we see on stage (1972, 187).

37. Taillepied, *A Treatise of Ghosts*, tr. Summers (1933), 44.

38. *Ovids Metamorphosis*, tr. Sandys (1632), 508; 527. A woodcut of the phenomenon was included in *A Lamentable List of Certaine Hidious, Frightfull, and Prodigious Signs* (1638), and is reproduced in Park and Daston (1981), 31.

39. *Some Memorials of John Hampden*, ed. Nugent (1854), 382-4.

40. Burton, *Anatomy of Melancholy*, ed. Jackson (1923), 1, 191; Taille-pied, *Treatise of Ghosts*, tr. Summers (1933), 89; Rabelais, *Gargantua and Pantagruel*, ed. Lewis (1929), 2, 216-19; Scot, *Discoverie of Witchcraft*, ed. Nicholson (1886, repr. 1973), 509-25.

41. *Julius Caesar*, ed. Dorsch, (1955), 142.

42. The speech also includes a pleasing blunder reminiscent and worthy of Crackstone: 'I did unhorse three *Turkie* Janizaries', he claims, ignorant that such men were, famously, infantrymen (E3v). See above, p. 147.

43. Taillepied, *Treatise of Ghosts*, tr. Summers (1933), 205 n.

44. *Lectures and Notes*, ed. Ashe (1907), 369-70.

45. Herr (1978), 16.

46. *Antony and Cleopatra*, ed. Ridley (1954), 150.

47. Daniel, *Complete Works*, ed. Grosart (1885-96), 2, 173-4.

48. *Henry V*, ed. Walter (1954), 33.

49. Kirk, *Secret Commonwealth* (1815), 3-4.

50. Henry's Welsh kinship with Fluellen is stressed at 4.7.103-9.

51. Freud, *Psychological Works*, gen. ed. Strachey (1953-74), 17, 250.

52. See Winter (1995), 54-77; on the relationship between film and military ghosts in the aftermath of the Great War see Winter (1995), 15-28, and of World War II see Lawson (1991), 30-33.

53. *The First Nine Books of ... Saxo Grammaticus*, ed. Powell (1894), 128.

# CHAPTER SIX

# The Question of these Wars

*'Der Friedhof ist ein Trümmerfeld'* [1]

'The purpose of playing', according to Hamlet, 'both at the first, and nowe, was and is ... to shew ... the very age and body of the time his forme and pressure' (3.2.20-4).[2] This book has sought to reveal the extent to which wartime exerted a distinctive pressure on Elizabethan drama. Its parameters have been set by the Queen's declaration of war in 1585 and the King's accession in 1603. *Hamlet* constitutes a convenient and resonant means by which to conclude its enquiry. First written and first performed in wartime (*c*.1600-02), its earliest printed texts did not appear until its author was a King's Man. Both contextually and in the story it tells, the play straddles war and peace. Yet to speak of 'the play' is to blur the significant cultural boundary between Elizabethan and Jacobean drama, between wartime performance and peacetime texts. It is the task of this chapter to suggest that war's 'forme and pressure' leaves its imprint in key textual disparities between the First Quarto (1603), Second Quarto (1604-05) and First Folio (1623) versions of the play.

Q2, the longest text, is also the one closest to an authorial first draft. Its metaphorical texture continually returns to war, yet much of this military flavour is missing from Q1, a text that, for all its casualties of transmission, records the shape of the play's wartime performances. The marks of this revision can more clearly be observed, like putlog holes in church interiors, in the systematically adapted structure of the First Folio text. Furthermore, the most substantial disparities between Q2 and F hang together by their common concern with war. It has been argued that revisions made between the First Quarto and Folio texts of *King Lear* serve to excise the 'extraneous political complication' of Cordelia's alliance with the invading 'Powers of France' in Acts Four and Five (G. Taylor, 1980, 30-31). This chapter will also examine changes made to a fourth-act army, but will seek to find grounds for that revision in the wars surrounding *Hamlet*'s composition and performance (as well as in the wars that *Hamlet* dramatizes), a context overlooked in the considerable critical attention recently given to the play's textual history.[3] That wartime can extend an influence over both the performance and text of *Hamlet* may be shown by two productions of the play from our own century.

Ernst Lubitsch's sardonic film-comedy *To Be Or Not To Be* (1942) appropriated *Hamlet* to tell its story of a troupe of actors mounting a production of the play in Warsaw in September 1939. There are many shrewdnesses to Lubitsch's choice of play: the play-within-the-film, (actors playing) players playing soldiers, the mingling of political leaders with clowns, and the theme of espionage, are all elements common to film and play. But perhaps most suggestively, both pieces begin amid the tense expectation of mobilization and prepared defence, and of imminent invasion. Further, the internal background to both works' narrative mirrors the context against which they both opened, in 1942 and c.1600. In the event we see little of Shakespeare's play in the film beyond its eponymous speech, but the eloquent consonance of its adaptation within it is as intelligently tempered to the times as Olivier's *Henry V* would be.

The second production of *Hamlet* dates from a year later, in July 1943, and was apparently likewise sensitive to the 'forme and pressure' of wartime, this time textually. Throughout its run it 'substitute[d] Greece for Poland in the dialogue' (Chwalewik, 15). The play's fictive geography and its unprovoked military campaign against 'the maine of *Poland* ... Or ... some frontire' (4.4.15-16) had become as inappropriate within a wartime context as Lubitsch had found them apt, for this particular production was staged in Berlin.[4]

In both these adaptations we may find a model for the creative chronology of the original *Hamlet*. Conceived and drafted in wartime, the play is informed by that context: but the pressures of war seem to have necessitated a judicious revision of Shakespeare's initial text for performance (Q1) before being printed *in extenso* (Q2) once the war was over. A more detailed exposition of this textual narrative will be the subject of the second half of this chapter. This will be integrated into a sequential account of the play, moving from Act One's expectation of war, via an account of the play's military texture, to Fortinbras's arrival in Act Four, and Osric's role in Act Five. More immediately, however, it is worth stressing the military tenor of the play and of its first auspices.

## 'Implements of war'[5]

A consensus exists that the composition of *Hamlet* belongs to c.1600-02 and that the play follows *Henry V* and *Julius Caesar*, both of which were performed in 1599.[6] The urgency of the European situation, so galvanizing to the tone and subject matter of *Henry V*, had not receded as the new century began. Invasion-scares, musters and forced conscriptions were renewed, with more force perhaps in the wake of Essex's failure in Ireland. It seems immediately clear that while the 'two Centinels' on their 'strikt and most observant watch', the 'dayly cost of brazon Cannon | And forraine marte, for implements of warre' and the 'impresse of ship-writes' (1.1.74-8) might reflect 'Denmark's contemporary war preparations under Christian IV' as the Arden editor notes (170), they also evoked present English anxieties. After all, the lines were probably written within a year of the 'chaining of streets and shutting of the gates' of London that Chamberlain recorded in August 1599 (see above, pp. 186-7). *Hamlet*'s first three lines catch at these uncertain times of national emergency and demonstrate a familiarity with military procedure assumed in their first audiences:

BARNARDO   Whose there?
FRANCISCO   Nay answere me. Stand and unfolde your selfe.
BARNARDO   Long live the King.

Many commentators have noted the immediate disruption of military propriety registered in this sequence. It is the first of the play's 'maimed rites'. The sentinel, as Garrard explained (1591, 12), must 'demand with a lowd voice, *Qui vala*? Who goes there? to which when answere is made, Friende': it is Francisco's part, then, to issue the challenge, not the relieving sentry, Barnardo's.

What has not been noted, however, is that in a play in part devoted to distinguishing between true and false friendship, it is a rich irony that the prescribed response is diverted by the distracting anxiety of the nocturnal patrol. When Henry V is challenged by Pistol, he responds in text-book fashion ('*Che vous la*? | A friend') and does so again when the procedure is repeated with Bates, Court and Williams ('Who goes there? | A Friend') (F 4.1.36-7; 90-92). Banquo's challenge to Macbeth, again at night, shortly before Duncan's murder, is identical: 'Give me my Sword; who's there? | A Friend' (2.1.9-10). Each of these exchanges is more than mere military realism. For by the time Henry meets Pistol, his friendship with Falstaff and Bardolph has been fatally sacrificed to the demands of his office, and the friendship he professes to the three soldiers is soon to deteriorate into argument and rebuke. Macbeth's professed response to Banquo is likewise soon to be (rather more radically) put into question. When Francisco later correctly issues his challenge ('stand ho, who is there?') it is Horatio, the 'fine Character of Friendship' Pope described,[7] who correctly completes the ritual: 'Friends to this ground' (1.1.15-16). On each of these occasions current military practice is both reflected and dramatically exploited. The same is true of Barnardo's response to Francisco, 'Long live the King'.

That phrase, as Hibbard's edition reasons (1987, 143), comprises the unfolding of the password, Robert Barret's 'watch Word' given to 'souldiers, standing Sentinell at their postes, whereby their watches are nightly governed' (1598, 253). The ironies of such a password 'in the light of all that follows' (the apparition of a dead king) have long been noticed.[8] But re-acquaintance with contemporary military procedure adds a further dimension to those ironies, as Barret again explains: 'the souldier being set at the Sentinell is not bound to acknowledge any person, for to permit him to approch unto him, but such as shall give him the Word which was given by the Generall, and so to the guardes' (107). Claudius's military credentials are secured in Act Four ('I have ... serv'd against the French', 4.7.82) so it seems characteristic of the subtlety of his methods that he builds into his newly acquired soldiers' nightly routine a compulsory pledge of loyalty, 'given by the Generall'.[9]

The same double-page spread that contains Barret's detailing of the sentry's duties deals with the common superstition of the sentry's aptitude for seeing ghosts, 'For many times, unto one man alone, feare or imagination doth cause few people to seeme many, and many things to seeme to be, which are not indeede' (106). We have seen how Shakespeare exploited that folk-belief in *Henry V* 's alliance of war with the uncanny on the night before Agincourt. On the eve of Bosworth and of Philippi 'feare or imagination' conjure forth ghosts to Richard and Brutus. Such theatrically recent precedents for Old Hamlet's ghost reinforce the sense of imminent battle first prompted by these uneasy sentries. In *Richard III*, *Julius Caesar* and later in *Macbeth*, ghosts walk abroad to trouble the consciences of their protagonists. In *Henry V*, by contrast, the rhetoric of patriotic emulation is rendered uneasily explicit as a sort of imaginative conjuration of the glorious war-dead.

The same tradition surely underlies the apparition of Old Hamlet, 'that faire and warlike forme', as Horatio calls it, 'In which the Majestie of buried Denmarke | Did sometimes march' (1.1.50-52). Daniel's *Civile Wars* (reprinted in 1599) imagines the ghost of Henry V looming 'Out of the clowdy darkenes of the night' to inspire valorous deeds in the present (see above, pp. 213-14). H.A. Mason's commentary on *Hamlet*'s ghost receives contemporary support: 'For a moment we might suppose that the Spirit who had taken on so glorious a shape was the Genius of the Danes ... a Great Dane in full fighting trim' (133-5). For more than a moment the military aspects of the ghost are sustained and reiterated. 'Such was the very Armor he had on', says Horatio, 'When he the ambitious *Norway* combated'. Marcellus confirms how 'twice before ... With martiall stauke hath he gone by our watch'; to Barnardo it is appropriate 'that this portentous figure | Comes armed through our watch' (1.1.63-4; 68-9; 112-13). And the same details ('Armed at poynt', 'with solemne march') are reported to Hamlet at 1.2.200-201, then pondered by the Prince: 'Arm'd say you? ... My fathers spirit (in armes)' (226; 255). The language Hamlet uses when at last he meets his father's shade (1.4.46-53) strongly recalls that employed to awaken remembrance in the early scenes of *Henry V*, and their invocation of the 'Warlike Spirit' of 'mightie Ancestors':

> Let me not burst in ignorance, but tell
> Why thy canoniz'd bones hearsed in death
> Have burst their cerements? why the Sepulcher,
> Wherein we saw thee quietly interr'd
> Hath op't his ponderous and marble jawes,
> To cast thee up againe? what may this meane
> That thou dead corse, againe in compleat steele
> Revisites thus the glimses of the Moone.

Hibbard usefully points up the contrast Old Hamlet strikes with the conventionally 'filthy whining ghost, | Lapt in some foul sheet' described in 1598/99,[10] but it is not just his silent dignity that is enhanced by the comparison. The equivalent figure in *Antonio's Revenge*, which arguably shares a source in an *Ur-Hamlet*,[11] describes his 'cerecloth',[12] but there is nothing to indicate a soldierly appearance for Andrugio's ghost. Old Hamlet's 'compleat steele', on the other hand, seems both visually and verbally to echo the form of Marlowe's paradigmatic warrior Tamburlaine, encased in his 1590 Octavo portrait in the armour he assumes in his first play: 'This compleat armor, and this curtle-axe | Are adjuncts more beseeming *Tamburlaine*' (1.2.42-3). Less the shrill fury of revenge, Old Hamlet rather appropriates the trappings of the propagandist imperative marshalled in a series of contemporary exhortations.

The ghost of Nicholas Burdet in the 1587 *Mirror for Magistrates* looks as he did when 'slaine at *Pontoise*'; Horatio recognizes Old Hamlet from the time 'he the ambitious *Norway* combated' (1.1.64). Nashe described the inspiration to be had by exhuming Talbot from 'his Tombe ... on the Stage', and having 'his bones newe embalmed' by his audiences' tears; Hamlet questions his father's 'canoniz'd bones' and 'dead corse', cast out from its 'Sepulcher'. Gates appealed to the 'children of olde *English* Fathers ... famous in Militarie feates'; 'Ile call thee *Hamlet*', cries his son, 'King, father, royall Dane' (1.4.44-5). Such patriotic rhetoric is echoed in *Hamlet*'s early scenes, and until the truth is revealed at 1.5.25, the Prince shares with his audiences the insistence of a military past enjoining him to take up arms against an invasive expeditionary force. Some of that now dissipated suspense survives in the recruitment of *Hamlet* to Thomas Hood's playful poem about childhood games, 'Playing at Soldiers' (1831):

> Just like that ancient shape of mist,
> In Hamlet, crying ''List, O 'list!'
> Come, who will serve the king.[13]

The punningly replaced apostrophes ('[en]list' for 'list[en]') are Hood's, but the sense they elide is true to the contexts Shakespeare's scene exploits. Until we hear of Claudius's crime, in other words, war fever is the dominant impression of the play. Barbara Everett claims that 'audiences shuffle' or 'only half-listen' as Horatio summarizes Fortinbras's grievances (1989, 146-7), but the wartime context of 1600-02 would have set a chill on Horatio's view that the Ghost 'bodes some strange eruption to our state', or on Barnardo's markedly direct reference to the apparition 'That was and is the question of these warres' (1.1.72; 114). A brief survey of that context may restore some of the urgency felt by the play's original audiences.

The Franco-Spanish peace of Vervins was an 'accomplished fact', as we have seen, by May 1598 and a more comprehensive European peace was debated in England (MacCaffrey, 515). Among the benefits arising from such a settlement was advanced the alleviation of 'dangers of tumults at home', as Camden put it, 'for often payments, taxes, and leavies of men' (4, 122). As one theatre of war closed, however, another opened with a new urgency in the wake of the defeat of English forces at Yellow Ford that August. 'All this yeere', Camden wrote, 'was the *Irish* rebellion very hot' (4, 135), adding further burdens to England's commitment of resources to the Low Countries. The 1599 invasion-scare was the largest since 1588 (MacCaffrey, 133). Already 'very weary' with the wars in 1592, Elizabeth's subjects were seen as dangerously close to 'tumults' from 1599.[14] The extent of English losses in Ireland percolated home to London that July (Novarr, 234). In 1600 discontent at food-shortages in Norfolk was being levelled at the amount of supplies being sent to Irish garrisons (Pearce, 44); desertion and mutiny were reaching worrying levels;[15] and some arrested deserters were publicly executed.[16] In 1601, as one London City Council session minuted four years later, 'the commons [were] ... very deeply charged not only with the building of two gallies ... but also with sending over of soldiers into Ireland'.[17] This potentially volatile situation affected London dramatists in a variety of ways. Henslowe took advantage of the French peace by commissioning a four-part history of the French civil wars in 1598/99, but the Privy Council forbade discussion of the Irish campaign 'on pain of death' in the wake of the John Hayward affair, an edict which in part accounts for the discrepancies between Quarto and Folio versions of *2 Henry VI* and *Henry V* (Clare, 39-42; Patterson, 1988, 29-62). The Bishops' Order of June 1599 specified that 'noe English historyes be printed excepte they bee allowed by some of her majesties privie Counsell' (Patterson, 1984, 47), and the greater scrutiny afforded such plays may account for the frequency with which Camden's list of 'dangers of tumults' is reassuringly countered in the plays performed or printed in this period.

Barnaby Riche's final dialogue between his Captains Skill and Pill, *A Souldiers Wishe to Britons Welfare* (1604), stridently defends the 'Rents, Revenues, Impositions, Taxes, Subsidies, penalties, Lones, Confiscations' imposed on citizens by contrasting them with the 'superfluities' so taxed, the 'pryde and excesse of both men and women' (8). The resentment Camden recorded at 'often payments, [and] taxes' encountered a dramatized rebuke too in *Edward IV* (printed 1600), as Grudgen (a 'grumbling, grudging Churle') is shamed by Hobs: 'thou hast two ploughes going ... and wilt not spare the King foure or five pound' (E1r). Reluctance to enlist likewise meets reproach (as we have seen) in the rewards bestowed on veterans in *Edward I*, *Sir John Oldcastle*, and *The Fair Maid of the West*, as well as in *A Larum for London* (c.1600-02), a history play more directly concerned with 'the question of these warres' (see above, pp. 13-16). The similarly reassuring additions to the dusty old *Liberality and Prodigality* date from February 1600/01. John Cobbler's reluctant service in *The Famous Victories of Henry the Fift* (at long last published in 1598) is carefully rewarded 'with a packe full of apparell' (scene xix); and so is

Ralph in both *The Cobbler's Prophecy* and *The Shoemakers' Holiday*. In all these plays, as also in *Henry V* (that eerie blend of May Day and Halloween), Dekker's 'frolike spirits' (1.1.62) temper their grievance at veterans' neglect with an explicit obedience to patriotic service. Amidst such performances, in October 1599, 'the overthrow of *Turnholt*, was acted upon a Stage', probably by Shakespeare's company (see above, p. 92).

This representation of a two-year-old victory a month after Essex's ignominious return from Ireland, and two months after the panic in London of an invasion-scare, points towards an overlap in the Lord Chamberlain's dual roles of theatrical patron and Privy Councillor; towards a concerted enlistment of the resources of the stage for the furtherance of a patriotic imperative, the more pressing after fifteen years of expensively indecisive and unpopular war. Such subtly exhortatory corralling of an audience's loyalty should perhaps be seen as a counterpart to the actual enlistment of men, from the theatres themselves, that Gawdy described in May 1602, just two months after *Hamlet* was registered for publication 'as yt was latelie Acted'.

For most of its first act, *Hamlet* announces itself as part of this overtly topical and military dramatic trend. Barnardo and Francisco's nervous guard takes place against a backdrop of national mobilization of the sort renewed in London in the summers of 1599 and 1601 (*APC*, 32, 131-7; Camden, 4, 142). Fortinbras's disregard for the 'seald compact | Well ratified by lawe and herald[r]y' and by the 'bands of lawe' of earlier settlements, and his intent 'to recover of us by strong hand ... those foresaid lands | So by his father lost',[18] can be read as being obliquely suggestive of the desultory and profitless negotiations for peace in Europe; of the 'dissembled truces and submissions' by which Tyrone protracted his Irish rebellion, and, more generally, of the manner in which the flames of conflict, though sometimes dormant, were never quite extinct.[19] The prospect of invasion could threaten Denmark in the name of a thirty-year old grudge, much as the 'half-doing' of the 1588 Armada threatened repeated attempts upon England (Wiener, 52). *Hamlet*'s sentries encounter the spirit of a patriotic military authority of the kind familiar from a host of propagandist writings of the time, who commands a dutiful service from his son. The play sets up a parallel between Hamlet's duty to his father and his audiences' duty to their fatherland, only to reveal that duty (following Kyd's lead in *The Spanish Tragedy* and, perhaps, the *Ur-Hamlet*) to consist of private revenge. But that initial identification continues to reverberate beyond the revelation of Claudius's crime. It is only after the Ghost's narrative that Claudius receives news of his successful diversion of Fortinbras's enterprise, and for the rest of the play the Norwegian campaign will be interwoven with its events. What one critic calls *Hamlet*'s 'background of war' (Potter, 6), however, is not limited to Fortinbras's progress. War – more precisely the language of Elizabethan war – helps constitute the fabric of the play's metaphorical life and setting.

How was Denmark popularly conceived by Elizabethans? Nashe had caricatured the 'pride of the dane' in 1592 for standing 'so much upon their unweldy burliboand souldiery, that they account of no man that hath not a battle Axe at his girdle' (1, 177). That the Danes were regarded as especially belligerent in the period is confirmed, for example, by the list of allies that *Edward III* (another patriotic war-play reprinted in 1599) adds to its source: 'Some friends have we beside domesticke power', asserts its French King, 'The sterne Polonian, and the warlike Dane' (3.1.33-4). Subsequent stage-directions detail the entrance of the King of Bohemia 'with *Danes*, and a Polonian Captaine, with other soldiers' (39 SD), a reference that secures the equally warlike reputation of 'lofty Poland' (as its Captain describes it), 'nurse of hardie men' (44). Marlowe's Anjoy in *The Massacre at Paris* confirms this reputation, 'For *Poland* is as I have been enformde, | A martiall people' (454-5). Scholarly accusations of 'geographical solecism' in *Hamlet*, its 'misconceptions' that Poland bordered Denmark (Sjögren, 225), themselves misconceive the two countries' notional proximity, their commonly perceived expertise in war. Norway's military profile seems also to have been current among *Hamlet*'s first audiences, manifested in the chivalric idealism it displays in *Clyomon and Clamydes* (printed 1599), or the 'Norweyan Lord, surveying vantage, | With furbusht Armes, and new supplyes of men' in *Macbeth* (1.2.31-2), there allied with Irish 'Kernes and Gallowg[la]sses' (13). *Hamlet* is set in a European geography of military renown that frames an acknowledgement of wartime topicality sustained throughout the play's verbal texture.

*Hamlet*, as Zitner well puts it, is 'a play of weapons' (1). From the 'partizan' Marcellus offers to wield against the Ghost to Fortinbras's final command, 'Goe bid the souldiers shoote', from Old Hamlet's 'sleaded pollax' to the 'Rapier and Dagger' of the fencing-match, weaponry determines much of the plot and flavour of the play. Claudius's habitual firing of ordnance, we might add, is symptomatic of the way in which 'implements of warre' punctuate its narrative. It is perhaps unsurprising that the sentry Barnardo should be drawn to military metaphor in seeking to 'assaile' Horatio's ears 'That are so fortified against our story' (1.1.34-5), or that the old soldier King Hamlet should liken his murder to the sacking of a city (1.5.63-7). But such martial analogy is not confined to the cast's soldiers. Laertes, for example, counsels Ophelia to 'keepe ... in the reare of your affection | Out of the shot and danger of desire' (1.3.34-5), while Polonius instructs her to 'Set your intreatments at a higher rate | Then a commaund to parle' (1.3.122-3). The images are familiar from Sidneyan tropes of love,[20] but they, and Ophelia's promise to keep the advice 'As watchman to my hart' (1.3.46), are enlivened by their proximity to real sentries, and their talk of an 'angry parle' (1.1.65) and 'tearmes compulsatory' (106). Queen Gertrude is similarly conversant with military emergency, as she shows in the closet-scene: 'as the sleeping souldiers in th'alarme, | Your bedded haire ... Start up and stand an end' (3.4.120-22).

The metaphor is again strengthened by its reminiscence of the last time we saw the Ghost. And although, as Philip MacGuire argues, Claudius's diplomacy is implicitly contrasted with Old Hamlet's martial skill (163), the new king's service-record is carefully mentioned (4.7.82), and he accordingly views his own situation in terms of a battlefield, where sorrows resemble 'battalians', 'Like to a murdring peece' giving 'superfluous death' (4.5.79-96). From such a network of related imagery two distinct patterns emerge, both of which are relevant to the particular story *Hamlet* tells: the habitual failure of the play's weapons, and their invisible operation beneath the surface of events.

Marcellus's partisan (his halberd) is redundant against the ghost, 'as the ayre, invulnerable' (1.1.150), and indeed seems to have the effect of chasing it away rather than staying it. The image is repeated in Claudius's later, elaborate analogy for avoiding the fall-out from Polonius's murder:

> Whose whisper ore the worlds dyameter,
> As levell as the Cannon to his blanck,
> Transports his poysned shot, may misse our Name,
> And hit the woundlesse ayre.
> (4.2.41-4)[21]

John Hale's technical paraphrase of line 42 ('As level as the cannon sends its ball within the limit of its point-blank range') usefully gauges the technical nature of Shakespeare's image: the cannon of slander overshoots the mark in a trajectory 'familiar from the ballistic diagrams in Elizabethan gunnery books' (1983, 428). The metaphor is studiedly contemporary, and familiar too, as we have seen, from Tamburlaine's litany of 'martial tooles' (see above, p. 72). But while *Tamburlaine*'s weapons glory in their technological supremacy, it is the characteristic of *Hamlet*'s to misfire. Polonius excuses the spying he orders on his son by likening him to an unruly firearm, 'The flash and out-breake of a fierie mind ... Of generall assault' (2.1.33-5), and to Laertes himself Claudius reiterates the conceit of public opinion as another such weapon:

> so that my arrowes
> Too slightly tymberd for so [loud a Winde],[22]
> Would have reverted to my bowe againe,
> But not where I have aym'd them.
> (4.7.21-4)

In *Hamlet*'s Prince, too, its sequence of enterprises turned awry prompts a related image, when he seeks pardon of Laertes by urging him to imagine 'That I have shot my arrowe ore the house | And hurt my brother' (5.2.239-40). Near the beginning of *Henry V*, Canterbury sets the key-note of that play's mustered solidarity by imagining 'as an ayme or butt, |

Obedience' (1.2.186-7), and identifies the common purpose of the common-wealth (appropriately to a play about Agincourt) 'As many Arrowes loosed severall wayes | Come to one marke' (207-8). As characteristic points of disparity between the inspiritingly patriotic tenor of *Henry V* and the darker scrutiny of war in *Hamlet*, Claudius's and the Prince's lines describe a precisely opposite consequence of taking arms, as Laertes soon spells out when, fatally wounded, he in turn seeks Hamlet's pardon: 'The treacherous instrument is in my hand', he says, and 'Hath turn'd it selfe on me' (5.2.322-4).

The murderous fall-back Claudius contrives in the poisoned wine is correspondingly mooted via another image of ballistic self-destruction. 'This project', he says (the word alive to its etymon, now registered in its subsequent cognate, 'projectile'), 'Should have a back or second that might hold | If this did blast in proofe' (4.7.151-3): which is, in the event what happens to Claudius's second weapon, poisoning Gertrude and precipitating his own death. Horatio's final summary of the play's events, his list of 'casuall slaughters' and 'purposes mistooke, | Falne on th'inventers heads' (5.2.387-90), is one of the last links in a persistent chain of imagery that insists on the 'superfluous death' that resort to arms brings with it. The image occurs in the Folio's earliest-written history, where Queen Margaret checks Suffolk's curses which 'like an over-charged Gun, recoile, | And turnes the force of them upon thy selfe' (*2 Henry VI*, 3.2.334-6). Elsewhere it seems to have become something of a commonplace, 'for crafte recoyles in the end', as Middleton's Dick Follywit muses, 'like an overcharg'd musket, and maymes the very hand that puts fire too't'.[23] But the image accretes into a guiding principle of *Hamlet*'s 'play of weapons'.

Familiarity has perhaps dulled the edge of 'To be, or not to be', but its meditation on 'the slings and arrowes of outragious fortune' announces kinship with this metaphorical texture: weapons are as capricious and arbitrary as fortune. The speech's characteristic imagery prompted Pope to suggest emendation of the following line ('Or to take Armes against a sea of troubles') as follows: 'Perhaps *siege* ['against a siege of troubles'], which continues the metaphor of *slings, arrows, taking arms*; and represents the being encompass'd on all sides with troubles' (6, 400). However literalist this sounds, Pope is shrewd to identify the source of so much of the play's verbal life in the sieges of Elizabethan warfare. When, for example, the Ghost *'cries under the Stage'* (1.5.156 SD), Hamlet imagines him as an infantryman specializing in mines and trenches: 'Well sayd olde Mole, can'st worke i['']th['']earth so fast, | A worthy Pioner' (170-1). Jenkins's edition charts the mountain of debate sponsored by the old mole's potentially satanic identity (457-9), advanced by Battenhouse who noted that 'the characteristic activity of moles, as of devils, is to undermine' (1957, 146). Such a formulation, however, diminishes the relevance of the pioneer's military role, whose associations with the mole are well-documented. Lord Grey of Wilton's *Commentary* (which reappeared almost verbatim in

Holinshed's 1577 *Chronicles*) describes enduring an artillery bombardment 'whytche by night had dryven us of new to beecoome moalewarppes';[24] Dekker's *Wonderfull Year* (1604) likened the 'Grave-makers' busied by plague to 'Pioners of the Campe, that are imployed onely (like Moles) in casting up of earth and digging of trenches' (45).

The specific militarism of this context surely also illuminates Hamlet's earlier contemplation of 'some vicious mole of nature' (1.4.24). All modern editors gloss this Bradleyan mole as a dermatological blemish, a birth-mark perhaps suggested by the proximity of 'birth' (25) to 'complextion' (27);[25] but the clauses's conclusion should also be noticed: 'Oft breaking downe the pales and forts of reason' (28) suggests a quibble on the 'labouring Pyoner | Begrim'd with sweat, and smeared all with dust' described in *Lucrece* (1380-81). The invisible mischief wrought by such troops is perfectly analogous to the dissembled intents and disguised corruptions with which the play seems obsessed. That is certainly how Hamlet conceives of his mother's self-deception, filming over 'the ulcerous place | Whiles ranck corruption mining all within | Infects unseene' (3.4.149-51); and how, in the same scene, he anticipates thwarting the probing of his so-called friends:

> let it worke,
> For tis the sport to have the enginer
> Hoist with his owne petar, an't shall goe hard
> But I will delve one yard belowe their mines,
> And blowe them at the Moone: ô tis most sweete
> When in one line two crafts directly meete.
> (3.4.207-12)

Jonson later associated these volatile explosives with the campaign that was rumbling on in the years between *Hamlet*'s composition and its Second Quarto. His 1623 'Execration' wishes that instead of burning his library Vulcan had 'fixt in the *Low-Countrey's*', where he could 'Blow up, and ruine, myne, and countermyne, | Make your Petards, and Granats, all your fine | Engines of Murder' (lines 203-7). The poem's sardonic wit ('and receive the praise | Of massacring Man-kind so many wayes') finds a precedent in the mordant relish of Hamlet's resolve. It is here that the 'two crafts' of his play's military imagery 'in one line ... directly meete', as weaponry's capacity for self-destruction is squarely located in the most common field of Elizabethan war, the 'trench warfare', 'usually futile', of mine and countermine (see above, p. 3).

It is here, too, that *Hamlet*'s complex textual pedigree insists on being considered. For this speech's 'petar', Hamlet's earlier scrutiny of nature's 'vicious mole', Claudius's lines on the 'Cannon to his blanck', and Barnardo's conspicuous analysis of the Ghost as the 'question of these warres', are all occasions unique to Q2. It is only in that text, too, that Hamlet delivers his most concentrated inspection of the theory and practice of modern war, as Fortinbras's troops march towards Poland. We should accordingly turn our attention to the play's textual provenance.

## 'Is there no offence in't?' [26]

We have said that the composition of *Hamlet* belongs to 1600-02, and it is generally agreed that Q2 (1604-05) is also the most direct version available of that authorial draft. Hibbard takes its title-page's claim to be 'the true and perfect Coppie' at face-value, and Q2 as a faithful rendering of an 'authentic manuscript giving a complete version of the play as Shakespeare first wrote it', but which had not been acted due to its length (1987, 89-90). Edwards posits the existence of authorial 'deletion marks' in that manuscript that went unobserved by Q2's compositors and argues for a self-patrolling Shakespeare, reining in a tendency to prolixity in passages 'unwittingly preserved' in Q2 (1985, 11-14). Most modern editors agree that Q2 should be viewed as the original from which the other texts deviate, most pronouncedly in Q1 (1603). Long dismissed as a 'bad Quarto', Q1's reputation, via study and stage, has recently increased. Through its gauze of memorial and compositorial faults, Q1 retains the outline of the *Hamlet* adapted and cut from the Q2 manuscript for theatrical performance between 1601 and 1602, via a theatre transcript and prompt-book.[27] Ambiguities are simplified there, pace is accelerated, and its two hours' traffic streamlines and de-complicates its plot. The Folio text also constitutes a revision of the posited authorial papers behind Q2. Q1 makes all the same cuts as F, and passages peculiar to F are approximated there. Such details (together with its improvements in stage-directions) argue for F being the product of a 'logical and coherent process of revision designed to make a better acting version'.[28] If this textual chronology is read within the context of the European events which variously impinged on its first audiences, the logic and coherence of that revision may indeed be discerned, but not simply in the name of a 'better' version.

Shakespeare's first full authorial text of *Hamlet* was written around 1600 when invasion-scares and 'often payments, taxes, and leavies of men' fuelled popular discontent. His own *Henry V* was published that year in a simplified form which allied it more squarely to the exhortatory patriotism of a number of contemporary (pseudo-)historical plays, apparently to counter such discontent. The authorial text of *Hamlet*, preserved in Q2, seems not to have been performed as it stands, however, and was not printed until Elizabeth was dead and James had at last negotiated a European peace (1604-05). Yet the play had been performed around 1601-02, while Mountjoy's campaign in Ireland and the Siege of Ostend were commanding the resources and attention of London audiences – unignorably so, when we remember Gawdy's letter. Entered as 'latelie Acted' in the Stationers' Register in July 1602, that performance-text was printed as Q1 in 1603, and a version of it (perhaps an 'intermediate transcript')[29] which retained the most substantial cuts was published in the Folio in 1623. While *Hamlet* is always a 'play of weapons', that appraisal is truer of Q2 than of F, and truer of F than Q1.

Scholarly attention has recently returned with renewed vigour to the apparatus of Elizabethan dramatic censorship, but the consideration of *Hamlet* in this field has as yet been cursory. While Richard Dutton reports that 'censorship has never been suspected as a cause' of Q1's 'inadequacies' (88), Janet Clare passingly speculates on the 'expedient self-censorship' she suggests lies behind the absence from Q2 of Hamlet's reference to Denmark as a prison, 'which no doubt might have invited imputations of an affront to the Queen, Anne of Denmark' (108). More broadly, however, it seems notable that the text of *Hamlet* that was licensed for performance by the Master of Revels, performed by Privy Councillor Hunsdon's troupe (the Lord Chamberlain's Men) between 1601 and 1602, and printed in 1603 as Q1, is a markedly domesticated version of the play preserved in Q2. Between authorial text and wartime performance, between Q2 and Q1/F, the play seems to have undergone a systematic diminution of its original preoccupation with war. Q2 records a reflection on 'the question of these warres' too sensitive to be performed while they continued, but palatable and timely in their wake.

It is true that the verbal texture and sophistication of Q1 is blunted on almost every page, and that the reduction of Q2's military imagery is not a unique casualty. Yet without Polonius likening his children to beleaguered cities or to firearms; without Claudius equating his plots or public opinion with artillery, or sorrow with military units; without the 'strength and armour of the mind' mentioned by Rosenkrantz (3.3.12), or the 'proofe and bulwark against sence' by Hamlet (3.4.38); without these, and a host of other details, the inward martial contours of *Hamlet*'s narrative are altered. In Q2, for example, the intimacies of the closet-scene (3.4) are qualified by a series of images that suggest a consonance between Hamlet's interview with Gertrude and the 'warlike state' of which she is 'joyntresse' (1.2.9, not in Q1). Polonius's death prompts Hamlet's lines on the 'bulwark against sence' quoted above, that recall Barnardo's attempt to assail Horatio's ears before the Ghost's entrance. That entrance is repeated here, and it in turn prompts Gertrude's reminiscence of 'souldiers in th'alarme'. When the old mole exits, Hamlet speaks of 'corruption mining all within', and tugs Polonius's corpse away after announcing his intention to delve beneath his schoolfriends' mines. These military references are at one with the rest of the play's preoccupations, but they chime too with how Belleforest describes the scene's sequence (followed verbatim by his 1608 translator): 'having discovered the ambushe, and given the inventer thereof his just rewarde [Hamblet] came againe to his mother'.[30] That image seems to have been rendered more precisely modern in Q2 Hamlet's 'petar', but Polonius's just reward is also apt to his earlier instructions to Reynaldo/Montano, 'By indirections [to] find directions out'. The poetic justice of his death is the more pronounced in Q2 by dint of the 'assaies of bias' he mentions in that context to Reynaldo (Q2) but not to Montano (Q1) (2.1.65-6), since that image derives as much from ballistics as from bowls. It prefigures Claudius's 'Cannon to his blanck', just as Polonius's death prefigures Claudius's, and both men are caught in their own ambush.

All of these military resonances are absent from Q1. That text enhances the sense of *Hamlet* as a domestic tragedy, like its own Murder of Albertus, or Marston's treatment of the same source. What Q1 uniquely adds to the closet-scene is a stage-direction that spells out that domestication, 'Enter the ghost in his night gowne'. The illustration of the scene in Rowe's 1709 edition was engraved before re-discovery of Q1 was made, and the armoured form it portrays makes explicit the substitution Q1 effects of the 'habit as he lived' (3.4.137) for the martial costume so highlighted in Act One.[31]

The domestication of *Hamlet* afforded by such Q1 variants is one familiar to modern audiences through film: both Olivier's 1948 and Zeffirelli's 1990 *Hamlet*s dispense with Fortinbras altogether, and although Q1 does not go that far, Fortinbras's role is certainly qualified within it. He closes proceedings in all three texts but his assumption of control in Q1 is couched within the conclusive security of a rhyming couplet as he orders the elevation of Hamlet's body; in Q2 that finality is disrupted by a further order (an order that measures the distance in military technology now travelled from Old Hamlet's single combat) issued after the command to clear the stage of *all* the bodies:

> Take up the bodie[s], such a sight as this
> Becomes the fieldes [field], but here doth [showes] much amisse.
> [Goe bid the souldiers shoote.]
> (Q1 [Q2] 5.2.406-8)

As Philip McGuire shows, the excision from Q1 of most of 4.4 also frees this ending from the 'more troubling, more nuanced' response that Q2 provokes, in the wake of Hamlet's recent and radical scrutiny of Fortinbras's martialism there (175). That excision is one of a series shared by Q1 and F. Precise documentary comparison should perhaps be restricted to Q2 and F, the texts less prey to circumstantial variables. Q2 Horatio's lines on Caesar's fall, Q2 Barnardo's direct association of the ghost with 'these warres', Q2 Hamlet's lines on his schoolfellows' petard and his Q2 'How all occasions' soliloquy form that series, and I should like to close this chapter and this book by arguing for their common treatment of war, and hence their common absence from F due to an expedient and artful self-censorship.

After Barnardo's 'question of these warres', 'How all occasions' draws attention most immediately to a scrutiny of war. The scene in which it occurs has been acknowledged by many critics to be of central importance.

To Emrys Jones, for example, it forms the fulcrum of the play, dividing Hamlet's course of revenge from Laertes's: Fortinbras's entrance anticipates his assumption of power at the end, illustrating the 'structural rhyming' of the parts thus formed (1971, 80). Philip McGuire notes the subtle counterpointing of the progress of Norwegian and Danish princes, each embarked on a journey orchestrated by Claudius's petition of a foreign monarch, respectively the kings of Norway and England (162-3). Giorgio Melchiori likewise sees the scene as the tragedy's 'real turning point', a technical *catastasis* and 'central ideological support' of the original draft (198). The cutting of so pivotal a scene has accordingly been subject to much critical attention, whether in the cause of Shakespeare's thwarted purpose (Collier, Greg), on aesthetic grounds ('not one of the great soliloquies', according to Edwards), or purely pragmatic ones (the excision of the soliloquy grants the actor playing Hamlet 'a much needed rest', observes Hibbard).[32] Hibbard grants the speech its 'felicity of phrasing' but further justifies its cut by asserting how the 'very similar situation' it reiterates from the end of 2.2 renders it 'redundant' (109). But the thematic and structural symmetries of Hamlet's thoughts on the players and on the soldiers is surely precisely the point, and the 'natural symmetry' that Jenkins discerns between the two speeches (139) is announced by the staged action before Hamlet even opens his mouth, a dramatic reiteration retained even in the Folio text.

The principle of this structural echo is the widely perceived set of resources held in common by theatrical and military companies in the period, the kinship of player with soldier. Part of what Emrys Jones calls the 'quietly eloquent point' of Fortinbras's Folio entrance 'with an Armie' (1971, 80), is the noisily resonant echoes it sounds of the earlier entrance of the available extras to play the players, filling the stage and providing relief from the claustrophobic machinations of Elsinore. The resemblance between the two spectacles is caught in the stage-direction that Q1 provides, 'Enter Fortenbrasse, Drumme and Souldiers', which maintains an order of procession that occurs elsewhere in the context of strolling players: 'Faith sir', says Parolles in his slur on Dumaine's military expertise, 'ha's led the drumme before the English Tragedians' (see above, p. 182). That parallel lends force to the self-regardingly 'tragicke spectacle' that Horatio enjoins us to witness after the final entrance of 'Fortenbrasse with his traine' in Act Five of Q1. His promised relation of 'the first beginning of this Tragedy' links Hamlet's story to Pyrrhus's. But his summary, in Q2/F, of 'casuall slaughters' reinforces the military auspices of the play's close there, an emphasis assisted by the inclusion of 'How all occasions' in Q2. The structural chiming of players' and soldiers' entrances is underpinned in that text by the precisely comparable nature of the soliloquies prompted by them.

In both speeches Hamlet's tone is one of self-rebuke: he is a 'dull and muddy metteld raskall', for his 'dull revenge' (2.2.562; 4.4.33), and in each he rehearses the injuries done him. He reflects on imputations of cowardice, and gauges the slender grounds upon which 'this player heere', or 'this Army of such masse and charge', act out their roles, 'But in a fixion, in a dreame of passion', 'for a fantasie and tricke of fame' (2.2.545-6; 4.4.47-61), 'and all for nothing', 'Even for an Egge-shell' (2.2.551; 4.4.53). In so closely relating the object of Fortinbras's campaign to the players' insubstantial illusion, Q2 *Hamlet* signals its most radical divergence from the sorts of patriotic wartime plays emulated by its opening. The truth behind the sorts of propagandist assertions made by, say, *A Larum for London* or the Turnhout play, as they relate to the European wars, may be judged from MacCaffrey's recent study of them: 'That whole history had been one of frustration and futility from the English point of view' (296), he writes, and the terms recur throughout his book (96, 131, 137, 168, 289, 571). His deflating appraisal of the Battle of Nieuport in July 1600, that 'The cost of the victory had outweighed its profits' (291), recalls Shakespeare's imagining of another – and contemporary – military venture:

> Truly to speake, and with no addition,
> We goe to gaine a little patch of ground
> That hath in it no profit but the name
> To pay five duckets, five, I would not farme it.
> (4.4.17-20)

Barnardo's 'question of these warres' is echoed and diminished into what Hamlet now calls the 'question of this straw' (26), a 'widespread proverbial motif', as R.M. Frye notes, 'rich in connotations of triviality' (1984, 201).

The Norwegian Captain's lines prompt in Hamlet a sequence of responses that tally with the self-destructive technology elsewhere detailed in Q2's imagery. 'This is th'Imposthume of much wealth and peace', he says of Fortinbras's expedition, 'That inward breakes, and showes no cause without | Why the man dies' (27-9). This medical analogy, of a fatal internal rupture, significantly reverses the contemporary commonplace of war as a curative emetic, the 'medecine to a body that is choaked up with corrupt humours' which Riche described in the year in which Q2 *Hamlet* was first published (1604, 4). The forces of Tyranny in Marston's *Histrio-Mastix* (1598) must 'Wait ... till their ulcers breake, | Or else be launced by the hand of *Warre*' (F1r). But instead of lancing the boil on the body politic, Fortinbras's expedition itself 'Infects unseene', embodying the 'ulcerous place' Hamlet had earlier imagined, undermined by rank corruption (3.4.149-51). 'Why the man dies': the operation was successful, but the patient is dead.

The self-defeating 'implements of warre' presented throughout this play find their consequence (as so often since) on Poland's frontier, as Hamlet darkly reckons the economic and human cost of war:

> The iminent death of twenty thousand men,
> That for a fantasie and tricke of fame

> Goe to their graves like beds, fight for a plot
> Whereon the numbers cannot try the cause,
> Which is not tombe enough and continent
> To hide the slaine.
> (4.4.60-5)

Here is the 'superfluous death' of which Claudius spoke, wrought by a 'murdring peece': the wielding of weapons or of armies results in the destruction of both, and the same analogy strikes Fortinbras when he enters in Act Five, 'That thou [death] so many Princes at a shot | So bloudily hast strook' (5.2.371-2). That sentiment is the more appropriate in Q2 since it is there that Hamlet deduces a final reason for action from the example of Fortinbras's enterprise; and there, too, that the ironies of the play's habitual 'purposes mistooke' extend the more fully to that 'delicate and tender Prince' and his 'quarrell in a straw' (4.4.48; 55).

In taking arms against a sea (or siege) of troubles, Hamlet aims at Claudius and kills Polonius; Claudius aims at Hamlet and kills Gertrude; Laertes aims at Hamlet and kills himself. And Fortinbras, for so much of Act One the apparent motive behind Old Hamlet's inspiriting visitation, aims at Poland but gains the throne of Denmark. 'Such a sight as this, | Becomes the field' so much more truly in Q2 since his nominal strength-in-arms is allowed its full capacity to perfect the play's baleful scrutiny of what Shakespeare's later Prologue calls 'the chance of Warre' (F *Troilus and Cressida*, Pr.31).

Thomas Dekker, with a different emphasis to MacCaffrey, later characterized the battle of Nieuport as 'that brave *Romane* tragedy acted in our time'.[33] It is not Nieuport, however, but Ostend that has been made the basis of an interpretation of *Hamlet*'s negotiation of contemporary war. The Siege of Ostend lasted from July 1601 to September 1604, 'And there was not in our age', according to Camden, 'any siedge and defence maintained with greater slaughter of men, nor continued longer' (4, 197). In the 1930s Dover Wilson suggested that *Hamlet*'s 'little patch of ground' (4.4.18) drew on reports of this celebrated campaign, and cited Camden's account as analogous. The passage is indeed suggestive:

> Happy had it beene for a number of those military men on both sides, if the sea had beene let in, and had quite swallowed it up. For the most warlike souldiers of the Low-Countries, *Spaine, England, France, Scotland,* and *Italy,* whilest they most eagerly contended for a barren plot of sand, had as it were one common Sepulcher, but an eternall monument of their valour.
> (4, 198-9)

What dissuades whole-hearted acceptance of a direct influence, however, as

Jenkins notes, is the incompatibility of the siege's notoriety with the likely composition of the manuscript underlying Q2. One historian, A.H. Burne, described the defenders' pride in their resistance finding expression in festivities held 'as every anniversary of its opening came round' (246), yet the siege's first anniversary fell in the same month as *Hamlet* was entered as 'latelie Acted' in the Stationers' Register. Wilson's attractive hypothesis is thus difficult to accept. But the refutation need not be as absolute as Jenkins (527-8), following Chambers (1944, 68-75), maintains. For just as the particulars of 4.4 were to prompt textual emendation for its wartime performance in 1943 Berlin, so the simultaneous 'war conditions' under which Chambers tells us he composed 'The Date of *Hamlet*' (71) affected the performance and text of its subject.

Though not directly inspired by and pitched towards Ostend, it is surely clear that between composition (*c*.1600-01) and publication (1603), the Norwegian Captain's profitless 'patch of ground' and Hamlet's vision of the 'iminent death of twenty thousand men' must have assumed a topical dimension that made cruder, more overt, the play's commentary on war. At some point before 26 July 1602 (when it was registered for publication) the play must have been submitted to the Master of Revels to be licensed for performance. The first publicly available news of *The Oppugnation and fierce Siege of Ostend* [News-Pamphlet 20] reached London around August 1601, and the degree of interest it aroused is demonstrated by the swift succession of reprints that followed that news-letter. *Newes from Ostend, of, The Oppugnation* [News-Pamphlet 21] added 'other Newes and Accidents as have lately hapned at Ostend' (t.p.) 'Since the former Impression of this Pamphlet' (B4r). *Further Newes of Ostend* [News-Pamphlet 22] brought 'the former Edition' (t.p.) further up to date to include events up to 25 August 1601. At least three other pamphlets were published on the subject in early 1602.[34] Grimeston's *True Historie of the Memorable Siege of Ostend* was swiftly published after its 'yeelding up' in 1604, and the campaign's notoriety, the keen interest it aroused at home, was the subject of an illuminating quip in *Westward Hoe* (1604): 'the booke of the siedge of *Ostend*, writ by one that dropt in the action, will never sell so well'.[35]

One such 'booke', *Further Newes of Ostend* (1601), reports that 'The 1200. men that were pressed out of *Kent*, *Essex*, and other places of *England* ... are sent to *Ostend*', and takes care to praise the Dutch 'who (notwithstanding their continuall taxations laid upon them for the maintenance of these long warres) do most liberally, and freely contribute', 'which is a worthy mirrour to us' (A4v-B1r). That call to patriotic forbearance is one we may now recognize from the variety of plays performed in the period (*Oldcastle*, *Edward IV* and so on), a period, as Janet Clare describes it, that featured an 'increased surveillance' of drama (93). Richard Dutton agrees that 'each successive measure' imposed on London's dramatic companies between 1597 and 1600 constituted 'an attempt to reduce to precise limits the threat posed to public order in the capital by the actors' (111-12). It is this threat, he argues, that had earlier lain behind Tilney's censorship of *Sir Thomas More* and the uneasy topicality of its riot-scene, in the wake of the race riots in London in 1593. 'A high proportion', he observes, 'of interventions made by Tilney and his successors seem to relate to matters of immediate moment, to the over-specific shadowing of particular people and current events, rather than to considerations of doctrine' (85). In a later climate of 'dangers of tumults at home' and the realities of desertion and mutiny abroad, of enforced conscription and 'continuall taxations ... for the maintenance of these long warres', Hamlet's meditation on the costly 'fantasie and tricke of fame' was striking enough. But if read by a censor in or after the summer of 1601, its 'over-specific shadowing' of 'matters of immediate moment' would have pointed in one direction only: to Ostend. It is unlikely enough that the licensing system operated by the Lord Chamberlain and the Master of Revels would have allowed the Lord Chamberlain's Men to perform the sequence. But there is an additional point of intersection between Shakespeare's theatres of war that makes it even more so.

Tilney's successor as Master of Revels was Sir George Buc, to whom James granted the reversion in 1603 (Dutton, 144). Dutton has recently challenged G.E. Bentley's assertion that Buc acted as Tilney's deputy 'from 1597'.[36] Letters written between 1597 and 1599 none the less prove an association between Buc and the Revels Office before 1603, an association pertinent to our enquiry since between 19 August and 1 September 1601, Sir George Buc was engaged on a diplomatic mission to Flanders, to debate with Sir Francis Vere the viability of a successful defence of Ostend (Eccles, 431-7). His mission (as Vere wrote) 'hath bene to very good purpose for the setting us on worke' (436).

How extraordinary that the very question upon which Hamlet's soliloquy turns (is this little patch of ground worth defending?) is the question that an associate of the play's licensing office was employed to ask of Ostend, at the very time that the script of *Hamlet* was submitted to that office. 'Why then the *Pollacke* never will defend it. | Yes, it is already garisond' (4.4. 23-4). Both in general and particular ways, then, by the late summer of 1601, parts of *Hamlet* had (however inadvertently) come to show the 'age and body of the time his forme and pressure'. One has only to speculate on the consequences of Q2 *Hamlet* being performed in May 1602, and that performance being succeeded by the enforced recruitment from its audiences ('and all for flaunders') that Gawdy described, to find reason enough for the absence of most of 4.4 from Q1 and F.

It seems at least feasible to construct a textual chronology of *Hamlet* along the following lines. Around 1600-01, Shakespeare completed his authorial manuscript of the play. By the time a license for its performance was sought from the Master of Revels, the general tone of its speculation on war, notably of 'How all occasions', had become pointedly topical, all the more unsuitable for performance by the Lord Chamberlain's Men. Its challenging enquiry into the value of military enterprise in the summer of 1601 could not but seem to allude at once to the widely reported Siege of Ostend and the recruitment for service there from London's citizenry. In advance of the censorship that would almost certainly follow its submission to Tilney, the manuscript underwent a systematic revision. Thus revised, licensed and performed in 1601-02, the play was registered (in 1602) and printed (in 1603) – unconditionally since license for performance had already been granted – as Q1 in a state that included those revisions amongst its other casualties of transmission. By the time Q2 came to be published, the urgencies and sensitivities of wartime had waned. The new king had spoken of the 'great and tedious warre' that he was soon to bring to a formal close,[37] in a speech itself published in 1604 and 'discussed all over the country' (Patterson, 1984, 66). 'It is probable', writes Clare, 'that when it could be claimed that a play had once been licensed, that play could then be ... published after a safe interval without observing the strictures of the censor' (xi). But by the time of Q2 those strictures had disappeared, 'And peace proclaimes Olives of endlesse age' (Sonnet 107).[38] Sir George Buc himself attended the peace-celebrations in Spain between April and June 1605 (Eccles, 452). By the time of peace, references to Ostend become the stuff of overt and frivolous jokes in City Comedy.[39]

Something of the same transition (from war to peace) perhaps informs the thorny textual history of *Troilus and Cressida*. Critical consensus dates the play's composition to late 1602, and it was entered in the Stationers' Register in February 1602-03, 'as yt is acted by my lo: Chamberlens Men', with the proviso that the publisher obtain 'sufficient aucthority for yt'. It was not printed, however, until 1609, when it was prefaced (in later imprints) by an Epistle that claims this 'new play' was 'never stal'd with the Stage, never clapper-clawd with the palmes of the vulger' nor 'sullied, with the smoaky breath of the multitude' (1609, ¶2r-v). Critics have long accepted that the play was probably originally written for private performance at the Inns of Court for the privileged and 'cultured audience' Bullough describes, 'which prided itself on its unshockable "realism"' (6, 86). Gary Taylor's persuasive discussion of the play's 'Bibliography, Performance, and Interpretation' may be consolidated by reference to the contextual chronology of *Hamlet* we have assembled. Q *Troilus and Cressida*, argues Taylor, represents the 'foul-paper text' of its private première (*c*.1602-03), soon thereafter somehow surreptitiously sold to the publisher (with an explanatory epistle) by an associate of the Inns of Court. Publication was at last sanctioned in 1609 by a 'deputy to Sir Geo. Bucke' – the delay perhaps for want of the 'sufficient aucthority' demurred to in the first entry – and the anonymous 1603 epistle printed with it. Meanwhile, the play had been tinkered into a promptbook tailored for subsequent public performance at the Globe, a version now legible in F (1982, 118-21).

Three aspects of this précis concern us: the private auspices of its première; the delay in its publication; and the possible date of its Globe performances. It is surely unthinkable that such a study in military stalemate (its searing distinction between battle and the 'very darkest abyss of war' that reasserted its reputation in the 1920s)[40] could have found sufficient authority for publication or public performance so long as Elizabeth's wars continued. Composed within a year of the playhouse press-gangs Gawdy witnessed in May 1602, and within six months of the revised *Hamlet*'s registration in July 1602, *Troilus and Cressida* builds its grim entirety – the profound flippancy of its tragedy – from the 'question of this straw' Hamlet had originally pondered. 'After so many houres, lives, speeches spent' (2.2.1), the 'meere oppugnancie' (1.3.111) of the play's military critique gathers its less-than-oblique animus from *The Oppugnation and fierce Siege of Ostend*. Since Q2 *Hamlet* at last achieved print under King James, it seems a feasible assumption that *Troilus and Cressida* was indeed 'acted by the Kings Majesties servants at the Globe', as the cancelled Q title-page states, rather than by the Lord Chamberlain's Men, who had only ever privately performed it in wartime.

While *Othello* and *Measure for Measure* are self-consciously set in the aftermath of war (the former developing into the sort of domestic tragedy Q1 *Hamlet* became), *All's Well That Ends Well* perhaps signals its Jacobean status in the bruised workings of its title. It certainly parades, with *Troilus and Cressida*, the 'noisy virility but ultimate emptiness' of war it was now respectable and safe to assert (R. Parker, 103), now that the 'tedious warre' had ended, and all was well with Stow's 'true Merchant, and honest Citizen' (1631, 845). The play's tonal kinship with *Hamlet* has been noticed, and strengthens the view that its composition dates from the period that at last saw the publication of the 'original' *Hamlet*, 'enlarged to almost as much againe as it was' by the restoration of its systematically critical references to war.

It is a curious fact that one of the play's least readily explicable variants, unique to Q1, concerns the performance of the play's own wartime troupe. 'This play', as Hamlet glosses *The Mousetrap* only there, 'is | The image of a murder done in *guyana*, *Albertus* | Was the Dukes name' (F4r). Q2 (and F) have '*Vienna*' for the exotic Guyana, the exotic '*Gonzago*' for Albertus (3.2.232-4). But Albertus was the archduke's name who, defeated at Nieuport in 1600, laid siege to Ostend in July 1601. Archduke Albert's marriage to the Infanta Isabella has been persuasively associated with the Duke of Vienna's courtship of Isabella in *Measure for Measure* (Marcus, 1988, 189-94). Both figures take their part in *A Dialogue and Complaint Made Upon the Siedge of Oastend* (1602), 'All a true discourse', it is claimed, 'of that which is hapned in the same towne ... from the fourth day of the moneth of February 1602[/1603]' (News-Pamphlet 27). 'What misfortune', bemoans Albert there, 'to see this small place which hath stayed the valour of so many good souldiours, and cause an armie to be consumed before this pettie place' (A2r). Can these tinkerings with Q2

*Hamlet*'s authorial draft be interpreted as a compensatory gesture from a grudgingly self-censored wartime company and playwright, as Hamlet's 'little patch of ground' crept into 'this pettie place'?

The *Hamlet* first written (Q2) casts a cold eye on 'the question of these warres', and builds its critique upon the modulated structure of 'the question of this straw'. The *Hamlet* first published (Q1) sheathes the blade of that scrutiny, and seems to pre-empt the wartime censorship that must have seemed inevitable in the light of the European events that overtook – and confirmed – its own fiction. The influence of wartime over *Hamlet*'s stage-history can be glimpsed in the suppression we have noted of its references to Poland in the production that was mounted in Berlin in July 1943. September 1943 saw the première in Zurich of another play that was the subject of authorial revision during the course of a war. Like *Hamlet*, Brecht's *Leben des Galilei* exists in 'three principal versions'; like *Hamlet*, the span of these versions, from composition to publication via performance, straddles European war and peace; and like *Hamlet*, the specific events of the war it had always pondered came to overtake its author's abstract contemplation, prompting revision in the light of such developments.[41] 'The "atomic" age made its début at Hiroshima', Brecht recalled in 1946, 'in the middle of our work. Overnight the biography of the founder of the new system of physics read differently' (125). The first draft of *Hamlet* (Q2) also came to 'read differently', if not overnight, then over the course of the similarly 'horrible bloudie and unheard of Siege of Ostend' (Burne, 238).

The shift in emphasis between Q1 *Hamlet* (1603) and Q2 *Hamlet* (1604-05), between war and peace, is perhaps reflected in the title-page of Barnaby Riche's first Jacobean work, which itself exists in two versions. Q1 tempers its sustained critique of militarism in the interests of what Riche first called *A Souldiers Wishe to Britons Welfare*; Q2 presents, with Riche, both *A pleasing view for Peace* and *A looking-Glasse for Warre*, and at last harvests *The Fruites of Long Experience*. It might be countered that my hypothesis of self-censorship ignores the possibility of a non-authorial interference with Shakespeare's 'original' script, one perhaps undertaken by Tilney's own blue pencil. It is the aim of the remainder of this chapter to demonstrate the aesthetic integrity with which the cuts made to Q2 were dismantled from about its original design. The articulation of their framework is provided by the *Georgics* of Virgil.

## Unearthing skulls

We have commented on the consequences of the judicious excision of most of 4.4 upon Fortinbras's final assumption of power. That sequence, however, exerts an influence elsewhere in *Hamlet*, that is fully discernible in Q2. The Prince contemplates there the 'iminent death of twenty thousand men' (4.4.60). Editors have frowned over Shakespeare's apparent confusion of the war's economic and human cost reckoned by the Norwegian Captain: 'Two thousand soules, & twenty thousand duckets' (4.4.25). Whether Shakespeare's or Hamlet's inattention, the muddle remembers the play's first casualty, Polonius, 'dead for a Duckat' (3.4.23). The disposal of his corpse preoccupies the first three scenes of Act Four, with their queasy quibbles of 'politique wormes' and the 'variable service' of human flesh (4.3.20-24): 'but if indeed you find him not within this month, you shall nose him as you goe vp the stayres into the Lobby' (35-7). The war-dead Hamlet next considers (dead for twenty thousand duckets) are to be sacrificed for a 'patch of ground', 'not tombe enough and continent | To hide the slaine'. The lines gain a shiver from Old Hamlet's 'Sepulcher' (not tomb enough to prevent his 'dead corse' being 'cast up' again); and adumbrate the skulls later exhumed in Elsinore's graveyard.

When, much later, Shakespeare came to compose his final address to Mars in *The Two Noble Kinsmen* (1613) he re-imagined such a 'plot':

> Thou mighty one, that with thy power hast turnd
> Greene Neptune into purple.
> Whose havocke in vaste Feild Comets prewarne,
> Unearthed skulls proclaime, whose breath blowes downe,
> The teeming Ceres foyzon.
> (5.1.49-52)[42]

War is presaged by comets and its aftermath is registered in upturfed skulls. *Hamlet*'s events are also presaged by supernatural disturbances and find a final motive for action in 'Unearthed skulls'. Both Arcite's lines and the graveyard scene of *Hamlet* appear to be indebted to Virgil's *Georgics*, a 'deep source' (as one critic notes) of the preceding history-cycles (Bulman, 37). 'And know you this', it reads in Fleming's 1589 translation,

> the time will come when as the husbandman
> Ha[v]ing turnd up the ground with crooked plow in these same quarters,
> Shall find darts eaten [sore and gnawne] with rough and rugged rust;
> Or with his heavie harrow he shall emptie helmets hit
> And at the bones so great in graves digd up [found out, or hurt]
> He shall much marvell [seeing them so big, and ours so small.][43]

The fields of Philippi, like the patch of ground contested by Norwegian and Pole in *Hamlet*, are 'not tombe enough ... To hide the slaine'. Virgil's prediction follows on from his catalogue of what Fleming glosses as the 'strange & wonderfull accedentes' (16) that presaged Caesar's assassination. In its 'sound of ratling arms', 'colping ravens', gaping grounds and 'blazing stars' (16-17; 1, 470-88) we may recognize the components of the military supernatural, from both classical and Renaissance sources (not least from

*Julius Caesar*) (see above, pp. 209-12). They are also familiar from Horatio's comparable catalogue of auguries 'A little ere the mightiest *Julius* fell' (1.1.116-28), a passage which was, like 'How all occasions' and Barnardo's 'question of these warres', subsequently cut from Shakespeare's authorial manuscript.

There is something of a thesaurus's prolixity to Horatio's 'harbindgers ... And prologue to the *Omen* comming on' (1.1.125-6), rather like Taille-pied's catalogue of 'marvels the Romans used to term *Ostenta, Portenta, Monstra, Prodigia*';[44] but whether that tone shadows Horatio's scholarship or Shakespeare's incompletely assimilated source, there is surely more to their Q2 presence than 'an advertisement for *Julius Caesar*', deleted when no longer being performed suggested in Hibbard's edition (1987, 355). Perhaps the slightly half-baked list does diminish the force of the ghost's subsequent entrance – although the ghost's silence, it might be argued, is better enhanced by Horatio's verbiage explaining it. Its removal nevertheless affects the compositional structure of the play Shakespeare drafted. McGuire argues that Horatio's lines by-pass the ghost's association with Fortinbras, pointing to the internal rather than external threat: Old Hamlet was murdered, like Caesar, rather than killed in battle (158). But such a view overlooks the simultaneous excision in F and Q1 both of Barnardo's complementary explanation, and Hamlet's thoughts on Fortinbras's army. The Georgic prediction and aftermath of war, reiterated in *The Two Noble Kinsmen*, is lifted like scaffolding from around what Hibbard calls the play's 'most extraordinary scene' (320), 5.1, perhaps universalizing its scope, but none the less denying it the topicalities of the Q2 play's martial texture.

James Bulman has demonstrated the debt owed to the *Georgics* by Shakespeare's vision of history (37-47). *Hamlet*, described as 'a résumé of the Histories' by Barbara Everett (1989, 129), accordingly inherits a sporadic network of agricultural imagery.[45] We have noted in Chapter Two the mythic equation of husbandry and war in the myth of the Iron Age: 'No husbandmen did dresse the ground before good *Jupiter*', reads Virgil's Georgic account of that myth, 'Ne lawfull was it for to marke or part the field with bounds' (tr. Fleming, 5; 1, 125-6). Just as Tamburlaine's aspirations are gauged by their measurement of land, so it is the recovery of land which constitutes the grounds for Fortinbras's invasive mobilization at the outset of *Hamlet*. The same titanic aspiration as lends Marlowe's hero his role-model recurs in *Hamlet*. This is how Fleming's *Georgics* narrates the tale:

Thrise did they trie and give assay upon mount *Pelius*,
To lay the mountaine *Ossa* and forsooth on *Ossa* mounnt
To roll the hill *Olympus* full of trees bedeckt with leaves.
Thrise father [*Jupiter*] with lightnings and with thunderbolts
Cast downe those hils pilde on a heape [and floong them flat to ground.]
(10; 1, 281-3)

It is in *Hamlet*'s graveyard that this, the origin of warfare, is revisited. 'Now pile your dust upon the quicke and dead', cries Laertes, 'Till of this flat a mountaine you have made | To'retop old *Pelion*, or the skyesh head | Of blew *Olympus*' (5.1.244-7). Hamlet, like him and like Horatio, knows his Virgil:

> And if thou prate of mountaines, let them throw
> Millions of Acres on us, till our ground
> Sindging his pate against the burning Zone
> Make Ossa like a wart.
> (5.1.275-8)

Both men find a vessel for their grief over Ophelia in the primordial myth of war. 'Millions of Acres': the haunting phrase gains force if read against its association (unique to Q2) with the 'little patch of ground' contested by Norway and Poland, fighting 'for a plot'. For that is precisely what Laertes and Hamlet are doing, if we consider Q1's overt stage-directions (*'Leartes leapes into the grave ... Hamlet leapes in after Leartes'*, I1v) and Q2/F's concealed direction (5.1.273).

Without Horatio's 'prologue to the *Omen* comming on', or the battleground-cum-graveyard imagined in 4.4, Hamlet and Laertes's unseemly brawl is little more than just that; and Hamlet's earlier tracing of 'the noble dust of *Alexander*', or of 'Imperious *Caesar* dead, and turn'd to Clay' (5.1.197-8, 206), loses the uniquely military strand of the *memento mori* tradition they had embodied, for example, in *Love's Labour's Lost*. Without Q2's critique of military endeavour, Hamlet's homily on the next skull he contemplates fails fully to resound its hollow emptiness:

> hum, this fellowe might be in's time a great buyer of Land,
> with his Statuts, his recognisances, his fines, his double
> vouchers, his recoveries, to have his fine pate full of fine
> durt, will vouchers vouch him no more of his purchases &
> doubles then the length and breadth of a payre of
> Indentures? The very conveyances of his Lands will
> scarcely lye in this box, & must th'inheritor himselfe have
> no more, ha.
> (5.1.101-10)

The documents that detail the possession of land are scarcely contained by the coffin the land-owner now occupies. How poignant a reflection on Fortinbras's previous attempts to reclaim his inheritance and 'recover ... by strong hand | And tearmes compulsatory, those foresaid lands' (1.1.104-6), 'Lost by his father, with all bands of lawe' (1.2.24). It is 'conveyance of a promisd march' that Fortinbras requests in both F and Q2 (4.4.3), but his destination, 'not ... continent | To hide the slaine', provides a counterpart to this most lengthy of eulogies only in Q2. Hamlet's legalese, 'his double vouchers, his recoveries ... his purchases & doubles', finds its jargonized counterpart in the terms of war guyed in John Davies's 'In Gallum', which wittily contrasts a lawyer's 'foorching, vouchers, and counterpleas' with a soldier's (Hotspur-like) 'warlike wordes', 'Of parapets, curteynes and Pallizadois'.[46] The parallel may serve to tease out the one element of *Hamlet* that survives the judicious tempering of its authorial manuscript more or less intact; indeed, betrays its origins with more pertinence in the one wartime text of *Hamlet* we have: Young Osric.

Dr Johnson's view of Osric as a foppish and vacuously 'busy trifler', though enduring, is hard to justify.[47] 'Ostricke' in Q2, 'Osricke' in F, the curiously sinister figure who appears in Act Five to lure Hamlet to his death is characterized merely as 'a Bragart Gentleman' in Q1 (I2r). 'Spiced', 'the muske-cod smels', again uniquely to Q1 (I2v). Importantly, however, such odorous attributes had precedents in contemporary life and art. Thomas Digges criticized the corrupt captains of the modern army, marching upwind of their 'stinking', lice-ridden soldiers, while yet 'perfumed perhaps with Muske and Syvet' (1604, 11). Hotspur's contempt for such men, 'perfumed like a Milliner' (*1 Henry IV*, 1.3.35) repeats such soldiers' distaste. Earlier, though, in Kyd's *Soliman and Perseda*, the braggartly Basilisco also 'weres Civet, | And when it was askt him, where he had that muske, | He said, all his kindred smelt so' (1.3.220-21). Osric, more plumed and verbose in Q2, declares that kinship with Basilisco more manifestly in Q1, and presides over *Hamlet*'s last act in a manner now familiar from the pedigree of the *miles gloriosus* we have traced. Like Pistol or Basilisco, this comic archetype ('a Bragart Gentleman') finds himself on the serious stage of war. Like them, and like Parolles,[48] Osric bestrides a theatre of war and punctures the mingled weave of fiction and reality that term implies. He arbitrates at an exhibition fencing match (of the kind staged in London's Elizabethan playhouses)[49] which is in truth 'a disguised duel' (Kiernan, 10) no less mortal than the combat in which Old Hamlet 'did slay this *Fortenbrasse*' (1.1.89). Osric's announcement of Young Fortinbras's return, 'with conquest come from Poland', are the last words Hamlet hears (5.2.355). He presides over *Hamlet*'s final maimed rites just as Armado (also characterized simply as 'Braggart' in Folio and Quarto texts of Act Five) presides over the Nine Worthies parade in *Love's Labour's Lost*, a pageant likewise interrupted by news, on a stage that seems to have doubled as a news-room (see above, p. 137). Death dances attendance to all these soldiers. 'Quiddits will not answer death', Basilisco had mused after his litany of dead Worthies. Shortly before Hamlet's over-curious consideration of Caesar and Alexander, the Prince asks an equivalent question of the 'skull of a Lawyer', 'where be his quiddities now'? (5.1.96-7). Shakespeare has Osric bear the burden of such rumination since Osric mediates between player and soldier, between Yorick (whose name his recalls) and Fortinbras (a prospective land-owner). 'He hath', says Hamlet, 'much land and fertill ...

tis a chough, but as I say, spacious in the possession of durt' (5.2.86-9).[50] 'His fine pate full of fine durt', Osric's bony name, the play's nosing out of his striking smell ('And smelt so pah', 5.1.194), and his ownership of land, all contribute to the sense in which his grinning if unsmiling honour gathers about itself *Hamlet*'s – perhaps Shakespeare's – richest meditation on war.

If *Hamlet* came unintentionally to comment upon a contemporary battlefield, its graveyard seems grounded in a far older theatre of war. Saxo Grammaticus relates how Hamblet is successfully dispatched to England, accompanied by two retainers. A banquet is thrown at which the Prince mysteriously abstains from food or drink. When questioned, Hamblet replies (in Belleforest's 1608 translation):

> What, think you, that I wil eat bread dipt in humane blood, and defile my throate with the rust of yron, and use that meat that stinketh and savoureth of mans flesh, already putrified and corrupted, long since cast into a valt?[51]

The King of England learns of this gnomic utterance and sends for his baker, pork-butcher, and brewer to test its truth. He discovers that the pigs he had served had fed off a thief's carcass; that the water used in brewing his beer came from a river in which 'a great store of swords and rustie armours' had been dumped (245); and that the bread was made from wheat grown on land near

> a field ful of dead mens bones, in times past slaine in a battaile, as by the great heapes of wounded sculles mighte well appeare, and for that the ground in that parte was become fertiler then other grounds, by reason of the fatte and humours of the dead bodies, that every yeer the farmers used there to have in the best wheat they could finde to serve his majesties house.
> (243-5)

The episode has both an oblique and a direct bearing on Shakespeare's *Hamlet*. It is in England that Hamblet divines the irrepressible presence of war's aftermath, in the Georgic spectacle of 'greate heapes of wounded sculles' manuring the earth. Hamlet never reaches England, but in Fortinbras's expedition, in Yorick's skull, and in Osric (elements of the play that Hibbard tells us have 'no counterpart' in Saxo),[52] the savour of his divination reaches our senses. It is at the precise moment at which Shakespeare deviates from Saxo's narrative that he has Hamlet contemplate Fortinbras's 'little patch of ground', the 'field ful of dead mens bones'. The next time we see him, his 'gorge rises' at another pile of 'wounded sculles' (5.1.181). And thereafter it is Osric who relates the King's wager of a great store of swords to be fought for with swords. But the 'forme and pressure' of all this can only fully be felt in Q2, the text of the play at last published in peacetime.

The *Hamlet* first published was a late and minor casualty of the wars that accompanied most of Shakespeare's working life. In the *Hamlet* he first wrote, Shakespeare's art of war came to rest in a grave. The theatre of war in which it never fully played was constantly attentive to the rumours, that are now the ghosts, of war. 'Examples grosse as earth exhort me, | Witnes this Army ...' (4.4.46-7): was this passage 'ruthlessly slashed' from his working manuscript for its concern to alert us to the unsuccessful burial of war?[53] That is the question.

In 1919 Paul Valéry imagined a Hamlet 'Standing now, on an immense sort of terrace of Elsinore that stretches from Basel to Cologne, bordered by the sands of Nieuport, the marshes of the Somme ... our Hamlet of Europe is watching millions of ghosts'.[54] The twentieth century perhaps uniquely feels the presence of these ghosts. And these skulls: 'Hamlet hardly knows what to make of so many skulls', continues Valéry: 'His terribly lucid mind contemplates the passage from war to peace'. *Hamlet*'s terrible lucidity has endured in the 'great heapes of wounded sculles' which have, from Katyn to Srebenica, proclaimed renewed 'havocke in vaste Feild'; but the play's 'passage from war to peace' is embedded in the fertile ground of Q2, the one text that insists on a quite opposite transition.

'Bleste be the man that spares thes stones, | And curst be he that moves my bones':[55] Shakespeare's epitaph provides an appropriately resonant exit from the theatre of world war in which he worked. Another 'Sepulcher' was exhumed, it seems, in June 1941, and 'op't his ponderous and marble jawes'. Though the gravediggers were solemnly warned not to proceed, 'when his coffin was opened, they found written inside, the threat that "whoever opens my tomb shall unleash an invader more terrible than I." A day later on 22 June 1941, the Nazis invaded the Soviet Union'.[56] It was the tomb of Tamburlaine the Great.

## Notes

1. Remarque, *Im Westen Nichts Neues* (1979), 55.
2. Quotation will be from Q2 *Hamlet* until further notice, and reference is to the lineation of *Hamlet*, ed. Jenkins (1982) (see above, p. ix).
3. Werstine (1988) argues for distinct treatments of character and plot in Q2 and F; Mowat (1988) also argues against conflation by studying the editorial tradition; Loewenstein (1988) seeks to find grounds for the play's textual variants in the so-called War of the Theatres; Q1 *Hamlet* has been issued in an annotated edition (eds Holderness and Loughrey, 1992), performed unemended, and studied from a variety of perspectives in *The 'Hamlet' First Published*, ed. Clayton (1992).

4. See also Strobl (1997), 21: 'Some time after ... the Battle of Britain, Goebbels began to instigate definite restrictions. As of November 1941 all Shakespeare productions required his personal authorisation'.

5. *Hamlet*, 1.1.77.

6. *Hamlet*, ed. Jenkins (1982), 1-3; ed. Edwards (1985), 1-8; ed. Hibbard (1987), 3-5.

7. *Works of William Shakespear*, ed. Pope (1725), 6, Index, Section 3.

8. Dover Wilson quoted in *Hamlet*, ed. Jenkins (1982), 165.

9. It might be added that as well as loyalty, Claudius's password is designed to instil a sense of untroubled continuity to his reign: 'The King is dead ...'.

10. *Hamlet*, ed. Hibbard (1987), 146-7, citing *A Warning for Fair Women*.

11. Baines (1983), 277, n. 1.

12. Marston, *Selected Plays*, ed. Jackson and Neill (1986), 139 (3.1.32).

13. Hood, *Poetical Works*, ed. Jerrold (1906), 439.

14. Unton, *Correspondence*, ed. Stevenson (1847), 320.

15. *Historical Manuscripts Commission Calendar of the Manuscripts of the Marquis of Salisbury*, 10, 268; *APC*, 31, 100.

16. As the title of one ballad indicates: 'A warning for all Souldiers that will not venture their lyves in her Majestye's cause and and their Countries right: wherein is declared the lamentation of *William Wrench*, who, for running away from his captaine, with two other more, were executed for the same fact, in severall places about *London*, upon the viii. of *September* last, 1600', *Shirburn Ballads*, ed. Clark (1907), 200.

17. Corporation of London Record Office, Journal 26, 337 (10 June 1605).

18. *Hamlet*, 1.1.89-90; 1.2.24; 1.1.105-7.

19. On Boulogne's peace-talks of July 1600, see Camden (1630), 4, 154-9; 'dissembled ... submissions', Camden, 4, 221. MacCaffrey (1992) describes Tyrone in terms reminiscent of Fortinbras's grievance: '[from his return to Ireland in 1568, Tyrone] set his sights on recovering what he saw as his rightful heritage, the chieftaincy of the O'Neills and the lands that went with it' (446).

20. Compare for example the 'dribbed shot' and 'mine of time' in *Astrophil and Stella* 2, in Sidney, *Poems*, ed. Ringler (1962), 165.

21. King Philip's lines from *King John* provide a common precedent for and link between Marcellus's partizan and Claudius's cannon: 'Our Cannons malice vainly shall be spent | Against th'inv[u]l[n]erable clouds of heaven' (2.1.251-2).

22. The Q2 compositor seems to have been influenced by the play's military preoccupations in mis-setting 'loud a Winde' (F) as 'loved Arm'd'.

23. *A Mad World, My Masters* (*c*.1604), Q 1608, E3v. See also Dekker, *2 Honest Whore* (*c*.1605): 'It will so overcharge her heart with griefe, | That like a Cannon, when her sighes goe off, | She in her duty will recoyle, | Or breake in pieces, and so dye' (2.2.25-8).

24. Wilton, *Commentary*, ed. Egerton (1847), 23.

25. Jenkins cites as analogous the 'Mole' on Guiderius's neck, 'that naturall stampe' (*Cymbeline*, 5.6.366-8) (1982, 209); Hibbard cites Oberon's 'blots of Nature's hand' (*A Midsummer Night's Dream*, 5.2.39) in support of his gloss, 'natural blemish' (1987, 357); Edwards ('natural mark') (1985, 102), Spencer ('natural blemish') (1980, 234), Lott ('natural blemish') (1968, 34), and Evans et al. ('small natural blemish') (1974, 1148; 2nd ed. 1997, 1196) all concur, and none cross-refers to the 'olde Mole'.

26. *Hamlet*, 3.2.227-8.

27. *Hamlet*, ed. Edwards (1985), 31.

28. *Hamlet*, ed. Hibbard (1987), 109.

29. Fredson Bowers, quoted in *Hamlet*, ed. Edwards (1985), 21.

30. Gollancz (1926), 206-7.

31. *Works of Mr. William Shakespear*, ed.Rowe (1709-10), 5, 2365.

32. *New Variorum ... Hamlet*, ed. Furness (1877, repr. 1963), 323; *Hamlet*, ed. Hibbard (1987), 107; ed. Edwards (1985), 17; ed. Hibbard (1987), 109.

33. *Work for Armourers* (1607), *Non-Dramatic Works*, ed. Grosart, 4, 104.

34. News-Pamphlets 24, 26 and 27.

35. Dekker, *Dramatic Works*, ed. Bowers (1961-2), 2, 372 (4.2.186-7).

36. Bentley (1971), 152; Dutton (1991), 145-51.

37. *The Political Works of James I*, ed. McIlwain (1965), 270.

38. On the poem's topicalities, see *The Sonnets and A Lover's Complaint*, ed. Kerrigan (1986), 313-19.

39. See Dekker, *1 Honest Whore* (1604), where 'the constancy of a woman' is passingly considered 'harder to come by than ever was *Ostend*' (4.1.29); and see above, n.35.

40. O.W. Campbell (1921), 48; and see *Troilus and Cressida*, ed. Muir (1984), 10-11.

41. The 'three principal versions' are the first draft (November 1938), which was the text of the 1943 première; the American version written with Charles Laughton, 1944-7; and the conflated revision composed for the Berliner Ensemble, 1953-5. See Brecht, *Life of Galileo*, tr. Willett, eds Willett and Manheim (1980), vi-xxii, and 162-7.

42. Quotation is from the 1634 Quarto (reordering 5.2.52).

43. *The Bucolicks*, tr. Fleming (1589), 17 (Fleming's substantial parentheses); Virgil, *Georgics*, 1, 493-7, *Works*, tr. Fairclough (1935).

44. Taillepied, *A Treatise of Ghosts*, tr. Summers (1933), 88.

45. See for example 1.1.135-6, 3.4.64-5.

46. *Poems*, ed. Kruger (1975), 139; see above, p. 161.

47. *Johnson on Shakespeare*, ed. Sherbo (1968), 2, 1005.

48. Parolles too enters Act Five, 'stink[ing]', 'but not a Muscat' (5.2. 12-20): his sinister potential is redeemed by a metaphorical ducking in Fortune's sewer.

49. Aylward (1951), 201-04; Gurr (1987), 264; Brownstein (1971), 17-24.

50. I am aware that such a reading is supported by the 'intricate con-
    volutions of sheer stupidity' that comprise the central section of
    Nabokov's *Bend Sinister* (1947): ' " 'But to return to Osric. Garrulous
    Hamlet has just been speaking to a skull of a jester; now it is the skull
    of jesting death that speaks to Hamlet. Note the remarkable
    juxtaposition: the skull – the shell; "Runs away with a shell on his
    head." Osric and Yorick almost rhyme, except that the yolk of one has
    become the bone (os) of the other ... Who is this master of ceremonies?
    He is Young Fortinbras' most brilliant spy.' Well, this gives you a fair
    sample of what I have to endure."' (1974, 99). John McEnery's
    portrayal of Osric in Zeffirelli's *Hamlet* (1990) is a studiedly uncomic
    performance: he sourly ignores Hamlet's quibbles, and betrays an
    impatient and sinister impertinence. The less said about the role in
    Branagh's (otherwise atmospheric) *Hamlet* (1996) the better.
51. Gollancz (1926), 235-7.
52. *Hamlet*, ed. Hibbard (1987), 109.
53. *Hamlet*, ed. Hibbard (1987), 109.
54. Valéry, *An Anthology*, ed. Lawler (1977), 100.
55. Schoenbaum (1977), 306.
55. *The Times*, 27 March 1992, 13 ('Uzbeks resurrect Tamerlane as latter-
    day saint').

# Bibliography

## Primary sources

*Acts of the Privy Council of England*, eds J. Dasent et al., 46 vols (1890-1964)

*Calendar of State Papers, Domestic Series, of the Reign of Elizabeth, 1581-90*, ed. R. Lemon (1865)

*A Collection of Seventy-Nine Black-Letter Ballads and Broadsides*, eds T. Wright and J. Halliwell (1867)

*Historical Manuscripts Commission Calendar of the Manuscripts of the Marquis of Salisbury, Preserved at Hatfield House*, 18 vols (1883-1940)

*A Pepysian Garland: Black-Letter Broadside Ballads of the Years 1595-1639*, ed. H. Rollins, Cambridge (1922)

*The Shirburn Ballads, 1585-1616*, ed. A. Clark, Oxford (1907)

*Stuart Tracts, 1603-1693*, ed. C. Firth (1903)

*Tudor Royal Proclamations*, eds P. Hughes and J. Larkin, 3 vols (1964-69)

*The Whole Volume of Statutes at large, which anie time heeretofore have beene extant in print since Magna Charta* (1587)


Alciati, Andrea, *Emblemata cum Commentariis*, Padua (1621)

*Arden of Faversham*, ed. M. White (1982)

Ascham, Roger, *Toxophilus, The Schole of Shootinge* (1545)

'R.B.', *A Mirrour to all that love to follow the Warres* (1589)

Bacon, Francis, *The Essayes or Counsells, Civill and Morall*, ed. M. Kiernan, Oxford (1985)

Barret, Robert, *The Theorike and Practike of Moderne Warres* (1598)

Barnes, Barnabe, *The Divils Charter* (1607)

Barwick, Humfrey, *A Breefe Discourse, Concerning the Force and Effect of all Manuall Weapons of Fire* (1591)

Batman, Stephen, *The Golden Booke of the Leaden Goddes* (1577)

Beard, Thomas, *The Theatre of Gods Judgements: or, A Collection of Histories out of Sacred, Ecclesiasticall, and Prophane Authours* (1597)

Beaumont, Francis, *The Knight of the Burning Pestle*, ed. S. Zitner, Manchester (1984)

Beaumont, Francis and John Fletcher, *Dramatic Works*, gen. ed. F. Bowers, 7 vols, Cambridge (1966-89)

Becon, Thomas, *Early Works*, ed. J. Ayre, Cambridge (1843)

du Bellay, William, *Instructions for the Warres, Amply, Learnedly, Politiquely, Discoursing the Method of Military Discipline*, tr. Paul Ive (1589)

du Bellay, Martin and Guillaume, *Mémoires*, eds V. Bourilly and F. Vindry 4 vols, Paris (1908-19)

Birchensha, Ralph, *A Discourse Occasioned upon the Late Defeat Given to the Arch-rebels, Tyrone and Odonnell* (1602)

Blandy, William, *The Castle, or Picture of Pollicy shewing forth the most lively, the Face, Body and Partes of a Commonwealth, the Duety, Quality, Profession of a ... Souldiar* (1581)

Blundeville, Thomas, *A Briefe Description of Universal Mappes and Cardes* (1589)

Bourne, William, *The Arte of Shooting in Great Ordnaunce* (1587)

Braun, Georg and Frans Hogenberg, *Civitates Orbis Terrarum, 1572-1618*, facs. ed. R. Skelton, 3 vols, Amsterdam (1965)

Breton, Nicholas, *The Wil of Wit, Wits Will, or Wils Wit* (1597)

—— *Characters Upon Essaies Morall, And Divine* (1615)

—— *A Mad World My Masters, and Other Prose Works*, ed. U. Kentish-Wright, 2 vols (1929)

Browne, William, *Britannia's Pastorals: The Second Booke* (1616)

Burton, Robert, *The Anatomy of Melancholy*, ed. J. Jackson, 3 vols (1932)

Byrd, William, *My Ladye Nevells Booke*, ed. H. Andrews (1926)

'W.C.', *The True Reporte of the Skirmish Fought Betweene the States of Flaunders ...* (1578) [News-Pamphlet 2]

Caesar, Gaius Julius, *The eyght bookes ... conteyning his martiall exploytes in the Realme of Gallia*, tr. Arthur Golding (1565)

Camden, William, *Annals, or the Historie of the Most Renowned and Victorious Princesse Elizabeth, Late Queene of England*, tr. 'R.N.' (1635)

Caxton, William, *Caxton's Mirrour of the World*, ed. O. Prior (1913)

Chamberlain, John, *Letters*, ed. N. McLure, 2 vols, Philadelphia (1939)

Chapman, George, *Bussy D'Ambois*, ed. N. Brooke, Manchester (1964)

—— *The Conspiracy and Tragedy of Byron*, ed. J. Margeson, Manchester (1988)

—— *The Widow's Tears*, ed. A. Yamada (1975)

—— *The Tragedies*, ed. T. Parrott (1910)

—— *The Comedies: A Critical Edition*, gen. ed. A. Holaday (1970)

—— *The Poems*, ed. P. Bartlett, Oxford (1941)

Chaucer, Geoffrey, *The Complete Works*, ed. F. Robinson, 2nd ed., Oxford (1966)

Chettle, Henry, *The Tragedy of Hoffman*, MSR, Oxford (1950)

*Choice, Chance, and Change, or Conceites in Their Colours* (1606)

Churchyard, Thomas, *A Lamentable and Pitiful Description of the Wofull Warres in Flaunders* (1578)

—— *A Generall Rehearsall of Warres* (1579)

—— *Churchyards Challenge* (1593)

—— *A Pleasant Discourse of Court and Warres* (1596)

—— *The Fortunate Farewel to the Most Forward and Noble Earle of Essex* (1599)

Clayton, Giles, *The Approoved Order of Martiall Discipline* (1591)

Clowes, William, *A Profitable and Necessarie Booke of Observations, for all that are burned with ... Gun pouder* (1596)

*Clyomon and Clamydes*, MSR, Oxford (1913)

Collins, Arthur, *Letters and Memorials of State*, 2 vols (1746)

Comes, Natalis, *Mythologie, où Explication des Fables*, tr. J. Baudouin, 2 vols, Paris (1627)

Coningsby, Thomas, *Journal of the Siege of Rouen*, ed. J. Nichols (1847)

Cooper, Thomas, *Thesaurus Linguae Romanae et Britannicae* (1565)

Daniel, Samuel, *The Complete Works*, ed. A. Grosart, 5 vols (1885-96)

Davies, Sir John, *The Poems*, ed. R. Krueger, Oxford (1975)

Davies, Richard, *Chester's Triumph in Honor of her Prince*, Manchester (1844)

Dekker, Thomas, *The Shomakers Holiday, or The Gentle Craft* (1600)

—— *The Wonderfull Yeare, 1603* (1604)

—— *The Honest Whore, with The Humours of the Patient Man* (1604)

—— *The Artillery Garden* (1616)

—— *Warres, Warres, Warres* (1628)

—— *The Second Part of The Honest Whore* (1630)

—— *The Shoemakers' Holiday*, ed. D. Palmer (1975)

—— *Dramatic Works*, ed. F. Bowers, 4 vols, Cambridge (1961-62)

—— *Non-Dramatic Works*, ed. A. Grosart, 5 vols (1884-86)

Devereux, Robert, Earl of Essex, *Lawes and Orders of Warre, Established for the Good Conduct of the Service in Ireland* (1599)

Digges, Leonard, *A Boke Named TECTONICON, briefely shewynge the exacte measurynge and speady reckenynge all maner Lande* (1562)

Digges, Leonard and Thomas, *A Geometricall Practise, Named PANTOMETRIA, divided into Three Bookes, Longimetra, Planimetra, and Stereometra* (1571)

—— *An Arithmeticall Militare Treatise, Named STRATIOTICOS: Compendiously Teaching the Science of Numbers ... Requisite for the Profession of a Souldiour* (1579)

'T.D.' [Thomas Digges], *A Briefe Report of the Militare Services Done in the Low Countries, by the Erle of Leicester* (1587)

Digges, Thomas and Dudley, *Foure Paradoxes, or Politique Discourses* (1604)

Donne, John, *Poetical Works*, ed. H. Grierson, Oxford (1929)

Drayton, Michael, *Poly-Olbion, Or a Chorographicall Description of*

*Tracts, Rivers, Mountaines, Forests ... of Great Britaine* (1613)
—— *The Second Part ... of Poly-Olbion* (1622)
Dudley, Robert, Earl of Leicester, *Lawes and Ordinances* (1586)
'I.E.', *A Letter from a Souldier ... in Ireland* (1602) [News-Pamphlet 28]
Eden, Richard, *The History of Travayl in the West and East Indies and Other Countreys Lying Either Way*, 'newly set in order, augmented, and finished' by Richard Willes (1577)
Eliot, John, *Ortho-Epia Gallica: Eliots Fruits for the French* (1593)
Elyot, Sir Thomas, *The Boke Named the Governour*, ed. H. Croft (1880)
Erasmus, Desiderius, *A Booke Called ... Enchiridion Militis Christiani, and in Englysshe The Manuell of the Christen Knyght* (1533)
—— *The Complaint of Peace*, tr. Thomas Paynell (1559)
—— *Ten Colloquies*, tr. C. Thompson, New York (1957)
—— *The Adages*, ed. M. Phillips, Cambridge (1964)
Euclid, *The Elements of Geometrie*, tr. Henry Billingsley, 'with a very fruitfull Praeface Made by M. J. Dee' (1570)
Farrant, Richard, *The Wars of Cyrus (1594): An Early Classical Narrative Drama of the Child Actors*, ed. J. Brawner, Urbana, Illinois (1942)
Fenne, Thomas, *Fennes Fruites* (1590)
Fraunce, Abraham, *The Third Part of the Countesse of Pembrokes Yvychurch* (1592)
Frontinus, Sextus Julius, *The Stratagemes, Sleyghtes, and Policies of Warre*, tr. Richard Morysine (1539)
'C.G.', *A Watch-worde for Warre: Not so New as Necessary* (1596)
'I.G.', *A Refutation of the Apology for Actors* (1615)
Gale, Thomas, *Certain Workes of Chirurgerie* (1563)
Garrard, William, *The Arte of Warre: Beeing the Onely Rare Booke of Myllitarie Profession* (1591)
Gascoigne, George, *The Posies ... corrected and augmented* (1575)
—— *The Spoyle of Antwerp* (1576)
—— *A Hundreth Sundrie Flowres: From the Original Edition of 1573*, ed. R. Miller, 2nd ed. (1975)
—— *Complete Works*, ed. J. Cunliffe, 2 vols, Cambridge (1907-10)
Gates, Geoffrey, *The Defence of Militarie Profession* (1579)
Gawdy, Philip, *Letters of Philip Gawdy of West Harling, Norfolk, and of London to Various Members of his Family, 1579 -1616*, ed. I. Jeayes (1906)
Gilbert, Humphrey, *A Discourse of a Discoverie for a Newe Passage to Cataia* (1576)
—— *Queene Elizabethes Achademy*, ed. F. Furnivall (1869)
Gosson, Stephen, *The Trumpet of Warre: A Sermon Preached at Paules Crosse the seventh of Maie 1598* (1598)
Greene, Robert, *The Tragical Reign of Selimus*, MSR, Oxford (1908)
—— *Friar Bacon and Friar Bungay*, MSR, Oxford (1926)
—— *Friar Bacon and Friar Bungay*, ed. D. Seltzer (1964)

—— *James the Fourth*, ed. J. Lavin (1967)

—— *Works*, ed. A. Grosart, 15 vols (1881-86), repr. New York (1964)

*Grettir the Strong, The Saga of*, tr. G. Hight, ed. P. Foote (1972)

Greville, Fulke, *Prose Works*, ed. J. Gouws, Oxford (1986)

Grimeston, Edward, tr., *A True Historie of the Memorable Siege of Ostend, and what passed on either side* (1604) [News-Pamphlet 29]

Hall, Edward, *The Unyon of the Twoo Noble and Illustre Famelies of Lancastre & Yorke* (1550)

Hall, Joseph, *Characters of Vertues and Vices: In Two Bookes* (1608)

Harriot, Thomas, *A Briefe and True Report of the New Found Land of Virginia*, Frankfurt (1590)

Harvey, Gabriel, *Works*, ed. A. Grosart, 3 vols (1884-85)

—— *Marginalia*, ed. G. Smith, Stratford-upon-Avon (1913)

Hawes, Stephen, *The Pastime of Pleasure*, ed. W. Mead (1928)

Hayward, Sir John, *Annals of the First Four Years of the Reign of Queen Elizabeth*, ed. J. Bruce (1840)

Henslowe, Philip, *Henslowe's Diary*, eds R. Foakes and R. Rickert, Cambridge (1961)

Heywood, Thomas, *The First and Second Partes of King Edward the Fourth* (1600)

—— *The Second Part of If You Know Not Me, You Know No Bodie* (1606)

—— *An Apology for Actors, Containing Three Briefe Treatises* (1612)

—— *The Foure Prentises of London* (1615)

—— *The Fair Maid of the West, or A Girle worth Gold* (1631)

—— *A Woman Killed With Kindness*, ed. B. Scobie (1985)

—— *Dramatic Works*, eds B. Field and J. Collier, 2 vols (1853)

Hilliard, Nicholas, *A Treatise Concerning the Arte of Limning*, eds R. Thornton and T. Cain, Ashington (1981)

Holinshed, Raphael, *The First and Second Volumes of Chronicles*, 2 vols (1587)

Horace (Quintus Horatius Flaccus), *The Odes and Epodes*, tr. C. Bennett (1927)

Ive, Paul, *The Practise of Fortification* (1589)

James I and VI, *BAΣIΛIKON ΔΩPON : His Majestys Instructions to his Dearest Sonne, Henry the Prince*, ed. C. Edmonds (1887)

—— *The Political Works ... Reprinted from the Edition of 1616*, ed. C. McIlwain, New York (1965)

Johnson, Richard, *The Nine Worthies of London, Explayning the Honourable Exercise of Armes, the Vertues of the Valiant* (1592)

Jonson, Ben, *Every Man in His Humour*, ed. M. Seymour-Smith (1966)

—— *Poetaster*, ed. T. Cain, Manchester (1995)

—— *Works*, eds C. Herford and P. and E. Simpson, 11 vols, Oxford (1925-52)

—— *Complete Poems*, ed. G. Parfitt, Harmondsworth (1975)

—— *Conversations with William Drummond of Hawthornden*, ed. R. Patterson (1923)

Kellie, Sir Thomas, *Pallas Armata, or Militarie Instructions for the Learned*, Edinburgh (1627)

*Kemps Nine Daies Wonder, Performed in a Daunce from London to Norwich* (1600)

Kirk, Andrew, *Secret Commonwealth, or A Treatise Displayeing the Chiefe Curiosities as they are in use among ... the People of Scotland ... 1691*, Edinburgh (1815)

Kyd, Thomas, *The Spanish Tragedie* (1592)

—— *Soliman and Perseda* (1599)

—— *The Spanish Tragedy*, ed. P. Edwards, Manchester (1959)

—— *The Spanish Tragedy*, ed. J. Mulryne, 2nd ed. (1989)

—— *The Spanish Tragedie*, ed. J. Pitcher, Harmondsworth (1998)

—— *Works*, ed. F. Boas, Oxford (1901)

*A Larum for London, or the Siedge of Antwerpe*, MSR, Oxford (1913)

Lavater, Lewes, *Of Ghostes and Spirites*, tr. 'R.H.' (1572)

Legh, Gerard, *The Accedens of Armory* (1568)

Leigh, Valentine, *The Moste Profitable and Commendable Science of Surveying of Landes* (1577)

*Liberality and Prodigality, The Contention Between*, MSR, Oxford (1913)

Linche, Richard, *The Fountaine of Ancient Fiction* (1599)

Lingham, John, *A True Relation of all suche Englishe Captaines ... as have beene slaine* (1584) [News-Pamphlet 4]

Lloyd, Lodowick, *The Stratagems of Jerusalem: With the Martiall Lawes and Militarie Discipline* (1602)

Lloyd, Richard, *A Briefe Discourse of the most renowned actes and right valiant conquests of ... the Nine Worthies* (1584)

*Locrine, The Lamentable Tragedy of*, MSR, Oxford (1908)

Lodge, Thomas, *A Fig for Momus: Containing Pleasant Varietie, included in Satyres, Eclogues, and Epistles* (1595)

—— *Wits Miserie, and the Worlds Madnesse* (1596)

—— *The Wounds of Civil War*, ed. J. Houppert, Nebraska (1969)

de Loier, Peter, *A Treatise of Specters or Straunge Sights* (1605)

de Loque, Bertrand, *Discourses of Warre and Single Combat*, tr. John Eliot (1591)

Lyly, John, *Works*, ed. R. Bond, 3 vols, Oxford (1902)

*Nicholas Machiavel's Prince*, tr. Edward Dacres (1640)

Machiavelli, Niccolò, *The Arte of Warre*, tr. Peter Whitehorne, ed. W. Henley, Tudor Translations 39 (1905)

—— *The Florentine History*, tr. Thomas Bedingfield, ed. W. Henley, Tudor Translations 40 (1905)

—— *The Prince*, tr. G. Bull, Harmondsworth (1961)

Markham, Francis, *Five Decades of Epistles of Warre* (1622)

Marlowe, Christopher, *Doctor Faustus: Parallel Texts, 1604-1616*, ed.

Greg, Oxford (1950)

—— *Doctor Faustus*, ed. J. Jump (1962)

—— *Edward II*, ed. W. Merchant (1967)

—— *Tamburlaine*, ed. J.Harper (1971)

—— *The Jew of Malta*, ed. N. Bawcutt, Manchester (1978)

—— *Tamburlaine the Great*, ed. J. Cunningham, Manchester (1981)

—— *Works*, ed. C. Brooke, Oxford (1910)

—— *Complete Works*, ed. F. Bowers, 2nd ed., 2 vols, Cambridge (1981)

—— *Complete Works*, ed. R. Gill, 2 vols (1987-91)

Marston, John, *The Scourge of Villainie* (1599)

—— *Histrio-Mastix* (1610)

—— *The Malcontent*, ed. M. Wine (1965)

—— *The Plays*, ed. H. Wood, 3 vols (1934-39)

—— *Selected Plays*, eds M. Jackson and M. Neill, Cambridge (1986)

—— *The Poems*, ed. A. Davenport, Liverpool (1961)

Mercator, Gerard and Judocus Hondius, *Atlas, or a Geographicke Description of the Regions, Countries and Kingdomes of the World*, tr. Henry Hexham, Amsterdam (1636); facs. ed. R. A. Skelton, 2 vols, Amsterdam (1968)

Middleton, Thomas, *A Mad World, My Masters* (1608)

—— [or Cyril Tourneur] *The Revenger's Tragedy*, ed. B. Gibbons (1967)

—— *A Chaste Maid in Cheapside*, ed. A. Brissenden (1968)

—— *A Fair Quarrel*, ed. R. Holdsworth (1974)

—— *Selected Plays*, ed. D. Frost, Cambridge (1978)

Middleton, Thomas and Thomas Dekker, *The Roaring Girl*, ed. P. Mulholland (1987)

*Military Discourse Proving Whether it bee better for England to give an invador present battaile, or to temporize and deferre the same*, Dulwich College MSS 29 [*c*.1595]

*The Mirror for Magistrates*, ed. L. Campbell, Cambridge (1938)

*A Myrrour for English Souldiers: Or, An Anotomy of an Accomplished an at Armes* (1595)

de Montaigne, Michel, *The Essayes Or Morall, Politike and Militarie Discourses*, tr. John Florio (1603)

—— *The Essays*, tr. E. Trechmann (1955)

More, Sir Thomas, *Utopia*, tr. G. Logan, ed. Logan and R. Adams, Cambridge (1989)

Munday, Anthony, *Fedele and Fortunio*, MSR, Oxford (1909)

—— *John a Kent & John a Cumber*, MSR, Oxford (1923)

Munday, Anthony, and others, *Sir Thomas More*, eds V. Gabrieli and G. Melchiori, Manchester (1990)

Nashe, Thomas, *Works*, ed. R. McKerrow, rev. ed. F. Wilson, 5 vols, Oxford (1958)

—— *The Unfortunate Traveller and Other Works*, ed. J. Steane, Harmondsworth (1972)

News-Pamphlets: 1574-1605

1. *Certayne Newes of the Whole Discription, Ayde, and helpe of the Christian Princes and Nobles, the which for the comfort and deliverance of the poore Christians in the low Countries, are gathered together, and are nowe with their armies in the fielde* (1574)

2. *'W.C.', The True Reporte of the Skirmish fought betwene the States of Flaunders, and Don Joan, Duke of Austria, with the number of all them that was slayne on both sides, which battel was fought the first day of August being Lammas Day 1578* (1578)

3. *A Discourse of the Present State of the Wars in the Lowe Countryes. Wherein is Contayned the pittiful spoyle of Askot: And the Articles of Peace to bee concluded betwene the States and Don John of Austrea 24. of. August. 1578* (1578)

4. John Lingham, *A True Relation of all suche Englishe Captaines and Lieutenants,as have beene slaine in the lowe Countries of Flaunders, together with those now living, as also of such as are fled to the Enimie* (1584)

5. *The Besieging of Bergen op Zoom* [News-Map] (1589)

6. *True Newes from one of Sir Fraunces Veres Companie Concerning Delftes-Ile,and sundry other townes in the Lowe Countries, yeelded to the Generall since May last* (1591)

7. *A True Reporte of the Service in Britanie, Performed Lately by the Honorable Knight Sir John Norreys and other Captaines and Gentlemen Souldiers before Guingand* (1591)

8. *Newes from Sir Roger Williams, With a Discourse printed at Rheines,containing the most happie Victorie lately obtained by the Prince de Conty* (1591)

9. *A Breefe Description of the Battailes, Victories, and Triumphes, Atchived by the D. of Parma, and the Spanish Armye sent by the King of Spayne, under his conduct to the succour of the rebellious Leaguers of Fraunce,* tr. 'E.A.' (1591)

10. *The Politique Takinge of Zutphen Skonce, with the Winning of the Towne, and beleaguring of Deventer. With the honourable enterprise of Sir Roger Williams* (1591)

11. *A Journall, or Briefe Report of the Late Service in Britaigne, by the Prince de Dombes Generall of the French Kings Army in those parts, assisted with her Majesties forces at this present there* (1591)

12. *A True Declaration of the Streight Siedge laide to the Cytty of Steenwich, and the Skirmishes and Battailes which happened on both sides, very strange and adventurous,* tr. 'I.T.' (1592)

13. *A Journall, Wherein is Truely Sette Downe from Day to Day, What was doone, and worthy of noting in both the Armies, from the last comming of the D. of Parma into Fraunce, untill the eighteenth of*

*May 1592*, tr. 'E.A.' (1592)

14. *The Honorable Victorie obteined by Grave Maurice his Excellencie against the Cittie of Rhyne-berg, the 20. of August 1597* (1597)

15. *A Discourse More at Large of the Late Overthrowe given to the King of Spaines armie at Turnehaut, in Januarie last, by Count Morris of Nassawe, assisted with the English forces* (1597)

16. *A Briefe Chronicle, and perfect rehearsall of all the memorable actions happened not only in the Low Countries, but also in Germanie, Italie, Fraunce, Spaine, England, Turkey, and other Countries since ... 1500, to this present yeare 1598* (1598)

17. *The Battaile Fought Betweene Count Maurice of Nassaw, and Albertus Arch-duke of Austria nere Newport in Flaunders, the xxij of June 1600. With the names of such men of accompts as have beene either slaine, hurt, or taken prisoners* (1600)

18. *A True Relation of the famous and renowned Victorie latelie atchieved by the Counte Maurice of Nassau, neere to Newport in Flaunders against the Arch-Duke Albertus* (1600)

19. John Rider, *The Coppie of a Letter Sent from M. Rider, Deane of Saint Patricks, concerning the Newes out of Ireland, and of the Spaniards landing and present estate there* (1601)

20. *The Oppugnation and fierce Siege of Ostend, by the Archduke Albertus his Forces, commanded by the Duke of Ossuna, who came before the said Towne, the fift day of June past* (1601)

21. *Newes from ostend, of, The Oppugnation, and Fierce Siege, made by the Archeduke Albertus his Forces, commanded by the Duke of Ossuna who came before the saide Towne, the fift day of Julie last past ... Now newly imprinted; whereunto are added such other Newes and Accidents as have lately hapned at Ostend* (1601)

22. *Further Newes of Ostend. Wherein is declared such accidents as have happened since the former Edition, dilligently Collected out of Sundry Letters and advertisements* (1601)

23. *A True Report of all the Proceedings of GRAVE MAURIS before the Towne of Bercke: With all the Accidentes that happened in the Besiedge of the same, since the 12 day of June last 1601* (1601)

24. *A Breefe Declaration of that which is happened as well within as without Oastend sithence the vii of Januarie 1602. As also when the Enemy did give Foure, Five, or more Assaults upon the same Towne. Also the Names of the Commaunders ... and the Names of the said Conductors which have beene slaine* (1602)

25. *A True Discourse of all the Sallyes which the Souyldiers of the Citie of Grave have made since the Siedge: And in what manner ... necessaries of reliefe, came to relieve the Citye* (1602)

26. *Extremities Urging the Lord Generall Sir Fra: Veare to the Antiparle with the Archduke Albertus. Written by an English Gentleman of verie good account from Ostand* (1602)

27.   *A Dialogue and Complaint Made Upon the Siedge of Oastend, Made by the King of Spaine, the Archduke, the Infanta, the Pope, the Prince Morrice, and the eldest sonne of Savoye ... All a true discourse of that which is hapned in the same towne of Oastend, from the fourth day of the moneth of February 1602* (1602)

28.   'I. E.', *A Letter from a Souldier of Good Place in Ireland, to his friend in London, touching the notable Victorie of her Majesties Forces there, against the Spaniards, and Irish Rebels: And of the yeelding up of Kynsale, and other places there held by the Spanyards* (1602)

29.   *A True Historie of the Memorable Siege of Ostend, and what passed on either side, from the beginning of the Siege, unto the yeelding up of the Towne,* tr. Edward Grimeston (1604)

30.   *A True Reporte of the Great Overthrowe lately given unto the Spaniards in their resolute assault of Bergen op Zoam in the Lowe Countries* (1605)


Norden John, *A Prayer for the Proceedings and Good Successe of the Earle of Essex and his Companies in their present expedition in Ireland* (1599)

Novarese, Girolamo, *Moste Briefe Tables to know redily how manie ranckes of footemen ... go to the making of a just battaile,* tr. 'H.G.' (1588)

Nun, Thomas, *A Comfort Against the Spaniard* (1596)

Ockland, Christopher, *The Valiant Actes and Victorious Battailes of the English Nation,* tr. 'J. S.' (1585)

*Sir John Oldcastle, The Life of,* MSR, Oxford (1908)

*An Oration Militarie to all Naturall Englishmen, Whether Protestants, or otherwise* (1588)

*Ordonances and Instructions for the Musters* (1590)

Ortelius, Abraham, *Theatrum Orbis Terrarum,* Amsterdam (1570); facs.ed. R. Skelton, Amsterdam (1964)

——   *The Theatre of the Whole World: Set Forth by That Excellent Geographer Abraham Ortelius,* tr. 'W.B.' (1606); facs. ed. R. Skelton, Amsterdam (1968)

Overbury, Sir Thomas, *The Overburian Characters,* ed. W. Paylor, Oxford (1936)

Ovid (Publius Ovidius Naso), *The .xv. Bookes ... entytuled Metamorphosis,* tr. Arthur Golding (1567)

*Ovids Metamorphosis Englished, Mythologiz'd and Represented in Figures,* tr. George Sandys, Oxford (1632)

*The Three Parnassus Plays, 1598-1601,* ed. J. Leishman (1949)

Peele, George, *The Honour of the Garter* (1590)

——   *The Battle of Alcazar,* MSR, Oxford (1907)

——   *David and Bathsebe,* MSR, Oxford (1907)

—— *King Edward the First*, MSR, Oxford (1911)

—— *Works*, ed. A. Bullen, 2 vols (1888)

Pickeryng, John, *Horestes*, in *Three Tudor Classical Interludes*, ed. M. Axton, Cambridge (1982)

Pictorius, Georgius, *Apotheoses Tam Exterarum Gentium Quam Romanorum Deorum*, Basel (1558); facs. ed. S. Orgel (1976)

Platter, Thomas, *Thomas Platter's Travels in England*, tr. C. Williams (1937)

Plautus, Titus Maccius, *Works*, tr. P. Nixon, 5 vols (1916-38)

*Plutarch's Lives of the Noble Grecians and Romans*, tr. Thomas North, ed. W. Henley, Tudor Translations 7-12, 6 vols (1895-96)

Polemon, John, *All the Famous Battels that have bene fought in our age throughout the Worlde* (1578)

—— *The Second Part of the Booke of Battailes* (1587)

Preston, Thomas, *Cambises*, in *Minor Elizabethan Tragedies*, ed. T. Craik (1974)

Pricket, Robert, *Unto the Most High and Mightie Prince, his Soveraigne Lord King James, A Poore Subject sendeth, A Souldiors Resolution* (1603)

Proctor, Thomas, *Of the Knowledge and Conducte of Warres* (1578)

Puttenham, George, *The Arte of English Poesie*, eds G. Willcock and A. Walker, Cambridge (1936)

Rabelais, François, *The Heroic Deeds of Gargantua and Pantagruel*, tr. T. Urquhart and P. le Motteux, ed. D. Lewis, 2 vols (1929)

Ralegh, Sir Walter, *A Discourse of the Originall and Fundamentall Cause of Naturall, Customary, Arbitrary, Voluntary and Necessary Warre* (1650)

Rankins, William, *A Mirrour of Monsters: Wherein is plainely described the manifold vices, & spotted enormities, that are caused by the infectious sight of Playes* (1587)

—— *Seaven Satyres Applyed to the Weeke* (1598)

Rastell, John, *Three Rastell Plays*, ed. Richard Axton (1979)

*Richard the Third, The True Tragedy of*, MSR, Oxford (1929)

Riche, Barnaby, *A Right Exelent and Pleasaunt Dialogue betwene Mercury and an English Souldier: Contayning his Supplication to Mars* (1574)

—— *Allarme to England, foreshewing what perilles are procured, where the people live without regard of Martiall Lawe* (1578)

—— *His Farewell to Militarie Profession* (1581)

—— *A Path-Way to Military Practise* (1587)

—— *A Martiall Conference, Pleasantly Discoursed Betweene Two Souldiers, the one Captaine Skil, trained up in the French and Low Country services, the other Captaine Pill, only practised in Finsburie Fields* (1598)

—— *A Souldiers Wishe to Britons Welfare: or a Discourse, fit to be read of all Gentlemen and Souldiers* [*The Fruites of Long Experience. A Pleasing View for Peace. A Looking-Glasse for Warre. Or, Call it What You List*] (1604)

—— *Faultes, Faults, and Nothing Else But Faultes* (1606)

Rider, John, *The Coppie of a Letter* (1601) [News-Pamphlet 19]

Ripa, Cesare, *Iconologia, Overo Descrittione d'Imagini Delle Virtu*, Padua (1611)

—— *Iconologia: or, Morall Emblems* (1709)

le Roy, Loys, *Of the Interchangeable Course, or Variety of Things in the Whole World*, tr. Robert Ashley (1594)

'W.S.', *A Discourse of the Common Weal of this Realm of England*, ed. E. Lamond, Cambridge (1897)

Sackville, Thomas and Thomas Norton, *Gorboduc*, in *Specimens of the Pre-Shakespearean Drama: 37 Plays from the Norwich Pageants to Kyd's 'Spanish Tragedie'*, ed. J. Manly, 2 vols (1974)

Saxo Grammaticus, *The First Nine Books of the Danish History*, tr. O. Elton, ed. F. Powell (1894)

Scot, Reginald, *The Discoverie of Witchcraft*, ed. B. Nicholson (1886)

Shakespeare, William, *The First Part of the Contention betwixt the two famous Houses of Yorke and Lancaster* (1594)

—— *Lucrece* (1594)

—— *The ... Lamentable Romaine Tragedie of Titus Andronicus* (1594)

—— *The True Tragedie of Richard Duke of Yorke* (1595)

—— *The Tragedy of King Richard the Third* (1597)

—— *The Historie of Henrie the Fourth* (London, 1598)

—— *A Pleasant Conceited Comedie Called Loves Labors Lost* (1598)

—— *The Second Part of Henrie the Fourth* (1598)

—— *The Most Excellent Historie of the Merchant of Venice* [Q1] (1600)

—— *A Midsommer Nights Dreame* (1600)

—— *The Cronicle History of Henry the fift* (1600)

—— *A Most Pleasaunt and excellent conceited Comedie, of Syr John Falstaffe, and the Merrie Wives of Windsor* (1602)

—— *The Tragicall Historie of Hamlet Prince of Denmarke* [Q1] (1603)

—— *The Tragicall Historie of Hamlet Prince of Denmarke* [Q2] (1605)

—— *True Chronicle Historie of the life and death of King Lear* (1608)

—— *The Late ... Play, Called Pericles, Prince of Tyre* (1609)

—— *The Famous Historie of Troylus and Cresseid* (1609)

—— *The Tragoedy of Othello, The Moore of Venice* (1622)

—— [and John Fletcher], *The Two Noble Kinsmen* (1634)

—— *All's Well That Ends Well*, ed. G. Hunter (1962)

—— *A New Variorum Edition of Hamlet*, ed. H. Furness, New York, (1963)

—— *Hamlet*, ed. B. Lott (1968)

—— *Hamlet*, ed. T. Spencer, Harmondsworth (1980)

—— *Hamlet*, ed. H. Jenkins (1982)

—— *Hamlet, Prince of Denmark*, ed. P. Edwards, Cambridge (1985)

—— *Hamlet*, ed. G. Hibbard, Oxford (1987)

—— *The Tragicall Historie of Hamlet Prince of Denmarke*, eds G. Holderness and B. Loughrey, Hemel Hempstead (1992)

—— *The First Part of King Henry IV*, ed. A. Humphreys (1960)

—— *Henry IV, Part 1*, ed. D. Bevington, Oxford (1987)

—— *A New Variorum Edition of the Second Part of Henry IV*, ed. M. Shaaber (1940)

—— *The Second Part of King Henry IV*, ed. A. Humphreys (1966)

—— *King Henry V*, ed. J. Walter (1954)

—— *Henry V*, ed. G. Taylor, Oxford (1984)

—— *The Cronicle History of Henry the Fift*, eds G. Holderness and B. Loughrey, Hemel Hempstead (1993)

—— *King Henry V*, ed. T. Craik (1995)

—— *The First Part of King Henry VI*, ed. J. Wilson, Cambridge (1952)

—— *The First Part of King Henry VI*, ed. A. Cairncross (1962)

—— *The Second Part of King Henry VI*, ed. A. Cairncross (1957)

—— *The Third Part of King Henry VI*, ed. A. Cairncross (1964)

—— *Julius Caesar*, ed. T. Dorsch (1955)

—— *Love's Labour's Lost*, ed. R. David (1951)

—— *Love's Labour's Lost*, ed. J. Kerrigan, Harmondsworth (1982)

—— *Othello*, ed. M. Ridley (1958)

—— *Othello*, ed. E. Honigmann (1997)

—— *King Richard III*, ed. A. Hammond (1981)

*Shakespeare's Sonnets*, ed. S. Booth, Yale (1977)

—— *The Sonnets, and A Lover's Complaint*, ed. J. Kerrigan, Harmondsworth (1986)

*Shakespeare's Sonnets*, ed. K. Duncan-Jones (1997)

—— *Troilus and Cressida*, ed. K. Palmer (1982)

—— *Troilus and Cressida*, ed. K. Muir (1982)

—— and John Fletcher, *The Two Noble Kinsmen*, ed. N. Bawcutt, Harmondsworth (1977)

*The First Folio of Shakespeare*, Norton Facsimile, ed. C. Hinman (1968)

*The Works of Mr William Shakespear*, ed. Nicholas Rowe, 7 vols (1709-10)

*The Works of William Shakespear*, ed. Alexander Pope, 6 vols (1725)

*The Riverside Shakespeare*, eds G. Evans et al, Boston (1974; 2nd ed., 1997)

*The Complete Works of William Shakespeare*, gen. eds S. Wells and G. Taylor, Oxford (1986)

*The Shakespeare Apocrypha*, ed. C. Brooke (Oxford, 1908)

*Shakespeare's Edmund Ironside*, ed. E. Sams, Aldershot (1986)

Sidney, Sir Philip, *An Apologie for Poetrie* (1595)

—— *The Poems*, ed. W. Ringler, Oxford (1962)

Silver, George, *Paradoxes of Defence* (1599)

Smythe, Sir John, *Certain Discourses Military* (1590)

Spenser, Edmund, *The Faerie Queene*, ed. A. Hamilton (1977)
—— *Prose Works*, ed. R. Gottfried, Baltimore (1949)
Stow, John, *A Survay of London, Contayning the Originall, Antiquity, Increase Modern Estate, and Description of that Citie* (1598)
—— *Annales, or a Generall Chronicle of England Begun by John Stow Continued ... by Edmund Howes* (1631)
*Jack Straw, The Life and Death of,* MSR, Oxford (1957)
Styward, Thomas, *The Pathwaie to Martiall Discipline* (1581)
Sun Tzu, *The Art of War*, tr. Y. Shibung, ed. T. Hanzhang, Ware (1993)
Sutcliffe, Matthew, *The Practice, Proceedings, and Lawes of Armes, Described out of the Doings of the most valiant and expert Captaines* (1593)
Taillepied, Noël, *A Treatise of Ghosts, Being the Psichologie, or Treatise upon Apparitions and Spirits*, tr. M. Summers (1933)
Taylor, John, *A Dogg of Warre* (n.d.)
Terence (Publius Terentius Afer), *Works*, tr. J. Sargeaunt, 2 vols (1912)
Tourneur, Cyril, *A Funerall Poeme. Upon the Death of ... Sir Francis Vere* (1609)
—— *The Atheist's Tragedie* (1611)
—— *The Atheist's Tragedy*, ed. B. Morris and R. Gill (1976)
—— *Works*, ed. A. Nicoll (1929)
*Trial of Chivalry, The History of the* (1605), facs. ed. J. Farmer (1912)
Udall, John, *The True Remedie Against Famine and Warres* (1586)
Udall, Nicholas, *Roister Doister*, ed. G. Scheurweghs, Louvain (1939)
Unton, Sir Henry, *Correspondence of Sir Henry Unton, Knt, Ambassador from Queen Elizabeth to Henry IV, King of France, in the Years 1591 and 1592*, ed. J. Stevenson (1847)
Valeriano, G.P. Bolzani, *Hieroglyphica*, Lyon (1602)
Vegetius, Flavius Renatus, *Knyghthode and Battaile: A XVth Century Verse Paraphrase of Flavius Vegetius Renatus' Treatise 'De Re Militari'*, eds R. Dyboski and Z. Arend (1935)
—— *The Foure Bookes of Flavius Vegetius Renatus, briefelye contayninge a plaine forme, and perfect knowledge of Martiall policye, feates of Chivalrie*, tr. John Sadler (1572)
Vennar, Richard, *Englands Joy* (1601)
Vere, Sir Francis, *The Commentaries* (1657)
Virgil (Publius Vergilius Maro), *Works*, tr. H. Fairclough, 2 vols (1935)
—— *Virgil's Aeneid Translated into Scottish Verse*, tr. Gavin Douglas, ed. D. Coldwell, 4 vols (1957)
—— *The Bucoliks ... Together with his Georgiks or Ruralls*, tr. Abraham Fleming (1589)
Ward, Robert, *The Anatomy of Warre, or, Warre with the wofull fruites ... laid out to the life* (1642)
Webster, John, *The White Devil*, ed. J. Brown, Manchester (1960)
—— *The Duchess of Malfi*, ed. J. Brown, Manchester (1964)

—— *Complete Works*, ed. F. Lucas, 4 vols (1927)

—— *Works: An Old-Spelling Critical Edition*, ed. D. Gunby et al., volume 1, Cambridge (1995)

Whetstone, George, *The English Myrror: A Regard Wherein al Estates may behold the Conquests of Envy* (1586a)

—— *The Honourable Reputation of a Souldier, with a Morall Report of the Vertues, Offices, and (by abuse) the disgrace of his Profession ... De Eerweerdighe Achtbaerheyt van een Soldener*, Leiden (1586b)

Whitehorne, Peter, *Certaine Waies for the Ordering of Souldiours in battelray, and setting of battailes, after diverse fashions* (1588)

Whitney, George, *A Choice of Emblemes*, ed. H. Green (1866)

Williams, Sir Roger, *Works*, ed. J. Evans, Oxford (1972)

Wilson, Robert, *The Pleasant and Stately Moral of the Three Lordes and Three Ladies of London* (1590)

—— *The Cobbler's Prophecy*, MSR, Oxford (1914)

de Wilton, Arthur, Lord Grey, *A Commentary of the Services and Charges of William, Lord Grey of Wilton*, ed. P. Egerton (1847)

Worsop, Edward, *A Discoverie of Sundrie Errours and Faults* (1582)

Wyatt, George, *The Papers of George Wyatt Esquire of Boxley Abbey in the County of Kent*, ed. D. Loades (1968)

Wyrley, William, *The True Use of Armorie, Shewed by Historie and Plainly Proved by Example* (1592)

## Secondary sources

Adams, R. (1962) *The Better Part of Valor: More, Erasmus, Colet, and Vives, on Humanism, War and Peace, 1496-1535*, Seattle

Adnitt, H. (1880) 'Thomas Churchyard', *Transactions of the Shropshire Archaeological and Natural History Society* 3

Aers, D., Hodge, B. and Kress, G. (1981) eds, *Literature, Language and Society in England, 1580-1680*, Dublin

Agnew, J-C. (1986) *Worlds Apart: The Market and the Theater in Anglo-American Thought, 1550-1750*, Cambridge

Alden, R. (1899) *The Rise of Formal Satire in England Under Classical Influence*, Philadelphia

Alexander, F. (1933) 'A Note on Falstaff', *The Psychoanalytic Quarterly* 2

Allmand, C. (1976) ed., *War, Literature, and Politics in the Late Middle Ages*, Liverpool

Alpers, S. (1983) *The Art of Describing: Dutch Art in the Seventeenth Century*

Altman, J. (1991) '"Vile Participation": The Amplification of Violence in the Theater of *Henry V* ', *Shakespeare Quarterly* 42

Anderson, D. (1974) 'Tamburlaine's "Perpendicular" and the T-in-O Maps', *Notes And Queries* 219

Andrews, J. (1985) ed., *William Shakespeare: His World, His Work, His Influence*, 3 vols, New York

Andrews, K. (1983) *Trade, Plunder, and Settlement: Maritime Enterprise and the Genesis of the British Empire, 1480-1630*, Cambridge

Anglo, S. (1969) *Machiavelli: A Dissection*

—— (1990) *Chivalry in the Renaissance*, Woodbridge

Ardolino, F. (1990) '"In Paris? Mass, and Well Remembered!": Kyd's *The Spanish Tragedy* and the English Reaction to the St. Bartholomew's Day Massacre', *Sixteenth Century Journal* 21

Arendt, H. (1970) *On Violence*

Armstrong, P. (1995) 'Spheres of Influence: Cartography and the Gaze in Shakespearean Tragedy and History', *Shakespeare Studies* 23

Armstrong, W. (1958) '*Tamburlaine* and *The Wounds of Civil War*', *Notes and Queries* 203

Auberlen, E. (1980) '*King Henry VIII*: Shakespeare's Break with the "Bluff-King-Harry" Tradition', *Anglia* 98

Axton, M. (1977) *The Queen's Two Bodies: Drama and the Elizabethan Succession*

Axton, M. and Williams, R. (1977) eds, *English Drama: Forms and Development*, Cambridge

Aydelotte, F. (1913) *Elizabethan Rogues and Vagabonds*, Oxford

Aylward, J. (1951) 'Playing a Prize', *Notes and Queries* 196

Babington, A. (1997) *Shell-Shock: A History of the Changing Attitudes to War Neurosis*

Baines, B. (1980) 'Kyd's Silenus Box and the Limits of Perception', *Journal of Medieval and Renaissance Studies* 10

—— (1983) '*Antonio's Revenge*: Marston's Play on Revenge Plays', *SEL* 23

Bakeless, J. (1942) *The Tragicall History of Christopher Marlowe*, 2 vols, Harvard

Baker, H. (1935), 'Ghosts and Guides: Kyd's *Spanish Tragedy* and the Medieval Tragedy', *Modern Philology* 33

Bald, R. (1959) ' "Will, My Lord of Leicester's Jesting Player"', *Notes and Queries* 204

Barber, C. (1959) *Shakespeare's Festive Comedy: A Study of Dramatic Form and its Relation to Social Custom*, Princeton

Barber, R. (1974) *The Knight and Chivalry*, 2nd ed.

Bardens, D. (1965) *Ghosts and Hauntings*

Barish, J. (1991) 'Shakespearean Violence: A Preliminary Survey', *Themes in Drama* 13

Barkan, L. (1975) *Nature's Work of Art: The Human Body as Image of the World*, New Haven

Barnie, J. (1974) *War in Medieval Society: Social Values and the Hundred Years War 1337-99*

[Barton] Righter, A. (1962) *Shakespeare and the Idea of the Play*

Barton, A. (1984) *Ben Jonson, Dramatist*, Cambridge

―― (1994) *Essays, Mainly Shakespearean*, Cambridge

Battenhouse, R. (1957) '*Hamlet*, 1.5.162: "Well said Old Mole"', *Notes and Queries* n.s. 215

Baudrillard, J. (1991) *La Guerre du Golfe N'a Pas Eu Lieu*, Paris

Beier, A. (1985) *Masterless Men: The Vagrancy Problem in England, 1560-1640*

Belsey, C. (1985) *The Subject of Tragedy: Identity and Difference in Renaissance Drama*

Bender, H. (1956) 'The Pacifism of the Sixteenth Century Anabaptists', *Mennonite Quarterly Review* 30

Bentley, G. (1941-68) *The Jacobean and Caroline Stage*, 7 vols, Oxford

―― (1971) *The Profession of Dramatist in Shakespeare's Time, 1590-1642*, Princeton

―― (1984) *The Profession of Player in Shakespeare's Time, 1590-1642*, Princeton

Berek, P. (1982) '*Tamburlaine*'s Weak Sons: Imitation as Interpretation Before 1593', *Renaissance Drama* n.s. 13

Berger, H. (1984) 'Sneak's Noise, Or Rumor and Detextualisation in *2 Henry IV* ', *Kenyon Review* n.s. 6

Berger, T. (1988) 'Casting *Henry V* ', *Shakespeare Studies* 20

Bergeron, D. (1971) *English Civic Pageantry, 1558-1642*

Bergonzi, B. (1980) *Heroes' Twilight: A Study of the Literature of the Great War*

Bernheimer, R. (1956) 'Theatrum Mundi', *Arts Bulletin* 38

Berry, E. (1979) '"True Things and Mock'ries": Epic and History in *Henry V* ', *Journal of English and Germanic Philology* 78

―― (1989) 'The Poet as Warrior in Sidney's *Defence of Poetry*', *SEL* 29

Berry, H. (1979) ed., *The First Public Playhouse: The Theatre in Shoreditch, 1576-1598*, Montreal

Berry, R. (1969) 'The Words of Mercury', *Shakespeare Survey* 22

―― (1986) 'Hamlet's Doubles', *Shakespeare Quarterly* 37

Bevington, D. (1962) *From 'Mankind' to Marlowe: The Growth of Structure in the Popular Drama of Tudor England*, Cambridge, Mass.

―― (1968) *Tudor Drama and Politics: A Critical Approach to Topical Meaning*, Cambridge, Mass.

―― (1984) *Action is Eloquence: Shakespeare's Language of Gesture*

Birringer, J. (1984) 'Marlowe's Violent Stage: "Mirrors" of Honor in *Tamburlaine*', *ELH* 51

Blake, A. (1987) ' "The Humor of Children": John Marston's Plays in the Private Theatres', *Review of English Studies* n.s. 38

Blankert, A. (1978) *Vermeer of Delft: Complete Edition of the Paintings*, Oxford

Boas, F. (1950) *Queen Elizabeth in Drama and Related Studies*

Bohannan, P. (1967) ed., *Law and Warfare: Studies in the Anthropology of Conflict*, New York

Boitani, P. (1984) *Chaucer and the Imaginary World of Fame*, Cambridge

Booth, S. (1983) *'King Lear', 'Macbeth', Indefinition and Tragedy*

Bornstein, D. (1972) 'Military Strategy in Malory and Vegetius' *De Re Militari'*, *Comparative Literature Studies* 9

—— (1975) 'Military Manuals in Fifteenth-Century England', *Medieval Studies* 37

Boughner, D. (1936) 'Pistol and the Roaring Boys', *Shakespeare Association Bulletin* 11

—— (1939) 'The Background of Lyly's Tophas', *PMLA* 54

—— (1940) 'Don Armado and the *Commedia dell'Arte*', *Studies in Philology* 37

—— (1954) *The Braggart in Renaissance Comedy: A Study in Comparative Drama from Aristophanes to Shakespeare*, Minneapolis

Bowers, F. (1940) *Elizabethan Revenge Tragedy, 1587-1642*, Princeton

Boyce, B. (1947) *The Theophrastan Character in England to 1642*, Cambridge, Mass.

Boynton, L. (1967) *The Elizabethan Militia, 1558-1638*

Bradbrook, M. (1962) *The Rise of the Common Player: A Study of Actor and Society in Shakespeare's England*, Cambridge

—— (1978) *Shakespeare: The Poet in his World*

Bradner, L. (1957) 'The Latin Drama of the Renaissance (1340-1640)', *Studies in the Renaissance* 4

Brady, C. (1986) 'Spenser's Irish Crisis: Humanism and Experience in the 1590s', *Past and Present* 111

Bramson, L. and Goethals, G. (1964) eds, *War: Studies from Psychology, Sociology, Anthropology*, New York

Brecht, B. (1980) *The Life of Galileo*, tr. J Willett, eds J. Willett and R. Manheim

Briggs, J. (1983) 'Marlowe's *Massacre at Paris*: A Reconsideration', *Review of English Studies* n.s. 34

Briggs, K. (1959) *The Anatomy of Puck: An Examination of Fairy Beliefs Among Shakespeare's Contemporaries and Successors*

Brissenden, A. (1981) *Shakespeare and the Dance*

Bristol, M. (1985) *Carnival and Theater: Plebeian Culture and the Structure of Authority in Renaissance England*

Brockbank, J. (1961) 'The Frame of Disorder – *Henry VI* ', *Stratford-upon-Avon Studies* 3

Brook, G. (1976) *The Language of Shakespeare*

Brooke, N. (1961) 'Marlowe as Provocative Agent in Shakespeare's Early Plays', *Shakespeare Survey* 14

Brooks-Davies, D. (1983) *The Mercurian Monarch: Magical Politics from Spenser to Pope*, Manchester

Brower, R. (1971) *Hero and Saint: Shakespeare and the Graeco-Roman Heroic Tradition*, Oxford

Brown, K. (1968) 'Hamlet's Place on the Map', *Shakespeare Studies* 4

Brown, L. (1951) *The Story of Maps*

Brown, N. (1969) *Hermes the Thief: The Evolution of a Myth*, New York

Brown, R. (1974) *A Casebook of Military History*

Brownstein, O. (1971) 'A Record of Inn-Playhouses from c.1565-1590', *Shakespeare Quarterly* 22

Bryant, J. (1974) 'Falstaff and the Renewal of Windsor', *PMLA* 89

Bryson, F. (1938) *The Sixteenth-Century Italian Duel: A Study in Renaissance Social History*, Chicago

Bullough, G. (1957-75) ed., *Narrative and Dramatic Sources of Shakespeare*, 8 vols

Bulman, J. (1985) 'Shakespeare's Georgic Histories', *Shakespeare Survey* 38

Burelbach, F. (1968) 'War and Peace in *The Shoemakers' Holiday*', *Tennessee Studies in Literature* 13

Burne, A. (1938-39) '"The Horrible Bloudie and Unheard of Siege of Ostend"', *Journal of the Royal Artillery* 65

Burns, N., and Reagan, C. (1975) eds, *Concepts of the Hero in the Middle Ages and the Renaissance*, New York

Burrow, J. (1986) *The Ages of Man: A Study in Medieval Writing and Thought*, Oxford

Butler, M. (1984) *Theatre and Crisis: 1632-1642*, Cambridge

Calderwood, J. (1960) 'Commodity and Honour in *King John*', *University of Toronto Quarterly* 29

Campbell, O. (1925) '*Love's Labour's Lost* Restudied', *University of Michigan Publications: Language and Literature* 1

—— (1938) *Comicall Satyre and Shakespeare's 'Troilus and Cressida'*, San Marino, California

Campbell, O.B. (1921) '*Troilus and Cressida*: A Justification', *London Mercury* 4

Carroll, W. (1976) *The Great Feast of Language in 'Love's Labour's Lost'*, Princeton

Carter, C. (1966) ed., *From the Renaissance to the Counter-Reformation: Essays in Honour of Garret Mattingley*

Chadwick, M. (1960) 'Defence Measures for the West Riding, 1586', *Yorkshire Archaeological Journal* 40

Chambers, E. (1923) *The Elizabethan Stage*, 4 vols, Oxford

—— (1930) 'The Date of Marlowe's *Tamburlaine*', *T.L.S.*, 28 August 1930

—— (1944) *Shakespearean Gleanings*, Oxford

Charlton, H. (1938) *Shakespearian Comedy*

Charney, M. (1988) *Hamlet's Fictions*

de Chickera, E. (1962) 'Divine Justice and Private Revenge in *The Spanish*

*Tragedy'*, *Modern Language Review* 57

Christian, R. (1972) *Ghosts and Legends*, Newton Abbot

Chwalewik, W. (1968) ed., *Anglo-Polish Texts for the Use of Shakespeare Students*, Warsaw

Clare, J. (1990) *'Art Made Tongue-Tied by Authority': Elizabethan and Jacobean Dramatic Censorship*, Manchester

Clark, I. (1988) *Waging War: A Philosophical Introduction*, Oxford

Clark, J. (1950) *The Dance of Death in the Middle Ages and the Renaissance*, Glasgow

Clark, P. (1985) ed., *The European Crisis of the 1590s: Essays in Comparative History*

—— and Slack, P. (1972) eds, *Crisis and Order in English Towns, 1500-1700: Essays in Urban History*

Clarkson, J. and Cochran, T. (1941) eds, *War as a Social Institution: The Historian's Perspective*, New York

von Clausewitz, C. (1968) *On War*, ed. A. Rapoport, tr. J. Graham, Harmondsworth

Clayton, T. (1992) ed., *The 'Hamlet' First Published (Q1, 1603): Origins, Form, Intertextualities*

Clements, R. (1944) 'Pen and Sword in Renaissance Emblem Literature', *Modern Language Quarterly* 5

Clephan, R. (1910) 'The Military Handgun of the Sixteenth Century', *Archaeological Journal* 67

Cockle, M. (1978) *A Bibliography of Military Books Up to 1642*, 3rd ed.

Coddon, K. (1989) '"Suche Strange Desygns": Madness, Subjectivity, and Treason in *Hamlet* and Elizabethan Culture', *Renaissance Drama* n.s. 20

Cohen, D. (1993) 'The Culture of Violence in *2 Henry IV* ', *Shakespeare Studies* 21

Cole, D. (1962) *Suffering and Evil in the Plays of Christopher Marlowe*, Princeton

Coleman, D. (1977) *The Economy of England, 1450-1750*

Coleridge, S. T. (1907) *Lectures on Shakespeare and Other English Poets*, ed. T. Ashe

—— (1912) *Poetical Works*, ed. E. Coleridge, Oxford

Contamine, P. (1986) *War in the Middle Ages*, tr. M. Jones, Oxford

Cook, E. (1986) *Seeing Through Words: The Scope of Late Renaissance Poetry*

Cooper, A. (1949) *Sergeant Shakespeare*

Cooper, H., Munich, A. and Squier, S. (1989) eds, *Arms and the Woman: War, Gender, and Literary Representation*

Cooper, J. (1978) *An Illustrated Encyclopaedia of Traditional Symbols*

Cope, J. (1965) '*Bartholomew Fair* as Blasphemy', *Renaissance Drama* 8

—— (1973) *The Theater and the Dream: From Metaphor to Form in Renaissance Drama*

Copeman, W. (1960) *Doctors and Disease in Tudor Times*

Cordner, M., Holland, P. and Kerrigan, J. (1994) eds, *English Comedy*, Cambridge

Cork, R. (1994) *A Bitter Truth: Avant-Garde Art and the Great War*

Council, N. (1973) *When Honour's at the Stake: Ideas of Honour in Shakespeare's Plays*

—— (1974) 'Prince Hal: Mirror of Success', *Shakespeare Studies* 7

—— (1975-76) '*O Dea Certe*: The Allegory of *The Fortress of Perfect Beauty*', *Huntington Library Quarterly* 39

—— (1980) 'Ben Jonson, Inigo Jones, and the Transformation of Tudor Chivalry', *ELH* 47

Cranfield, G. (1978) *The Press and Society from Caxton to Northcliffe*

Cranfill, T. and Bruce, D. (1953) *Barnabe Riche: A Short Biography*, Austin, Texas

Crewe, J. (1982) *Unredeemed Rhetoric: Thomas Nashe and the Scandal of Authorship*

Crone, G. (1978) *Maps and Their Makers: An Introduction to the History of Cartography*, 5th ed., Folkestone

Cronin, V. (1973) *Napoleon*, Harmondsworth

Cruickshank, C. (1966) *Elizabeth's Army*, 2nd ed., Oxford

Cunningham, J. and Warren, R. (1978) '*Tamburlaine the Great* Re-Discovered', *Shakespeare Survey* 31

Curren-Aquino, D. (1989) ed., *'King John': New Perspectives*

Cust, R. (1986) 'News and Politics in early Seventeenth-Century England', *Past and Present* 112

Dabbs, T. (1991) *Reforming Marlowe: The Nineteenth-Century Canonization of a Renaissance Dramatist*

Davies, C. (1977) 'The English People and War in the Early Sixteenth Century', in Duke and Tamse (1977)

Davis, H. (1949) 'The Military Career of Thomas North', *Huntington Library Quarterly* 12

Davis, N. (1983) *The Return of Martin Guerre*

Dean, L. (1947) 'Tudor Theories of History Writing', *Contributions in Modern Philology (University of Michigan)* 1

Dessen, A. (1978) 'The Logic of Elizabethan Stage Violence: Some Alarms and Excursions for Modern Critics, Editors, and Directors', *Renaissance Drama* n.s. 9

van Deursen, A. (1977) 'Holland's Experience of War During the Revolt of the Netherlands', in Duke and Tamse (1977)

Dodsworth, M. (1985) *Hamlet Closely Observed*

Dollimore, J. (1984) *Radical Tragedy: Religion, Ideology and Power in the Drama of Shakespeare and his Contemporaries*, Brighton

Donagan, B. (1988) 'Codes and Conduct in the English Civil War', *Past and Present* 118

Dop, J. (1981) *Eliza's Knights: Soldiers, Poets, and Puritans in the Nether-*

*lands,1572-1586*, Leiden

van Dorsten, J. (1962) *Poets, Patrons, and Professors: Sir Philip Sidney, Daniel Rogers, and the Leiden Humanists*, Leiden

—— , Baker-Smith, D. and Kinney, A. (1986) eds, *Sir Philip Sidney: 1586 and the Creation of a Legend*, Leiden

Draper, J. (1931) 'Captain General Othello', *Anglia* 55

—— (1931-2) 'Othello and Elizabethan Army Life', *Revue Anglo-Americaine* 9

—— (1976) '*Measure for Measure* and the Stews', *West Virginia University Bulletin: Philological Papers* 23

Duke, A. and Tamse, C. (1977) eds, *War and Society: Papers Delivered to the Sixth Anglo-Dutch Historical Conference*, The Hague

Duncan-Jones, K. (1983) 'Was the 1609 *Shake-Speares Sonnets* Really Unauthorised?', *Review of English Studies* n.s. 34

—— (1991) *Sir Philip Sidney: Courtier Poet*

Dusinberre, J. (1975) *Shakespeare and the Nature of Women*

—— (1990) '*King John* and Embarrassing Women', *Shakespeare Survey* 42

Dutton, R. (1991) *Mastering the Revels: The the Regulation and Censorship of English Renaissance Drama*

Earle, E., Craig, G. and Gilbert, F. (1944) eds, *Makers of Modern Strategy: Military Thought from Machiavelli to Hitler*, Princeton

Eccles, M. (1933) 'Sir George Buc, Master of the Revels', in Sisson (1933)

Edelmann, C. (1990) 'Shakespeare's "Brawl Ridiculous"', *Shakespeare Survey* 42

Edwards, P. (1970) *Thomas Kyd and Early Elizabethan Tragedy*, 2nd ed.

—— , Ewbank, I. and Hunter, G. (1980) eds, *Shakespeare's Styles: Essays in Honour of Kenneth Muir*, Cambridge

Ehrmann, J. (1968) 'Homo Ludens Revisited', *Yale French Studies* 41

van Elbe, J. (1939) 'The Evolution of the Concept of the Just War in International Law', *American Journal of International Law* 33

Eliot, T.S. (1932) *Selected Essays, 1917-1932*

Elliot, R. (1960) *The Power of Satire: Magic, Ritual, Art*, Princeton

Empson, W. (1986) *Essays on Shakespeare*, ed. D. Pirie, Cambridge

Engler, B. (1992) 'Shakespeare in the Trenches', *Shakespeare Survey* 44

Erickson, P. and Kahn, C. (1985) eds, *Shakespeare's 'Rough Magic': Renaissance Essays in Honor of C. L. Barber*

Erskine-Hill, H. (1983) *The Augustan Idea in English Literature*

Esper, T. (1965) 'The Replacement of the Longbow by Firearms in the English Army', *Technology and Culture* 6

Evans, M. (1975) 'Mercury versus Apollo: A Reading of *Love's Labour's Lost*', *Shakespeare Quarterly* 26

Everett, B. (1977) '*Hamlet*: A Time to Die', *Shakespeare Survey* 30

—— (1989) *Young Hamlet: Essays on Shakespeare's Tragedies*

Falls, C. (1950) *Elizabeth's Irish Wars*

—— (1955) *Mountjoy: Elizabethan General*

Farmer, H. (1945) 'The Martial Fife: The Bi-Centenary of its Re-Introduction', *Journal of the Society for Army Historical Research* 23

—— (1950) '16th-17th-Century Military Marches', *Journal of the Society for Army Historical Research* 28

Farnham, W. (1950) *The Medieval Heritage of Elizabethan Tragedy*, Oxford

Feest, C. (1980) *The Art of War*

Feingold, M. (1984) *The Mathematicians' Apprenticeship: Science, Universities and Society in England, 1560-1640*, Cambridge

Feld, M. (1974-75) 'Middle Class Society and the Rise of Military Professionalism: The Dutch Army, 1589-1609', *Armed Forces and Society* 1

Feldman, A. (1953) 'Playwrights and Pike Trailers in the Low Countries', *Notes And Queries* 189

Ferguson, A. (1960) *The Indian Summer of English Chivalry*, Durham, North Carolina

—— (1986) *The Chivalric Tradition in Renaissance England*

Fergusson, F. (1949) *The Idea of Theater: A Study of Ten Plays: The Art of Drama in Changing Perspectives*, Princeton

Fernández, J. (1973) 'Erasmus and the Just War', *Journal of the History of Ideas* 34

Fernández-Armesto, F. (1989) *The Spanish Armada: The Experience of War in 1588*, Oxford

Ferrari, G. (1987) 'Public Anatomy Lessons and the Carnival: The Anatomy Theatre of Bologna', *Past and Present* 117

Fineman, J. (1977) 'Fratricide and Cuckoldry: Shakespeare's Doubles', *The Psychoanalytic Review* 64

Finkelpearl, P. (1965-66) 'John Marston's *Histrio-Mastix* as an Inns of Court Play: An Hypothesis', *Huntington Library Quarterly* 29

—— (1969) *John Marston of the Middle Temple: An Elizabethan Dramatist in his Social Setting*, Cambridge, Mass.

Fisch, H. (1974) 'Shakespeare and the Puritan Dynamic', *Shakespeare Survey* 27

Fischer, S. (1985) *Econolingua: A Glossary of Coins and Economic Language in Renaissance Drama*

Fletcher, A. and Stevenson, J. (1985) eds, *Order and Disorder in Early Modern England*, Cambridge

Foakes, R. (1965) *Illustrations of the English Stage, 1580-1642*

—— (1992) 'The Reception of Hamlet', *Shakespeare Survey* 45

Foulkes, R. (1986) ed., *Shakespeare and the Victorian Stage*, Cambridge

Fowler, A. (1989) 'Spenser and War', in Mulryne and Shewring (1989)

Frank, J. (1961) *The Beginnings of the English Newspaper, 1620-1660*, Cambridge, Mass.

Freeman, A. (1967) *Thomas Kyd: Facts and Problems*, Oxford

Freeman, J. (1980) *Milton and the Martial Muse: 'Paradise Lost' and European Traditions of War*, Princeton

Freeman, R. (1948) *English Emblem Books*

Freud, S. (1953-74) *Complete Psychological Works*, gen. ed. J. Strachey, 24 vols

Friedenreich, K., Gill, R. and Kuriyama, C. (1988) eds, *'A Poet and a Filthy Play-Maker': New Essays on Christopher Marlowe*, New York

Frye, R. (1980) *Milton's Imagery and the Visual Arts: Iconographic Tradition in the Epic Poem*, Princeton

—— (1984) *The Renaissance Hamlet: Issues and Responses in 1600*, Princeton

Fussell, P. (1975) *The Great War and Modern Memory*, Oxford

—— (1989) *Wartime: Understanding and Behaviour in the Second World War*, Oxford

Gagen, J. (1968) 'Hector's Honor', *Shakespeare Quarterly* 19

Gallie, W. (1978) *Philosophers of Peace and War: Kant, Clausewitz, Marx, Engels and Tolstoy*, Cambridge

Garber, M. (1984) '"Here's Nothing Writ": Scribe, Script, and Circumscription in Marlowe's Plays', *Theatre Journal* 36

—— (1987) *Shakespeare's Ghost Writers: Literature as Uncanny Causality*

Gardner, H. (1942) 'The Second Part of *Tamburlaine the Great*', *Modern Language Review* 37

Gasper, J. (1990) *The Dragon and the Dove: The Plays of Thomas Dekker*, Oxford

Geckle, G. (1972-73) 'John Marston's *Histriomastix* and the Golden Age', *Comparative Drama* 6

Gibbons, B. (1980) *Jacobean City Comedy*, 2nd ed.

Gilbert, W.S. (1962) *The Savoy Operas*

Gilman, E. (1978) *The Curious Perspective: Literary and Pictorial Wit in the Seventeenth Century*

—— (1986) *Iconoclasm and Poetry in the English Reformation: Down Went Dagon*

Girard, R. (1986) 'Hamlet's Dull Revenge', in Parker and Quint (1986)

Gittings, C. (1984) *Death, Burial and the Individual in Early Modern England*, Beckenham

Goldberg, J. (1983) *James I and the Politics of Literature: Jonson, Shakespeare, Donne, and their Contemporaries*, Baltimore

—— (1986) *Voice Terminal Echo: Postmodernism and English Renaissance Texts*.

—— (1988) 'Rebel Letters: Postal Effects from *Richard II* to *Henry IV* ', *Renaissance Drama* n.s. 19

Goldman, M. (1972) *Shakespeare and the Energies of Drama*, Princeton

Gollancz, I. (1926) *The Sources of 'Hamlet': With Essay on the Legend*

Goring, J. (1975) 'Social Change and Military Decline in Mid-Tudor England', *History* 60

Gould, G. (1919) 'A New Reading of *Henry V* ', *The English Review* 29

Gould, T. (1991) 'The Uses of Violence in Drama', *Themes in Drama* 13

Grantley, D. and Roberts, P. (1996) eds, *Christopher Marlowe and English Renaissance Culture*, Aldershot

Graves, R. (1929) *Goodbye To All That*

Greenblatt, S. (1973) *Sir Walter Ralegh: The Renaissance Man and his Roles*

—— (1980) *Renaissance Self-Fashioning from More to Shakespeare*, Chicago

—— (1986) 'Psychoanalysis and Renaissance Culture', in Parker and Quint (1986)

—— (1988a) *Shakespearean Negotiations: The Circulation of Social Energy in Renaissance England*, Oxford

—— (1988b) ed., *Representing the English Renaissance*

Greer, G. (1986) *Shakespeare*, Oxford

Greg, W. (1955) *The Shakespeare First Folio: Its Bibliographical and Textual History*, Oxford

Grennan, E. (1978) 'Shakespeare's Satirical History: A Reading of *King John*', *Shakespeare Studies* 11

Grimal, P. (1986) *The Dictionary of Classical Mythology*, tr. A. Maxwell-Hyslop, Oxford

Gurr, A. (1977) '*Henry V* and the Bees' Commonwealth', *Shakespeare Survey* 30

—— (1980) *The Shakespearean Stage, 1574-1642*, 2nd ed., Cambridge

—— (1987) *Playgoing in Shakespeare's* London, Cambridge

—— (1989) 'The Shakespearean Stages, Forty Years On', *Shakespeare Survey* 41

Haining, P. (1982) *A Dictionary of Ghosts*

Hale, J. (1961) *The Art of War and Renaissance England*, Washington

—— (1962) 'War and Public Opinion in the Fifteenth and Sixteenth Centuries', *Past and Present* 22

—— (1977) *Renaissance Fortification: Art or Engineering?*

—— (1983) *Renaissance War Studies*

—— (1985a) *War and Society in Renaissance Europe, 1420-1620*

—— (1985b) 'Shakespeare and Warfare', in J. Andrews (1985)

—— (1988) 'A Humanistic Visual Aid: The Military Diagram in the Renaissance', *Renaissance Studies* 2

—— (1990) *Artists and Warfare in the Renaissance*

Hallett, C. (1977) 'Andrea, Andrugio, and King Hamlet: The Ghost as Spirit of Revenge', *Philological Quarterly* 56

Halliday, F. (1956) *Shakespeare in his Age*

Hallin, D. (1986) *The 'Uncensored War': The Media and Vietnam*, Oxford

Halliwell-Phillipps, J. (1883) *Outlines in the Life of Shakespeare*, 3rd ed.

Hanford, J. (1921) 'Milton and the Art of War', *Studies in Philology* 18

Hanning, R. and Rosand, D. (1983) eds, *Castiglione: The Ideal and the Real in Renaissance Culture*

Hanson, V. (1991) ed., *Hoplites: The Classical Greek Battle Experience*

Hapgood, R. (1965) 'The Life of Shame: Parolles and *All's Well*', *Essays in Criticism* 15

Harbage, A. and Schoenbaum, S. (1964) *Annals of English Drama, 975-1700*

Harrison, G. (1941) *A Jacobean Journal, Being a Record of Those Things Most Talked of During the Years 1603-1606*

—— (1955) *The Elizabethan Journals, Being a Record of Those Things Most Talked of During the Years 1591-1603*

Harriss, G. (1985) *Henry V: The Practice of Kingship*, Oxford

Hartigan, R. (1966) 'Saint Augustine on War and Killing: The Problem of the Innocent', *Journal of the History of Ideas* 27

Hattaway, M. (1982) *Elizabethan Popular Theatre: Plays in Performance*

—— (1996) 'Christopher Marlowe: Ideology and Subversion', in Grantley and Roberts (1996)

Hatto, A. (1940) 'Archery and Chivalry: A Noble Prejudice', *Modern Language Review* 35

Hawkes, T. (1986) *That Shakespeherian Rag: Essays on a Critical Process*

—— (1992) *Meaning by Shakespeare*

Hawkins, H. (1966) '"All the World's a Stage": Some Illustrations of the *Theatrum Mundi*', *Shakespeare Quarterly* 17

Hayes, J. (1987) 'The Elizabethan Audience on Stage', *Themes in Drama* 9

Hazlitt, W. (1882) *Bibliographical Collections and Notes on Early English Literature, 1474-1700*

Heath, E. (1973) ed., *Bow versus Gun, Being a Reprint of* [Smythe (1590) and Barwick (1594)], Wakefield

Heinemann, M. (1992) '"Demystifying the Mystery of State": *King Lear* and the World Upside Down', *Shakespeare Survey* 44

Helgerson, R. (1986) 'The Land Speaks: Cartography, Chorography and Subversion in Renaissance England', *Representations* 16

Heller, J. (1964) *Catch-22*

Henry, L. (1953) 'The Earl of Essex as Strategist and Military Organiser (1596-7)', *English Historical Review* 68

Herr, M. (1978) *Dispatches*

Hesse, H. (1974) *If The War Goes On ... : Reflections on War and Politics*, tr. R. Manheim

Hill, C. (1965) *Intellectual Origins of the English Revolution*, Oxford

Hill, E. (1985) 'Senecan and Vergilian Perspectives in *The Spanish Tragedy*', *ELR* 15

Hill, J. (1970) 'Braggadocchio and Spenser's Golden World Concept: The Function of Unregenerative Comedy', *English Literary History* 37

Hilliard, S. (1986) *The Singularity of Thomas Nashe*

Hobbs, W. (1980) *Stage Combat: 'The Action to the Word'*

Hodges, D. (1985) *Renaissance Fictions of Anatomy*, Amherst, Mass.

Hoffman, E. (1974) *Frame Analysis: An Essay on the Organisation of Experience*, Cambridge, Mass.

Holderness, G. (1992) *Shakespeare Recycled: The Making of Historical Drama*, Hemel Hempstead

Holleran, J. (1962) 'Spenser's Braggadocchio', in *Studies in English Renaissance Literature*, ed. W. McNeir, Baton Rouge

Holmes, M. (1969) *Elizabethan London*

Homan, S. (1969) 'Chapman and Marlowe: The Paradoxical Hero and the Divided Response', *Journal of English and Germanic Philology* 68

Honigmann, E. (1980) 'Shakespeare's "Bombast"', in Edwards et al. (1980)

—— (1985) 'Shakespeare and London's Immigrant Community Circa 1600', in *Elizabethan and Modern Studies Presented to Professor Willem Schrickx*, Ghent

—— (1986) ed., *Shakespeare and his Contemporaries: Essays in Comparison*, Manchester

Hood, T. (1906) *Poetical Works*, ed. W. Jerrold

Hopper, K. (1995) *Flann O'Brien: A Portrait of the Artist as a Young Post-Modernist*, Cork

Hosley, R. (1963) ed., *Essays on Shakespeare and Elizabethan Drama in Honour of Hardin Craig*

Hotson, L. (1948) 'Ancient Pistol', *Yale Review* 38

Howard, M. (1976) *War in European History*, Oxford

—— (1978) *War and the Liberal Conscience*, Oxford

—— (1992) *Strategic Deception in the Second World War*

Howell, R. (1975) 'The Sidney Circle and the Protestant Cause in Elizabethan Foreign Policy', *Renaissance and Modern Studies* 19

Huizinga, J. (1949) *Homo Ludens: A Study of the Play Element in Culture*, tr. R. Hull

—— (1955) *The Waning of the Middle Ages: A Study of the Forms of Life, Thought, and Art in France and the Netherlands in the Fourteenth and Fifteenth Centuries*, tr. F. Hopman, Harmondsworth

Hunt, M. (1911) *Thomas Dekker: A Study*, New York

Hunter, G. (1961) '*The Warres of Cyrus* and *Tamburlaine*', *Notes and Queries* 206

—— (1962) *John Lyly: The Humanist as Courtier*

—— (1964) 'Elizabethans and Foreigners', *Shakespeare Survey* 17

Hussey, S. (1982) *The Literary Language of Shakespeare*

Hutson, L. (1989) *Thomas Nashe in Context*, Oxford

Ide, R. (1980) *Possessed by Greatness: The Heroic Tragedies of Shakespeare and Chapman*

James, H. (1991) 'Cultural Disintegration in *Titus Andronicus*: Mutilating Titus, Vergil, and Rome', *Themes in Drama* 13

James, M. (1986) *Society, Politics and Culture: Studies in Early Modern*

*England*, Cambridge

Jaquot, J. (1957) 'Le Théâtre du Monde de Shakespeare à Calderon', *Revue de Littérature Comparée* 31

Jardine, L. (1983) *Still Harping on Daughters: Women and Drama in the Age of Shakespeare*, Brighton

Johnson, F. (1942) 'Thomas Hood's Inaugural Address as Mathematical Lecturer of the City of London (1588)', *Journal of the History of Ideas* 3

Johnson, J. (1975) *Ideology, Reason, and the Limitation of War:Religious and Secular Concepts, 1200-1740*

Johnson, P. (1974) *Elizabeth I: A Study in Power and Intellect*

Johnson, S. (1968) *Johnson on Shakespeare*, ed. A. Sherbo, 2 vols, Yale

Johnson, S.F. (1963) '*The Spanish Tragedy* or Babylon Revisited', in Hosley (1963)

Jones, A. and Stallybras, P. (1942) 'The Politics of *Astrophil and Stella*', *Studies in English Literature* 3

Jones, D. (1963) *In Parenthesis*

Jones, E. (1968) '*Othello, Lepanto*, and the Cyrus Wars', *Shakespeare Survey* 21

—— (1971) *Scenic Form in Shakespeare*, Oxford

—— (1977) *The Origins of Shakespeare*, Oxford

Jones, G. (1978) '*Henry V*: The Chorus and the Audience', *Shakespeare Survey* 31

Jones, T. (1980) *Chaucer's Knight: The Portrait of a Medieval Mercenary*

Jones-Davies, M. (1990) ed., *Shakespeare et la Guerre*, Paris

—— (1991) ed., *Langues et Nations au Temps de la Renaissance*, Paris

Jorgensen, P. (1948) 'Vertical Patterns in *Richard II* ', *Shakespeare Association Bulletin* 23

—— (1949) 'Shakespeare's Coriolanus: Elizabethan Soldier', *PMLA* 64

—— (1949-50) 'Moral Guidance and Religious Encouragement for the Elizabethan Soldier', *Huntington Library Quarterly* 13

—— (1950) 'My Name is Pistol Call'd', *Shakespeare Quarterly* 1

—— (1950-51) 'Military Rank in Shakespeare', *Huntington Library Quarterly* 14

—— (1951) 'Enobarbus' Broken Heart and *The Estate of English Fugitives*', *Philological Quarterly* 30

—— (1952) 'Theoretical Views of War in Elizabethan England', *Journal of the History of Ideas* 13

—— (1956a) *Shakespeare's Military World*, Los Angeles

—— (1956b) 'Alien Military Doctrine in Renaissance England', *Modern Language Quarterly* 17

—— (1961) 'The "Dastardly Treachery" of Prince John of Lancaster', *PMLA* 76

—— (1976) 'Valor's Better Parts: Backgrounds and Meanings of Shakespeare's Most Difficult Proverb', *Shakespeare Studies* 9

Joseph, B. (1971) *Shakespeare's Eden: The Commonwealth of England, 1558-1629*

Judges, A. (1965) ed., *The Elizabethan Underworld: A Collection of Tudor and Early Stuart Tracts and Ballads*, 2nd ed.

Kantorowicz, E. (1951) '*Pro Patria Mori* in Medieval Political Thought', *American Historical Review* 56

—— (1957) *The King's Two Bodies: A Study in Medieval Political Theology*, Princeton

Kaplan, J. (1971) 'Pistol's "Oath": *Henry V*, II.I.101', *Shakespeare Quarterly* 22

Kay, D. (1987) ed., *Sir Philip Sidney: An Anthology of Modern Criticism*, Oxford

—— (1990) *Melodious Tears: The English Funeral Elegy from Spenser to Milton*, Oxford

Keegan, J. (1976) *The Face of Battle*

—— (1993) *A History of Warfare*

Keen, M. (1984) *Chivalry*, Yale

Keller, A. (1950) 'Calvin and the Question of War', *Modern Language Quarterly* 11

—— (1952) 'Anti-War Writing in France, 1500-60', *PMLA* 67

Kelso, R. (1929) 'The Doctrine of the English Gentleman in the Sixteenth Century', *University of Illinois Studies in Language and Literature* 14

Kernan, A. (1958) 'John Marston's Play *Histriomastix*', *Modern Language Quarterly* 19

—— (1959) *The Cankered Muse: Satire of the English Renaissance*, New Haven

Kernodle, G. (1944) *From Art to Theatre: Form and Convention in the Renaissance*, Chicago

Kerrigan, J. (1981) 'Hieronimo, Hamlet and Remembrance', *Essays in Criticism* 31

—— (1987) 'Shakespeare as Reviser', in Ricks (1987)

—— (1990) '*Henry IV* and the Death of Old Double', *Essays in Criticism* 40

—— (1994) 'A Complete History of Comic Noses', in Cordner et al. (1994)

—— (1996) *Revenge Tragedy: Aeschylus to Armageddon*, Oxford

Keuning, J. (1963) 'The "Civitates" of Braun and Hogenberg', *Imago Mundi* 17

Kiernan, V. (1988) *The Duel in European History: Honour and the Reign of Aristocracy*, Oxford

Knapp, R. (1973) 'Horestes: The Uses of Revenge', *ELH* 40

Kocher, P. (1942) 'Marlowe's Art of War', *Studies in Philology* 39

—— (1947) 'Contemporary Pamphlet Backgrounds for Marlowe's *The Massacre at Paris*', *Modern Language Quarterly* 8

Kökeritz, H. (1953) *Shakespearean Pronunciation*

Korn, A. (1954) 'Puttenham and the Oriental Pattern-Poem', *Comparative Literature* 6

Kreider, P. (1935) *Elizabethan Comic Character Conventions as Revealed in the Comedies of G. Chapman*, Ann Arbor

Lake, D. (1981) '*Histriomastix*: Linguistic Evidence for Authorship', *Notes and Queries* 226

Langer, U. (1986) 'Gunpowder as Transgressive Invention in Ronsard', in Parker and Quint (1986)

Lawson, M. (1991) 'Heaven on Earth', *The Independent Magazine*, 28 December 1991

Leech, C. (1954) 'The Theme of Ambition in *All's Well That Ends Well*', *ELH* 21

—— (1986) *Christopher Marlowe: Poet for the Stage*, ed. A. Lancashire, New York

Leggatt, A. (1971) '*All's Well That Ends Well*: The Testing of Romance', *Modern Language Quarterly* 32

—— (1974) *Shakespeare's Comedy of Love*

Leslie, M. (1983) *Spenser's 'Fierce Warres and Faithfull Loves': Martial and Chivalric Symbolism in The Faerie Queene*, Cambridge

Lever, J. (1953) 'Shakespeare's French Fruits', *Shakespeare Survey* 6

Levin, H. (1970) *The Myth of the Golden Age in the Renaissance*

Levin, R. (1965) '*The Staple of News*, The Society of Jeerers, and Canters' Colleges', *Philological Quarterly* 44

—— (1984) 'The Contemporary Perception of Marlowe's *Tamburlaine*', *Medieval and Renaissance Drama in England* 1

Levine, M. (1968) *Tudor England, 1485-1603*, Cambridge

Levy, F. (1982) 'How Information Spread Among the Gentry, 1550-1640', *Journal of British Studies* 21

Lewis, C. (1954) *English Literature in the Sixteenth Century Excluding Drama*, Oxford

Lievsay, J. (1941) 'Braggadochio: Spenser's Legacy to the Character-Writers', *Modern Language Quarterly* 2

Limon, J. (1985) *Gentlemen of the Company: English Players in Central and Eastern Europe, 1590-1660*, Cambridge

Lindley, D. (1984) ed., *The Court Masque*, Manchester

Linnell, R. (1977) *The Curtain Playhouse*

Loades, D. (1974) 'The Theory and Practice of Censorship in Sixteenth-Century England', *Transactions of the Royal Historical Society*, 5th series 24

Loewenstein, J. (1984) *Responsive Readings: Versions of Echo in Pastoral, Epic, and the Jonsonian Masque*

—— (1988) 'Plays Agonistic and Competitive: The Textual Approach to Elsinore', *Renaissance Drama* n.s. 19

Lonsdale, R. (1984) ed., *The New Oxford Book of Eighteenth Century*

*Verse*, Oxford

Loomis, R. (1919) 'The Allegorical Siege in the Art of the Middle Ages', *American Journal of Archaeology*, 2nd series 23

Low, A. (1985) *The Georgic Revolution*, Princeton

Luciani, V. (1948-49) 'Ralegh's *Discourse of War* and Machiavelli's *Discorsi*', *Modern Philology* 46

McCabe, R. (1982) *Joseph Hall: A Study in Satire and Meditation*, Oxford

MacCaffrey, W. (1992)   *Elizabeth I: War and Politics, 1588-1603*, Princeton

McCann, F. (1952) *English Discovery of America to 1585*, New York

McCoy, R. (1989) *The Rites of Knighthood: The Literature and Politics of Elizabethan Chivalry*

MacDonald, M. (1981)  *Mystical Bedlam: Madness, Anxiety, and Healing in Seventeenth-Century England*, Cambridge

McFarlane, K. (1962) 'England and the Hundred Years War', *Past and Present* 22

McGee, A. (1987) *The Elizabethan Hamlet*

MacGuire, P. (1992) 'Which Fortinbras, Which *Hamlet*?', in Clayton (1992)

MacIntyre, J. (1982) 'Shakespeare and the Battlefield: Tradition and Innovation in Battle Scenes', *Theatre Survey* 23

MacLure, M. (1979) ed., *Marlowe: The Critical Heritage, 1588-1896*

McNab, A. (1994) *Bravo Two Zero*

McNeill, W. (1983) *The Pursuit of Power: Technology, Armed Force, and Society Since A.D. 1000*, Oxford

Majewski, W. (1982) 'The Polish Art of War in the Sixteenth and Seventeenth Centuries', in *A Republic of Nobles: Studies in Polish History to 1864*, tr. J Federowicz, eds Federowicz, M. Bogucka and H. Samsonowicz, Cambridge

Maple, E. (1964) *The Realm of Ghosts*

Marcus, L. (1986) *The Politics of Mirth: Jonson, Herrick, Milton, Marvell, and the Defence of Old Holiday Pastimes*

—— (1988) *Puzzling Shakespeare: Local Reading and its Discontents*

—— (1989) 'Textual Indeterminacy and Ideological Difference: The Case of *Doctor Faustus*', *Renaissance Drama* n.s. 20

Markham, C. (1888) *The Fighting Veres*

Marotti, A. (1982) '"Love is not Love": Elizabethan Sonnet Sequences and the Social Order', *ELH* 49

—— (1986) *John Donne, Coterie Poet*

Marx, S. (1995) 'Holy War in *Henry V* ', *Shakespeare Survey* 48

Mason, H. (1967-68) 'The Ghost in *Hamlet*: A Resurrected "Paper"', *The Cambridge Quarterly* 3

Maus, K. (1986) 'Taking Tropes Seriously: Language and Violence in Shakespeare's *Rape of Lucrece*', *Shakespeare Quarterly* 37

Melchiori, G. (1992) '*Hamlet*: The Acting Version and the Wiser Sort', in Clayton (1992)

de Mendonca, B. (1968) '*Othello*: A Tragedy Built on a Comic Structure', *Shakespeare Survey* 21

Mithal, H. (1958) '"Will, my Lord of Leicester's Jesting Player"', *Notes and Queries* 203

Morris, H. (1985) *Last Things in Shakespeare*, Tallahassee, Florida

Morsberger, R. (1974) *Swordplay and the Elizabethan and Jacobean Stage*, Salzburg

Mowat, B. (1988) 'The Forms of *Hamlet*'s Fortunes', *Renaissance Drama* n.s. 19

Mullaney, S. (1980) 'Lying Like Truth: Riddle, Representation and Treason in Renaissance England', *ELH* 47

Mulryne, J. (1991) 'Nationality and Language in Thomas Kyd's *The Spanish Tragedy*', in Jones-Davies (1991)

—— and Shewring, M. (1989) eds, *War, Literature and the Arts in Sixteenth-Century Europe*

Musgrove, S. (1959) 'The Birth of Pistol', *Review of English Studies* n.s.10

Nabokov, V. (1974) *Bend Sinister*, Harmondsworth

Neale, J. (1930) 'Queen Elizabeth and the Netherlands, 1586-7', *English Historical Review* 45

Nef, J. (1950) *War and Human Progress: An Essay on the Rise of Industrial Civilisation*, New York

Neill, M. (1984) 'Changing Places in *Othello*', *Shakespeare Survey* 37

Nelson, K. and Olin, S. (1979) *Why War? Ideology, Theory and History*

Nicholl, C. (1984) *The Cup of News: The Life of Thomas Nashe*

—— (1992) *The Reckoning: The Murder of Christopher Marlowe*

—— (1996) '"At Middleborough": Some Reflections on Marlowe's Visit to the Low Countries in 1592', in Grantley and Roberts (1996)

Nicoll, A. (1983) *The World of Harlequin: A Critical Study of the Commedia dell'Arte*, Cambridge

Norbrook, D. (1984) *Poetry and Politics in the English Renaissance*

Nosworthy, J. (1979) 'The Importance of Being Marcade', *Shakespeare Survey* 32

Novarr, D. (1959-60) 'Dekker's Gentle Craft and the Lord Mayor of London', *Modern Philology* 57

Nugent, Lord (1854) *Some Memorials of John Hampden, His Part and His Times*, 3rd ed.

Nuti, L. (1988) 'The mapped Views of Georg Hoefnagel: The Merchant's Eye, the Humanist's Eye', *Word and Image* 4

O'Brien, Flann [Brian O'Nolan] (1967) *The Third Policeman*

Olivier, L. (1984) *Henry V (1945)*, ed. A. Sinclair

—— (1987) *Confessions of an Actor*

Olsson, Y. (1968) 'In Search of Yorick's Skull: Notes on the Background of *Hamlet*', *Shakespeare Studies* 4

Oman, C. (1937) *A History of the Art of War in the Sixteenth Century*

Ong, W. (1956) 'System, Space and Intellect in Renaissance Symbolism',

*Bibliothèque d'Humanisme et Renaissance* 18

Ordish, T. (1894) *Early London Theatres - In The Fields*

Orgel, S. (1970-71) 'The Poetics of Spectacle', *New Literary History* 2

Ornstein, R. (1972) *A Kingdom for a Stage: The Achievement of Shakespeare's History Plays*, Cambridge, Mass.

Orrell, J. (1968) *The Human Stage: English Theatre Design, 1567-1640*, Cambridge

Orsini, N. (1946) '"Policy", or the Language of Elizabethan Machiavellianism', *Journal of the Warburg and Courtauld Institutes* 9

Outhwaite, R. (1982) *Inflation in Tudor and Early Stuart England*, 2nd ed.

Owen, W. (1985) *The Poems*, ed. J. Stallworthy

*The Oxford Dictionary of Quotations* (1979) 3rd ed., Oxford

Palmer, J. (1964) 'Magic and Poetry in *Doctor Faustus*', *The Critical Quarterly* 6

Park, K. and Daston, L. (1981) 'Unnatural Conceptions: The Study of Monsters in Sixteenth- and Seventeenth-Century France and England', *Past and Present* 92

Parker, G. (1972) *The Army of Flanders and the Spanish Road, 1567-1659: The Logistics of Spanish Victory and Defeat in the Low Countries' Wars*, Cambridge

―― (1975) 'War and Economic Change: The Economic Costs of the Dutch Revolt', in Winter (1975)

―― (1979) *Europe in Crisis, 1598-1648*

―― (1988) *The Military Revolution: Military Innovation and the Rise of the West, 1500-1800*, Cambridge

―― (1990) *Spain and the Netherlands, 1559-1659: Ten Studies*, Glasgow

Parker, P. and Hartman, G. (1985) eds, *Shakespeare and the Question of Theory*

Parker, P. and Quint, D. (1986) eds, *Literary Theory/Renaissance Texts*

Parker, R. (1984) 'War and Sex in *All's Well That Ends Well*', *Shakespeare Survey* 37

Parr, J. (1944) 'Tamburlaine's Malady', *PMLA* 59

―― (1948) 'John Rastell's Geographical Knowledge of America', *Philological Quarterly* 27

Patrides, C. (1963) '"The Bloody and Cruell Turke": The Background of a Renaissance Commonplace', *Studies in the Renaissance* 10

Patterson, A. (1984) *Censorship and Interpretation: The Conditions of Writing and Reading in Early Modern England*

―― (1988) 'Back by Popular Demand: The Two Versions of *Henry V* ', *Renaissance Drama* n.s. 19

Pearce, B. (1942) 'Elizabethan Food Policy and the Armed Forces', *Economic History Review* 12

Pearl, S. (1984) 'Sounding to Present Occasions: Jonson's Masques of 1620-1625', in Lindley (1984)

Pearson, J. (1980) *Tragedy and Tragicomedy in the Plays of John Webster*, Manchester

Peet, D. (1959) 'The Rhetoric of *Tamburlaine*', *ELH* 26

Pendry, E. (1974) *Elizabethan Prisons and Prison Scenes*, Salzburg

Perkins, D. (1960) 'Issues and Motivations in the Nashe-Harvey Quarrel', *Philological Quarterly* 39

Porter, J. (1986) 'More Echoes from Eliot's *Ortho-Epia Gallica*, in *King Lear* and *Henry V* ', *Shakespeare Quarterly* 37

—— (1988) *Shakespeare's Mercutio: His History and Drama*

Potter, A. (1983) '*Hamlet* and the Background of War', *Unisa English Studies* 21b

Praz, M. (1928) 'Machiavelli and the Elizabethans', *Proceedings of the British Academy* 14

Price, J. (1975) ed., *The Triple Bond: Plays, Mainly Shakespearean, in Performance*

Prosser, E. (1971) *Hamlet and Revenge*, 2nd ed., Stanford, California

Proudfoot, R. (1984) '*Love's Labour's Lost*: Sweet Understanding and the Five Worthies', *Essays and Studies* n.s. 37

—— (1985) '*The Reigne of King Edward the Third* (1596) and Shakespeare', *Proceedings of the British Academy* 71

Prouty, C. (1942) *George Gascoigne: Elizabethan Courtier, Soldier, and Poet*, New York

Pugliatti, P. (1993) 'The Strange Tongues of *Henry V*', *Yearbook of English Studies* 23

Purdon, N. (1974) *The Words of Mercury: Shakespeare and English Mythography of the Renaissance*, Salzburg

Raab, F. (1964) *The English Face of Machiavelli: A Changing Interpretation, 1500-1700*

Rabkin, N. (1977) 'Rabbits, Ducks, and *Henry V*', *Shakespeare Quarterly* 28

Rachum, I. (1979) *The Renaissance: An Illustrated Encyclopaedia*

Raimondi, E. (1977) 'Machiavelli and the Rhetoric of the Warrior', *Modern Language Notes* 92

Remarque, E. (1979) *Im Westen Nichts Neues*, Frankfurt

Revard, S. (1972) 'Milton's Gunpowder Poems and Satan's Conspiracy', *Milton Studies* 4

Rhodes, N. (1979) *Elizabethan Grotesque*

Ribner, I. (1953) 'The Idea of History in Marlowe's *Tamburlaine*', *ELH* 20

—— (1954) 'Marlowe and Machiavelli', *Comparative Literature* 6

—— (1955) 'Greene's Attack on Marlowe: Some Light on *Alphonsus* and *Selimus*', *Studies in Philology* 52

Richards, K. and Richards, L. (1990) *The Commedia dell'Arte: A Documentary History*, Oxford

Richardson, J. (1973) *Sarah Bernhardt*

Ricks, C. (1987) ed., *English Drama to 1710*

—— (1996) *Essays in Appreciation*, Oxford

Riggs, D. (1971) *Shakespeare's Heroical Histories: 'Henry VI' and its Literary Tradition*, Cambridge, Mass.

Roberts, G. (1996) 'Necromantic Books: Christopher Marlowe, *Doctor Faustus* and Agrippa of Nettesheim', in Grantley and Roberts (1996)

Roberts, J. (1921-22) 'The Nine Worthies', *Modern Philology* 19

Roberts, M. (1967) 'The Military Revolution, 1550-1660', in Roberts, *Essays in Swedish History*

Roberts, R. (1962) 'The Personnel and Practice of Medicine in Tudor and Stuart England: Part I: The Provinces', *Medical History* 6

—— (1964) 'The Personnel and Practice of Medicine in Tudor and Stuart England: Part II: London', *Medical History* 8

Robinson, G. (1966) 'Wounded Sailors and Soldiers in London during the First Dutch War (1652-1654)', *History Today* 16

Rosenberg, E. (1955) *Leicester, Patron of Letters*, New York

Rostenberg, L. (1960) 'Thomas Thorpe, Publisher of *Shake-Speares Sonnets*', *Papers of the Bibliographical Society of America* 54

Rowse, A. (1955) *The Expansion of Elizabethan England*

Rudwin, M. (1931) *The Devil in Legend and Literature*

Russell, J. (1986) *Peacemaking in the Renaissance*

Salingar, L. (1974) *Shakespeare and the Traditions of Comedy*, Cambridge

Salmon, E. (1984) ed., *Bernhardt and the Theatre of her Time*, Westport, Connecticut

Sanders, W. (1968) *The Dramatist and the Received Idea: Studies in the Plays of Marlowe and Shakespeare*, Cambridge

Sassoon, S. (1947) *Collected Poems*

Scarry, E. (1985) *The Body in Pain: The Making and Unmaking of the World*, Oxford

Schama, S. (1987) *The Embarrassment of Riches: An Interpretation of Dutch Culture in the Golden Age*

Schelling, T. (1963) 'Deterrence: Military Diplomacy in the Nuclear Age', *Virginia Quarterly Review* 39

Schoenbaum, S. (1977) *William Shakespeare: A Compact Documentary Life*, Oxford

Schrickx, W. (1956) *Shakespeare's Early Contemporaries: The Background of the Harvey-Nashe Polemic and 'Love's Labour's Lost'*, Antwerp

Schwoerer, L. (1974) *'No Standing Armies!' The Antiarmy Ideology in Seventeenth Century England*

Scofield, M. (1980) *The Ghosts of Hamlet: The Play and Modern Writers*, Cambridge

Scouloudi, I. (1938) 'Alien Immigration into and Alien Communities in London, 1558-1640', *Proceedings of the Huguenot Society in London* 16

Scutter, H. (1950) 'Satan's Artillery', *Notes and Queries* 195

Seaton, E. (1924) 'Marlowe's Maps', *Essays and Studies* 10

Seznec, J. (1980) *La Survivance des Dieux Antiques: Essai sur la Rôle Mythologique dans l'Humanisme et dans l'Art de la Renaissance*, Paris

Shaaber, M. (1929) *Some Forerunners of the Newspaper in England, 1476-1622*

Shaaber, M. (1976-77) 'Pistol Quotes St Augustine?', *English Language Notes* 14

Shapiro, J. (1988) '"Metre Meete to Furnish Lucans Style": Reconsidering Marlowe's *Lucan*', in Friedenreich et al. (1988)

Shapiro, M. (1977) *Children of the Revels: The Boy Companies of Shakespeare's Time and their Plays*, New York

Shaw, P. (1947) 'The Position of Thomas Dekker in Jacobean Prison Literature', *PMLA* 62

Shell, M. (1982) *Money, Language, and Thought: Literary and Philosophical Economies from the Medieval to the Modern Era*

Shepherd, S. (1981) *Amazons and Warrior Women: Varieties of Feminism in Seventeenth-Century Drama*, Brighton

—— (1986) *Marlowe and the Politics of Elizabethan Theatre*, Brighton

Sher, A. (1985) *Year of the King*

Shire, H. (1978) *A Preface to Spenser*

Siegel, P. (1968) *Shakespeare in His Time and Ours*

Siemon, J. (1985) *Shakespearean Iconoclasm*, Berkeley, California

Sisson, C. (1933) ed., *Thomas Lodge and Other Elizabethans*, Cambridge, Mass.

Sjögren, G. (1968) 'The Danish Background in *Hamlet*', *Shakespeare Studies* 4

Slavin, A. (1985) 'Printing and Publishing in the Tudor Age', in J. Andrews (1985)

Smallwood, R. (1972) 'The Design of *All's Well That Ends Well*', *Shakespeare Survey* 25

Smeed, J. (1985) *The Theophrastan 'Character': The History of a Literary Genre*, Oxford

Smith, C. (1986) 'Shakespeare on French Stages in the Nineteenth Century', in Foulkes (1986)

Smith, H. (1945) 'Tamburlaine and the Renaissance', *University of Colorado Studies in the Humanities* 2

Smith, I. (1956) '"Gates" on Shakespeare's Stage', *Shakespeare Quarterly* 7

Smith, L. (1966) *The Elizabethan Epic*

Smuts, R. (1987) *Court Culture and the Origins of a Royalist Tradition in Early Stuart England*, Philadelphia

Southern, R. (1973) *The Staging of Plays Before Shakespeare*

Soyinka, W. (1965) *The Road*, Oxford

Spalding, T. (1880) *Elizabethan Demonology: An Essay*

Stallworthy, J. (1988) ed., *The Oxford Book of War Poetry*, Oxford

Spencer, T. (1957) 'Shakespeare and the Elizabethan Romans', *Shakespeare Survey* 10

Steane, J. (1964) *Marlowe: A Critical Study*, Cambridge

Stephen, M. (1988) ed., *Never Such Innocence: A New Anthology of Great War Verse*

Stern, V. (1979) *Gabriel Harvey: His Life, Marginalia and Library*, Oxford

Stevenson, R. (1985) *Treasure Island*, ed. E. Letley, Oxford

Stoessinger, J. (1985) *Why Nations Go To War*, 4th ed., Basingstoke

Stoll, E. (1927) *Shakespeare Studies, Historical and Comparative in Method*

Stone, L. (1965) *The Crisis of the Aristocracy, 1558-1641*, Oxford

Strauss, G. (1966) 'A Sixteenth Century Encyclopaedia: Sebastian Münster's *Cosmography* and its Editions', in Carter (1966)

Strindberg, A. (1992) *Miss Julie*, tr. H. Cooper

Strobl, G. (1997) 'Shakespeare and the Nazis', *History Today* 47

Strong, R. (1973) *Splendour at Court: Renaissance Spectacle and Illusion*

—— (1977) *The Cult of Elizabeth: Elizabethan Portraiture and Pageantry*

—— and van Dorsten, J. (1964) *Leicester's Triumph*

Summers, C. (1974) *Christopher Marlowe and the Politics of Power*, Salzburg

Summerson, J. (1957-58) 'Three Elizabethan Architects', *John Rylands Library Bulletin* 40

Supple, J. (1984) *Arms and Letters: The Military and Literary Ideals in the 'Essais' of Montaigne*, Oxford

Tawney, R. and Power, E. (1924) eds, *Tudor Economic Documents Illustrating the Economic and Social History of Tudor England*, 3 vols

Taylor, E. (1930) *Tudor Geography, 1485-1583*

—— (1934) *Late Tudor and Early Stuart Geography, 1583-1650*

—— (1947) 'The Surveyor', *Economic History Review* 17

—— (1954) *The Mathematical Practitioners of Tudor and Stuart England*, Cambridge

Taylor, G. (1980) 'The War in *King Lear*', *Shakespeare Survey* 33

—— (1982) '*Troilus and Cressida*: Bibliography, Performance, and Interpretation', *Shakespeare Studies* 16

—— (1985) *Moment by Moment by Shakespeare*

—— (1990) *Reinventing Shakespeare: A Cultural History from the Restoration to the Present*

—— and Warren, M. (1983) eds, *The Division of the Kingdoms: Shakespeare's Two Versions of 'King Lear'*, Oxford

Taylor, G.C. (1930) 'Milton on Mining', *Modern Language Notes* 45

Thompson, H. (1997) *Peter Cook: A Biography*

Thompson, I. (1985) 'The Impact of War', in P. Clark (1985)

Thoms, W. (1859) 'Was Shakspeare Ever a Soldier?', *Notes and Queries* 7

Thomson, P. (1969) 'Rant and Cant in *Troilus and Cressida*', *Essays and Studies* n.s. 22

Thrower, N. (1972) *Maps & Man: An Examination of Cartography in Relation to Culture and Civilisation*, New Jersey

Toy, S. (1955) *A History of Fortification from 3000 B.C. to A.D. 1700*

Trewin, J. (1984) 'Bernhardt on the Stage', in Salmon (1984)

Tyler, S. (1987) 'Minding True Things: The Chorus, The Audience, and *Henry V* ', *Themes in Drama* 9

Underdown, D. (1985) *Revel, Riot and Rebellion: Popular Politics and Culture in England, 1603-1660*, Oxford

Ure, P. (1950) 'The Main Outlines of Chapman's *Byron*', *Studies in Philology* 47

Vagts, A. (1960) *A History of Militarism, Civilian and Military*

Vale, M. (1981) *War and Chivalry: War and Aristocratic Culture in England, France and Burgundy at the End of the Middle Ages*

Valéry, P. (1977) *An Anthology*, ed. J. Lawler

Vendler, H. (1997) *The Art of Shakespeare's Sonnets*

Vickers, B. (1974-81) ed., *Shakespeare: The Critical Heritage*, 6 vols

Virilio, P. (1989) *War and Cinema: The Logistics of Perception*, tr. P. Camiller

Virilio, P. and Lotringer, S. (1983) *Pure War*, tr. M. Polizotti, New York

Waggoner, G. (1954) 'An Elizabethan Attitude Toward Peace and War', *Philological Quarterly* 33

Waith, E. (1962) *The Herculean Hero in Marlowe, Chapman, Shakespeare and Dryden*

Walter, J. (1985) 'A "Rising of the People"? The Oxfordshire Rising of 1596', *Past and Present* 107

Walzer, M. (1978) *Just and Unjust Wars: A Moral Argument With Historical Illustrations*

Watson, C. (1960) *Shakespeare and the Renaissance Concept of Honor*, Princeton

Waugh, E. (1928) *Decline and Fall*

Webb, H. (1943) 'Barnabe Riche: Sixteenth Century Military Critic', *Journal of English and Germanic Philology* 42

—— (1951) 'The Military Background of *Othello*', *Philological Quarterly* 30

—— (1952) 'Miltary Newsbooks During the Age of Elizabeth', *English Studies* 33

—— (1954) 'The Science of Gunnery in Elizabethan England', *Isis* 45

—— (1955) 'Elizabethan Field Artillery', *Military Affairs* 19

—— (1965) *Elizabethan Military Science: The Books and the Practice*, Madison, Wisconsin

Weil, J. (1977) *Christopher Marlowe: Merlin's Prophet*

Welsh, A. (1979-80) 'The Task of Hamlet', *Yale Review* 69

Wernham, R. (1932) 'Queen Elizabeth and the Siege of Rouen, 1591', *Transactions of the Royal Historical Society*, 4th series, 15

—— (1976) 'Christopher Marlowe at Flushing in 1592', *English Historical Review* 91

—— (1984) *After the Armada: Elizabethan England and the Struggle for Western Europe, 1588-1595*, Oxford

Werstine, P. (1988) 'The Textual Mystery of *Hamlet*', *Shakespeare Quarterly* 39

West, R. (1969) *The Invisible World: A Study of Pneumatology in Elizabethan Drama*, New York

Whigham, F. (1984) *Ambition and Privilege: The Social Tropes of Elizabethan Courtesy Theory*

—— (1985) 'Elizabethan Aristocratic Insignia', *Texas Studies in Literature and Language* 27

Wickham, G. (1959-81) *The Early English Stage*, 3 vols

Wiener, C. (1971) 'The Beleagured Isle: A Study of Elizabethan and Early Jacobean Anti-Catholicism', *Past and Present* 51

Wilkins, H. (1935) *Mysteries of the Great War*

Wilson, C. (1970) *Queen Elizabeth and the Revolt of the Netherlands*

Wilson, F. (1920) '"An Ironicall Letter"', *Modern Language Review* 15

Wilson, J. (1932) *The Manuscript of 'Hamlet' and the Problem of its Transmission: An Essay in Critical Bibliography*, Cambridge

—— (1935) *What Happens in 'Hamlet'*, Cambridge

Wilson, M. (1950) *Sir Philip Sidney*

Wilson, R. (1996) 'Visible Bullets: *Tamburlaine the Great* and Ivan the Terrible', in Grantley and Roberts (1996)

Winter, J. (1975) ed., *War and Economic Development: Essays in Memory of David Joslin*, Cambridge

—— (1995) *Sites of Memory, Sites of Mourning: The Great War in European Cultural History*, Cambridge

Woodcock, T. and Robinson, J. (1988) *The Oxford Guide to Heraldry*, Oxford

Wright, C. (1940) 'The Amazons in Elizabethan Literature', *Studies in Philology* 37

Wright, Q. (1969) *A Study of War*, 2nd ed.

Yates, F. (1967) 'The Hermetic Tradition in Renaissance Science', in Singleton (1967)

—— (1969) *Theatre of the World*

—— (1973) *Astraea: The Imperial Theme in the Sixteenth Century*

Young, K. (1941) 'The Psychology of War', in Clarkson and Cochran (1941)

Young, M. and Stamp, R. (1989) *Trojan Horses: Deception Operations in the Second World War*

Zitner, S. (1969-70) 'Hamlet, Duellist', *University of Toronto Quarterly* 39

# Index